D1081706

Women
in
American
Law

Women in American Law

VOLUME 1

From Colonial Times
to the New Deal

Edited by
MARLENE STEIN
WORTMAN

HM

Holmes & Meier Publishers, Inc.
NEW YORK LONDON

First published in the United States of America 1985 by
Holmes & Meier Publishers, Inc.
30 Irving Place
New York, N.Y. 10003

Great Britain:
Holmes & Meier Publishers, Ltd.
Unit 5   Greenwich Industrial Estate
345 Woolwich Road   Charlton, London SE 7

Copyright © 1985 by Marlene Stein Wortman
All rights reserved

Book design by Stephanie Barton

Library of Congress Cataloging in Publication Data

Wortman, Marlene Stein.
Women in American law.

Bibliography: v. 1, p.
Includes index.
Contents: v. 1. From colonial times to the New Deal.
1. Woman—Legal status, laws etc.—United States—
History.   I. Title.
KF478.W67   1985   346.7301'34   83-22527
ISBN 0-8419-0752-8 (v. 1)   347.306134
ISBN 0-8419-0753-6 (pbk. : v.1)

Manufactured in the United States of America

Contents

UNIT 2
Family Roles   59

DOCUMENTS

UNIT 3
Occupational Choice   89

DOCUMENTS

CHAPTER 2
The Age of Jackson, Reconstruction, and the Gilded Age (1830–1890)   115

UNIT 1
Marriage and Property   117

DOCUMENTS

Preface

This anthology is a response to questions about the past raised by young people exploring the social implications of legal decision making based on gender stereotypes. We would lead very different lives today if those who made and administered the law in the eighteenth or nineteenth century had chosen to follow different principles about the distribution of rights, power, and authority in family and society. Primary source materials enable us to enter into the minds and feelings of people long dead and to examine the choices before them.

The legal documents presented here not only illustrate the principles and processes of legal decision making, but also depict the realities of women's social experience. Judicial cases, statutes, administrative rulings, legal treaties, contracts, wills, and legislative reports individually and collectively describe how men and women were expected to behave, how they actually did behave, and how the law responded to social realities. Nonlegal documents illustrate established cultural images of women and the family, aspects of social reality, and feminist perspectives for each historical period. When read in conjunction with legal documents, they capture the relationship between law and culture and provide a basis for examining legal choices. Illustrations develop some of the themes of written documents and make visible some of the women who participated in shaping the course of change.

Both law-related and cultural documents have been grouped in each chronological chapter around the same topics: Marriage and Property, Family Roles, Occupational Choice, and Crime and Deviance. They provide the basis for exploring the issue of Protection versus Equal Rights. The historical period covered by each chapter is broad enough to encompass new developments and cultural conflict. Because I hope to provoke questions about the adequacy of traditional representations of an age, and because I want to highlight the relationship between law and politics, I have used traditional political categories to characterize the periods. The chronological-topical format permits the reader to see the interrelationship between legal policy in different areas within one time frame and at the same time explore continuity and change in one topic area.

Documents rarely speak for themselves. They need explanations that relate them to the specific historical culture and to patterns of continuity and change. For this purpose, headnotes are grouped together in the form of introductions to each topic area or unit. This approach combines freedom of inquiry with more structured historical analysis and interpretation. At times the headnotes provide a summary as well as an analysis of the action in the document to help the reader become more comfortable with legal reasoning. The introductions also permit readers to decide which documents they want to examine in depth.

The way people speak and organize their thoughts directs attention to cultural and social differences. In editing the documents, I have chosen to retain the original grammar and spelling where it does not unduly interfere with understanding. Unusual or archaic words are explained within brackets or defined in the glossary of legal terms. The places where a text has been rewritten or summarized are indicated through an editorial note and brackets. To save space and facilitate reading, many internal citations as well as footnotes have been omitted. They have been retained where they are an integral part of a sentence, where they help characterize the legal mode of argument, and where they point to important cases. Minor changes in spelling and capitalization have been made here and there without notation. At times parts of two documents have been spliced together in an effort to capture the essence of materials too long for inclusion in an anthology of this scope. These are indicated in the footnotes.

As the citations and bibliography show, this book is deeply indebted to those who prepared documentary supplements in complementary areas and who have published books and articles in women's history, family history, and legal history. I have not attempted to unearth new documents in women's social history, but rather to use those already available. I have concentrated instead on developing legal materials that amplify our understanding of women's experience and the role of law in shaping that experience. I hope those not already familiar with the works from which I drew documents will read those collections as well.

Acknowledgments

Many people have contributed to this interpretative anthology. I wish to thank those who generously shared documents they had found in the course of research for books and articles. They have helped to shape not only the content but, through their writing and comments, the thinking underlying various sections. Mary Lynn Salmon contributed most of the examples of antenuptial contracts and statutory and case law from South Carolina, Maryland, Pennsylvania, and Connecticut for the chapter on the Colonial, Revolutionary, and Early Federal Period. Norma Basch enriched the section on the property acts, and Noralee Franklin contributed the examples of black labor contracts for the section on Reconstruction. Mary Bularzik contributed material on Massachusetts for the sections on differential treatment in the criminal justice system in the nineteenth century and Progressive Era. Peter Tyor provided copies of case records on admission to the Wisconsin Home for the Mentally Retarded for the section on crime and deviance in the Progressive Era.

This volume is the outcome of a larger project, "Perspectives on Women in America's Legal Development," that included law-related source material from the New Deal to the present and was sponsored by the Institute for Research in History. All phases of this project, from the design and development of materials through the piloting and preparation of the manuscript, were made possible by a grant from the National Endowment for the Humanities, Division of Education Programs. The idea for the project originated with Linda Irene-greene, an attorney in Teaneck, New Jersey. She and Adrienne Eisenbud Lesser, a curriculum specialist, were codirectors of this project.

Women in American Law was greatly influenced by the students and teachers involved in the project. Discussions in workshops with Mildred Alpern, Alexandra Sullivan, Martin Levine, and Donald Elwell of Spring Valley High School in Spring Valley, New York, with Marlene Nussbaum and Mary Butz at Edward R. Murrow High School in Brooklyn, with

Joseph Cummings at Murray Bergtraum High School in Manhattan, and with Jean Dresden Grambs, Professor of Education at the University of Maryland, College Park, furthered my thinking about how to integrate materials into the social studies curriculum. Their comments, along with the extensive logs kept by students at Spring Valley High School, helped me make difficult decisions about presentation and the writing of headnotes. Ultimately, I am responsible for the approach used here and although I have followed current interpretations found in both legal and women's history, many writers may disagree with interpretations of their areas of special interest.

In any project of this size there are many whose contributions are less visible, but none the less crucial. I would like to thank Lois Banner, Stanley Katz, Ruth Bader Ginsburg, Linda Biemer, Allen Davis, Nancy Erikson, Frances Arick Kolk, Joan Hoff Wilson, Carol Ruth Berkin, and Leigh Bienen for their support and advice on documents. I have relied heavily not only on those who have written about our past, but on those who have preserved its records. I am greatly obliged to the following libraries for giving permission to use their manuscript collections and books and for the aid provided by reference librarians: the Schlesinger Library on the History of Women in America at Radcliffe, the Norman E. Himes Collection at the Widener Library, the Harvard University Law School Library, the New York Public Library, and the Miriam Y. Holden Collection on Women's History at Princeton University. Numerous institutions provided photographs: the Library of Congress, the National Archives, the Sophia Smith Collection at Smith College, the Boston Museum of Fine Arts, the Frick Art Reference Library, the Bryn Mawr Library, and the Graphics Division of the Princeton University Library.

In closing I would like to show my appreciation to my family, who accepted with good humor and love additional household tasks so I could retreat into the past. I would also like to thank William N. Zeisel. This book has benefited greatly from his editorial skills.

Marlene Stein Wortman
Princeton, New Jersey
March 1984

Women and
American Law

Women, Law, and Society: An Overview

Historians traditionally have identified American culture and character with equality of opportunity—ensuring everyone an equal start and removing all handicaps and special privileges that tend to give one person an advantage over another. The record of national achievements became proof of the social and individual benefits of a political and legal system committed to freedom of individual choice. Equality of opportunity, according to this analysis, challenged individuals to pit their skills and talents against others and released the creative energies of people denied status and position in the old world. More recent studies have directed attention to the process by which minority groups were excluded from the opportunity structure on the basis of cultural and physical characteristics. The findings of both the idealistic and the realistic schools of history provide a basis for identifying in law some groups as "suspect classes." The United States Supreme Court has defined a suspect class as one "saddled with such disabilities, or subjected to such a position of political powerlessness as to command extraordinary protection from the majoritarian political process." This has usually meant blacks and aliens.

Feminists have argued that sex should also be treated as a suspect classification. They point out that the contemporary system of occupational segregation and rewards is the outcome of the nineteenth century's solution to the problems of organizing society, and not the result of biology. Current surveys, while recognizing the diversity of the American experience, provide little insight into this process. To discover what is unique about women's experience and how this is related to the way they have been treated in comparison to men in different institutional settings, one must turn to recent scholarship about women's social, cultural, and legal history.

Historians recently have focused much attention on images of womanhood that articulate woman's nature and establish what is and is not

3

appropriate female behavior and work. Images of woman's nature and what was encompassed by her gender role have changed in response to social, economic, and ideological developments. But, however different the images were, they all preserved the original notion that women were destined to serve others. When incorporated into the process of socialization and into legal and social policy, the images shape expectations and opportunities.

Colonial society believed that women were created to be men's helpmates; their role encompassed economic and domestic responsibilities. This model emphasized a married woman's total subordination to the family patriarch in decision making and her total exclusion from the public world of politics. Revolutionary and Jacksonian America sharply differentiated between male and female personalities and spheres of action. Women were depicted as physically delicate, sexually passive, and selfless. They were the opposite of the colonial image. Woman's role was to supply the immediate physical and emotional needs of husbands and children, to socialize the new republic's citizens, and insure the continuity of culture and morality. Income-producing work was deemed a male prerogative. The twentieth century brought new variations and linked women's role to anatomy.

Models of womanhood gain their legitimacy from the presumption that they represent the natural order and are in tune with social reality. But at the time it was fashioned, the model of separate gender roles at best described the life of the urban white American-born middle and upper classes. White and black working-class and farm family histories show women contributing to the family economy while they carried out their functions as mothers and wives.

Women pressed for more personal autonomy and equality, first as individuals and then through organizations. Their aspirations were often expressed through disguised rebellions and shrewd manipulations of gender images. In the nineteenth century, the image of true womanhood and the ideology of domesticity represented an adjustment to available options that secured a separate identity and cultural equality for white middle- and upper-class women. The image of selflessness and purity legitimized participation in humanitarian societies that drew attention to female victimization inside and outside the family. The ideology of domesticity presented the ideal family as a system of human relationships based, not on competition and domination, but on love and justice. It provided a model for criticizing and reforming the real family and society.

The nineteenth-century strategy expanded the boundaries of women's world and heightened women's sense of self-worth by using rather than questioning social definitions of sex roles. It brought them recognition as citizens and new opportunities in a segregated occupational and public-service sphere. But it also restricted their personal liberty and, in the twentieth century, their career choices as well. The documents in this collection vividly portray the role of law in distributing power and responsibility, as well as work, on the basis of gender. They provide the factual basis for approaching such key contemporary issues as whether gender, like race, should be considered a suspect classification, and whether we need an Equal Rights Amendment.

The law, according to legal sociologists and political scientists, is more than the complex of rules for settling disputes between litigants in court. It is also an instrument of the state for securing social control. It defines the relationships among society's members by indicating which types of behavior are permitted and which are proscribed, by allocating authority, by specifying who may legitimately exercise coercion over whom, and by establishing appropriate sanctions. The legal system affects the distribution of power, status, and opportunity by the way it confers rights and applies the concept of "property rights." Legal rules reflect contemporary pressures of the needs and interests of the community or of groups within the community, as well as the ideals of society, and its sense of justice and injustice.

The law in the United States is the constitution of the federal government and all the states. It is legislation, both federal and state. It is regulations promulgated by federal and state agencies to implement that legislation. And, it is interpretations by the courts of those constitutions, legislation, and regulations. Law is also the custom and tradition which accumulate in those areas where there is no legislation. This is known as the common law. It is judicially interpreted law, derived from principles and customs of long usage, and based on precedent originally inherited from England. The common law is found in written decisions of judges and in legal treatises. Equity, a separate, but complementary system of jurisprudence, also inherited from England, provides individual remedies where there is no common or statutory law or where the application of the law in particular situations results in injustice. Equitable relief is dispensed by judges and does not involve a trial by jury. Equity courts, usually called chancellery courts, although more flexible than law courts, are not necessarily more just.

Legal sociologists and philosophers disagree on whether the law can promote or impede social change in a particular direction. Those who see the primary job of the legal system as mitigating elements of conflict and smoothing the course of social interaction argue that the law has no significant shaping power of its own. They claim that the legal rules that guide individual expectations and the process of judicial adjudication are essentially modifications or restatements of social mores. Judges do not make the law. They find it through a logical system of principles embodied in precedents, and they adapt it, through a process of interpretation, to fit new circumstances. Legal formalists point out that strict adherence to general rules and procedural forms is a protection against politically expedient or idiosyncratic decision making.

Legal realists, on the other hand, direct attention to actual court behavior and to the social consequences of legal outcomes. They point out that since all legal actions are taken within a general context of competing pressures from opposed interest groups, judicial or administrative rules and statutes are never neutral. Some interests are maintained or advanced, others are repudiated or set back. Judges always have choices, and judicial precedent and principle can be found or developed to support almost any outcome or policy. A judge's decision as to which principle and which party will prevail is grounded in personal conceptions of justice, social background, and general policy predilections. When judges take the opportunity which a case affords, not only to decide that case, but to establish rules of a general application, they are performing a legislative role and making social policy. Even when courts narrowly define their powers, they are involved in social action. They are in effect deciding in behalf of the status quo.

In this more policy-oriented conception of the legal decision-making process, the law is seen as an instrument for controlling individual purposes and bringing them in line with particular goals. Legal forms and processes may be used with almost equal ease to expand the freedom of different groups or to maintain the dominance of some social and economic segments of society over others. The historically close relationship between legal and socioeconomic status suggests that a pronounced change in the substance of law or in key legal procedures can encourage social change in a particular direction. This can happen when there are divergent views within society on the rights of excluded groups and when there is pressure for change. The short-run effects of any legal enlargement of the rights of excluded groups will be felt largely in the reduction of overt discrimination, not in the reduction of personal prejudice. But the concrete conditions produced through the law's implementation may in the long run lead to changes in attitudes.

The structural features of the legal system tend to perpetuate the existing distribution of social power. Change in social policy through judicial action tends to be slow and incremental. Judges for the most part are limited by adversary procedure to the consideration of only those particular issues that are raised by the litigants. One judicial opinion can introduce a new precedent, but only a series of courts implementing it can change the law over time. Legislatures can produce broader and quicker solutions to social problems. But the checks and balances built into the elective and legislative process discourage action in the absence of a clear consensus. This also results in legislation remaining on the books long after the consensus that gave rise to it has changed.

The problem of anachronistic statutes that do not fit the values or behavior of current majorities looms large in the area of women's rights. The only way to repeal an offending statute in the face of legislative inertia is to show that it conflicts with the fundamental law of the land. Excluded groups challenging the existing distribution of rights, obligations, and powers generally will focus their efforts on those branches at either the state or federal level which appear most responsive.

The issue of what are fundamental personal rights has been bound historically to the question of states rights. The framers of the federal constitution and the first ten amendments created a national government of limited powers. They specifically rejected attempts to place restrictions on the way states chose to order and control their domestic, economic, and political institutions. Thus, the political majority was sovereign within the states. Although the United States Supreme Court in 1803 asserted the general power to declare acts of both the state and federal legislatures void, it limited the scope of judicial review to commercial law. In *Barron* v. *Baltimore* (1833) the Court affirmed that it could not intervene if the states chose to deny to any class of persons the liberties enumerated in the Bill of Rights.

The passage of the fourteenth amendment in 1868 altered the constitutional settlement. It reads:

> No State shall make or enforce any law which shall abridge the privileges or immunities of citizens of the United States: nor shall any State deprive any person of life, liberty or property, without due process of law; nor deny to any person within its jurisdiction the equal protection of the laws. . . . The Congress shall have power to enforce, by appropriate legislation, the provisions of this article.

This language is broad and can be interpreted to mean that all subjects of state legislation were now within the scope of judicial review, that class and caste legislation was prohibited, and that Congress had the power to correct unjust legislation of the states.

The Court rejected this interpretation in 1873. It held that the only change introduced by the amendment was to require that statutes establishing rights and obligations of individuals not treat blacks and whites differently. A few years later, however, the Court expanded the scope of judicial review by interpreting the due process clause to mean that the legislatures' power to make social policy did not permit it to arbitrarily or unreasonably restrict individual property and contract rights. It also included corporations within the meaning of persons.

By the end of the century, the Court identified the fourteenth amendment's protection of liberty almost exclusively with liberty of contract and placed that right above majority rule. In the twentieth century, this view became a bar to state protective labor legislation. The Court, as progressive jurists pointed out, by ignoring both the imbalance in power and the social effect was in practice undermining the principle of equal protection of the laws. In *Muller* v. *Oregon* (1908), however, the Court took judicial notice of social reality and excepted women's contractual rights from the general rule. It found that the inherent differences between the sexes justified legislation that was designed to protect women but would not be acceptable if applied to men. As a general practice, the Supreme Court exercised restraint and intervened only when in its judgment a state's actions to protect the interests of its citizens threatened national economic development.

In the nineteenth century, judicial involvement in the making of economic and social policy came, not through constitutional law, but through the promulgation and enforcement of common-law rules. Until the 1920s most law ordering the way we do things was made by courts. The judiciary in the early nineteenth century did not see its task as simply interpreting and enforcing the received common law. Judges saw law as an instrument for achieving policy goals. To promote rapid economic development, they transformed inherited doctrines and rules involving property and contract, tort, and commercial law. They created what became the doctrine of liberty of contract. White male entrepreneurs, legal historians agree, became the primary beneficiaries of legal innovations that reduced community control and the rights of vested interests.

To preserve family unity and social stability, the judiciary left intact most of the common-law rules that placed married women's property and persons in the hands of their husbands. These rules were designed to restrict a married woman's participation as an independent person in the marketplace and to enforce her domestic obligations. Equity, however, created legal instruments that enabled individual women to hold separate property. When social reality made clear that women and their families were becoming victims of the law, many states extended to them limited property rights through statutory law.

The state judiciaries transformed family law. They transferred from the father to the courts the authority to make decisions about child custody and guardianship. The great expansion of married women's legal capacities came in the form of familial privileges like maternal custody preference, not in the form of legal rights. Mothers who violated judicial expectation about appropriate female behavior, that is, mothers who were found to be at fault, received no legal assistance.

Between the Civil War and the end of the 1920s, the state judiciaries adopted a formalistic approach to law and came to treat the transformed common law as immutable and eternal. They used their power of review and interpretation to limit legislative attempts to redistribute wealth, power, and opportunity. They strictly construed statutes that expanded women's property and contract rights. But they left intact statutes that were designed to preserve women's family role.

Over the course of the twentieth century, both the focus and structure of law changed considerably. The center of lawmaking shifted from the courts to the legislatures and administrative agencies and then from the states to the federal government. With this shift came a new emphasis on improving the quality of life and distributing social benefits more widely. This involved not only expanding social welfare, but state action to reduce the existing imbalance of power. An increasing range of private economic activities became subject to statutory and administrative rulings.

After 1937 a liberal majority on the United States Supreme Court completed the constitutional revolution and demoted liberty of contract from its status as a fundamental freedom. Through a process of judicial deference to legislative supremacy, the Court sustained the principle that the power of government can legitimately be used to curtail the freedom of powerful groups within society for the benefit of the relatively powerless. The Court's general approach to its power of review, together with the Muller precedent that had made sex a valid basis for differential treatment of rights, led it to uphold the constitutionality of public policies that restricted women's opportunities in the interests of men.

Within a few years, the Court shifted its involvement to the domain of civil liberties and civil rights. The change in the judicial agenda began in the 1920s and made itself fully felt in the 1960s and 1970s. The Court expanded the number and scope of fundamental personal freedoms protected against infringement by both the federal and state governments. It gave new meaning to the concept of equal protection of the laws. Laws inevitably create distinctions as to how various people will be treated. To determine which laws discriminate impermissibly, the Court created the category of suspect classes. Racial and cultural minorities that had been subjected to a history of purposeful unequal treatment and excluded from the political process were defined as suspect classes. Statutes that excluded a group from the possession of a "fundamental" right fell within the suspect-class category. When using race, religion, and nationality as a basis for differential treatment, states had to show a compelling purpose, one that could not be accomplished by other means. Statutes that made arbitrary distinctions were also deemed offensive to the equal protection of the laws guarantee of the fourteenth amendment.

Federal and state governments, responding to pressure from women's organizations in the 1960s, broadened the civil rights mandate to include prohibitions against sex discrimination. The Supreme Court, however, did not direct federal and state courts to adopt a higher standard in reviewing gender-based discrimination until 1971. Sex discrimination remained constitutionally permissible, but it no longer could be arbitrary.

Most of the judicial opinions in this collection are those of appellate courts. This means that the cases had already been decided by a judge or by a judge and jury, and the losing party, dissatisfied with the outcome, had appealed to the next highest court. An appeals court usually consists of a

panel of judges who read the briefs and hear legal arguments by the lawyers
for both parties and ask questions about the law relevant to the case. One
judge writes the opinion of the majority. Other judges who agree with the
decision, but for different reasons, will write concurring opinions. Those
who do not agree may write one or more dissenting opinions. The United
States Supreme Court is the last court of appeal.

In handing down decisions, appellate judges are addressing several audiences. There is the public at large, whose lives may be influenced in a general
way by the impact of the decision. Then there is a professional constituency—the lower courts, similarly situated potential litigants, and their counsel. They are influenced by a decision in a more specific sense. An appellate
decision can be a signal to this group that their conduct must be adjusted in
accordance with the decision. An appellate court's failure to make clear
pronouncements and to be consistent about the rights of a particular group
like women can expose the group to careless and bad treatment by society.

When reading a case, you should look for the basic facts upon which it
is decided, the rules of law upon which the court bases its opinion, and the
reasoning that supports the application of those rules to the facts of the case.
Individual decisions are guided by legal doctrines that embody broad policy
goals. In many cases, judges are rather explicit about the social consequences
they think will flow from a change in a particular rule.

Although court decisions are exercises of power, the burden of judicial
opinion writing is to show that the decision has not been grounded on other
than "legal" considerations. Judges, however, do sometimes insert into their
opinions their views of how people ought to behave in the "natural order" of
life. This is likely to occur when there is great pressure for social change.
Such statements, although technically not part of the decision, shed light on
which competing cultural value was promoted or sustained by a particular
legal rule. At stake in many of the cases in this collection is the issue of
whether American society should continue to be organized on the principle
of a gender division of roles or on the principle of individual free choice.

The cases and statutes together with the cultural documents in this
volume trace the process of institutionalizing one conception of gender role
and gender capacity. They illustrate the conflicts that arose time and again
over the structure of authority in family and society and the response of the
legal system to challenges to the established order. In describing specific
situations—disputes between real people about immediate issues—they
make concrete the generalizations about the impact of the legal system on
the course of American development and women's lives.

CHAPTER 1

[
*The Colonial,
Revolutionary, and
Early Federal Period*
]

UNIT 1

[*Marriage and Property*]

THE CONCEPT OF COVERTURE

European settlers in the American colonies tended to recreate the patriarchal family order that existed in their countries of origin. The family, indeed all of society, was marked by a status system that included finely graded positions of authority and subordination. The household, which served as the basic unit of production, was sometimes called a "little commonwealth" and was responsible for the well-being of the nuclear family, its servants, and, upon occasion, widows, orphans, the poor, and even criminals in need of rehabilitation. The male head of the household was expected to manage this little society and protect it. The wife and children, in exchange, were expected to respect, obey, and help him in his task. The wife, with the aid of daughters and sometimes servants, provided domestic service and produced part of the food, clothing, and other necessaries of daily life.[1]

In depicting the structure of family authority, colonial society drew on feudal images associated with kings and subjects, masters and servants. Settlers explained the origins of a wife's subordinate status by referring to God's purpose in creating woman, to Eve's sin, and to nature. The selections from the Bible and from wedding sermons illustrate the religious perspective about where authority in the family resided and about proper wifely behavior. The marriage ceremony performed for blacks, modified to fit the system of slavery, fashioned a different model of relationship for husband and wife.

Patriarchy was buttressed by a political system that excluded women from the process of making and administering the laws. Marital property laws enforced the moral authority of the husband over the family. They placed in the hands of the husband control over the real property (land and buildings) a wife brought into the marriage. He could use this property as he pleased, but could not sell or give it away because it descended to his wife's legal heirs. The law, however, gave him ownership of his wife's personal property—other forms of tangible wealth—including her wages. These he could dispose of as he saw fit. The selections from *The Lawes Resolution of Women's Rights* (1632) and from William Blackstone's "The Principle of Unity of Husband and Wife" in *Commentaries from the Laws of England* (1765) illustrate the close interconnection between law and culture. Traditional images of family and gender roles became embodied in "coverture," the legal principle of marital unity. From this concept flow the particular rights, obligations, and legal disabilities of a wife.

The goal of the law of husband and wife, as presented by Blackstone, was to provide a wife with a protector against a harsh outside society. In giving the protector great powers to carry out his role, the law created a problem it could not fully ignore. Who would protect a wife from a guardian who through incompetence or selfishness failed to carry out his obligations properly during marriage and left her destitute in widowhood? The law created provisions for economic security in widowhood that did not rely on moral obligation, but on the rights that flowed from property ownership. It gave the wife a life interest in a portion of all her husband's real property for use during widowhood. Called a dower right, this did not include the power to dispose of the property as she would like. The vested interest in her husband's real property created by this dower right meant that he could not lawfully sell any family property without her consent, since to do so would deprive a wife of her property, which was intermingled with his.

Because a wife remained in every other way under her husband's "coercion," the law established a procedure to insure that her consent had been voluntary. The rule requiring voluntary consent was not gender based, but was part of the system of laws to protect the fundamental right to property. The particular procedural protection described by Blackstone, however, was limited to married women and necessary because of their "inferior" status. In giving a wife this partial property right as a defense, the law treated the principle of marital unity as a legal fiction. It recognized the wife as a separate person in this instance, and placed the responsibility for protecting her interests in her own hands. Whether the procedural protection was sufficient in practice to balance her other legal disabilities will be explored in the next section.

The law of husband and wife was part of the English common law, which was adopted by all the states after the Revolution as the basis of their legal system. The common law is a form of jurisprudence based on customs in long usage and found only in the records of judicial decisions and some legal treatises. These provide the precedents judges applied to similar situations. By providing the first readable and concise discussion of the principles and goals that animated the English system of laws, customs, and arrangement of government institutions, Blackstone made the "mysterious science of the law" comprehensible to a broader public.

The *Commentaries* served as a primary reference on women's position through most of the nineteenth century. Their failure to discuss developments in equity jurisprudence, administered by a different set of courts, produced a somewhat less than accurate picture of married women's legal rights and obscured the inadequacies of the common-law protections that had given rise to new legal defenses. Equity did not alter the status of married women as a class in law, but it did recognize legal instruments that enabled some wives with money and legal knowledge to hold property separately during marriage and so escape the full implications of coverture.

Over the course of the seventeenth and eighteenth centuries Anglo-American society rejected as arbitrary and too often corrupt a system of government in which the monarch could act, in relation to society, as the father of a family. What emerged was a republican ideology and form of government, enshrined in state and federal constitutions that was designed to restrict unilateral decision making by the executive. Property law became the vehicle for assuring the individual a greater measure of personal autonomy against the central authority and for redistributing decision-making power more broadly within the community. The law accomplished this goal by legally committing to private hands control over most economic resources.[2]

Considering the importance placed by both the English and the colonists on property as an instrument of protection against arbitrary rule, could the property rights granted to wives provide them the same security? The law of husband and wife embodied two models of individual protection, one based on the concept of property ownership and the other on the concept of guardianship. How the law worked in practice, will be explored in the following sections, along with related developments in equity.

THE FICTION OF LEGAL PROTECTION

The documents in this section explore the emerging conflict between two goals of judicial policy in the eighteenth and early nineteenth century. One involved promoting economic development by facilitating entrepreneurial activity, and the other involved protecting wives from an abuse of power by their legal guardians. The protection of wives' property could and did come into conflict with a policy of nurturing a market economy in land. The way the courts and legislatures handled the conflicts in a modernizing economy reveals the legal system's priorities in practice.

Land itself was the main vehicle of credit for development in colonial and revolutionary America. The rise in population through natural increase and immigration made land speculation a useful mechanism for capital accumulation in a money scarce economy. For the market system to work effectively, however, creditors and purchasers needed procedures for conveying land and securing full title that were simpler than the common-law legal forms.

Property Transactions

Under common law when a husband sold a piece of property the proceeds went to him alone to use as he saw fit. Since any property sold or mortgaged included a wife's dower portion, the common law required her previous consent and a private interrogation by a judge to make sure that her consent was voluntary. If a husband sold property without going through this procedure, a wife could sue whoever owned the property at the time for the return of her portion. In practice such a suit was most likely to be instituted when the wife became a widow, or when a wife's legal heir had been deprived of part of his or her inheritance. The common-law rules for property conveyance and protecting wives had been fashioned for a static society, not one where population and property turned over frequently. The *Maryland Act for the Enrolling of Conveyances* (1674), an example of an early attempt to simplify the procedure for establishing full legal title, incorporates the law's concern with protecting wives by including the common-law requirement for a secret judicial examination.

Bisset v. *Bisset* (Maryland, 1761) directs attention to the question of whether the system of private examination of the wife was really an adequate defense against coercion. In this case a widow tried to reclaim property from her stepson by bringing clear evidence that her agreement was gained through coercion. The judge could decide either on the basis of evidence and fairness or on the basis of law. *Lloyd* v. *Taylor* (Pennsylvania, 1768) refers to a more common situation—husbands selling property without bothering to get their wives' agreement. Legal and social evidence suggests that the practice of not consulting wives on important economic decisions was common in all the colonies. In making their decisions on individual cases, the judges were concerned with the possibly destabilizing effect of encouraging wives, in similar situations, to seek redress of their grievance.[3]

The effect of the common law of marital property was to distribute the benefits of land speculation to the husband and the risks to the wife. Once a wife consented to the sale of real property she had no legal way of insuring that she would receive the benefits from that sale in widowhood. If wives in any large number chose to assert their common-law rights and refused to agree to the sale or mortgaging of family property, this would have depressed the land market and constricted credit. One solution to this problem was to give legal recognition to agreements where the husband undertook to give the wife a share in the proceeds of a sale. An equity court could recognize this type of postnuptial agreement, barred under common law by the rule that husbands and wives could not make contracts with each other. *Dibble* v. *Hutton* (1802) describes Connecticut's response to this legal innovation.

Neglected Wives

While Connecticut was more reluctant than other states to recognize legal instruments that might limit a husband's capacity to make unilateral decisions, the attitude toward married women's status and role that animated *Dibble* v. *Hutton* was shared by judges and legislators elsewhere and influenced the way they responded to the potential welfare problem created by desertion. The common-law prohibition against a wife owning property meant that if her husband deserted her she could be thrown into the ranks of the poor, even if she had been born into an affluent family. One solution to helping ladies in distress, embodied in the Pennsylvania statute *An Act for the Relief of the Poor* (1771), was to provide the deserted wife with another legal protector, who could attach the family property. The alternative would be to give the deserted wife the legal power to attach family property and function as the head of the household. Courts and statutes allowed this possibility, but generally only after a wife had been abandoned for a number of years. (See "*An Act Concerning Feme Sole Traders,*" Pennsylvania, 1718.)

The Widow's Portion

A wife's greatest insurance against destitution when her husband died was her dower right, which came to her if her husband did not leave a will or if he left her a smaller share of the family wealth than she would receive if she asserted her dower right. The common-law dower right provided her with a one-third life interest in all the real property her husband owned during their marriage, if there were children, and a one-half life interest if there were none. The husband's equivalent of dower under the common law was "curtesy," which was a full life interest in the real estate his wife brought to the marriage, if there were children. Dower meant that the wife was allowed to live off part of the property that belonged to the legal heirs. She could not sell or give away that property, nor could she alter it to increase profits; this was considered wasting another's property. A wife, in practice, was a tenant.

Dower underwent important changes in the post-Revolutionary period, as part of the process of promoting economic development. Widows benefited and lost by new ways of calculating the widow's thirds, and gained greater freedom of action when some state courts, such as Maryland and South Carolina, permitted them to take their portion in a cash equivalent.[4] In *Conner* v. *Shepherd* (Massachusetts, 1818) the Supreme Court eliminated a widow's right to dower in unimproved lands. The court based this precedent on the common-law "doctrine of waste" and presented it as a protection rather than a restriction of dower rights. In other situations involving tenants, the courts had modified the doctrine of waste so as to encourage immediate development. If the courts had followed the same principle concerning widows and allowed them to develop unimproved property, such land would have provided enterprising women with potentially larger incomes. This, however, would have limited the freedom of legal heirs, usually males, to make decisions about land use and development. Since the doctrine of *Conner* v. *Shepherd* was an exception to a general legal policy of encouraging improvements by those in possession of the land, the case raises the question as to whether the purpose was in fact to provide greater protection or to limit the role of women in making economic decisions.[5]

Husbands who left wills were free to decide how they would distribute their property. They could not leave a widow less than what she would have received under either dower or intestacy laws, which were usually more liberal and included something out of a husband's personal estate, as well as real estate. Patterns of will making appear to have changed between the seventeenth and nineteenth centuries. In seventeenth-century Maryland for example, where, because of disease and patterns of migration, there was a dearth of kin and adult sons, husbands bequeathed the use and disposition of their property to their wives.[6] As the colonies became more populated and civilized, wills came more often to be used to restrict the widow's role in managing the estate and supervising the children. A common means of enforcing these restrictions was through the appointment of co-executors. Some husbands gave their widows use of the family estate only as long as they remained single.

The *Will of Jeronimus Rapelye* (1754) is an example of the way husbands distributed their assets among wives, sons, and daughters. The smaller portions provided to female family members, far from representing personal feelings, reflected social beliefs that the major function of inheritance was to give male descendants status and freedom of action. Because Jeronimus Rapelye chose to turn his real property into cash, his widow could dispose of her inheritance as she pleased. If you look at her cash portion you will see how dower set the standard for distribution. This came to be known as the "widow's thirds."

The selection from Tapping Reeve's treatise, *The Law of Baron and Feme* (1816), on the concept of "paraphernalia," describes a widow's rights to personal objects ranging from clothing to jewelry. It illustrates the priorities and outlook of American common law and the deep conflict of objectives in marital property law.

ESCAPE FROM COVERTURE

Run Away or Suffer

The documents in this section present solutions to the problem of unbearable marriages and show the important economic role of wives. Newspaper advertisements for runaway wives, abounding in the late eighteenth century, provide a glimpse of the social reality to which the law would eventually have to address itself. Advertisements such as that of Joseph Perkins in *The Pennsylvania Chronicle* (1767) were a legal necessity because the common law made a husband responsible for his wife's debts. The rebuttal of his wife, however, was not typical. The more usual response, particularly for women not living in or near metropolitan areas, appears in the selection from *The Diary of Abigail Gardner Drew* (Nantucket, circa 1800). These selections direct attention to the social function of marital property laws.

Marriage Settlements

Diaries, letters, advertisements for runaway wives, court cases, and statutes all point to the ineffectiveness of the common law protections for women who found themselves married to men who were incompetent, irresponsible, or scoundrels. One legal solution was to let wives own and control property separately from their husbands. Such arrangements, in the form of trusts, jointures, and antenuptial agreements, appeared first in sixteenth-century England. There the aristocracy feared that husbands might take money brought into marriage and transfer it to their own families. These devices for evading the full implications of coverture were accepted by equity courts, called chancery courts, which had been established to ameliorate the inflexibility of common-law courts and their complicated legal forms.

The antenuptial agreement was a contract made between a man and a woman who intended to marry. It took effect after marriage and set forth the wife's rights to property. The most common form held property in trust for the wife and any children of the union. Typically, such a contract was made when both spouses-to-be were entering upon their first marriage; they generally reflected the interests of the bride's male relatives and were intended less to give the bride control over her finances than to provide her with a comfortable marriage and a tolerable widowhood.[7] The Bequest to Sarah Amelia Tart, by her Father (South Carolina, 1794), signed by Amelia's fiancé, George Bampfield, is an example of such an agreement. Fathers could and did leave bequests to their daughters, as well.

It was also possible to make an agreement or bequest that gave the wife control over and the use and disposition of property she brought into marriage or acquired during marriage. This kind of contract was more likely to be made by a widow than by a young woman embarking on her first marriage.[8] The *Marital Agreement between Ebenezer Vereen and Catharin McKiver* (South Carolina, 1784) gives Catharin the power to will her property to whomever she pleases, but leaves control over it to her husband during the marriage. The *Marital Agreement between Eliza Johnson and Christopher Walten* (South Carolina, 1813) is an instance of a woman using this legal device to gain almost full control over property she brought into the marriage or had acquired as a result of her efforts during marriage.

Antenuptial contracts were wordy and repetitious in order to avoid loopholes or misinterpretation. Whatever rights a woman did not secure for herself before marriage, and which under common law belonged to the husband, remained his. The documents below show how much foresight and legal knowledge a woman needed to gain a large measure of personal autonomy within marriage.

In making antenuptial agreements, women often were more concerned to reserve the right to bequeath their property to people of their own choice than to control its use during marriage. The making of a will did not involve the question of protection, but independent control over the distribution of property. Because inheritance was such an important source of capital for the next generation, the ability to choose a beneficiary had always been viewed as central to the issue of power and status. It was believed that the right of wives to bequeath their estates would alter the structure of authority within the family and society and undermine family unity. Two cases, *Barnes* v. *Hart*, Pennsylvania (1791) and *Fitch* v. *Brainerd*, Connecticut (1805) examine the judicial response to the idea of independent control over property in the early federal period.

During the eighteenth century, Pennsylvania had accepted the idea of separate property, but only in the form of a trust. In *Barnes* v. *Hart* the court took the next logical step and recognized a simple agreement of the type described above. In her agreement Margaret Henderson retained possession of her property, allowed her husband to use it during their marriage, and reserved the right to make her own will. She died childless before her husband and left her property to various nieces and nephews. Her husband's nephew, who was the legal heir, contested the will. The tortuous argument of the judge in upholding this will indicates how important a legal innovation this was. The change from antenuptial agreements created only by trusts, to simple agreements between engaged couples, was in keeping with the legal thrust toward simplicity and practicality. (Margaret could have accomplished the same end by establishing a trust estate.) Another factor making this precedent possible was the fact that in upholding the agreement the court was supporting the decision of the husband, Matthew Henderson: it was thus both preserving the historic principle of a husband's freedom of decision and accepting change.[9]

States varied widely in the degree of independence they were willing to accord wives. Connecticut stood at the conservative end of the spectrum. *Fitch* v. *Brainerd* (1805) provides insight into the underlying social perspective that made change toward greater property rights such a slow process. In this case Elizabeth Mary Fitch appealed a superior court decision approving the will of Abigail Mary Brainerd, who left her property to her husband. The appeals court, by overturning this lower-court decision, rejected the precedent. Under common law the property would have descended to Elizabeth Mary Fitch, who was the heir at law.

In their representation of the case, the lawyers provided a social history of the attitudes that shaped the status of women's rights before the Revolution and limited the pace of change in the early federal period. The lawyers for Fitch depicted a broad set of rights, including suffrage, that would flow from the court's acceptance of the right to make a will. The lawyer for the appellee, Jehu Brainerd, on the other hand, tried to minimize the social implications of this precedent by showing that it involved no real change. *Fitch* v. *Brainerd* presents one of the clearest descriptions of how courts find principles through precedents, and of how judges perceive the differences between the powers of a court and the legislature.

The American Revolution accelerated the trend toward arranging marriage settlements that accorded wives more autonomy. Judicial recognition of such instruments reflected greater respect for women's capabilities and greater sensitivity to the issue of abuse of power. In the course of their dispute with England the colonists detailed the way the king and his agents perverted their authority to selfish ends. It became an axiom of the new political science that the concentration of liberty in the hands of one or a few persons produces tyranny, licentiousness, and oppression. This theory expressed for women their own anxieties about their situation. *The letters from Lucy Ludwell Paradise to Thomas Jefferson* (1789) are an example of the private attempt by a few women to raise the issue of legal rights for their sex. Lucy Paradise uses her own experience to draw attention to the general danger of arbitrary government by husbands and the need for protection.

Her language, designed to evoke chivalry, stands in striking contrast to the thrust of her petition. In advocating the marriage settlement as a model for reform, Lucy Paradise was expressing the egalitarian ethos of the Revolution. Turning the marriage settlement into law would extend privileges enjoyed by a few to all women and institute the principle of equal protection of the law.

Republican visionaries such as Jefferson disregarded pleas for a married woman's property act. They believed that the separation of spheres and functions was as God-given and natural as the right to life, liberty, and property. Highly conscious of the symbolic significance of the law, they may have feared that the granting of a fundemental property right, historically associated with the male world and with freedom of action, would legitimize female participation in economic and political affairs. As politicians they knew that any attempt to restrict men's property rights would jeopardize the republican experiment.

DAUGHTERS, WARDS, AND SERVANTS

Social attitudes and the nature of the economy placed single women at the bottom of the social scale. Spinsterhood, therefore, was not an attractive alternative to marriage. As we have seen, a wife's dependent status and inadequate legal protection made her peculiarly vulnerable to the effects of her husband's failings; thus the crucial decision in her life involved the selection of her spouse. Parents had great social and legal authority in matters of marriage, indeed, their consent to any match was necessary until the child reached age twenty-one. A father could not force a child to marry someone she disliked, but at least in New England, he had the legal authority to decide who could court his daughter. In making judgments about suitors, fathers tended to stress economic qualifications while mothers and daughters placed more emphasis on the role of affection in marriage. The way men and women approached matrimony reflected the different boundaries of their lives. Parental involvement in this period was deemed a protection against rash decisions. The legal requirements of a father's consent to marriage, like that of a master in the case of a servant, however, were rooted in the concept of children as property.[10] *The Laws of the Colony of New Plymouth on Marriage* (1658) describe the legal authority of parents, guardians, and masters. Although the law refers to parents and encourages joint decision making, ultimate legal authority in case of a disagreement rested with the father, who had custody of the children and control over family property.

Indentured female servants were less likely to face marriage with the same level of trepidation as girls from higher social ranks. Marriage almost always represented a rise in social and economic status and greater opportunities for personal satisfaction. Indentured servants were in essence temporary slaves, the personal property of their masters. They could, in most cases, be freely sold, hired out, and assigned to others in a will or in payment for a debt. At the end of their term they received some kind of compensation called "freedom dues." A contract of indenture generally was for between four and seven years. The colonies relied on indenture to finance immigration and assure a cheap labor force. They used the welfare and penal codes to augment the supply of willing servants. Orphans and abandoned children were bound into service, as were persons convicted of crimes against property. Extra service was imposed on servants for various types of wrongful conduct, such as absenteeism, desertion, and bastardy.

The selection from *The Laws of Virginia* (1705) dealing with bastardy is an example of the way class, gender, and race shaped the legal approach to a problem that arose in part because masters had an economic interest in keeping maidservants from marrying. The goal of the statute is to protect the community against bearing the welfare costs of bastardy and discourage illicit relations that inevitably led to childbearing. The law serves neither of these goals well because the penalties and enforcement procedures are designed to protect male freedom of action by shifting the burden to mothers. The men who benefited most from what was deemed a sin were the masters. The women penalized most were those involved in miscegenation.

The statute imposes an extra service penalty on the mother that assures the master recovery of services and costs associated with pregnancy and some punitive damages. By requiring the female servant to pay off her debt before leaving service, future husbands were relieved of this debt which otherwise they would be required by law to assume. In the colonial context a service penalty was not unfair, and it was practical. The state, however, provides the parish no comparable enforcement procedure, leaving the putative father free to decide whether to pay the required child support. It is easier for the parish to recover by binding out the child.

In this statute extra service is not simply a damage payment for a breach of contract, but punishment for a crime. Since it is applied no matter what the circumstance, it takes a female servant's liberty away without due process. The penalty structure, by implication, establishes the mother as the culpable person and the father as an accessory. This is indicated by the fact that even if the master is the father, the maidservant must not only complete her indenture, but serve extra time with another master. Since the master is viewed as an accessory, he cannot benefit from his seduction and must absorb a loss of service. This assignment of who is the responsible party comports more with cultural definitions of woman as Eve than with the English Common Law's conception of the rights, powers, and obligations of a master. The fact that the term of extra service was minimal may have reflected simply justice or it may have reflected the fact that there was a shortage of marriageable white women. The penalty for miscegenation indicates what lawmakers thought would reduce bastardy, and what they might have applied if there had been no slave labor force and a different sex ratio.

ESCAPE FROM SLAVERY

The Massachusetts slave cases show that white colonists' own fears or fantasies about being reduced to slavery by England's tax policies made many of them sensitive to the idea of reducing blacks into slaves. In the late 1760s a number of slaves turned to the courts to obtain their freedom. They may have been encouraged to test the legal status of slavery by English court decisions that freed slaves brought to England from the colonies and by the rhetoric of the accelerating revolutionary movement that portrayed the objects of free government and the law as the protection of inalienable rights to life, liberty, and property.

To gain a legal hearing and redress of grievances, slaves presented themselves to the Massachusetts courts as free individuals. They brought suits for damages against their masters on the grounds of trespass to person, that is, false imprisonment. Freedom was determined as an incident of the right of a free person to maintain this kind of civil action. In practice juries almost always found blacks to be free, not slaves. Because slavery was culturally, as well as legally accepted as an institution, slaves had to rest their case for freedom more on grounds of evidence than on human rights. *Slew* v. *Whipple* (1766) illustrates this reliance on evidence, precedent, and legal procedure in slave pleadings. More particularly it shows how, on the merits of the case, the common-law status of married women could be used to limit the access of female, but not male blacks to a jury trial.

While the slave cases did not lead to the abolition of slavery or of the slave trade, as in England, they set forth the policy that a free black could not be enslaved against his or her will within Massachusetts. It was not until the Massachusetts Constitution of 1780, and Judge William Cushing's construction of its "free and equal" clause as a prohibition of slavery in *Quock Walker's Case* (1783), that there was a firm legal basis for manumission when, on the facts, the plaintiff was clearly a slave.[11]

DOCUMENTS

THE CONCEPT OF COVERTURE

[1]
The New Testament, Ephesians 5:22–24

Wives should regard their husbands as they regard the Lord, since as Christ is head of the Church and saves the whole body, so is a husband the head of his wife; and as the Church submits to Christ, so should wives to their husbands, in everything.

From *The Jerusalem Bible: The Reader's Edition* (Garden City, New York: Doubleday, 1966).

[2]
"A Wedding Ring Fit for the Finger"

It is between a man and his wife in the house as it is between the Sun and the Moon in the Heavens: when the great light goes down, the lesser light gets up. When the one ends in setting, the other begins in shining. The wife may be sovereign in her husband's absence, but she must be subject in his presence.

From William Secker, "A Wedding Ring, Fit for the Finger" (Boston, 1750). From *Womanhood in America* by Mary P. Ryan. Copyright © 1983 by Mary P. Ryan. Used by permission of Franklin Watts, Inc.

[3]

A Marriage Ceremony for Slaves in Colonial Massachusetts (1710–1771)

You, S., do now, in the presence of God and these Witnesses, take R. to be your WIFE, Promising that, so far as shall be consistent with your relation which you now sustain as a Servant, you will Perform your part of a Husband towards her; and in particular you Promise that you will LOVE her; and that, as you shall have your Opportunity and Ability, you will take a proper CARE of her in Sickness and Health, in Prosperity and Adversity: And that you will be True and FAITHFUL to her, and will Cleave to her ONLY, SO LONG as God, in his Providence, shall continue your and her abode in Such Place (or Places) as that you can conveniently come together.

[The minister addresses similar words to the woman and then continues.]

I, then, agreeable to your Request, and with the Consent of your Masters and Mistresses, do Declare that you have License given you to be conversant and familiar together, as HUSBAND and WIFE, so long as God shall continue your Places of abode as aforesaid; and so long as you shall behave your-selves as it becometh Servants to do: For you must both of you bear in mind that you Remain Still, as really and truly as ever, your Master's Property, and therefore it will be justly expected both by God and Man that you behave and conduct your-selves as Obedient and faithful Servants towards your respective Masters and Mistresses for the Time being.

And Finally, I exhort and charge you to beware lest you give place to the Devil, so as to take Occasion, from the License now given you, to be lifted up with PRIDE and thereby to fall under the displeasure not of Man only but of God also; for it is written that God resisteth the Proud but he giveth Grace to the humble.

Cited in George Elliott Howard, *A History of Matrimonial Institutions,* vol. 2 (Chicago: University of Chicago Press, 1904), pp. 225–26.

[4]
The Lawes Resolutions of Women's Rights (1632)

In this consolidation which we call wedlock is a locking together. It is true that man and wife are one person; but understand in what manner. When a small brooke or little river incorporateth with Rhodanus, Humber, or the Thames, the poor rivulet looseth her name; . . . it possesseth nothing during coverture. . . . A woman, as soon as she is married, is called *covert;* . . . she hath lost her streame. I may more truly . . . say to a married woman, Her new self is her superior; her companion, her master . . . Eve, because she had helped to seduce her husband, had inflicted upon her a special bane. See here the reason of that which I touched before—that women have no voice in Parliament. They make no laws, they consent to none, they abrogate none. All of them [women] are understood [as] either married, or to be married, and their desires are to their husbands. . . . The common laws here shaketh hand with divinitye.

From "The Lawes Resolutions of Women's Rights: Or, the Laws Provision for Women" (London, 1632). From *Women's Life and Work in the Southern Colonies,* by Julia Cherry Spruill *Laws or Lawes?* Copyright 1938 The University of North Carolina Press. Reprinted by permission of the publisher.

[5]
William Blackstone on the Principle of the Unity of Husband and Wife (1765)

By marriage, the husband and wife are one person in law: that is, the very being or legal existence of the woman is suspended during the marriage, or at least is incorporated and consolidated into that of the husband, under whose wing, protection, and *cover,* she performs every thing; and is therefore called in our law-French a *feme-covert* . . . or under the protection and influence of her husband, her *baron* or lord; and her condition during her marriage is called her *coverture.* . . . For this reason, a man cannot grant any thing to his wife, or enter into covenant [except through the intervention of a trustee] with her, for the grant would be to suppose her separate existence; and to covenant with her would be only to covenant with himself: and therefore it is also generally true, that all compacts made between husband and wife, when single, are voided by the intermarriage. A woman indeed may be

From William Blackstone, *Commentaries on the Laws of England,* 1765 (facsimile of first edition, vol. 1, Chicago: University of Chicago Press, 1979), pp. 430–33.

attorney for her husband; for that implies no separation from, but is rather a representation of, her lord. And a husband may also bequeath any thing to his wife by will; for that cannot take effect till the coverture is determined by his death. The husband is bound to provide his wife with necessaries by law, as much as himself; and if she contracts debts for them, he is obliged to pay them: but any thing besides necessaries, he is not chargeable. Although if a wife elopes, and lives with another man, the husband is not chargeable even for necessaries; at least if the person who furnishes them is sufficiently apprised for her elopement. If the wife be indebted before marriage, the husband is bound afterwards to pay the debt; for he has adopted her and her circumstances together. If the wife be injured in her person or her property, she can bring no action for redress without her husband's concurrence, and in his name, as well as her own: neither can she be sued, without making the husband a defendant. There is indeed one case where the wife shall sue and be sued as a feme sole, *viz.* where the husband has abjured the realm, or is banished: for then he is dead in law; and, the husband being thus disabled to sue for or defend the wife, it would be unreasonable if she had no remedy, or could make no defence at all. . . .

BUT, although our law in general considers man and wife as one person, yet there are some instances in which she is separately considered; as inferior to him, and acting by his compulsion. And therefore all deeds executed, and acts done, by her, during her coverture, are void, or at least voidable; except it be a fine, or the like matter of record, in which case she must be solely and secretely examined, to learn if her act be voluntary. She cannot by will devise lands to her husband, unless under special circumstances; for at the time of making it she is supposed to be under his coercion. . . .

THESE are the chief legal effects of marriage during the coverture; upon which we may observe, that even the disabilities which the wife lies under are for the most part intended for her protection and benefit. So great a favourite is the female sex of the laws of England.

THE FICTION OF LEGAL PROTECTION
Property Transactions

[6]
"An Act for the Enrolling of Conveyances and Servicing the Estates of Purchasers" (Maryland, 1674)

. . . Whereas any married woman, or *feme covert,* shall happen to be named a Party, Grantor in any such Writing indented [a deed, for example], the same shall not be of Force to debar her, or her Heirs, except (upon her Acknowledgment of the same.) The Person or Persons taking such, her Acknowledgment, shall examine her privately and secretly, out of the Hearing of her Husband, "Whether she do make such Acknowledgment willingly and freely, and without being induced thereunto, by any Force or Threats used by her Husband, or through fear of his Displeasure?" And that upon such Examination, she shall own the said Acknowledgment to be free and voluntary. . . .

From Thomas Bacon, ed., *Laws of Maryland At Large, with Proper Indexes. Now First Collected into One Compleat Body* (Annapolis, 1765), ch. 2.

[7]
Bissett *v.* Bissett *(Maryland, 1761)*

This is a bill filed by Ann Bissett in Chancery (an equity court) to transfer back to her the land she had given away under duress, while married to David Bissett. The language has been changed in places to facilitate reading—Ed.

Bill of Complaint of Ann Bissett against James Bissett. She says that her former husband, John Atkinson, appointed her Executrix in his will and devised to her all his real and personal estate. On December 14, 1754 she obtained a survey of the tracts of land and found that she had 1184 acres. . . . Then she married David Bissett, "who had not any real but a very inconsiderable Personal Estate. And the said David Bissett, soon after your Oratrix's [female petitioner's] intermarriage with him, . . . of

From Chancery Court Records, vol. 10 (1761–1764) (Annapolis: Maryland Hall of Records), pp. 60–73; 1 Harris and McHenry (Ma.) 211 (1762).

persuasion, endeavored to induce your Oratrix to give him the whole of her Real Estate. Your Oratrix objected and Absolutely refused. The said David Bissett, to gain to himself the whole Inheritance of your Oratrix his then wife (which your Oratrix is now too well convinced was the Principal if not the Sole Motive with him for his Marriage with your Oratrix), did threaten your Oratrix with Ill-usage if she would not Consent to make over her Real Estate to him. To force and induce your Oratrix to make such conveyance said David Bissett did often cruelly beat and with Opprobrious Language abuse your Oratrix, menacing and threatening her at the same time with a repetition of such Ill-Usage unless she consented to such Conveyance. . . . David Bissett's . . . settled Moroseness and Sourness of Temper towards her was inconsistent with and repugnant to the Rights of Marriage by which she was rendered extremely miserable. She was taught to Esteem as a Master the Man who She had but lately raised from Small estate by taking him to Husband. She at length, on the Importunity of the said David Bissett and through fear of him from his ill-treatment, did tell him that She would make over her lands to him. Thereupon Deeds of Lease and Release were Devised and Drawn" and executed in June 1755. They conveyed [the land] to John Matthews in fee . . . "and immediately upon the Execution of the said Lease and Release . . . John Matthews did convey all the said Lands to the aforesaid David Bissett. . . ." She notes that she made her acknowledgement of the conveyance as is required by law. . . . "Your Oratrix does expressly charge and so the Truth really is that the Acknowledgments were not made willingly and freely and without being induced thereto by Fears and Threats of Ill-usage from her said Husband and from the Beatings, threatenings and other abuse. . . ."

David Bissett died intestate after he obtained these conveyances. His eldest brother James Bissett (the Defendant) took out letters of administration on the estate. He refused to reconvey to the complainant, though he knew in his conscience the lands were rightfully hers, and that she had been forced to give them up.

Answer of James Bissett. He cites the deeds as all valid. "The said Acknowledgements and Private Examination taken in the very Terms, Very Words and Spirit of the said Act of Assembly must be conclusive and effectually Bar any complainant from having the Relief prayed for in this Court. Otherwise property would be rendered altogether Vague and incertain. . . ." He says David Bissett used no threats (etc.) to force his wife to convey, but that she did so willingly and "cheerfully."

[The Chancellor determined] "that no evidence could be received to invalidate an acknowledgement of a deed, taken by two justices agreeably to the act of the assembly."

[8]
Lloyd *v.* Taylor *(Pennsylvania, 1768)*

Mercy Masters owned property in Philadelphia when she married Peter Lloyd. Peter Lloyd and Mercy his wife conveyed the land to Ralph Ashton in 1727, and Ralph reconveyed the land in question to Peter Lloyd. Afterwards, in 1738, on judgment against Peter Lloyd, the land was taken in execution and sold by the sheriff to the defendant for 1300 pounds. Plaintiff, son of Mercy Lloyd, claims the land, insisting that his mother, being feme covert, could not legally convey her estate without an examination by writ—Ed.

But, it appearing in evidence that it had been the constant usage of the Province formerly for *femes covert* to convey their estates in this manner, without an acknowledgment or separate examination; and that there were a great number of valuable estates held under such titles which it would be dangerous to impeach at this time of day. THE COURT gave a charge to the jury in favor of the defendants, founded on the maxim *communis error facit jus* [common error makes law]. And the Jury accordingly found for the Defendant.

1 Dallas (Pa.) 17 (1768).

[9]
Dibble *v.* Hutton *(Connecticut, 1802)*

Mary Hutton, widow of Samuel Hutton, petitioned the Chancery Court to order the executor of her deceased husband's will to pay her money she felt was due her. She claimed that during her marriage she and her husband jointly owned fifty-five acres of land. Samuel had owned three-quarters of the land and Mary one-quarter. Samuel wanted to sell the land but could not do so unless Mary agreed to sell her portion. In order to convince her to do so, Samuel promised to give Mary one-quarter of the proceeds of the sale for her private use. As a result of his promise, the land was sold to Caleb Comstock and Benoni St. John on January 6, 1798. Samuel received notes in the amount of 192 pounds, 10 shillings in return for the land, and he immediately gave Mary part of the notes. She kept the notes until Samuel died on 16 September 1799.

In May 1792, Samuel had made a will giving Mary nothing more than that part of his real estate to which she was entitled under dower rights. He appointed Nehemiah Dibble as executor of the will. After Samuel's death, Mary claimed that

1 Day (Conn.) 221 (1802).

she was owed one-quarter of the 192 pounds, 10 shillings, but Dibble disagreed. He demanded the notes and threatened Mary with a lawsuit if she did not relinquish them so that he could include them in the inventory of Samuel's estate. Mary gave him the notes but refused to give up her claim to them. Dibble has since received the money from the notes but has not given Mary what she believes is due her.—Ed.

BY THE COURT. The petitioner's claim . . . rests on the ground of the husband and wife's contract, or a combined view of the facts contained in the bill. Hence, the questions made relate to the competency of a husband and wife to contract with each other; the competency of the wife to have an estate for her separate use; and the equity of the particular case.

By the common law, the husband and wife are considered as one person in law, the existence of the wife being merged in that of the husband, or suspended during the coverture. As a consequence of this union of persons, . . . husband and wife cannot contract with each other, nor the husband make a grant or gift to the wife, nor the wife have personal estate, to her sole and separate use.

If these principles are to be received and applied . . . to this claim, they, at once, determine all the questions that arise in considering the case. They preclude the idea of the husband's and wife's competency to contract with each other, and the wife's competency to have, during *coverture,* personal estate to her separate use; And these being precluded, no equity arises out of the facts in the case, which, consistently with those principles of the common law, can be recognized by a court of chancery. Nor, indeed, is any equity perceived to exist in this case, to distinguish it from the ordinary transaction of the wife's estate being sold and the avails thereof coming, in personal estate, to the husband.

It is, however, insisted that those principles of the common law have been qualified, and modified, in the courts of chancery, in England, in such manner, as to recognize the wife's right and competency to have personal estate to her separate use, and the validity of certain contracts between husband and wife; and that those qualifications and modifications which have taken place in the English courts of chancery, ought to be adopted in ours. . . .

In tracing the history of the English chancery on this subject, it is found, that the doctrine of the wife's separate personal estate, a little more than a century past, since the emigration of our ancestors into this country, first insinuated itself into practice. It was not received without difficulty; but has gradually gained ground, and soon introduced the principle of contract between husband and wife. . . . It owes its rise to that state of manners and society which it has followed and accommodated.

By a kind of fiction, the husband is considered a trustee for the wife, as to her separate estate; and on the ground of its being a trust estate, chancery has taken cognizance of it; and a husband and wife have become suitors and litigant parties against each other before the court. The chancellor adapts the proceedings and decree of the court to the intimate relation between the parties.

The principle, that governs with respect to contracts between husband and wife, does not appear to be definite. Some kinds of contracts are recognized and enforced, but a wide latitude is left for the discretionary power of the chancellor. The system is complex, originating numerous, complicated questions as to the relative rights and property of husband and wife, and changing the form of legal proceedings.

It is unnecessary to enter on a detail of those manners, different ranks, and general state of society in England, which induced the system; they greatly differ from ours. At the time of the emigration of our ancestors from England, the principles of the common law, on this subject were in full force, unqualified by the modifications of the court of chancery: they have never been received and applied in the unqualified sense, both in our courts of law and chancery.

. . . The maxims of the ancient common law, on this subject, are plain and simple; our state of manners and society do not require that they should be relaxed or qualified. The principles, therefore, which govern in the English courts of chancery, ought not to be engrafted into our chancery system; but those of the common law remain unimpaired. [The petition granted by two lower courts was unanimously overturned with this opinion.]

Neglected Wives

[10]
"An Act for the Relief of the Poor"
(Pennsylvania, 1771)

And whereas it sometimes happens that men separate themselves, without reasonable cause, from their wives, and desert their children, and women also desert their children, leaving them a charge upon the said city, or upon some borough, township or place aforesaid, although such persons may have estates which should contribute to the maintenance of such wives or children: *Be it therefore enacted,* That it shall and may be lawful for the Overseers of the poor of the said city, having first obtained a warrant or order from two Magistrates of the said city, or for the Overseers of any borough, township or place, where such wife or children shall be so left, or where such wife or children shall be so neglected, having first obtained a warrant or order of any two Justices of the Peace of the county, to take and seize so much of the goods and chattels, and receive so much of the annual rents and profits of the lands and tenements of such husband, father or mother, as such two Magis-

From *Laws of the Commonwealth of Pennsylvania,* vol. 1 (Philadelphia, 1810), pp. 344–45.

trates or Justices shall order and direct, for providing for such wife, and for maintaining and bringing up such child or children.

Which warrant or order being confirmed at the next Quarter Sessions for the city or county respectively, it shall and may be lawful for the Justices there to make an order for the Overseers to dispose of such goods and chattels, by sale or otherwise, or so much of them, for the purposes aforesaid, as the court shall think fit, and to receive the rents and profits, or so much of them as shall be ordered by the said Sessions, of his or her lands and tenements, for the purposes aforesaid.

And if no estate, real or personal, of such husband, father or mother, can be found, wherewith provision may be made as aforesaid, it shall and may be lawful to and for the said Justices, in their Court of Quarter Sessions for the city or county respectively, to order the payment of such sums, as they shall think reasonable for the maintenance of any wife or children so neglected, and commit such husband, father or mother to the *common gaol,* there to remain, until he or she comply with the said order, give security for the performance thereof, or be otherwise discharged by the said Justices.

And on complaint made to any Magistrate of the city of Philadelphia, or to any Justice of the Peace in any county, of any wife or children being so neglected, such Magistrate or Justice shall take security from the husband, father or mother, neglecting as aforesaid, for his or her appearance at the next General Quarter Sessions, there to abide the determination of the said Court, and for want of security to commit such persons.

The Widow's Portion

[11]
Conner *v.* Shepherd *(Massachusetts, 1818)*

THIS was a writ of *dower,* in which it was agreed that the demandant's husband was seised [i.e., legally owned and possessed], during coverture, of the premises described in her writ, . . . and in the year 1802 conveyed the same to the tenant; that after the death of her said husband, . . . in May, 1816, she duly demanded her dower to be assigned to her, which the tenant refused to do; that the premises consist of two hundred acres of land, which were, at the time of the said conveyance, wholly uncultivated and covered with wood and timber, in which state they still remain, and the land is valuable only for the purpose of being cleared and cultivated.

15 (Mass.) 164 (1818).

[ARGUMENTS]

BOUTELLE, *for the demandant.* At the common law a widow is entitled to her dower in all the lands and tenements in which her husband was seised . . . during coverture. The provision of the colony law was to the same effect, including "all such houses, lands, tenements, and hereditaments" as the husband was seised of, etc. By the statute of the commonwealth, 1783, the widow of a person deceased shall in all cases be entitled to her dower in the *real estate,* using the most comprehensive term; and the statute of dower recognizes the right to dower in lands, tenements, and hereditaments, generally. . . . It has been settled in New York that tenant for life of wild and uncultivated land, wholly covered with wood and timber, may fell part of the wood and timber, so as to fit the land for cultivation. . . .

In the action of *Nash* v. *Boltwood* the land in which dower was demanded had been conveyed by the husband of the demandant, when it was in a wild and unimproved state, incapable of any yearly rent or profit; and although, after the conveyance, great improvements had been made by the grantee and those claiming under him, the demandant had judgment.

It was said, by Sir *Joseph Jekyll,* that a widow has not merely a civil but also a moral right to dower; and the position is well maintained by that learned jurist.

WILLIAMS *for the tenant.* The intent of dower is for the sustenance and support of the widow, but she can derive none from land in an uncultivated state; and the very act of rendering the land capable of yielding any sustenance to her would amount to a forfeiture of her estate. The law of *England* is equally extensive, in its description of the kinds of property in which a wife is dowable, as our statutes. Yet in that country there are exceptions, as of a castle for defense . . .; and the like reason of inconvenience applies to the case of land in a state of nature.

It was adjudged, in the case of *Leonard* v. *Leonard,* that, in the assignment of dower, commissioners are to regard the rents and profits only of the estate out of which dower is to be assigned. But in the case at bar, there can be no rents or profits. In the case of *Sargent et al.* v. *Towne,* it was said by this Court that a life estate in wild land cannot be considered as of any value. It would, then, be of no benefit to the demandant, were she to have judgment in this action.

[DECISION]

The opinion of the Court was delivered by PARKER, C. J. Upon this question we have had considerable difficulty. By the common law, the widow is dowable of all the real estate of which her husband was seised during the coverture, with the exception only of a castle erected for public defense, . . . and some other kinds of estate not known in this country. The question whether forests, parks, and other property of a similar nature, are also exceptions, seems never to have occurred; probably because there is no instance, in *Great Britain,* of any such property held separately and distinct from improved and cultivated estates.

In this country, on the contrary, there are many large tracts of uncultivated territory owned by individuals who have no intention of reducing them to a state of improvement, but consider them rather as subjects of speculation and sale, or as a future fund for their posterity, increasing in value with the population and improvement of the country. If dower could be assigned in estates of this nature, the views of those who purchase such property would be obstructed; and an impediment to their transfer would be created, and in many instances the inheritance would be prejudiced, without any actual advantage to the widow to whom the dower might be assigned. For, according to the principles of common law, her estate would be forfeited if she were to cut down any of the trees valuable as timber. It would seem, too, that the mere change of the property from wilderness to arable or pasture land, by cutting down the wood and clearing up the land, might be considered as waste; for the alteration of the property, even if it became thereby more valuable, would subject the estate in dower to forfeiture—the heir having a right to the inheritance in the same character as it was left by the ancestor.

It is no extravagant supposition that lands actually in a state of nature may, in a country fast increasing in its population, be more valuable than the same land would be with that sort of cultivation which a tenant for life would be likely to bestow upon it; and that the very clearing of the land, for the purpose of getting the greatest crops from the least labor, which is all that could be expected from a tenant in dower, would be actually, as well as technically, waste of the inheritance.

There would seem, then, to be no reason for allowing dower to the widow in property of this kind. If she did not improve the land, the dower would be wholly useless; if she did improve it she would be exposed to disputes with the heir, and to the forfeiture of her estate, after having expended her substance upon it.

But this is not all. It is well understood by the common law, and the principle has been repeatedly settled in this Court, that the dower of the widow is not to be assigned, so as to give her one third of the land in quantity, but so that she may enjoy one third of the rents and profits, or income, of the estate. Now, of a lot of wild land, not connected with a cultivated farm, there are no rents or profits. On the contrary, it is an expense to the owner, by reason of the taxes. The rule, therefore, by which dower is to be assigned cannot be applied to such property.

. . . Upon the whole, seeing no possible benefit to the widow from an assignment of dower in such property; and, on the contrary, believing that it would operate as a clog upon estates designed to be the subject of transfer; and finding that the principles upon which the estate in dower rests at common law are not applicable to a case of the kind before us—we feel constrained to say that the demandant cannot maintain her present action. . . .

[12]

Abstract of the Will of Jeronimus Rapelye (Flushing, New York, 1754)

In the name of God, Amen. I, Jeronimus Rapelye, of Flushing, in Queens County, yeoman, being now sick, I leave to my wife Ann my best bed, my silver teapot, and my riding chair, and a horse suitable to draw the same, and my cabinet and 350 pounds. I leave to my son John all that certain messuage, dwelling house and farm or plantation which I lately purchased of Samuel Farrington, and where my son John liveth, situated in the township of Flushing; also a negro woman; and also the horses, cattle, and utensils I have already given to him and which with the farm I value at 850 pounds. I also leave him my silver tankard for his birth right, and my wife shall have the use of it so long as she continues my widow. I leave to my son Richard 800 pounds, and a negro man. I leave to my daughter Ann 200 pounds, which with 100 pounds lately given to her by her grandmother, and a negro wench which I value at 50 pounds, also given by her grandmother, makes her portion 350 pounds. I leave to my daughter Idagh 330 pounds, and a negro girl which I value at 30 pounds. To my daughter Elizabeth 330 pounds, and a negro girl which I value at 30 pounds. I leave to my son Stephen 890 pounds when he is 21. I leave to my wife and children all the rest of my wrought plate. My son John is to have the care of the portions of my two eldest daughters, Ann and Idagh. I order that as soon as convenient my executors shall sell the farm and lands whereon I now live in Flushing, and all my other lands and meadows (except the farm which I have given to my son John), together with my dwelling house and building, and all the rest of my movable estate, the proceeds to be applied towards payment of debts and legacies, and the rest to my wife and children. I make my wife Ann and my nephew Garrit Rapelye, of New York, and my trusty friend and brother in law Elbert Hoogland, of Flushing, executors.

> Dated August 28, 1754
> Witnesses, Thomas Willitt, Thomas Willitt, Jr., Benjamin Hinchman
> Proved at Jamaica [Queens],
> September 23, 1754

From *Collections of the New-York Historical Society*. Cited in W. Elliott Brownlee and Mary M. Brownlee, eds., *Women in the American Economy: A Documentary History, 1675 to 1929* (New Haven: Yale University Press, 1976), pp. 66–67. Reprinted by permission.

[13]

Tapping Reeve on the Concept of "Paraphernalia" (1816)

WE will now inquire what advantages the wife may gain, eventually by marriage, in point of property, during the coverture. She gains nothing during his life; but upon the death of her husband intestate, she is entitled to one third part of his personal property, which remains after paying the debts due from the estate of the husband, if he left any issue; but if he left no issue, she is entitled to one half of the residuum of the personal estate, after the debts are paid, but the husband, if he had chosen so to do, might have devised such estate from her [willed it to another]. . . .

There is one species of personal property in which she acquires a different interest from that which she may acquire in his other property, which is termed *paraphernalia*. This is of two kinds: the first consists of her beds and clothing, suitable to her condition in life; the second consists of her ornaments and trinkets, such as her bracelets, jewels, her watch, rich laces, and the like. As to the former, they cannot, with propriety, be considered as his estate, for they are not liable, upon the principles of the common law, without any aid from any statute, to the payment of his debts, and never ought to be inventoried as part of his estate; neither can they be devised from her by will.

As to the second kind, these cannot be devised from her by the husband, though he may take them from her, and dispose of them during the coverture. On the death of the husband, they vest in the wife, liable, indeed, to be taken by the executor of the husband, for the payment of his debts, provided that there are not sufficient assets beside to discharge his debts, but the whole of the personal estate must be exhausted before any resort can be had to them by the executor. Her right must yield to that of creditors; but in no instance to that of volunteers, for her *paraphernalia* can never be taken to pay legacies. . . .

She is often viewed as a creditor to her husband's estate, in respect of her *paraphernalia:* as when the husband, in his lifetime, being under the necessity of raising money, pledges her jewels, etc., and dies, leaving personal property more than sufficient to pay his debts, she shall have aid of this personal estate to redeem her *paraphernalia* thus pledged. So too, where real estate is devised for the payment of debts, and the executor takes the *paraphernalia,* on account of a deficiency of assets in the personal funds to pay the debts, she shall have the same right against this estate so devised for the payment of debts, to refund to her the real value of her *paraphernalia,* as a creditor can have, who is not paid his debt for the want of assets. Where a real estate is given in trust (whether by deed or will) for the payment of debts, if her *paraphernalia* be taken by the executor, she shall be considered as a creditor to the value of her *paraphernalia.* . . .

From *The Law of Baron and Feme, of Parent and Child, of Guardian and Ward, of Master and Servant, and of the Powers of Courts of Chancery* (New Haven, 1816), p. 98.

ESCAPE FROM COVERTURE
Run Away or Suffer

[14]
Advertisements by Joseph Perkins and Elizabeth Perkins (Pennsylvania, 1767)

Whereas Elizabeth Perkins, Wife to me, the Subscriber, of the township of Will-ingburg and County of Burlington, hath not only eloped from my Bed and Board, but otherwise behaves in a very unbecoming manner toward me; and as I am apprehensive from what I have already experienced, she may endeavor to run me in Debt, I am obliged to take this public Method to forewarn all Persons from trusting her on my Account, as I am determined I will not pay a single Farthing of her contracting from the Date hereof. And I hope no Person will encourage her on such Occasions, as it may be a Prejudice to me, and will render them liable to prosecu-tion.

Joseph Perkins
August 10–17

Joseph Perkins, of the township of Willingborough and county of Burlington, my graceless husband, having maliciously advertised to the world that I have eloped from his bed and board, run him in debt, and otherwise behaved in an unbecoming manner toward him, I am obliged to take this method solemnly to declare, that those charges against me have not the least foundation in truth, which can be easily made to appear; and were entirely occasioned by my refusing to assign over to him the little interest I have, that he might squander it away in disorderly company, as he hath done the greatest part of his own; and by my declining to entertain and encourage the infamous guests he frequently brought to his house, where, amidst the most notorious scenes and disorder, I often met with treatment which would have shocked a savage of the Ohio, which at last obliged me to fly to my mother's house in this city, which I unfortunately left, as the only sanctuary I could expect to find from his persecutions. There being a greater probability of his running me in debt, than my injuring him in that manner, I desire that no person may trust him from any

From the *Pennsylvania Chronicle,* 1767, in Gerda Lerner, ed., *The Female Experience: An American Documentary* (Indianapolis: Bobbs-Merrill, 1977), pp. 75–76.

expectation that I will pay his debts, for I have determined never to pay a Farthing of his contracting from the date hereof.

Elizabeth Perkins
Philadelphia
August 18–25

[15]
Diary of Abigail Gardner Drew
(Nantucket, Rhode Island, circa 1800)

I would willingly fly . . . but [it] is more than I can bear to have the one who occasions my unhappiness to enjoy . . . that property I have endured so many hardships to obtain, and I turned once more in to the wide World, bereft of Interest and friends.

Cited in Mary Beth Norton, *Liberty's Daughters: The Revolutionary Experience of American Women, 1750–1800* (Boston: Little Brown, 1980), p. 48. Courtesy American Antiquarian Society.

Marriage Settlements

[16]
Bequest to Sarah Amelia Tart by her Father
(South Carolina, February 26, 1794)

I Nathan Tart of the Parish of St. Thomas send Greeting. Whereas a Marriage is intended to be shortly had and solemnized between George Bampfield . . . and my Daughter Sarah Amelia Tart; and I am disposed to give to my said Daughter the three following slaves, vizt. Juliet, Hard Times and Margery. Now know ye that I, in Consideration of the natural Love and affection which I have and bear to my said Daughter Sarah Amelia Tart, . . . do give and grant and deliver to my said Daughter the said Slaves To have and to hold the same. And [I give] the Issue and Increase of

Recorded April 7, 1794, under "Marriage Settlements," no. 321 in *Records of the Secretary of State* (South Carolina Department of Archives and History, Columbia, S.C.) vol. 2, pp. 241–42.

such as are Female to the said Sarah Amelia Tart, to her own separate and sole use, free from the Debts and Engagements, of her intended husband, during the Term of her natural Life, and from and after her decease; then to him, the said George Bampfield absolutely and for ever if he shall survive her. But if she should survive him, then from and immediately after his Death to her, absolutely and forever— Provided nevertheless that it shall and may be lawful to and for the said Sarah Amelia Tart, with the consent and approbation of the said George Bampfield, to sell and dispose of the said Slaves and their Issue, and to vest the monies, which may arise from such sale, in the purchase of any other Property.

[17]

Marital Agreement between Ebenezer Vereen and Catharin McKiver (South Carolina, September 8, 1784)

To all persons whome it may concern: Know ye that as a Marriage is to be shortly solemnized Between Ebenezer Vereen and Catharin McKiver, and she being desirous of having all her Interest and fortune settled upon her in the following manner, with my full consent and approbation thereto, that is to say that all her fortune in Lands, Slaves, Chattels, Household Goods and Money that is now hers, or that may be hers hereafter, shall be wholly in her power at the time of her Death . . . to Will, Give or Dispose of in any form or manner without the least hindrance or obstruction of me the said Ebenezer Vereen; and then to be the property of those that she may think proper to will, give, or dispose of . . . for Their Use . . . forever. And I the said Ebenezer Vereen doth promise, Covenant and bind myself to perform any further Act or thing that shall be requested of my Counsel learned in Law, in behalf of the parties that may be concerned in this Case, for the more perfect selling and Securing the same for such uses and purposes as is herein mentioned. . . . In Witness I have here set my hand and seal this eighth day of September in the year of our Lord one thousand seven hundred and eightyfour.

First recorded Nov. 16, 1786, "Marriage Agreement" no. 209, in *Records of the Secretary of State* (South Carolina Department of Archives and History, Columbia, S.C.), vol. 1, pp. 326.

[18]

Marital Agreement between Eliza Johnson and Christopher Walten (South Carolina, December 31, 1813)

This Agreement made and Executed at Charleston in the District and State aforesaid, this thirty-first day of December in the year of our Lord one thousand eight hundred and thirteen, and in the thirty-eighth year of the Sovereignty and Independence of the United States of America, between Christopher B. Walten and Eliza Johnson, both of the City of Charleston—District and State aforesaid.

Witnesseth That Whereas the said Eliza owns and is in possession of various articles of House hold furniture and merchandise, all of which are in the House and Store, which she the said Eliza now occupies in Wentworth Street in the City of Charleston aforesaid. And whereas a Marriage is intended to be shortly had and solemnized between the said Christopher and Eliza, upon which contract of marriage the said Christopher hath agreed: that if the same shall take effect, that then notwithstanding the said marriage, that the said Christopher, his Heirs, Executors, Administrators or Assigns, shall not nor will intermeddle with or have any right, title or interest either in law or equity, in or to any part of the said furniture or Merchandise belonging to the said Eliza, within said House or Store or anywhere else, as to any debts that to her may be due or owing, nor shall the said furniture, goods, Merchandise or debts be in any way subject to his, the said Christopher's, control, or liable for any of his present or future debts or contracts. . . .

And the said Christopher doth furthermore agree to and with the said Eliza in consideration of the contemplated marriage that if the same should take place, be had and solemnized as aforesaid, that she the said Eliza shall remain, continue and be—so far as it respects said furniture, merchandise, and debts due and owing to her, and so far as respects all property which she may hereafter acquire, by her traffic or Industry, or debts which may become due to her—in the same situation; [that she be] entitled to the same rights and privileges, and be considered as a sole and separate dealer, independent and uncontrollable by her said intended Husband. . . . This indenture further witnesseth, that for making this agreement effectual in the Law . . . the said Christopher doth for himself, his Executors and Administrators, and for every of them, Covenant, promise and agree to and with the said Eliza, and the Executors, Administrators and Assigns of the said Eliza that . . . all the property, rights and debts which she the said Eliza may hereafter acquire, or which she now hath in possession . . . shall be accounted reckoned and taken as separate and distinct property of and from the property and Estate of him the said Christopher and be no way liable to or for the payment of his debts or subject to his control, but

Recorded Jan. 11, 1814, "Marriage Agreement" no. 493, in *Records of the Secretary of State* (South Carolina Department of Archives and History, Columbia, S.C.) vol. 6, pp. 294–96.

Elizabeth Murray (1726–1785), a successful millinery merchant in Boston, returned to trade during her first widowhood. Thereafter she never again entered marriage without an ante-nuptial agreement that secured her full freedom of action. She left the bulk of her fortune to women, to help them secure a measure of personal independence. Portrait by John Singleton Copley. Courtesy Museum of Fine Arts, Boston.

the same be ordered, disposed of, and employed to such person or persons, and to and for such use and uses intents and purposes and in such manner and form, as she the said Eliza may think proper to elect and appoint. In Witness whereof I have hereunto set my hand and seal the day and year first herein mentioned.

Christopher B. Walten

[19]
Barnes *v.* Hart *(Pennsylvania, 1793)*

Margaret Erwin owned a large tract of land, received an annuity of 25 pounds, and would inherit a large portion of her father's estate upon her mother's death. Before Margaret married Matthew Henderson, they agreed that the land and income would be for their joint use during their marriage and that if Margaret outlived Matthew, all would remain hers as if she had never married. They also agreed that if any part of her inheritance above the interest should be used by Matthew, she could recover that amount from his estate. And further, Margaret retained the power to dispose of her property by will.

Margaret and Matthew married and had no children. In January 1790, Margaret executed a will in which she left her property to her nieces and nephews and appointed executors with full power to dispose of both her real and personal property. Margaret died in March and her executors sold the land. The person who would have inherited, had she died without a will ("the heir at law") is suing to claim the land.—Ed.

McKEAN C. J. The question is whether a feme covert . . . can, in consequence of a power contained in articles executed between her husband and her before their marriage, . . . give away such estate by will, or instrument in nature of a will, during the coverture?

It is very clear that a feme covert, by virtue of an agreement between her and her husband before marriage, may dispose of her *personal* estate by will or testament, because it is to take effect during the life of her husband; for if he survived her he would be entitled to the whole, and therefore he alone could be affected by it.

It is also clear that a married woman cannot devise her real estate. It is expressly enacted, that "wills or any manors, land tenements, or other hereditaments, made by any woman covert, shall not be taken to be good or effectual in law."

The instrument of 1790, executed by *Margaret Henderson,* being then covert, is not strictly a will, but distinct from it, though in nature of a will. It takes its affect out of the articles or deed of 1774, which created the power to make such instrument, and was made in execution of such power. She takes notice in the preamble of it, that she was a married woman, and that as to what she was legally entitled to dispose of, her will was as therein mentioned. It is usually called an appointment. A feme covert can execute an appointment over her own estate. The reason, or ground of a wife's being disabled to make a will, is from her being under the power of her husband, not from want of judgment, as in the case of an infant, idiot, etc.

Matthew Henderson and his wife, before their marriage, agreed, that her real estate should remain her property, and might be disposed of by will and testament in writing by her, as she should think fit, as absolutely as if the said marriage had never

1 Yeates (Pa.) 221 (1793).

been solemnized. The intention of the parties is plain, and admits of no doubt. She has, accordingly disposed of it by . . . a will and testament, in execution of the power, and by the express consent of her husband, not to him or his relatives but amongst her own nearest kin. No fraud, force, flattery or improper use of the power he had over her as husband, has been exerted, nor is it alleged. This will bar him of any title to her estate, and why should it not bar the heir at law, in equity and reason? Here was a fair and lawful agreement between them, founded on a valuable and meritorious consideration. Mrs. *Henderson,* with her husband, could, during the coverture, have given away her real estate by fine or deed, (if she had been secretly examined, agreeably to the act of the assembly of *Pennsylvania*); . . . if he had refused to join with her, a court of equity, (if such a court had existed here,) would, on her application, have compelled him to carry their agreement into execution. It is a lamentable truth, there is no court clothed with chancery powers in *Pennsylvania;* but equity is part of our law, and it has been frequently determined in the Supreme Court, that the judges will, to effectuate the intention of the parties, consider that as executed, which ought to have been done. . . .

[20]
Fitch *v.* Brainerd *(Connecticut, 1805)*

THIS was an appeal from a decree of probate, approving the will of *Abigail Mary Brainerd.* It contained a devise of real estate to her husband; and the only exception relied upon was, that she was a feme-covert when she executed it. The Superior Court affirmed the decree.

SMITH *(of Woodbury) and* EDWARDS *(of New Haven) for the plaintiff in error* [Mary Elizabeth Fitch].

The question of law, which the record presents, is whether a feme-covert can devise her real estate?

This general question will be discussed by examining, first, what are the PRINCIPLES which govern it; and secondly, how far those principles have been supported or shaken by PRECEDENTS.

The legislature, by their various acts, have virtually declared that a feme-covert cannot make a will.

At an early period, the General Assembly passed an act authorizing all persons of sound mind and memory, who had arrived to the age of twenty one years, to make their wills. This act continued, without any alteration, through various revisions of the statutes, until that in the year 1784, when the words "not otherwise legally incapable," were inserted. At the original passing of this act, an exception of femes-

2 Day (Conn.) 163 (1805).

covert would have been futile; for at that time, and for many years afterwards, the whole property of a feme-covert, real as well as personal, vested absolutely in her husband. She could, therefore, have no property to devise. But, at the revision of 1784, her condition was changed. The act protecting "Heiresses" had, before that time, been passed, by which the lands of a feme-covert were secured to her, and her husband could no longer alienate them without her consent. It, therefore, undoubtedly occurred to the legislature, that to continue this act, without excepting femes-covert, while they were capable of holding lands, might raise a doubt whether they were not comprised in the general clause, "all persons". . . . The words "not otherwise legally incapable," were, therefore inserted, which were intended, at once, to except femes-covert and to exclude any implication, which an exception in a different form might have raised, that they were empowered to devise, by the general words in the old law. If the exception does not refer to femes-covert, what possible meaning can it have? There are certainly no *other* persons in society, of twenty-one years of age and of sound mind and memory, who are legally incapable of making their wills. That the legislature should make an alteration in a statute, without any object in view, is not to be admitted.

It ought furthermore, to be remarked, that if femes-covert are, by our statute, enabled to devise, they are equally capacitated not only to alienate "their lands and other estates," but "to give their vote, verdict, or sentence, in any matter or cause;" they may vote in freeman's meeting, may be jurors, and may even be judges of the courts. The evident absurdity of such a conclusion is a clear proof that it was not intended by the legislature. . . .

The question then arises, whether a feme-covert can, without the aid of the statute, or at common law, devise her real estate? In the inquiry on this subject, the common law of Connecticut will be principally regarded; for we have, it is conceived, a common law of our own.

When our ancestors first settled this country, they looked up to the great LAW-GIVER OF THE UNIVERSE as their immediate legislator; and from *him* they learned that when two persons are married, *of twain they become one flesh.* But, two persons cannot be formed into one unless the legal existence of one of them be *suspended.* And if a doubt could exist, which of the two should retain the sole legal existence and be the head of the family, that doubt is solved by the same high authority. So strongly, indeed, were our ancestors impressed with the necessity of a perfect union between husband and wife, that without any statute on the subject they adopted every principle of the ancient common law of England, which went to establish such union. The right of a feme-covert to hold lands, which by the English common law, forms an exception to the entire union of husband and wife, was at the same time rejected here. Our ancestors admitted of no exception. The whole estate of the wife, both real and personal, vested absolutely in her husband. These principles, being adopted by general consent, in obedience to what was supposed to be the divine law on the subject, became a part of the common law of Connecticut, and so remained for nearly a century. In the year 1723 "An act for preventing the sales of the real estates of heiresses without their consent" was passed, by which one exception was made to the matrimonial union. . . . Her being enabled to exercise power in the sale of [real estate], during coverture, formed a new feature in the marriage covenant. For this, however, there was a strong reason: the family might want the avails of them for support. The sale, also, is to be guarded by an acknowledgment before a justice. . . .

. . . If a statute was necessary to enable a feme-covert to convey by deed, is it not equally so to enable her to convey by will? And here, again, we clearly discover the sense of the legislature on this subject. Had they supposed that a feme-covert could make a will, as they were about to enable her to make a deed, it is inconceivable that they should have taken care to regulate the one and not the other,—that they should have taken care to protect her in making deeds, and yet afford her no protection in making wills. . . .

But the common law of England will afford our opponents no support. It is as much opposed to the doctrine which they contend for, as the statute of *34 Hen. VIII.*

That the legal existence of the wife is suspended or incorporated with that of her husband, may be proved, by innumerable English authorities; but it may be sufficient to refer the Court to the very explicit language of Judge BLACKSTONE on this subject. . . .

But our opponents will say, that a feme-covert can appoint a trustee to a trust estate; that she can devise her husband's personal estate, with his consent; that, with his consent, she may also devise her choses in action; and that she can even make an appointment, in pursuance of marriage articles. . . .

All the cases mentioned proceed upon the ground, that she has not a general disposing power. Though she has no power in herself, she can exercise a power derived from another, in appointing a trustee. Though she cannot dispose of her husband's personal estate, yet *he* may dispose of it, and when he consents to her disposition, it becomes, substantially, his own. The same may be said of her choses in action. The husband, during coverture, has absolute power over them, either to collect them or to give them away; and his consent, during that period, to any disposition of them amounts substantially to a disposition by him. As to the appointment in pursuance of marriage articles, it is only the exercise of a power with which he has vested her; the power of doing an act, which he has covenanted shall be binding on him. The same power might be given to a child of ten years old, and the act done by him, in the exercise of it would be equally binding.

After all, it must be admitted, that although the general common law of England has established the most perfect union of husband and wife, beyond the possibility of doubt, yet there has been a constant struggle, in that country, against what has been considered the tyranny of the marriage yoke. And, within a century past, a system of separate property has been introduced, which has become very general, whereby the wife is enabled to hold property to her *sole* and *separate* use, independent of her husband, and as to which she is, to all intents and purposes, a feme sole. . . . That notions of independence in wives should prevail in England, will not, therefore, appear strange to us. These notions, introduced by the civil law, have been encouraged by family pride, supported by overgrown wealth, and extended by dissipated manners and corrupt morals. . . .

The principle insisted upon by our opponents, and which must be adopted, if they prevail, is, that as to the interest of a feme-covert in land, which does not vest in her husband, she may be considered as a feme-sole. It follows, as a necessary consequence, that she may sell it to him, or to any other person, without his consent; and the avails, upon the same principle, must be her separate property, with which she may speculate in new lands, traffic in goods, or sport at the gaming table.

The will, indeed, does not take effect until coverture is determined; but it must be good at the time of making it, or never; and the same disabilities, which render persons incompetent to make any other disposition of property, render them equally so to make a will.

The doctrine which we contend against, is not only novel in this State; but is of very dangerous tendency. It is no less opposed to sound policy than to the principles of the common law.

The harmony and good order of society result naturally from peace and harmony in families, which will nowhere be found without an entire union of interests between husband and wife. Our happy state of society, of which we frequently, and very justly boast, will be found to rest, in a great measure on that domestic harmony, which is produced only by the two heads of the family becoming emphatically *one*. The difference between a state of things to be found in England, and what has, hitherto, existed in this State, is too striking to pass unnoticed. In that country, marriage articles securing property to the independent use of the wife, have been common for a considerable period; and it has also been common, whenever, any relation was about to give property to a female, to secure it to her, through the medium of trustees, to her sole and separate use: until very little property belonging to females remains subject to the general law of coverture. The wife, by the aid of her friends, has been enabled to evade that law, and has truly obtained her boasted independence, in its fullest extent. And what has followed? Precisely what might have been expected—divorces *a mensa et thoro,* and articles of separation; until nothing is more common, than to see my lord at one country seat, and my lady at another, pursuing respectively their own affairs, in their own way—but to the benefit of nobody. . . . A comment cannot be necessary, to show the impropriety of adopting principles, tending to establish interests, views and prospects, in married women, independent of, and distinct from their husbands.

But, let us follow this independent lady, and see her exercising the *rights of women.* She can make a will to her husband, say our opponents. On the same principles, she may sell to him; and, if he fail to pay, she must have the right to sue him; he may claim to have made a *private settlement;* a bitter lawsuit must be the consequence, with their different counsel and different witnesses.

Again: She may make a will to her husband, say the gentlemen. On the same principles, she can make a will to any other person, against his wishes; and after procuring her scrivener and witnesses, for this purpose, she may want an apartment in the house to do the writing in; but the house is his; and he may intrude upon them, though, as the will is to be made against his wishes he may be, of all others, the most unwelcome. He may finally turn them all out of doors; and what is this independent lady to do then? Why, as the law has given her the right to make her will, it implies every other right necessary to accomplish it. Of course, she must turn him out, the moment he intrudes; and, if he still interrupts her, she must sue him and recover exemplary damages! This is too ridiculous. . . .

Could any great benefit be promised to society from allowing femes-covert to devise their estate, the many evils resulting from it might be encountered; but so far is this from being the case, that it is doubtful whether sound policy dictates the making of wills at all; certainly the reason urged in favor of making them does not apply to femes-covert, as their industry adds nothing to their property.

We have endeavored to establish the general principle that a feme-covert can make no will, either *with* or *without* her husband's consent; but as it respects this case we might safely admit her to be competent, *with the consent of her husband,* the devise in question being directly to him. For whenever the law makes a man's consent necessary to the transfer of property, he cannot receive it, by force of such his consent, as grantor. The law will never permit a man to act in the double capacity of devisor and devisee. . . .

Having examined the principles which are involved in this case, we beg leave to direct the attention of the Court to the precedents.

The case of *Kellogg* v. *Adams* will doubtless be insisted on as settling the question in favor of the power which we oppose. But let us, in the first place, inquire, why are precedents resorted to? A remark of LORD MANSFIELD is full to this point: *"That precedents do not govern cases; they only serve to illustrate principles, and principles govern cases."* What, then, are the Court to do with a single precedent, which is opposed to every principle of law? The answer is obvious. They are bound, by their oaths of office, to disregard it, and to decide according to law. The precedent, however, will have its due weight, in proportion to the soundness of the reasons, on which it was founded, and the number and respectability of the judges, who acted upon it. In the case of *Kellogg* v. *Adams,* it is a little remarkable, that no reasons are to be found for the reversal of the judgment of the Superior Court, while the most forcible ones are preserved in support of it.

Nothing is more common in England, than for judges to declare, that former precedents are not law. Many cases might be cited to prove this. A long course of uniform decisions may, indeed, be considered as establishing a new principle; and, in that case, it is obvious that it is very unimportant, whether you follow the precedents, or the principle which they establish. . . .

The case of *Kellogg* v. *Adams* came before this Court at the close of the revolutionary war; a period peculiarly fitted to produce a decision, tending to loosen the bands of society. Suppose, that a single adjudication had, at that period, taken place in pursuance of the civil law, and in opposition to the law of England and of this country, that woman's personal estate did not vest in her husband, on marriage: would the Court now consider themselves bound by that precedent?

But why talk about the case of *Kellogg* v. *Adams,* since that of *Dibble* v. *Hutton-* ,was decided by this Court a year ago, by an unanimous opinion? . . .

Now, to say, that a feme-covert can have a legal existence when giving to her husband, without any consideration, and yet say that she has no legal existence to take benefit of a solemn contract made in her favor, for which she has given and he has received a most valuable consideration, would be a system of jurisprudence, to say no worse of it, not much in favor of the female sex. The truth is, these two precedents cannot stand, and both be considered as law; for one goes to destroy a principle, which the other sets up. And it is cheerfully submitted to the Court, to elect which of the two they will support.

INGERSOLL *and* DAGGETT *for the defendant in error* [Jehu Brainerd]. The question in this case is, can a feme-covert devise her real estate with the consent of her husband?

. . . The common law of England, also, is our law, in cases, to which it has been extended; and, it will be admitted, in all other cases, where a difference of circumstances, does not clearly warrant a departure.—It is, however, to be remembered, that where we have a statute regarding any subject, *that* is to govern.

We have a statute authorizing devises of real estate, made before 1672, when the first statute book which is to be found was printed.—With both the English statutes before them, our legislature made the law of Connecticut;—It was copied almost literally from theirs, and contains *all* the exceptions but that of *femes-covert.* It may be asked, why that exception was omitted. Suppose, in the English statutes, clergymen had been prohibited, and ours had been silent as to them; would not the argument have been strong, that they were authorized?

On the revision of the laws, in 1784, our statute was re-enacted, with an addition of these words after the exceptions, *viz.* "not otherwise legally incapable."

It has been strongly insisted that these words took away from femes-covert the power of devising, if they possessed it before.—But is this fair reasoning? It is not to be presumed that the legislature of 1784 intended to devest an important right, by such a clause inserted in a parenthesis and liable to so much just criticism. . . .

What is the incapacity of a feme-covert? Not idiocy, nor insanity, nor want of discretion; for, in these, to say the least, they are competent;—nor want of will, properly so called; for she may dispose of all her estate with her husband; who may sell and devise under a power; she may be punished for offenses to the commission of which freedom of will is essential.

The reason generally given is that she is *sub potestate viri* [under the power of her husband]; but this operates with equal force against her conveyance, in Great-Britain, by fine, and here by deed; And yet both are acknowledged and established, beyond debate. . . .

The reasons in favor of the power in question are as forcible in the case of women, as of men. It is not necessary to discuss the question, whether this is a natural right; it certainly results from the most correct and sound principles, by which property is regulated. And why may not a woman, equally with her husband, reward the affectionate treatment of a kind relative, rather than see her property descend to those who have been perverse, unkind, or cruel? Must she, *at all events,* submit to the thought that a kind husband is to be beggared, to aggrandize a cousin of the tenth degree?

Nor is there any just ground to apprehend any great evils, from the principle for which we contend.—Does experience teach us that women can be coerced to disinherit *their children?* It is believed that such would be a most singular occurrence. If, however, the power of a husband is so great as to compel a devise, will he not, with the same power, compel a disposition equally injurious, and more sure? Her *devise* is revocable;—her *deed,* irrevocable. . . .

Since the only ground assumed is, that a feme-covert, from the marriage relation, is *sub potestate viri;* the disability is as extensive upon her power, as that relation is operative upon her rights, and not more so. This is the rule, in all analogous cases; such as where men are under overseers, masters, conservators, etc. It is, also, a rule of right reason. Hence we insist that when a feme-covert, by the common law, has property, over which she may exercise a *disposing power, without affecting the rights of the husband,* she may, by the same common law, dispose of that property by will. She cannot destroy the husband's tenancy by the curtesy, nor can he devise away her dower.

We then will examine the wife's right to devise her personal property at common law. . . . We frequently find it said generally, that a woman cannot devise her personal property, *because it belongs to her husband.* With this principle we have no controversy; for the right of devising never extends to the property of another.

. . . It is said that there are several cases in which a feme-covert may dispose of her personal property by will. [There follows a list of situations and cases.] Thus, for nearly two hundred years, the right of a feme covert to devise *her* personal estate has been sanctioned by the English courts. This proves, that she is under no common law disability to devise.

It is said, in answer to these cases, that there is no such thing as separate property, by our law, in a feme-covert. If that be admitted, it does not militate against the argument. We are upon the question of the power to devise at common law; and such power is clearly established, by the foregoing cases, and by many others, which might be cited.

But it is saying a great deal, to say that there can be no such thing as *separate* property by our law. Are not jointures, and other covenants made in contemplation of marriage, by which the property of the man and woman is to be taken out of the general rules of law, very frequent? Are they not extremely beneficial, in many cases? And have not our courts repeatedly established them? And will not the increase of personal property render them more and more useful? [There follows a list of cases.]

It is also said, that if our statute does not prohibit femes-covert from devising, then they are permitted to "give their vote, verdict, or sentence in any matter or cause." To this it is sufficient to answer, that this argument equally destroys the right of a single woman to devise, unless those who urge it will contend that single women may sit as jurors.

It is also strongly urged, that good policy is against the right in question. As this argument would introduce the discussion of a question appropriate to another forum, it need not be answered here. When a court of justice leave a question of *law*, to inquire what *policy* dictates, they cease to be judges and commence legislators, or politicians.

But, however, this question might have been decided twenty years ago, we contend that it now ought to be considered at rest.

In 1786, the Superior Court adjudged, in the case of *Adams* v. *Kellogg*, that a feme-covert could not devise her real estate to her husband. This judgment was reversed, by the Court of Errors, in October, 1788, after an argument in May, 1788, and a continuance to advise, and a further argument in October. Among the gentlemen composing the Court of Errors, at that time, we may mention Governor HUNTINGTON and Doctor JOHNSON, whose names, where they were known, will give weight to a decision. In May, 1789, the question came before the legislature, between the same parties, on a petition for a new trial. Although there might be a sufficient reason for rejecting this petition, aside from the question, whether the decision was correct, yet the General Assembly went into the question of the power of a feme-covert to devise, and sanctioned the opinion before given by the Court of Errors. From that day to this, all the subordinate Courts, and the general body of the people, have considered the law as settled; and numerous wills have been made, by the advice of the best counsel, and approbated by the Courts of Probate. It is not too much to say, that property to the amount of many hundred thousand dollars, is now holden by this title.—Of course, to shake it, will induce all the evils of which instability in decisions is productive.

By the above decision, and a conformity thereto, by all the Courts of Probate, the statute relating to wills, has been, for seventeen years, construed to give, or, at least not to take away, the power of a feme-covert, to devise her real estate. Is not this, then, our law? . . .

In anticipation of these remarks, it has been said by the counsel for the plaintiff in error that the case of *Adams* v. *Kellogg* is the *only* instance in which this doctrine has been established.—We answer: 1) That case has been followed with numerous cases in the lower Courts, so that its authority ought not to be questioned. 2) One decision of this Honorable Court must be deemed sufficient, or it will be difficult to know, when the law may be considered as settled. 3) If this objection be valid, how will the law stand upon a reversal? Contrary decisions of the highest Court of law can only distract and confound.

. . . . If the purchaser and seller cannot rely on the principles, solemnly, and deliberately pronounced, by the highest Courts of law, there will be little confidence placed in any guarantee, which can be given.

BY THE COURT. The question is, can a feme-covert legally devise, or dispose of real estate by will? What she may do with respect to personal estate, in certain cases, with the consent of her husband or without, is not a part of this case, nor determinable on principles which apply to it.

It being well understood, that a right to devise is not a natural, but municipal, right, it must, so far as it exists, have a statute or custom for its creation. . . .

For though the common law of England hath not, *as such,* nor ever had, any force here; yet, in the progress of our affairs, whatever was imagined at the beginning, it long since became necessary, in order to avoid arbitrary decisions, and for the sake of *rules,* which habit had rendered familiar, as well as the wisdom of ages matured, to make that law our own, by practical *adoption*—with such exceptions as a diversity of circumstances, and the incipient customs of our own country, required. The same may be said of ancient English statutes, not penal, whose corrective and equitable principles had become so interwoven with the common law, as to be scarcely distinguishable therefrom. . . .

With respect to the common law, as it formerly stood, the uniform doctrine of elementary writers, and one which authorities well support and well account for, is that a feme-covert cannot devise,—except by special custom: and even such custom has been adjudged ill, on the ground, that it could not have had a *reasonable* commencement.

Our own statute next to be considered, is, omitting the parenthesis of 1784,— "That all persons of the age of twenty-one years, of right understanding and memory, whether excommunicated or other, shall have full power, authority and liberty to make their wills and testaments, and all other lawful alienations of their lands and other estates; and to give their vote, verdict, or sentence in any matter or cause."—Does it create the *right* of devising, or only declare the *age* competent for its exercise? The former construction has been resorted to, but the latter best comports with the provisions of the statute throughout; and is, indeed the only one that can rescue it from ridicule and absurdity. [The court then traces the statute.]

It remains only to inquire, has there been, from the early settlement of the state, a practice for femes-covert to devise: which might serve for a different exposition of the statute, or might, as a custom, have acquired the force of law?

Of such a practice there are neither memorials nor traditions. And we cannot presume from the condition of the early settlers, and still less from their character, that they would have introduced it. They, who could declare to the world, as prefatory to their first code of laws, *"we have endeavored not only to ground our capital laws on the* WORD OF GOD *but also all our other laws in the justice and equity held forth in that* WORD, *which is a most perfect rule,"* would not be likely to swerve from the maxims of *unity* and *subjection* attached by sacred writers to the matrimonial vow. . . . For near a century, femes-convert had no estate to devise.—The custom for them to devise, if such it may be called, is very recent, as well as very limited—confined, so far as is known, to a few instances and within the last twenty years.

There has, indeed been one ultimate decision, of a divided court, in favor of the right in question, in the case of *Kellogg* and *Adams;* but that decision, we are constrained to say, after much deliberation, was not law.

Whether the refinements of the present age, require a departure from the ancient law upon this subject; or whether the supposed benefits of a change would countervail its obvious mischiefs, are legislative, not judicial questions. In this case, the Court is unanimously of opinion, there must be a reversal.

[21]
Letters from Lucy Ludwell Paradise to Thomas Jefferson (1789)

January 31

Mrs. Paradise begs the favor of her friend Mr. Jefferson *to facilitate as Much as possible her going to England next week,* as she thinks the last letter received from their steward will ease the Minds of the Creditors; and she also thinks that Mr. Anderson will advance her the Money for her Subsistence. It will [be] necessary for Mr. Paradise to write a few lines to Dr. Bancroft and Mr. Anderson. She wishes, therefore, that her dear protector would insist upon his writing. I wish that the Creditors may be Made to understand, I bind myself in case of Mr. Paradise's death to pay all their debts, but none other, that shall be contracted after this paper is signed. Therefore, it will be Necessary for Mr. Paradise to live with More thought and Economy than he has hitherto done. Your excellency sees of what use a Settlement is for us poor helpless Women, and for my Sex's sake I hope you will have the Goodness to introduce it into Virginia, and by so doing we poor women shall *Immortalize your Name.*

May 5, 1789 (London)

The letter your Excellency sent me came from my friend Mrs. Washington. In it she tells me that the Constitution is likely to be received without tumult or disorder. . . . I have just heard that Mr. P. is often drunk and he has said it is my letters that Makes him drink. I am certain it is false, as your Excellency must have seen every letter I have written to him. I am resolved my Letters shall never make him drunk any More, as he never shall receive another from Me. . . . I hear he exposes himself at Paris to every person he sees and tells them that anything that troubles him Makes him drink. Why do not I drink? And thousands besides? That is only an excuse. What is he, not to feel pain and trouble? Then he might have

From Julian P. Boyd, ed., *The Papers of Thomas Jefferson*, Vol. 15: *27 March 1789 to 30 November 1789.* Copyright © 1958 by Princeton University Press. Excerpts from pp. 95–96 reprinted by permission of Princeton University Press.

avoided it, by not spending his Money and time with Women. This I know he did, to my certain knowledge, and I suppose he must wish to see them greatly. A Man has a right to amuse himself, but he has no right to bring his Wife to want, and his Children also.

I am not the object of Mr. P's affections. Pray my dear sir, remember my sex when you go to Virginia, and introduce [the] Marriage Settlement for to preserve my Sex from want in case of the Bad behavior of their husbands. . . .

DAUGHTERS, WARDS, AND SERVANTS

[22]
Laws of the Colony of New Plymouth on Marriage (reenacted 1658)

English modernized—Ed.

Because of the practice among different persons, unfit for marriage due to their youth and poor estate, of inveigling daughters and maids contrary to and without leave of parents, guardians and masters, it is therefore enacted by the Court, that if any shall make any motion of marriage to any man's daughter or maid servant, not having first obtained leave and consent of the parents or master, he shall be punished either by fine or corporal punishment, or both, at the discretion of the bench and according to the nature of the offence.

It is also enacted that if a motion of marriage be duly made to the master, and through any sinister end or covetous desire he will not consent thereunto, then an appeal may be made to the magistrates, who shall after examination present a decision that appears to be most equal for both sides.

From William Brigham, *The Compact with the Charter and Laws of the Colony of New Plymouth* (Boston, 1836), p. 61.

[23]

Laws of Virginia on Bastardy (1705)

English Modernized.—Ed.

XVIII. If any woman servant shall be delivered of a bastard child within the time of her service, be it enacted: that in recompense of the loss and trouble occasioned her master or mistress thereby, she shall for every such offense serve her said master or owner one whole year after her time by indenture, or pay her said master or owner one thousand pounds of tobacco.

The reputed father, if free, shall give security to the church-wardens of the parish where that child shall be, to maintain the child. But if a servant, he shall make satisfaction to the parish for keeping the said child after his time by indenture shall be expired.

And if any woman servant shall be got with child by her master, neither the said master nor his executors shall have any claim of service against her, for or by reason of such child; but she shall, when the time due to her said master by indenture shall be expired, be sold by the church-wardens for one year, or pay one thousand pounds of tobacco. And the said one thousand pounds of tobacco, or whatever she shall be sold for, shall be employed by the vestry to the use of the said parish.

And if any woman servant shall have a bastard child by a negro or mulatto, over and above the years of service due to her master or owner she shall, immediately upon the expiration of her time to her then present master or owner, pay down to the church-wardens of the parish fifteen pounds current money of Virginia, or be by them sold for five years, to the use aforesaid.

And if a free, Christian, white woman shall have such bastard child, pay to the church-warden fifteen pounds current money of Virginia, or be by them sold for five years to the use aforesaid. And in both the cases the church-wardens shall bind the said child to be a servant, until it shall be of thirty-one years of age.

From William Wallor Hening, ed., *The Statutes at Large; Being a Collection of All the Laws of Virginia from the First Session of the Legislature, in the Year 1619*, vol. 3 (Philadelphia, 1823), p. 452.

ESCAPE FROM SLAVERY

[24]
Slew *v.* Whipple *(Massachusetts, 1766)*

Jenny Slew brought suit for trespass to person against her master, John Whipple, Jr., and sought damages. Whipple attempted to have the court dismiss the case ("abate the writ"), but the judges divided evenly on the question of abatement; this allowed the case to come to a jury trial on its merits. The jury awarded Jenny Slew damages and legal costs.

The issue of Jenny Slew's marriage was complicated by her race. If she could convince the court she was either white or mulatto, her marriages to blacks were statutorily void, under the law forbidding miscegenation. To circumvent this point, Jeremiah Gridley, counsel for the defendant, states that "marriage is the law of nations. Justinian extends it even to the brutes." He is invoking natural and civil law to support an argument that if brutes can marry, so can slaves. Benjamin Kent, counsel for the plaintiff, states that he is not going to argue the question of whether some men can enslave others, but will rest his case on evidence. "Jenny Slew, it is commonly known, is the child of Betty Slew, a white woman, by a negro man, Mr. Goffe." His point is that because Jenny's mother was a white woman, Jenny could not be a slave, no matter what her father's status. This would not necessarily have been true if Jenny's mother was a free black and her father a slave.

Gridley next argues that when a person sues for trespass, she must prove that she had possession of her liberty and that it was taken away by force. Because trespass was a civil act that could be punished criminally as well, the burden of proof lay with the defendant. Kent, citing precedent, argues that in slave cases the defendant must provide evidence, such as a bill of sale, that he did not forcibly take away the plaintiff's liberty.

In his opinion, Judge Oliver states that this case is a contest between liberty and property, and that liberty is the more important of the two rights protected by common law. Judge Cushing, in his opinion, argues that if a person is free, he or she may bring a case of trespass at any time. He concludes that the child follows the status of the mother; that color is only a presumption of status, not evidence of slavery. The reasoning of Chief Justice Thomas Hutchinson and Justice Lynde, who supported the writ to abate, is missing from the original manuscript.

The documents describing the case are not transcripts, but the notes of John Adams. The summary presented here is based both on the document and on the footnotes to the case, which appeared in the *Legal Papers of John Adams.*—Ed.

Essex Superior Court (Salem, Mass., 1766) in L. Kinvin Wroth and Hiller B. Zobel, eds., *Legal Papers of John Adams,* vol. 2 (Cambridge, Mass.: Belknap Press, 1965), pp. 52–55.

I. COPY OF THE DECLARATION AND REPORT

Jenny Slew, of Ipswich, in the County of Essex, spinster, plaintiff v. John Whipple Jr., of said Ipswich, gentleman, defendant, in a plea of trespass: for that the said John upon the 29th January, 1762, at Ipswich aforesaid, with force and arms, took her, the said Jenny, held and kept her in servitude as a slave in his service, and has restrained her of her liberty from that time to the fifth of March last, without any lawful authority or right so to do, and did her other injuries against the peace, and to the damage of the said Jenny Slew, as she saith, 25 pounds.

Defendant pleaded that there is no such person in nature as Jenny Slew of Ipswich aforesaid, spinster, and this the said John is ready to verify, wherefore he prays judgment, etc.

Evidence was that she was originally called Jenny Slew, but that she had been severally times married to slaves, etc.

Writ did not abate. Two judges for abatement and two against it; so being divided could not abate.

II.   MINUTES OF ARGUMENT

Gridley: Marriage is the law of nations. Justinian extends it even to the brutes. . . .

Kent: I shall not enter into the right of some men to enslave others. This right in some places seems established. Not indeed a right to life, though this is assumed in West Indies, to the shame of human nature.

Evidence was that Jenny Slew was commonly reputed to be the child of Betty Slew, a white woman, by a Negro man.

Gridley: Shall trespass be maintained? Shall not the plaintiff who sues in Trespass for goods be compelled to prove his possession, and that it was by force taken out of his possession. She has never been in possession of her liberty, she has been out of possession of it for 50 years. Trespass is the highest action of the highest nature in law. No other civil action in which the party may be punished criminally.

Kent: In the case of the East Indian, at Charlestown, they pleaded in bar that she was a slave, and produced the bill of sale. Why did not they do so here?

J. Oliver: This is a contest between liberty and property—both of great consequences, but liberty of most importance of the two.

J. Cushing: It is not long since K[ing]'s attorney brought an action of trespass in such a case as this, and I think he was right, for if a person is free he may bring trespass at any time. *Partus sequitur ventrem* ["the offspring follows the womb"]. Color is a presumption.

UNIT 2

[*Family Roles*]

CULTURE, LAW, AND SOCIAL REALITY

Womanhood and Family Government

In the view of our Pilgrim and Puritan fathers, the well-being of the Commonwealth rested on well-ordered families. The chief problem of the state was to see that family governors did their duty and maintained harmonious domestic relations, since marital discord invariably spilled over to disrupt the peace of the community. Ministers urged parents and friends to prevent marriages based solely on physical attraction. On the other hand, Puritans, unlike their Victorian descendants, believed that women, as well as men, had passions that legitimately required fulfillment in marriage. Although a wife's subordination to her husband's commandments was necessary to preserve order, ministers recognized that harmony rested on love and mutual respect; they sought to mitigate some of the consequences of patriarchy by emphasizing the moral equality of men and women and their interdependence. The selections presented here from John Robinson's *Essay on Marriage* (1628) and from John Cotton's *Wedding Sermon* (1694) illustrate the prevailing view of marriage, domestic relations, and human nature. They help explain why New England diverged from England in its approach to divorce.

Legal Heritage and Innovation

English law, unlike that in other Protestant countries, treated the marital tie as sacred and therefore incapable of being dissolved. Issues such as annulment, separation, and alimony were handled by ecclesiastical courts. Since marriage affected the distribution of property and the legal responsibilities of husband and wife, the common law and statutes set forth the conditions and procedures for making and validating a marriage contract.

The selection from William Blackstone on the *English Common Law on Marriage and Divorce* (1765) describes the difference between canonical and legal impediments to marriage. It also describes how statutes altered the common law, in apparent attempts to protect and extend patriarchal property rights and ecclesiastical control. Since marriage emancipated a child from parental authority, statutes raising the age at which boys and girls needed parental consent to marry extended into adulthood the father's control over his children's wages and services. Note that if a mother was the guardian she did not have the same power to prevent her child's marriage as a male guardian. The statute that required either a license from a judge or a public announcement of an engagement, was meant to prevent secret marriages.

The absence of absolute divorce was a burden to men, but it affected the personal lives of women far more because of the legal consequences of marital property laws. Although a wife could get a legal separation on grounds such as extreme cruelty, adultery, bigamy, or desertion, she remained legally married; her alimony and property rights were valid only as long as she remained physically faithful to her husband, that is, while she was celibate. After 1669 the rich and powerful could obtain an absolute divorce, with the right to remarry, through an act of Parliament. Before Parliament would review a petition for divorce, however, a husband had to get a legal separation in the ecclesiastical court and successfully prosecute an action for damages against his wife's lover. A wife was required both to prove her husband's adultery and to show that he had aggravated his offense by extreme cruelty or some other infamous conduct. Parliamentary divorce became the model for legislative divorce in the colonies and, later, in the new republic.[12]

Ideology and social circumstances led the colonists to make important alterations in the law of marriage and divorce. Puritan New England permitted divorce and gave the innocent party the right to remarry. In the Massachusetts Bay Colony, the Court of Assistants was empowered to hear and determine all cases of divorce. In petitions brought by women the ground most often cited was desertion. Bigamy, adultery, and failure to provide support were the next. Successful divorce cases brought by women all reveal the husband to have had a character unfit for family government. Considering the Puritan view of human nature it is likely that courts were predisposed to grant divorces rather than legal separations in order to remove women from the path of temptation. The *Connecticut Act of 1656* presented here exemplifies the perspective guiding New England colonies. Connecticut's liberal divorce policy stood in marked contrast to its marital property laws. Liberal divorce may have been meant to mitigate the consequences of a policy that gave a husband unencumbered freedom of action in marriage and provided a wife less protection than allowed in the English common law.[13]

The southern colonies, initially settled by Anglicans, followed English law. Because separation and alimony could be handled only in ecclesiastical courts, and none existed in the colonies, equity courts, starting from the premise that every wrong ought to have some remedy, assumed power to grant separate maintenance in aggravated cases. Southern colonies also adjusted marrige laws to fit racial policies, as is evident from the *Virginia Statute on Racial Intermarriage* (1705) presented here; this shows how it was possible to circumvent the fact that, under Scriptural law, race was not a bar to marriage.

The middle colonies had no clearly defined policy, although in the years following the French and Indian Wars legislatures began to enact private bills of divorce. This procedure, which became institutionalized following the Revolution, was disallowed by the British government because divorces were enacted without any of the safeguards that surrounded the parallel practice of the English Parliament. The unwillingness to allow the colonial legislatures to handle this problem according to their own judgment added to the resentment against the new paternalism of the British system.[14]

Realities of Married Life

The Puritan ideal of community harmony was not reflected by daily reality. Pilgrims and Puritans were a contentious people, and court records present a picture of domestic violence and abandonment. The women appear full of anger, as is evident from the selections presented here from *Domestic Relations Cases of Plymouth Colony Court Records* (1654–1666). The selections also indicate that the courts took considerable pains to deal with domestic tensions before they reached the divorce stage. *The Letters and Poems of Elizabeth Smith Shaw* (1786), *Elizabeth Graeme* (1770), and *Grace Growden Galloway* (circa 1759–1760) provide a glimpse into the private thoughts of women in good financial circumstances who were unlikely to show their discontent publicly. They use a language that displays the impact of revolutionary ideology.

CREATING A REPUBLICAN SOCIETY
Revolutionary Ideology and Suffrage

Revolutionary rhetoric linked the protectionist policy of Britain to tyranny. Women supported in various ways the rebellion led by their husbands, fathers, and brothers. They joined the boycott against tea, raised money for provisioning the troops, acted as spies, and ran family farms and businesses. All of these activities stimulated a sense of self-worth and confidence that is generally absent from the letters and diaries of white women before the Revolution. Letters written by husbands during the war also show a new respect for wives.[15]

In her *Letters to John Adams* (1776), Abigail Adams illustrates this self-confidence and political involvement. She is arguing not for direct representation of women but for restrictions on the husband's common-law authority over his wife. The letters should be read within the context of the public debate over the tyranny of British paternalism, a discussion that offered women an analogy with which to express their discontent over the patriarchal model. *John Adams's Letters to Abigail Adams and to John Sullivan* (1776) illustrate the extent to which the republican ideology of the founding fathers rested on English political theory about the relationship between power and property.

In the postrevolutionary era only one state recognized the public role of women. On July 2, 1776, New Jersey adopted a state constitution that conferred the elective franchise on "all free inhabitants" who met certain requirements of age, property, and residence. Although the broad wording probably represented a simple oversight, some women with property exercised their new privilege. A 1790 election law codified existing practice by including the words "he or she." In 1806, however, New Jersey followed the rest of the Union and withdrew the franchise from women and blacks. The reason generally cited for the change was a corrupt referendum that saw an unusually large number of women and blacks voting. This is certainly a transparent rationalization, however, for there had to have been far larger numbers of corrupt white male votes. More likely, local politicians were disturbed because women were beginning to take advantage of their right and, in the tightly contested elections of this period between Federalists and Republicans, threatened to alter the balance of power. It was in the 1797 election at Elizabethtown that women first voted in large numbers, and their sudden presence at the polls almost defeated the favored Republican candidate for the state legislature. He later introduced the bill that ended woman suffrage in the state.[16] The *Poem about an Election at Elizabethtown, New Jersey* (1797), captures the deeper fear of women using the franchise to upset patriarchy.

Women's Civic Role

The Revolution denied women the vote but created a new civic role for them, that of training the young to be virtuous republicans—traditionally the father's task. The selection from a *Columbia College Commencement Oration on "Female Influence"* (1795) contains this vision. The image of womanhood found here gained its power from the spread of new ideas about childhood and the distrust by the founding fathers of a materialistic, hetero-geneous and mobile population cut off from traditional community ties. The image proved attractive to women, whose role, with the spread of commer-cial capitalism, was becoming restricted to domestic and childcare duties. The image provided a rationale for giving women a higher education and imbued their activities with considerable social meaning. Appearing first among the wealthy, the image gradually spread to other classes.[17]

In training Americans to their roles, the new republic relied increasingly on public education to supplement the home. The selections from *Primary School Readers* (1787–1812) show a clearly developed notion of separate spheres and a narrowing of the culturally permissible limits of women's lives. This view of women influenced the generation that came to maturity in the age of Jacksonian Democracy.

FAMILY CASE LAW

Separation, Divorce, and Alimony

For most women marriage was the central adult experience. Freedom meant the opporunity to choose a spouse or to leave an unhappy marriage. One way to circumvent a father's legal power to oppose his daughter's choice of a husband was to become pregnant. White premarital pregnancies showed a dramatic rise during the eighteenth century, reaching a peak in the revolu-tionary era that was not matched again until the 1960s.[18] In Massachusetts during the same period there was a noticeable rise in the number of women who initiated divorce petitions and a corresponding rise in the number of favorable decrees.[19]

What was probably the most common approach to divorce, a mutual agreement by the spouses to separate and allow each other to remarry, appears in *Fry* v. *Derstler* (1798). "Self-divorce," which seems to have been socially acceptable, would not normally have appeared in court records. In this case, however, Mr. Fry decided, eleven years after the event, to bring suit against his wife's second husband for "criminal conversation," that is, a civil action for damages arising out of adultery. According to the judge's charge to the jury, the success of Fry's suit hinged on whether his agreement to the divorce had been voluntary or, as he now claimed, extracted by coercion. The judge's charge derived from the common-law principle that gave the husband full freedom of decision.

The spread of a liberal divorce policy in the early federal period was accompanied by a shift in some of the ecclesiastical grounds for separation with alimony, which were now moved into the category of divorce. All states with divorce statues included adultery and bigamy, and most included impotence, which was really a ground for annulment. Fewer than half included willful desertion for three or four years and extreme cruelty. Only New Hampshire added failure to provide for three years, and only Vermont added long absence with the presumption of death. Thus in most states, women caught in unhappy marriages had to rely on legal separation, a status that was important only because it was tied to the issue of alimony and other property rights.[20]

The reference points for awarding legal separation and for divorce were provided by the English ecclesiastical courts, where decisions hinged not simply on a husband's misconduct but on a wife's blameless character. *Anonymous, South Carolina* (1810) describes the standards for determining alimony and the way legal separation standards served public policy goals of enforcing a particular norm of wifely behavior. The case differs from most successful petitions in that the wife's physical safety is not in jeopardy. As a result the wife's conduct in marriage becomes central to determining alimony. Note how the judge values the testimony of each witness, which affects the outcome. The case also illustrates, as do others in the section on property, that having equity remedies available did not necessarily provide women with more freedom of action.

Guardianship and Child Custody

Burk v. *Phips* (1793) concerns the law of guardianship and the limited rights which a mother had to her children. Under the common law, children were the property of their father. They were a valuable source of free labor—to parent or guardian—until they were twenty-one years old. The story told in this case is a good source for social history.

Commonwealth v. *Addicks* (1813) investigates child custody in cases of separation or divorce. The common law automatically gave the child to the father, even if he was guilty of adultery or other gross misconduct. *Addicks* is considered a landmark case because it introduces a new principle for determining child custody—the now familiar "in the best interests of the child" principle. This doctrine reflected new ideas about child nurture which, later in the nineteenth century, led courts to favor the mother. In practice, colonial courts would often give a very young girl to her mother, while preserving the father's primary right. The case demonstrates how common-law courts began making law and expanding their discretionary powers; they were reversing the theory that judges merely found existing law and applied it to particular cases. *Addicks* indirectly describes a common way in which the guilty party in divorce cases would circumvent the legal impediment to remarriage, and it shows the court's tolerance toward this practice.

DOCUMENTS

CULTURE, LAW, AND SOCIAL REALITY
Womanhood and Family Government

[25]
The Old Testament, Genesis 3:16

Unto the woman he said, I will greatly multiply thy sorrow and thy conception; in sorrow thou shalt bring forth children; and thy desire shall be to thy husband, and he shall rule over thee.

From *The Jerusalem Bible: The Reader's Edition* (Garden City, New York: Doubleday, 1966).

[26]
Rev. John Robinson, "An Essay on Marriage" (1628)

The language has been modernized and biblical references have been deleted—Ed.

Abstinence from marriage and the marriage bed is no more a virtue than abstinence from wine or other pleasing natural things. Both marriage and wine are of God and good in themselves; either of them may in their abuse prejudice the natural or spiritual life. . . .

The virtue of the wife is the husband's ornament; so is the husband's the wife's.

From Robert Ashton, ed., *The Works of John Robinson* (Boston: 1851), vol. 1, pp. 236–40.

After goodness, fitness in marriage is most to be regarded. Fitness of years is requisite, that an old head be not set upon young shoulders; nor the contrary, which is worse. . . . Seeing there is seldom or never found such conformity between man and wife, when differences arise one must give way; this, God and nature layeth upon the woman, rather than upon the man.

Many common graces and good things are requisite both for husband and wife: but more especially the Lord requires in the man love and wisdom and in the women subjection. . . .

In the wife is specially required a reverent subjection in all lawful things to her husband. . . . He ought to give honor to the wife, as to the weaker vessel; but if he pass the bounds of wisdom and kindness she must bear patiently the burden, which God has laid upon the daughters of Eve. God, always most just, hath ordained that her desire should be subject to her husband, who by her seduction became subject to sin. Many proud women think it a matter of scorn and disgrace to humble themselves to God and their husbands, and choose a sin of rebellion which shall not escape unpunished from God. Many fond husbands nourish them therein, and by pampering and puffing them up by delicate fare, costly apparel and idleness, teach them to despise both them, themselves and all others.

Marriage has different ends that make it convenient and one that makes it necessary, which is the preventing of that most foul and filthy sin of adultery. He who coupleth himself with a harlot becomes one body with her, which cannot be said of him that consorts with a thief or murderer or drunkard in their sins. As marriage is medicine against uncleanness, so adultery is the disease of marriage. Divorce is the medicine of adultery, though not for the curing of the guilty, but for the easing of the innocent, The divorce for adultery both under and before the law was to be made by the magistrate's sword.

[27]
Rev. John Cotton, "A Wedding Sermon" (1694)

Women are Creatures without which there is no comfortable Living for man: it is true of them what is wont to be said of Governments, *That bad ones are better than none:* They are a sort of Blasphemers, then, who despise and decry them, and call them *a necessary Evil,* for they are *a necessary Good;* such as it was not good that man should be without.

Cited in Edmund S. Morgan, *The Puritan Family: Religion and Domestic Relations in Seventeenth-Century New England* (rev. ed., New York: Harper Torchbooks, 1966), p. 29. By permission of Edmund S. Morgan.

Legal Heritage and Innovation

[28]
English Common Law on Marriage and Divorce (1765)

[on Marriage]

I. OUR law considers marriage in no other light than as a civil contract. . . . In general, all persons are able to contract themselves in marriage, unless they labor under some particular disabilities and incapacities. What these are, it will here be our business to inquire.

NOW, these disabilities are of two sorts: first, such as are canonical, and therefore sufficient by the ecclesiastical laws to avoid the marraige in the spiritual court; but these in our law only make the marriage voidable, and not *ipso facto* void, until sentence of nullity be obtained. Of this nature and pre-contract; consanguinity, or relation by blood; and affinity, or relation by marriage; and some particular corporal infirmities. . . . But such marriages not being void . . . but voidable only by sentence of separation, they are esteemed valid to all civil purposes, unless such separation is actually made during the life of the parties. . . .

THE other sort of disabilities are those which are created, or at least enforced, by the municipal laws. . . . These civil disabilities make the contract void . . . and not merely voidable. . . .

1. THE first of these legal disabilities is a prior marriage, or having another husband or wife living; in which case, besides the penalties consequent upon it as a felony, the second marriage is to all intents and purposes void: polygamy being condemned both by the law of the New Testament and the policy of all prudent states, especially in these northern climes. . . .

2. THE next legal disability is want of age. This is sufficient to void all other contracts, on account of the imbecillity of judgment in the parties contracting. . . . Therefore if a boy under fourteen or a girl under twelve years of age marries, this marriage is only inchoate and imperfect; and when either of them comes to the age of consent aforesaid, they may disagree and declare the marriage void, without any divorce or sentence in the spiritual court. This is founded on the civil law. . . .

3. ANOTHER incapacity arises from want of consent of parents or guardians. By the common law, if the parties themselves were of the age of consent, there wanted no other concurrence to make the marriage valid: and this was agreeable to the canon law. . . . By statute 26 *Geo. II* c. 33 . . . it is enacted that all marriages celebrated by license . . . where either of the parties is under twenty-one (not being a widow or

From William Blackstone, *Commentaries on the Laws of England,* 1765. Facsimile of first edition, volume 1, (Chicago: University of Chicago Press, 1979), vol. 1, pp. 421–29.

widower, who are supposed emancipated) without the consent of the father, or, if he
be not living, of the mother or guardians, shall be absolutely void. A like provision
is made as in the civil law, where the mother or guardian is *non compos* . . . to
dispense with such consent at the discretion of the lord chancellor: but no provision
is made, in case the father should labor under any mental or other incapacity. Much
may be, and much has been, said both for and against this innovation upon our
ancient laws and constitutions. On the one hand, it prevents the clandestine marriages of minors. . . . On the other hand, restraints upon marriage, especially among
the lower class, are evidently detrimental to the public, by hindering the increase of
people; and to religion and morality, by encouraging licentiousness and debauchery
among the single of both sexes. . . .

4. A FOURTH incapacity is want of reason. . . . Idiots and lunatics, by the old
common law, might have married. . . . This defect in our laws is however remedied
with regard to lunatics and persons under frenzies by the express words of the statute
15 *Geo. II* c. 30; and idiots, if not within the letter of the statute, are at least within
the reason of it.

LASTLY, the parties must not only be willing, and able, to contract, but actually
must contract themselves in due form of law, to make it a good civil marriage. Any
contract made . . . in words of the present tense, and in the case of cohabitation . . .
between persons able to contract, was before the late act deemed a valid marriage to
many purposes. . . . But these verbal contracts are now of no force to compel a future
marriage. Neither is any marriage at present valid that is not celebrated in some
parish church or public chapel, unless by dispensation from the archbishop of
Canterbury. It must also be preceded by publication of banns [public notice] or by
license from the spiritual judge. . . .

[on Divorce]

II. I AM next to consider the manner in which marriages may be dissolved; and this
is either by death or divorce. There are two kinds of divorce, the one total, the other
partial. . . . The total divorce, *a vinculo matrimonii* ["from the bond of matrimony"]
must be for some of the canonical causes of impediment before-mentioned; and
those, existing *before* the marriage, as is always the case in consanguinity; not
supervenient, or arising *afterwards,* as may be the case in affinity or corporal imbecillity. For in cases of total divorce the marriage is declared null, as having been
absolutely unlawful. . . . The issue of such marriage, as is thus entirely dissolved, are
bastards.

DIVORCE *a mensa et thoro* ["from bed and board"] is when the marriage is just
and lawful . . . and therefore the law is tender of dissolving it: but for some
supervenient cause it becomes improper or impossible for the parties to live together:
as in the case of intolerable ill temper or adultery in either of the parties. For the
canon law, which the common law follows in this case, deems so highly and with
such mysterious reverence of the nuptial tie, that it will not allow it to be unloosed

for any cause whatsoever that arises after the union is made. . . . The civil law, which is partly of pagan original, allows many causes of absolute divorce; and some of them pretty severe ones (as if a wife goes to the theater *or* the public games without the knowledge and consent of the husband), but among them adultery is the principal, and with reason named the first. But with us in England adultery is only a cause of separation from bed and board: for which the best reason that can be given is, that if divorces were allowed to depend upon a matter within the power of either of the parties, they would probably be extremely frequent; as was the case when divorces were allowed for canonical disabilities, on the mere confession of the parties. . . . However, divorces *a vinculo matrimonii,* for adultery, have of late years been frequently granted by act of parliament.

IN case of divorce *a mensa et thoro,* the law allows alimony to the wife; which is that allowance which is made to a woman for her support out of the husband's estate; being settled at the discretion of the ecclesiastical judge, on consideration of all the circumstances of the case. . . . It is generally proportioned to the rank and quality of the parties. But in case of elopement, and living with an adulterer, the law allows her no alimony.

[29]
Connecticut Statute on Divorce (1656)

Spelling modernized.—Ed.

It is ordered, etc. That if any married person proved an Adulterer or an Adulteress shall, by flight or otherwise, so withdraw or keep out of the Jurisdiction, that the course of Justice (according to the mind and Law of God here established) cannot proceed to due execution: upon complaint, proof, and prosecution made by the party concerned and interested, a separation or Divorce, shall, by sentence of the Court of Magistrates, be granted and published, and the innocent party shall in such case have liberty to marry again.

And if any man marrying a woman fit to bear Children, or needing and requiring conjugal duty, and due benevolence from her husband, it be found (after convenient forebearance and due trial) and satisfyingly proved, That the husband, neither at the time of marriage nor since, hath been, is, nor by the use of any lawful means, is like to be, able to perform or afford the same, upon the wife's due prosecution, every such marriage shall by the Court of Magistrates, be declared void and a nullity, the woman freed from all conjugal relation to that man, and shall have

From John W. Cushing, ed., *The Earliest Laws of the New Haven and Connecticut Colonies, 1639–1673* (Wilmington: M. Glazier, 1977), p. 28. Reprinted by permission of the publisher.

liberty in due season, if she see cause, to marry another: but if in any such case, deceit be charged and proved, that the man, before marriage, knew himself unfit for that relation and duty, and yet proceeded sinfully to abuse an Ordinance of God, and in so high a measure to wrong the woman, such satisfaction shall be made to the injured woman, out of the estate of the offender, and such fine paid to the Jurisdiction, as the Court of the Magistrates shall judge meet.

But if any husband, after marriage and marriage duty performed, shall by any providence of God be disabled, he falls not under this Law, nor any penalty therein. And it is further declared, That if any husband shall, without consent, or just cause shown, willfully desert his wife, or the wife her husband, actually and peremptorily refusing all Matrimonial society, and shall obstinately persist therein, after due means have been used to convince and reclaim, the husband or wife so deserted may justly seek and expect help and relief, according to 1 *Corinthians* 7:15. And the Court, upon satisfying evidence thereof, may not hold the innocent party under bondage.

[30]

Virginia Statute on Racial Intermarriage (1705)

XIX. And for a further prevention of that abominable mixture and spurious issue . . . [of] white men and women intermarrying with negroes or mulattoes, as by their unlawful coition with them, *Be it enacted,* . . . That whatsoever English or other white man or woman, being free, shall intermarry with a negro or mulatto man or woman, bond or free, shall by judgment of the county court be committed to prison and there remain during the space of six months, without bail. . . , and shall forfeit and pay ten pounds current money of Virginia to the use of the parish, as aforesaid.

XX. *And be it further enacted,* That no minister of the Church of England, or other minister or person whatsoever within this colony, shall hereafter wittingly presume to marry a white man with a negro or mulatto woman; or to marry a white woman with a negro or mulatto man, upon pain of forfeiting and paying, for every such marriage, the sum of ten thousand pounds of tobacco; one half to our sovereign lady the Queen, her heirs and successors, for and towards the support of the government, . . . and the other half to the informer.

From William Wallor Hening, ed., *The Statutes at Large; Being a Collection of All the Laws of Virginia from the First Session of the Legislature, in the Year 1619* (Philadelphia, 1823), vol. 3, p. 453.

Realities of Married Life

[31]
Domestic Relations Cases
(Plymouth Colony, 1654–1666)

Language modernized—Ed.

October 6, 1659: The court orders the wife of John Spring of Watertown, sometimes the wife of Thomas Hatch of Scituate, who has lived about three or four years at Scituate, away from her husband, to return with all convenient speed to her husband, or to repair to the house of Mr. Alden of Duxbury, on October 20, to give reason why she does not. In case she shall refuse to attend this order, the court will take a speedy course to send her to her said husband.

June 7, 1665: The Court saw cause to require bonds for the appearance of John Williams, Jr. and sent for his wife in reference to different complaints made about his disorderly living with his wife, his abusive and harsh carriages towards her, both in words and actions, in particular his keeping of himself from the marriage bed and his accusation of her to be a whore and his denial of the legitimacy of a child lately borne of his said wife by him. After hearing of several things to and fro betwixt them, and finding the said Williams unable to make out his charge against her, they were both admonished to apply themselves to such ways as might make for the recovering of peace and love betwixt them. For that end the Court requested Isacke Bucke to watch over them and so dismissed them from the Court for that time.

June 5, 1666 [continuation of case]: At this Court, Elizabeth, the wife of John Williams, appeared with a complaint against her husband, John Williams, for his great abusive and unnatural carriage towards her, both in word and deed, by defaming her in rendering her a whore and in persisting to refuse to perform his marriage duty unto her according to what both the law of God and man requireth.

The said John Williams obtained liberty of the Court to have the case tried by a jury, and accordingly a jury was impanelled for the trial of the said case. . . . The jury found the above complaint to be true and just and accordingly the Court proceeded to pass sentence against him as follows:

The Court, having seriously considered the matter, do judge that it is not safe or convenient for her to live with her husband, and gives her liberty at present to

From Nathaniel B. Shurtleff and David Pulsifer, eds., *Records of the Colony of New Plymouth, in New England* (Boston, 1855–1861), vol. 3, pp. 75, 174; and vol. 4 pp. 43, 125–126.

depart from him unto her friends until the Court shall otherwise order, or until he shall apply himself unto her in such a way as she may be better satisfied to return to him again. The Court orders him to apparel her suitably at the present, to furnish her with a bed and bedding and such like necessaries, and to give her ten pounds yearly to maintain her while she shall be thus absent from him. The Court requires that one-third part of their estate be secured for her livelihood and comfort, or some other form of security.

Secondly. For defaming and otherwise abusing his said wife, he must stand in the street or market place by the post with an inscription over him that may declare to the world his unworthy carriages toward his wife. (At the earnest request of his wife, this part of the sentence was remitted and not executed.)

Thirdly. Inasmuch as these, his wicked carriages, have been contrary to the laws of God and man, and also very disturbing and expensive to this government, we require him to pay a fine of twenty pounds to the use of this colony.

The Court orders the chief marshall to make distresse on [to take possession of] the goods of the said Williams for his fine to the county as provided by law; and as to the securing of one-third of his estate for his wife's maintenance or livelihood, the court orders that in case he refuses to set out one-third to his wife's order or to give her security for the payment of the ten pounds annually, then the chief marshall shall see to an equal division of the said estate, visa lands, goods and chattels into three parts. This shall be brought to his view by Elizabeth the wife of the said Williams, with the help of Captain Cudworth, Isacke Chettenden or any other of her neighbors. Once divided, one of the three parts shall be delivered to Elizabeth to be disposed of by her for the ends aforesaid. The marshall shall take care, in the performance of this order, that it be done in such a way as may be least prejudicial to the said estate.

[32]

Poem by Grace Growden Galloway (circa 1759)

never get Tyed to a Man,
for when once you are yoked,
Tis all a Mere Joke,
of seeing your freedom again.

Cited in Mary Beth Norton, *Liberty's Daughters: The Revolutionary Experience of American Women, 1750–1800* (Boston: Little Brown, 1980), p. 45. From the Joseph Galloway papers in the Library of Congress Manuscript Collection.

[33]

Letter from Elizabeth Graeme (February 27, 1770)

[A married woman's life is] [h]ard and painful even with a kind and tender partner, but if it is our fate to be conected with a Tyrant; it is then a temporary Hell.

Cited in Mary Beth Norton, *Liberty's Daughters: The Revolutionary Experience of American Women, 1750–1800* (Boston: Little Brown, 1980), p. 44. Reprinted by permission of the Historical Society of Pennsylvania. Society Collection.

[34]

Elizabeth Smith Shaw to Abigail Adams Smith
(November 27, 1786)

The sensations you experienced upon quitting your father's family were such as I can easily conceive. . . . To bid adieu to our former Habitation and to give up the kind Guardians [sic] of our youth, & place ourselves under quite a new kind of protection cannot but strike a reflecting Mind with awe & the most fearful Apprehensions—as it is *the* important crisis, upon which our Fate depends.

Cited in Mary Beth Norton, *Liberty's Daughters: The Revolutionary Experience of American Women, 1750–1800* (Boston: Little Brown, 1980). From the Shaw papers in the Library of Congress Manuscript Collection.

CREATING A REPUBLICAN SOCIETY

Revolutionary Ideology and Suffrage

[35]
Letters of Abigail Adams and John Adams (1776)

[Abigail to John, March 31, 1776]
I wish you would ever write me a Letter half as long as I write you, and tell me, if you may, where your fleet are gone? What sort of Defense Virginia can make against our common Enemy? Whether it is so situated as to make an able defense? Are not the gentry lords and the common people vassals, are they not like the uncivilized Natives Brittain represents us to be? . . .

. . . I have sometimes been ready to think that the passion for liberty cannot be equally strong in the breasts of those who have been accustomed to deprive their fellow creatures of theirs. Of this I am certain, that it is not founded upon that generous and Christian principle of doing to others as we would that others should do unto us. . . .

. . . I long to hear that you have declared an independency—and by the way, in the new Code of Laws which I suppose it will be necessary for you to make I desire you would Remember the Ladies, and be more generous and favorable to them than your ancestors. Do not put such unlimited power into the hands of the Husbands. Remember, all Men would be tyrants if they could. If perticular care and attention is not paid to the Ladies we are determined to foment a Rebelion, and will not hold ourselves bound by any Laws in which we have no voice or Representation.

That your sex are Naturally Tyrannical is a Truth so thoroughly established as to admit of no dispute, but such of you as wish to be happy willingly give up the harsh title of Master for the more tender and endearing one of friend. Why then, not put it out of the power of the vicious and the Lawless to use us with cruelty and indignity with impunity? Men of Sense in all Ages abhor those customs which treat us only as the vassals of your Sex. Regard us then as Beings placed by providence under your protection, and in immitation of the supreem Being make use of that power only for our happiness.

[John to Abigail Adams, April 14, 1776]
You justly complain of my short Letters, but the critical State of Things and the

From W. Elliot Brownlee and Mary M. Brownlee, eds., *Women in the American Economy: A Documentary History, 1675–1929* (New Haven: Yale University Press, 1976), pp. 79–83. Reprinted by permission.

Abigail Adams (1744–1818) urged her husband John, a representative to the Continental Congress, to write a new code of laws to protect women from the tyranny of men. Portrait by Gilbert Stuart. National Gallery, Washington, DC.

Multiplicity of Avocations must plead my excuse.—You ask where the Fleet is. The inclosed Papers will inform you. . . .

As to the Declarations of Independency, be patient. Read our Privateering Laws, and our Commercial Laws. What signifies a word?

As to your extraordinary Code of Laws, I cannot but laugh. We have been told that our Struggle has loosened the bands of Government everywhere: that Children and Apprentices were disobedient—that schools and colledges were grown turbulent—that Indians slighted their guardians and Negroes grew insolent to their Masters. But your Letter was the first Intimation that another Tribe more numerous and powerfull than all the rest were grown discontented.—That is rather too coarse a Compliment, but you are so saucy, I won't blot it out.

Depend upon it, We know better than to repeal our Masculine systems. Altho they are in full Force, you know they are little more than Theory. We dare not exert our Power in its full Latitude. We are obliged to go fair, and softly, and in practice you know we are the subjects. We have only the Name of Masters, and rather than give up this, which would compleatly subject Us to the Despotism of the Petticoat, I hope General Washington and all our brave Heroes would fight. I am sure every good politician would plot, as long as he would, against Despotism, Empire, Monarchy, Aristocracy, Oligarchy, or Ochlocracy.—A fine story indeed. I begin to think the Ministry as deep as they are wicked. After stirring up Tories, Landjobbers, Trimmers, Bigots, Canadians, Indians, Negroes, Hanoverians, Hessians, Russians, Irish Roman Catholics, Scotch Renegadoes, at last they have stimulated the [women] to demand new Privileges and threaten to rebell.

[36]
John Adams to John Sullivan (May 1776)

Our worthy friend, Mr. Gerry, has put into my hands a letter from you, of the sixth of May, in which you consider the principles of representation and legislation, and give us hints of some alterations, which you seem to think necessary, in the qualification of voters. . . .

It is certain, in theory, that the only moral foundation of government is, the consent of the people. But to what an extent shall we carry this principle? Shall we say that every individual of the community, old and young, male and female, as well as rich and poor, must consent, expressly, to every act of legislation? No, you will say, this is impossible. How, then, does the right arise in the majority to govern the minority, against their will? Whence arises the right of the men to govern the women, without their consent? Whence the right of the old to bind the young, without theirs? . . .

But why exclude women?

You will say, because their delicacy renders them unfit for practice and experience in the great businesses of life, and the hardy enterprises of war, as well as the arduous cares of state. Besides, their attention is so much engaged with the necessary nurture of their children, that nature has made them fittest for domestic cares. And children have not judgement or will of their own. True. But will not these reasons apply to others? Is it not equally true, that men in general, in every society, who are wholly destitute of property, are also too little acquainted with public affairs to form a right judgement, and too dependent upon other men to have a will of their own? . . .

Harrington has shown that power always follows property. This I believe to be as infallible a maxim in politics, as that action and reaction are equal, is in mechanics. Nay, I believe we may advance one step farther, and affirm that the balance of power in a society, accompanies the balance of property in land. The only possible

From Charles Adams, ed., *The Works of John Adams* (Boston: 1856), vol. 9, pp. 375–79.

way, then, of preserving the balance of power on the side of equal liberty and public virtue, is to make the acquisition of land easy to every member of society; to make a division of the land into small quantities, so that the multitude may be possessed of landed estates. If the multitude is possessed of the balance of real estate, the multitude will have the balance of power, and in that case the multitude will take care of the liberty, virtue, and interest of the multitude, in all acts of government. . . .

Your idea that those laws which affect the lives and personal liberty of all, or which inflict corporal punishment, affect those who are not qualified to vote as well as those who are, is just. . . .

The same reasoning which will induce you to admit all men who have no property, to vote, with those who have, for those laws which affect the person, will prove that you ought to admit women and children; for, generally speaking, women and children have as good judgements, and as independent minds, as those men who are wholly destitute of property; these last being to all intents and purposes as much dependent upon others, who will please to feed, clothe, and employ them, as women are upon their husbands, or children on their parents.

As to your idea of proportioning the votes of men, in money matters, to the property they hold, it is utterly impracticable. There is no possible way of ascertaining, at any one time, how much every man in a community is worth; and if there was, so fluctuating is trade and property, that this state of it would change in half an hour. The property of the whole community is shifting every hour, and no record can be kept of the changes. . . .

Depend upon it, Sir, it is dangerous to open so fruitful a source of controversy and altercation as would be opened by attempting to alter the qualifications of voters; there will be no end of it. New claims will arise; women will demand a vote; lads from twelve to twenty-one will think their rights not enough attended to; and every man who has not a farthing, will demand an equal voice with any other, in all acts of state. It tends to confound and destroy all distinctions, and prostrate all ranks to one common level.

[37]

Poem about an Election at Elizabethtown, New Jersey (1797)

What tho' we read, in days of yore,
    the women's occupation,
Was to direct the wheel and loom,
    not to direct the nation:
This narrow-minded policy
    by us hath met detection;
While woman's bound, man can't be free,
    nor have a *fair election*.

Oh! what parade those widows made!
    some marching cheek by jole, sir;
In stage, or chair, some beat the air,
    and press'd on to the *Pole,* sir:
While men of rank, who played this prank,
    beat up the widow's *quarters;*
Their hands they laid on every maid,
    and scarce spar'd wives, or daughters!

This precious clause of section laws
    we shortly will amend, sir;
And woman's rights, with all our might,
    we'll labor to defend sir:
To Congress, lo! widows shall go,
    like metamorphosed witches!
Cloath'd with the dignity of state,
    and eke, in coat and breeches!

Then freedom hail! thy powers prevail
    o'er prejudice and error;
No longer men shall tyrannize,
    and rule the world in terror:
Now one and all, proclaim the fall
    of Tyrants! — Open wide your throats,
And welcome in the *peaceful* scene,
    of government in petticoats!!!

From *The Newark* (New Jersey) *Centinel,* October 18, 1797. Cited in Edward R. Turner, "Women's Suffrage in New Jersey: 1790–1807," *Smith College Studies in History* (June 1916), 189.

Women's Civic Role

[38]

Columbia College Commencement Oration
"On Female Influence" (1795)

Let us then figure to ourselves the accomplished woman, surrounded by a sprightly band, from the babe that imbibes the nutritive fluid, to the generous youth just ripening into manhood, and the lovely virgin. . . .Let us contemplate the mother distributing the mental nourishment to the fond smiling circle, by means proportionate to their different powers of reception, watching the gradual openings of their minds, and studying their various turns of temper . . . the Genius of Liberty hovers triumphant over the glorious scene. . . . Yes, ye fair, the reformation of a world is in your power. . . . Contemplate the rising glory of confederated America. Consider that your exertions can best secure, increase, and perpetuate it. The solidity and stability of the liberties of your country rest with you; since liberty is never sure, 'till Virtue reigns triumphant. . . . Already may we see the lovely daughters of Columbia asserting the importance and the honor of their sex. It rests with you to make this retreat [from the corruptions of Europe] doubly peaceful, doubly happy, by banishing from it those crimes and corruptions which have never yet failed of giving rise to tyranny, or anarchy. While you thus keep our country virtuous, you maintain its independence. . . .

Cited in Linda K. Kerber, "Daughters of Columbia: Educating Women for the Republic, 1787–1805," in Jean E. Friedman and William G. Shade, eds., *Our American Sisters: Women in American Life and Thought* (2d ed., Boston: Allyn & Bacon, 1976), pp. 88–89.

[39]

Images of Women in Primary School Readers
(1787–1812)

On Women (1787)
Born to dignify retreat, unknown to flourish, and unseen to be great

Reprinted from *Guardians of Tradition: American Schoolbooks of the Nineteenth Century*, by Ruth Miller Elson, by permission of the University of Nebraska Press, Copyright © 1964 by the University of Nebraska Press.

On Woman's Influence (1797)
It is in the inculcation of high and pure morals . . . that in a free republic woman performs her sacred duty, and fulfills her destiny.

On Female Behavior (1787–1804)
But what can be more disgusting than to see innocent and timid females, whose excellence in part consists of their modesty and silence before superiors, encouraged to reverse the order of nature, by playing the orator on a public stage!

Girls should be taught to give up their opinions betimes, and not pertinaciously to carry on a dispute, even should they know themselves to be in the right.

Misconduct of daughters is more fatal to family peace, though perhaps not more heinous in a moral view.

On Higher Learning for Women (1790–1801)
The modest virgin, the prudent wife, or the careful matron are much more serviceable in life than petticoated philosophers, blustering heroines, or *virago* queens.

When a woman quits her own department she offends her husband, not merely because she obtrudes herself upon his business, but because she departs from that sphere which is assigned to her in the order of society, because she neglects *her* duty and leaves *her own* department vacant . . . the same rule which excludes a man from attention to domestic business, excludes a woman from law, mathematics and astronomy.

FAMILY CASE LAW

Separation, Divorce, and Alimony

[40]
Fry *v.* Derstler *(Pennsylvania, 1798)*

This was an action for criminal conversation. The defendant pleaded not guilty, and the act of limitations.

The plaintiff proved his marriage in 1785, and proof was likewise given of a criminal conversation [adultery] between the defendant and the plaintiff's wife, within a year or two after marriage. In 1787, the plaintiff's wife refused to leave her father's house and live with her husband; whereupon the plaintiff advertised in the public newspaper and likewise by many hand bills, that he warned everybody from

2 Yeates (Pa.) 278 (1798).

giving her credit on his account, and that he was determined never to cohabit with her again. About this time, the plaintiff got some arbitrators to attend at the house of his wife's father, to settle accounts between them. The wife there again refused to go and live with her husband, although he offered to take her. . . . It was then agreed that Fry and his wife should separate and either should be at liberty to marry whom they pleased; although some of the witnesses proved this was agreed to by Fry with great reluctance, as he wished to take his wife home with him. However from this time, they actually did live separately and had no connection with each other. About four months after the separation, the defendant married the plaintiff's wife, took her home, and they have ever since cohabited together as man and wife, having two children living. . . .

The court directed the jury that as to the criminal conversation before the separation, the defendant was secured by the act of limitations. As to the subsequent cohabitation of the plaintiff's wife with the defendant, it was after an agreement between the plaintiff and his wife to separate, and an actual separation in consequence. If the jury found a mutual agreement to separate, the plaintiff's action was not supportable.

The jury, however, found a verdict for the plaintiff, and gave 227 pounds damages.

Per cur. [an unsigned opinion of all members of the court]: The law is perfectly clear, that where husband and wife live in a state of separation, an action for criminal conversation cannot be maintained. Though the defendant may be punished by indictment for the offense, yet he is not amenable to the plaintiff in damages for depriving him of the society of his wife, whom he had before parted with, with his full consent. The case before us under all its circumstances requires re-examination. . . . New trial awarded.

This action came on again to be tried, before Shippen and Yeates, Justices, at Lancaster, on the 13th April, 1798, when some fresh evidence was given, and the point was submitted to the jury, whether the consent to separation on the part of the plaintiff was voluntary or constrained. If they were not satisfied of his consent, they wre instructed to find discreet and temperate damages, proportioned to the injury sustained, under all the circumstances of the case. The jury found for the plaintiff 150 pounds damages.

[41]
Anonymous *(South Carolina, 1810)*

This is a trial level case.—Ed.

This was a bill filed by a wife against her husband to recover alimony or some allowance, to support her in living apart from her husband, on the ground of ill-usage. The wife had carried in marriage a considerable fortune, and a settlement had been made which secured the estates to the children of the marriage but which gave the disposal of the income to the husband during their joint lives, for the benefit of both, and to the survivor during life.

[The case was] heard by Chancellor James who, after the argument, delivered the following decree:

In whatever points of view the present case is considered, whether as relating to the respectability of the parties litigant or the example it is to offer to the community, it is of utmost importance.

It is important to the parties litigant not in pecuniary point of view alone but also as it affects their peace and reputation; and to the community in showing how necessary it is for married persons to control their tempers and to guard against every cause of offense to each other, though such cause may appear to the one offering it not well founded or of little importance. . . .

The questions which appear proper for my decision are, first,—whether plaintiff is entitled to alimony on account of her good conduct as a wife; second—if her conduct should be such as not to entitle her to alimony out of the private estate of her husband, whether she is not entitled to it out of the trust estate. . . .

To excuse her departure from the bed and board of her husband, as stated in the answer, and not contradicted by the evidence, the wife has alleged that defendant suffered her to want the necessaries of life and that he ill-used her. . . . The witnesses which she relies upon to prove the want of necessaries are two: Mrs. Eliza White and Mrs. Croft.

Mrs. White deposed, "that complainant before her marriage with defendant and, whilst dependent, resided with her (about two years), lived in the greatest comfort, and was abundantly supplied with the necessaries and luxuries of life; and during her residence with complainant and defendant, after their marriage, which was about eighteen months, she was provided for very abundantly until after she left them. That dependent afterwards paid several visits and sometimes stayed two or three months upon a visit. On these occasions she found complainant scarcely provided for, and sometimes nearly destitute of the necessaries of life. That the defendant often left the complainant and would stay away three or four months at a time,

4 Desaus (S.C.) 95 (1810).

leaving her so scantily provided for that she was obliged to sell trifling articles in order to supply herself with necessaries."

Mrs. Croft deposed, "that she often visited the house of complainant while she was a widow, and she lived very happily and in a comfortable style. That since the marriage of complainant and defendant she has frequently visited the house of the defendant and has witnessed a want of those articles necessary for the comfort and convenience of a family in their situation, but cannot specify the articles wanted. That she has known complainant before her separation to have been refused credit in Georgetown; but does not know whether her not obtaining the articles she wished arose from an order of defendant or because they were not to be obtained in the store."

To contradict the evidence of these two witnesses, and to show that complainant never wanted the comforts and necessaries of life, defendant has in his answer denied the allegations to that effect in the bill, and has supported his answer by the testimony of Mrs. Charlotte A. Allston, Mrs. Marvin, Mr. Sessions, who was the overseer on the plantation, Mr. John Keith, Mr. Benjamin Huger, Dr. Blyth and Dr. Allston. Defendant in his answer states, "that he doth particularly deny it to be true that he at any time left the complainant unprovided with the necessaries of life, as in bill alleged; on the contrary, he doth affirm that his house was well provided not only with the necessaries but with most of the usual luxuries of life."

Mrs. Charlotte A. Allston deposed, "that in her visits to defendant's house she always witnessed the greatest abundance of all that could contribute to the comfort and support of a family; and that the style of living of complainant during the life of her first husband and during her widowhood was not preferable to that of her living when she resided with defendant."

Dr. Allston has deposed to the same effect.

Mrs. Marvin has sworn, "that she is well acquainted with the complainant but has little or no acquaintance with the defendant; that she visited their house sometime in the year 1802 or 1803, and that she observed the greatest abundance of every kind of comfort proper for a family such as that of the defendant's."

Mr. Sessions, the overseer, "served defendant three years, from 1800 till 1803, after the separation of his wife, the complainant, from him. . . . That as overseer he had the care of the livestock and poultry, which was as abundant as in most plantations; these were killed and used in the absence of defendant equally as when he was present." The witness, *Mr. Keith,* and his family, by invitations visited defendant and family. He states "that they stayed five or six days, and defendant's living appeared to be equal to his fortune."

Mr. Benjamin Huger deposed much to the same effect.

Dr. Blyth has sworn, "that he knew defendant for many years when he was a bachelor, when married to his first and when married to his second wife. That in all these situations he lived well; that he lived as well as his neighbors. And that there was no great difference between the style of living of complainant when she was a widow and when she was the wife of defendant." Besides these several witnesses, Mr.

Samuel Smith and Mr. Savage Smith, merchants, were examined, who proved "the complainant was permitted by her husband, the defendant, to take up goods in Georgetown, and that he gave her an unlimited credit there; so much so that Savage Smith as a friend told him, if he continued to contract such heavy debts he would be ruined."

Such is the testimony offered by complainant to show the want of the necessaries of life, and such that of the defendant to rebut the charge. In weighing the evidence, the court cannot have a doubt, nor hesitate to pronounce, that the testimony of these witnesses of complainant, however respectable, must fall to the ground when oppugned by the answer and by the testimony of nine other witnesses, eight of whom are at least as respectable as the witnesses for complainant. . . . But further to excuse her departure from her husband, the complainant has alleged his ill treatment of her. Upon this treatment her claim to alimony out of his private estate must be principally founded. To prove this she relies upon the evidence of the same two ladies, Mrs. White and Mrs. Croft. . . .

Mrs. White has sworn, "that the conduct of defendant towards complainant was total inattention and indifference. The witness hath often heard them quarrelling, but without hearing any distinct words or conversation, though deponent Mrs. White hath discovered, in their conduct towards each other, the visible effect of their private quarrels, after such had taken place. That in the opinion of deponent the jeering and ridicule by defendant of the complainant was of the most provoking and offensive kind, and calculated to wound her feelings, disgust her, and alienate her affections from him. That the defendant informed her he had purchased a plantation to the southward which he was then planting; that this place would afford him a good pretext for leaving complainant for a length of time; . . . that she was a virago and he could not live with her; but that he would visit her at stated periods, see that she was provided for, and if her conduct to him was still disagreeable he would stay away longer and longer at a time." . . .

Mrs. Croft deposed, "that she thinks defendant was very frequently absent from his family, and that she does not think that defendant was very affectionate to his wife. That she has heard them quarrelling at night after they had been in bed, though she could not distinctly hear their words; and that she has been at defendant's when the complainant was very sick, and his treatment of her on such occasions was not affectionate and tender."

To contradict this testimony of ill treatment, defendant has offered the evidence of Mr. Benjamin Huger, Dr. Blyth, Mrs. Charlotte A. Allston, and Mr. John Keith.

Mr. Huger stated, "That defendant is not of a bad or violent temper."

Dr. Blyth believes "defendant to be a good natured man;" and states "That he and his first wife lived happily together; no married people more so."

Mrs. Allston deposed, "That she has known defendant for many years and always found him a humane and amiable man. . . ."

Mr. Keith has sworn, "That he has been acquainted with defendant twenty years and always considered him a good tempered, benevolent man. . . ."

In considering the evidence, as to ill treatment offered by defendant to complainant, the court is of the opinion that it falls short of the *saevitia* of the ecclesiastical court, which must be translated "severity" or "cruelty." It is a pity that Mrs. White and Mrs. Croft had not descended to particulars so as to show in what the "inattention, indifference and the want of affection in defendant" consisted. . . . But from the latter part of the conversation which Mrs. White states she had with defendant, respecting the temper of his wife, and his observations to Miss Colcock upon the same subject, and from the first and last letters from complainant to defendant, dated respectively the 20th October, 1799, and 26th December, 1802, it is much to be suspected that complainant herself drove defendant from home to seek refuge from her bickerings. . . .

Both parties, as in most such cases, were no doubt in some respects blameable. Yet, taking the testimony of complainant's two witnesses in its utmost latitude, I cannot see that severity or cruelty for which it would seem that an ecclesiastical court, in England, would grant a divorce. Nor does there appear to me any agreement to live separate between them. The treatment, though somewhat neglectful, is not equal to that stated in the case *Jellineau* v. *Jellineau,* decided in this court. In that case, the defendant refused to send away the woman who was the bone of contention between them. At dinner one day he took away the plate from complainant when she was going to help herself to something to eat, and said: when he and his servant had dined, she might. He grudged her the bread she ate and said, "grass was good enough for her; that he was going to a magistrate to get a divorce and would buy a horsewhip and whip her well before she went away." In the present case, . . . there was no such improper and brutal conduct or treatment . . . and none such being proved, none such shall be presumed. . . . I have before said that the complainant has offered the above evidence adduced by her, to excuse her departure from the bed and board of her husband; that abrupt departures required some good excuses, and those offered do not appear sufficient or satisfactory. Had there been such a want of necessaries as is pretended, and such severity or cruelty as the law looks for before alimony is granted, it would not have been refused. But as the case stands, I cannot think myself warranted to granting it out of the private fortune of the husband.

It now remains for me to consider whether complainant is entitled to maintenance out of the trust estate. . . . The trust estate came from the complainant;—the whole of it belonged to her previous to the marriage. By the marriage settlement, "the rents and profits of it were to inure to the defendant and complainant during their joint lives, he to be entitled to take the same." Now, although the husband is entitled to the perception of these profits during their joint lives, yet it is conjointly with the wife, and her right, though legally vested in him.

Yet, in an equitable and moral point of view, and so far as her maintenance is concerned, it appears to be mutual and unextinguished. The defendant, too, appears to have been conscious of this, and in his first answer filed in this case it seems he fixes the amount, making an offer of a maintenance of 500 pounds, supposed to be one half the income of this trust estate. It is true, that in his amended answer he has retracted this offer, on account of the number of debts she has contracted on his account; but if he has suffered her to contract such debts, it is his own fault;—he is bound by Law to pay them;—this court will not interfere, nor will it suffer him to retract an offer, when he was equitably bound, and which he has once fairly made by his answer. Indeed, had he in his answer unequivocally made her the offer to return to him, perhaps, on the authority of the cases cited this court must have refused to grant her anything; but it appears from defendant's declaration to Miss Colcock that it is not his intention to take his wife back.

For these reasons the court considers the complainant entitled to receive the one half of the profits of the trust estate; but not retrospectively. Therefore, let the defendant account now and hereafter, annually with the commissioner, and pay over to him for the use of the complainant one half of the net profits of the trust estate, including any and all proceeds of the last year's crop not actually paid away; deducting from all future calculations the hire of the negroes she now has in her possession, unless the same should be delivered up to defendant; but that she be at liberty to retain any two of said negro slaves to wait upon her.

Let the defendant have the nurture and education of the child under his own control, but let the complainant have reasonable access to her. And let the costs of this suit be paid out of the income of the trust estate, to be born equally, complainant and defendant.

Guardianship and Child Custody

[42]
Burk *v.* Phips *(Connecticut, 1793)*

. . . On or about the first of March last past, her son Edward Burk, a minor about 16 years of age, being on board of the defendant's vessel at Charleston, in South Carolina, as a seaman, for a voyage of three months at customary wages; the defendant sold and executed a bill of sale or indenture of said Edward, to one Thomas Thomas for a term of years, and compelled him to enter on board said Thomas's vessel, bound to foreign parts, contrary to the mind and will of the plaintiff, or of said Edward; whereby she is deprived of the person, services, and company of her said son, to her damage 1500 pounds. . . .

1 Root (Conn.) 487 (1793).

[Defendant pleaded not guilty and the jury returned a verdict for the plaintiff, and 15 pounds damages. The defendant moved to set aside the verdict and the court agreed.]

First: There is no averment [no offer to prove] in the declaration that the plaintiff is a feme sole or that said Edward's father is living. Second: It doth not appear that she was guardian or any way entitled to the services of said boy; that as mother she is not, which differs the case from that of a father's commencing the action, for he is the natural guardian of his minor children, and entitled to their services.

[43]
Commonwealth *v*. Addicks *(Pennsylvania, 1813)*

Joseph Lee obtained a divorce from his wife Barbara on the grounds of adultery, after she gave birth to a child fathered by Addicks, the man she had been living with. She married Addicks in spite of a Pennsylvania law prohibiting marriage to the paramour during the life of the spouse, and thereafter Lee applied to the court for a writ of habeas corpus to have his children brought before the court and returned to his custody. It was determined through testimony that during the marriage he had: made no provision for either his wife or these children, although he had been applied to for this purpose; that during this period the mother had kept a boarding house and had educated the children herself, having applied in this matter the accomplishments she had acquired in the course of an excellent education in Canada; that the marriage with Addicks had taken place with a knowledge of the legal impediment; and that in no respect had her intercourse with him interfered with the attention that was due to the children, whose sex, as well as age, particularly required the care of a mother.—Ed.

J. R. Ingersoll, [for the father] on the other hand, made a statement to exculpate the husband and to show that his pecuniary circumstances, which at one time prevented him from giving aid to his family, now enabled him to educate and maintain the daughters, as he did a son of the same marriage, who had always been under his care.

One fact was not disputed, that the children were well treated and educated by the mother and had hitherto in no respect suffered under her care.

After holding the case under advisement for a day, the Chief Justice now delivered the Court's opinion.

Tilghman C. J. We have considered the law and are of the opinion that although we are bound to free the person from all illegal restraints, we are not bound to decide

5 Binney (Pa.) 519 (1813).

who is entitled to guardianship, or to deliver infants to the custody of any particular person. But we may in our discretion do so, if we think that under the circumstances of the case it ought to be done. For this we refer to the cases of *The King* v. *Smith*, 2 *stra*. 982, and *The King* v. *Delaval*, 3 *Burr* 1436. The present case is attended with peculiar and unfortunate circumstances. We cannot avoid expressing our disapprobation of the mother's conduct, although so far as regards her treatment of the children she is in no fault. They appear to have been well taken care of in all respects. It is to *them* that our anxiety is principally directed; and it appears to us, that considering their tender age, they stand in need of that kind of assistance which can be afforded by none so well as by a mother. It is on their account, therefore, that, exercising the discretion with which the law has invested us, we think it best, at present, not to take them from her. At the same time, we desire it to be distinctly understood that the father is not to be prevented from seeing them. If he does not choose to go to the house of their mother, she ought to send them to him when he desires it, taking it for granted that he will not wish to carry them abroad so much as to interfere with their education.

UNIT 3

[*Occupational Choice*]

VOCATIONAL TRAINING, CIRCA 1700

The system of apprenticeship and indentured servitude served several functions. It provided adolescent boys and girls with a general education and occupational skills and their masters and mistresses with cheap labor. The representative contracts presented in this section illustrate the obligations of master and servant and length of service. Although contracts for indenture varied in details they followed a form established in the Middle Ages. They also described the most common form of training received by white, black, and Indian women in the middle colonies during the early eighteenth century. Aprenticeships were available for women in only a few skilled crafts: millinery work, dressmaking, embroidery, hairdressing, and midwifery. Women were found in a large variety of other crafts, but they gained their skills by sharing in home manufacturing or working in family shops. The fragmentary statistical evidence shows that it was not uncommon for single and married women to operate their own shops, inns, and taverns.[21]

MARRIED WOMEN IN THE MARKET PLACE

It is clear from court records and statutes that married and deserted women who engaged in trade encountered problems as a result of their legal status. According to English and American common law, a single woman, called a feme sole, could make contracts in her own name and sue and be sued, all of which were necessary to conduct business. Once married, however, she could not make binding contracts and could engage in business only with the express permission of her husband, and as his agent. The selection from Tapping Reeve on *The Rationale for the Common Law of Contracts* explains the reason for this limitation; it makes comprehensible why, in many states, and until quite recently, married women did not have the same freedom of contract as their husbands.

Although the primary legal responsibility for support rested on the husband, many married women had to provide for themselves and their children. In some colonies, after a wife had been deserted for a few years she could petition the legislature for a special act allowing her to become a feme sole trader—that is, a married woman with the capacity to carry on a business independent of her husband. The wives of sailors were placed in this position so often that some colonies passed statutes, continuing into the nineteenth century, that enabled the whole group to become feme sole traders. The Pennsylvania statute, *An Act Concerning Feme Sole Traders* (1718), describes the plight of deserted wives and why their legal status was so important an issue. Note, however, that the statute is also a relief act for creditors and the community.

Regardless of their legal status, married women engaged in trade; businessmen who traded with them did not ask too many questions about their husbands. Nevertheless, the transactions left creditors and debtors without adequate legal protection. The South Carolina statute, *An Act Concerning Feme Covert Sole Traders* (1744), describes the frauds perpetrated as a result of the law of contract. This problem remained as long as states retained the marital disability (see, for example, *U.S. v. Yazell, 1966*). The phrase, "by reason of the absence of their husbands," suggests that the statute was passed to help deserted wives recover debts by giving them the power to sue. It complemented a 1712 statute enabling creditors to sue feme coverts, as though they were unmarried. The statute, by holding married women legally responsible for their debts, effectively gave them legal power to make contracts without the express permission of their husbands. But the statute did not really meet the problem of preventing fraud, nor did it give wives complete freedom to declare themselves sole traders. This was largely accomplished by *An Act to Regulate the Mode in which Married Women Shall Become Sole Traders or Dealers* (1823), according to which a married woman simply gave public notice of her intention to trade on her own account. The statute left unclear, however, whether a wife could declare herself a sole dealer if her husband openly opposed it.

Within a decade after the Revolution, the South Carolina courts acknowledged the right of a wife to earnings acquired in the course of her business, if she could prove that her husband had tacitly agreed to her acting as a feme sole trader. The policy is articulated in the case of *Catherine*

Megrath v. *Robertson* (1795). Ann Robertson died shortly after her husband, with neither heirs nor will. Witnesses established that she had acted as a feme sole trader with her husband's knowledge and that she was an independent-minded and highly successful entrepreneur. The lack of a marital agreement establishing a separate estate caused her property to descend to her husband's heirs. Her mother, Catherine, claimed she properly should inherit the property, which her daughter acquired through her own efforts. In deciding the case, the court firmly established that a wife only needed her husband's tacit approval to be viewed by the law as a feme sole trader. Its reasoning illustrates the way legal change is created without straying far from basic principles—in this case the husband's marital sovereignty.

EDUCATING WOMEN FOR THE REPUBLIC

The years immediately following the Revolution witnessed a great expansion in education, based on the belief that the success of the republican experiment rested on an educated and virtuous citizenry. As a result, between 1780 and 1830 the vast gap in literacy between men and women was closed in the Northeast. Where women's education was concerned, the central question revolved around how much and for what end. In *The Gleaner* (1798), Judith Sargent Murray, a friend of John and Abigail Adams, advocated an education designed to make women self-reliant and independent; one that would free them from the pressures to marry and allow them to avoid the fate of many widows—poverty.

The revolutionary fathers departed radically from colonial tradition when they recommended higher education for women; Puritans had feared that intellectual activity would make women discontented. Although the leaders of the republic firmly believed that order rested on the preservation of separate spheres for men and women, they altered the content of the women's sphere, allocating to them the role of the primary educator. They opened up a new occupation, that of schoolteacher. From the perspective of a generation brought up on the sayings of St. Paul, which prohibited women from teaching, this role for mothers and occupation for single women represented an important change in status. The new academies that opened for white women offered the type of rigorous liberal education once reserved for men destined to become community leaders. The unintended effect of this education may be seen in *The Salutory Oration of Miss Priscilla Mason to the Young Ladies Academy of Philadelphia* (1793). The speech conveys broad aspirations but also a heightened discontent with having no public theater for exercising talents and leadership.

By 1800 a conservative reaction had appeared in the face of the Revolu-

DOCUMENTS

VOCATIONAL TRAINING, CIRCA 1700

[44]
Indenture of Sarah Baker, an American Indian (1699)

Spelling modernized and abbreviations written out.—Ed.

Indenture of Sarah Baker, daughter of Marietta Damean, a free Indian Woman, with the Consent of her Mother, to Capt. Peter Matthews, Gent, and Bridgett, his wife, as a Servant for seven years from date, with usual covenants.

"And also shall teach or Cause to be taught and Instructed the Said Apprentice to Read the English tongue and to work plain work, and at the expiration of the Said Term to Give and Supply to their Said apprentice two good Suits of Apparel." Provided always that the Said Apprentice Shall not be Obliged to her Apprenticeship or any parte thereof out of the Province of New York without the consent of her said Mother. Any thing Above Mentioned to the Contrary Notwithstanding.

> Signed, etc. May 5th, 1699
> X (Sarah Baker, her mark)
> X (Marietta Damean, her mark)

In the presence of K. V. Renslaer, Will Sharpas.
Acknowledged before Jacobus V. Corlandt, Esq., Alderman

Cited in W. Elliot Brownlee and Mary M. Brownlee, eds., *Women in the American Economy: A Documentary History, 1675–1929* (New Haven: Yale University Press, 1976), pp. 73–74. By permission of Yale University Press.

[45]
Indenture of Margarett Colly, a White Woman (1702)

Indenture of Margarett Colly, daughter of James Colly, with the consent of her father, to John Crooke, Cooper, and Guartery, his wife, for seven years from date.

[Usual form.] Apprentice "Shall be taught to read English with Such Other Needle worke and Other matters fitting for a good housewife of her ability."

Signed, July 13th, 1702. Margarett Colly.
In the presence of Tho. Noell, Mayor.

Cited in W. Elliot Brownlee and Mary M. Brownlee, eds., *Women in the American Economy: A Documentary History, 1675–1929* (New Haven: Yale University Press, 1976), p. 76. By permission of Yale University Press.

[46]
Indenture of Maude, a Black Woman (1702)

Spelling modernized and abbreviations written out.—Ed.

This indenture witnesseth that Col. Lewis Morris of New York, in America, and Mary, his wife, for the Real Love, kindness and Affection that they bear unto Ann, the Daughter of Thomas Rudyard of New East Jersey, of their Own Voluntary good Will do give freely unto the Said Ann Rudyard the use and Service of One Negro maid named Maude, for and during the Space and Term of Eighteen Years from the day of the Date hereof. During all which time the said Maude is faithfully to serve the said Ann Rudyard as her Mistress in all things, Obeying and performing her just Commands to her utmost Endeavor. . . . And the Said Ann Rudyard doth hereby Covenant and promise for her Self, her Heirs, Executors, and Administrators, at the Expiration of the Said Term of Eighteen Years to give unto the Said Maude three Suits of Apparel, Either of Serge or Stuff with Linen answerable, and then to set her, the said Maude, at Liberty, giving her freedom from any and all manner of Service Whatsoever, to go and dwell where She, the Said Maude, Shall think Fit, and in the mean time to find her with Sufficient Meat, drink, lodging, and Apparel fit for Such a Servant to have, and in due manner to Chastize her According to desert.

Cited in W. Elliot Brownlee and Mary M. Brownlee, eds., *Women in the American Economy: A Documentary History, 1675–1929* (New Haven: Yale University Press, 1976), p. 76. By permission of Yale University Press.

In witness to all which the parties aforesaid to these presents have interchange-
ably set their hands and seals, the eighth day of the third month, called May. . . .

Ann Rudyard
Signed, sealed and delivered in the presence of
John Lawrence Jr., John Pett, William Bickley

MARRIED WOMEN IN THE MARKET PLACE

[47]

Tapping Reeve on the Rationale for the Common Law of Contracts (1816)

The right of a husband to the person of his wife . . . is a right guarded by the law
with the utmost solicitude; if she could bind herself by contracts, she would be liable
to be arrested, taken in execution, and confined in a prison; and then the husband
would be deprived of the company of his wife, which the law will not suffer.

From *The Law of Baron and Feme, of Parent and Child, of Guardian and Ward, of Master and Servant, and of the Powers of Courts of Chancery* (New Haven, 1816), p. 98.

[48]

"An Act Concerning Feme Sole Traders" (Pennsylvania, 1718)

WHEREAS it often happens that mariners and others, whose circumstances as well as
vocations oblige them to go to sea, leave their wives in a way of shop-keeping: and
such of them as are industrious, and take due care to pay the merchants they gain so
much credit with, as to be well supplied with shop-goods from time to time,
whereby they get a competent maintenance for themselves and children, and have
been enabled to discharge considerable debts, left unpaid by their husbands at their
going away; but some of those husbands, having so far lost sight of their duty to

From *Laws of the Commonwealth of Pennsylvania* (Philadelphia, 1810), vol. 1, pp. 99–101.

their wives and tender children that their affections are turned to those, who, in all probability, will put them upon measures, not only to waste what they may get abroad, but misapply such effects as they leave in this province: For preventing whereof, and to the end that the estates belonging to such absent husbands may be secured for the maintenance of their wives and children, and that the goods and effects which such wives acquire, or are entrusted to sell in their husband's absence, may be preserved for satisfying of those who so entrust them.

Be it enacted That where any mariners or others are gone, or hereafter shall go, to sea, leaving their wives at shopkeeping, or to work for their livelihood at any other trade in this province, all such wives shall be deemed, adjudged and taken, and are hereby declared to be, as feme sole traders, and shall have ability and are by this act enabled, to sue and be sued, plead and be impleaded at law, in any court or courts of this province, during their husbands' natural lives, without naming their husbands in such suits, plea or actions: and when judgments are given against such wives for any debts contracted, or sums of money due from them, since their husbands left them, executions shall be awarded against the goods and chattels in the possession of such wives, or in the hands or possession of others in trust for them, and not against the goods and chattels of their husbands; unless it may appear to the court where those executions are returnable, that such wives have, out of their separate stock or profit of their trade, paid debts which were contracted by their husbands or laid out money for the necessary support and maintenance of themselves and children; then, and in such case, executions shall be levied upon the estate, real and personal, of such husbands, to the value so paid or laid out, and no more.

II. *And be it further enacted,* That if any of the said absent husbands being owners of lands, tenements, or other estate in this province have aliened, or hereafter shall give, grant mortgage or alienate, from his wife and children, any of his said lands, tenements or estate, without making an equivalent provision for their maintenance, in lieu thereof, every such gift, grant, mortgage or alienation shall be deemed, adjudged and taken to be null and void.

III. *Provided nevertheless,* That if such absent husband shall happen to suffer shipwreck, or be by sickness or other casualty disabled to maintain himself, then, and in such case, and not otherwise, it shall be lawful for such distressed husband to sell or mortgage so much of his said estate, as shall be necessary to relieve him, and bring him home again to his family, anything herein contained to the contrary notwithstanding.

IV. But if such absent husband, having his health and liberty, stays away so long from his wife and children, without making such provision for their mainte-nance before or after his going away, till they are like to become chargeable to the town or place where they inhabit; or in case such husband doth live or shall live in adultery, or cohabit unlawfully with another woman, and refuses or neglects within seven years next after his going to sea, or departing this province, to return to his wife and cohabit with her again; then, and in every such case, the lands tenements and estate belonging to such husbands, shall be and are hereby made liable and subject to be seized and taken in execution, to satisfy any sum or sums of money which the wives of such husbands, or guardians of their children, shall necessarily expend or lay out for their support and maintenance; which execution shall be founded upon process of attachment against such estate, wherein the absent husband shall be made defendant; any law or usage to the contrary in any wise notwithstanding.

[49]
"An Act Concerning Feme Covert Sole Traders"
(South Carolina, 1744)

And whereas feme coverts in this Province who are sole traders do sometimes contract debts in this Province, with design to defraud the persons with whom they contract such debts, by sheltering and defending themselves from any suit brought against them, by reason of their coverture, whereby several persons may be defrauded of their just dues; and feme coverts, sole traders, are often under difficulties in recovering payment of debts contracted with them, by reason of the absence of their husbands, in whose name they are obliged to sue for all debts due to them, sometimes not being able to produce any power or authority from their husbands, *Be it therefore enacted* by the authority aforesaid, That any feme covert, being a sole trader, in this Province, shall be liable to any suit or action to be brought against her for any debt contracted as a sole trader, and shall also have full power and authority to sue for and recover, naming the husband for conformity, from any person whatsoever, all such debts as have or shall be contracted with her as a sole trader; and that all proceedings to judgment and execution by or against such feme covert, being a sole trader, shall be as if such woman was sole, and not under coverture; any law or custom to the contrary thereof in any wise notwithstanding.

From Thomas Cooper, ed., *The Statutes at Large of South Carolina* (Columbia, S.C., 1838), vol. 3, pp. 616, 620.

[50]

"An Act to Regulate the Mode in which Married Women Shall Become Sole Traders or Dealers" (South Carolina, 1823)

WHEREAS the practice of making married women sole traders or dealers, is productive of fraud on the community;

I. *Be it therefore enacted* by the Senate and House of Representatives, and by the authority of the same, That no woman having a husband living shall be entitled, either at law or in equity, to the rights of a free dealer, unless she shall give notice by publication in a public newspaper, of her intention to trade as a sole trader, which notice shall be published at least one month; and in case there is no newspaper published in the district, then the notice shall be published in the same way as sheriff's sales.

II. *And be it further enacted,* That no marriage settlement shall be valid until recorded in the office of the Secretary of State, and in the office of the register of mesne conveyances of the district where the parties reside; *provided* that the parties shall have three months to record the same, and if not recorded within three months, the same shall be null and void.

From David J. McCord, ed., *The Statutes at Large of South Carolina* (Columbia, S.C., 1839), vol. 6, pp. 212–13.

[51]

Megrath *v.* Robertson *(South Carolina, 1795)*

JOHN ROBERTSON and Ann his wife lived together many years in Charleston. He carried on business and acquired real and personal property, for which he took the titles and bills of sale in his own name. His wife also carried on a separate business, bought and sold property in her own name, and took the titles to the real estate and the bills of sale for the personal estate in her own name. There was no deed from the husband formally constituting the wife a sole dealer, nor any writing agreeing that acquisition of her industry should be her own separate property. But there was ample proof that she acted with her husband's privity, acquiescence and verbal permission; and she always claimed the propety acquired by her as her own. Some of the

1 Desaus (S.C.) 444 (1795).

witnesses proved he acquiesced merely for peace sake, as she was of a violent temper. But the majority of respectable and well informed witnesses stated that for many years she had acted and been considered a sole trader; was active and industrious, and made great profits in her separate dealings, and bought property for herself; that her husband knew and acquiesced in her conduct; that he sometimes borrowed money from her, and returned it. One of her debtors offering to pay the husband, he told him that he must go and settle with her, as she acted for herself, and had the note; which was accordingly done. The husband would sometimes caution her against bidding too much for property at auctions, but she repelled his interference, and said the money was her own and she would do as she pleased with it; to which he replied that was no reason she should ruin herself. In short the evidence was conclusive that she acted constantly, for many years as a *feme sole,* or as a sole trader; had a clerk to keep her accounts, and took titles in her own name, with the privity and acquiescence of her husband. But no writing could ever be produced of any arrangement to that effect.

John Robertson died intestate leaving his wife alive; but no children. She administered on his estate, made an inventory and sale of it. She died not long after, intestate leaving a considerable property, real as well as personal: and the defendants administered on her estate, as well as on John Robertson's. The administrators returned an inventory of her estate, of cash and other personal estate, to the amount of 2971 pounds. But the defendants thought themselves bound to submit the point to the court whether the property thus acquired by her, should be considered as her separate estate. . . . The complainant was proved to be the mother of Mrs. Robertson, and she filed this bill to have an account of her daughter's personal estate, and to have the titles of her real estate delivered up to her. Claiming as the nearest relation entitled to take according to the laws of this state, the daughter having died intestate without leaving alive either husband, children or father. . . .

The Court, after taking time to deliberate, delivered the following decree:

This is a case of a new impression. . . . The marital rights were and are very strong, and give absolute power to the husband over the personal property of his wife. In latter times they have been somewhat relaxed under written agreements or usage. There are three questions here. 1st. Whether John Robertson, one of the deceased, constituted his wife a sole trader. 2d. What benefit resulted to her from it? 3d. What portion of the estate of Ann Robertson . . . goes to the complainant who was her mother?

Upon full review of the evidence (which was very ample) relative to the acts of John Robertson and Ann his wife, it is evident that John Robertson permitted her to act a sole dealer, and to make contracts, and to purchase, and to sell on her own account, and to take titles in her own name. It is a maxim that no man shall be presumed to be ignorant of the law. There is no law here defining what is a sole dealer, and how a *feme covert* can be made a sole trader; nor is there in England. The custom of London authorizes it: and a clause in our attachment act recognizes the right in this country. . . . If the husband permits his wife to act as such, he relinquishes the control he had at common law. The case before the court, made out by the proofs, is the strongest possible, next to producing a deed from the husband authorizing the wife to act as a sole trader; and establishes her power so to act. 2d. As to what benefit resulted from it? She became sole mistress of the property which she acquired in the character of a sole trader, free from control of her husband. In this case he died first; she administered on his estate, and died soon after; whereupon the defendant administered on both estates. The difficulty is to discriminate the property. What has been brought home to the house must be considered the husband's, unless shown to be her's by documents, deeds, or employed in her trade; and except her wearing apparel. This must be the rule to discriminate. The inventory of the husband's estate may assist, as done on oath. As to the land, the titles were made to her of her houses; to him of his; they are conclusive. As she survived her husband, who died without children, she is entitled to the moiety of her husband's estate, under the statute of 1791, besides her separate estate as a sole dealer. 3d. Complainant is entitled as mother of Ann Robertson to the whole of her personal estate, and to the real [estate] of the British treaty now pending, be ratified by our government.

> The reference is to Jay's Treaty. The ninth article enabled British and American citizens holding property in each other's country to continue to do so. Mrs. Megrath was a British subject.—Ed.

EDUCATING WOMEN FOR THE REPUBLIC

[52]
Quotations from Judith Sargent Murray in The Gleaner *(1798)*

I would expect to see our young women forming a new era in female history.

. . .

I would give my daughters every accomplishment which I thought proper. . . . I would early accustom them to habits of industry and order. They should be taught with precision the art economical; they should be enabled to procure for themselves the neccessaries of life; independence should be placed within their grasp. . . . A woman *should reverence herself.*

Cited in Linda K. Kerber, "Daughers of Columbia: Educating Women for the Republic, 1787–1904," in Jean E. Friedman and William G. Shade, eds., *Our American Sisters: Women in American Life and Thought* (2d ed., Boston: Allyn & Bacon, 1976), pp. 76, 78–79.

Judith Sargent Stevens (1751–1820) challenged prevailing assumptions about the status of women and called for educating young girls to an independent life. Portrait by John Singleton Copley. Courtesy Frick Art Reference Library, New York.

[53]

The Salutatory Oration of Miss Priscilla Mason to the Young Ladies Academy of Philadelphia, May 15, 1793

Venerable Trustees of this Seminary, Patrons of the improvement of the female mind; suffer us to present the first fruits of your labors as an offering to you, and cordially to salute you on this auspicious day. . . .

A female, young and inexperienced, addressing a promiscuous assembly, is a novelty which requires an apology, as some may suppose. I, therefore, with submission, beg leave to offer a few thoughts in vindication of female eloquence.

I mean not, at this early day, to become an advocate for that species of female eloquence, of which husbands so much, and so justly, stand in awe,—a species of which the famous Grecian orator, Xantippe, was an illustrious example. Although the free exercise of this natural talent is a part of the rights of woman, and must be allowed by the courtesy of Europe and America too; yet it is rather to be *tolerated* than *established;* and should rest like the sword in the scabbard, to be used only when occasion requires.—Leaving my sex in full possession of this prerogative, I claim for them the further right of being heard on more proper occasions—of addressing the reason as well as the fears of the other sex.

Our right to instruct and persuade cannot be disputed, if it shall appear, that we possess the talents of the orator—and have opportunities for the exercise of those talents. Is a power of speech, and volubility of expression, one of the talents of the orator? Our sex possess it in eminent degree. . . .

Our high and mighty Lords (thanks to their arbitrary constitutions) have denied us the means of knowledge, and then reproached us for the want of it. Being the stronger party, they early seized the scepter and the sword; with these they gave laws to society; they denied women the advantage of a liberal education; forbid them to exercise their talents on those great occasions, which would serve to improve them. They doom'd the sex to servile or frivolous employments, on purpose to degrade their minds, that they themselves might hold unrivall'd, the power and pre-eminence they had usurped. Happily, a more liberal way of thinking begins to prevail. The sources of knowledge are gradually opening to our sex. Some have already availed themselves of the privileges so far, as to wipe off our reproach in some measure. . . .

But supposing now that we possess'd all the talents of the orator, in the highest perfection; where shall we find a theater for the display of them? The Church, the Bar, and the Senate are shut against us. Who shut them? *Man;* despotic man first

Cited in Ann Gordon, "The Young Ladies Academy of Philadelphia," in Mary Beth Norton and Carol Ruth Berkin, eds., *Women of America: A History* (Boston: Houghton Mifflin, 1979), pp. 89–91. Copyright © 1979 by Houghton Mifflin Company.

made us incapable of the duty, and then forbade us the exercise. Let us, by suitable education, qualify ourselves for those high departments—they will open before us. They *will*, did I say? They have done it already. Besides several churches of less importance, a most numerous and respectable Society has display'd its impartiality.—I had almost said gallantry in this respect. With *others*, women, forsooth, are complimented with the wall, the right hand, the head of the table,—with a kind of mock pre-eminence in small matters: but on great occasions the sycophant changes his tune and says, "Sit down at my feet and learn." Not so the members of the enlightened and liberal Church. They regard not the anatomical formation of the body. They look to the soul, and allow all to teach who are capable of it, be they male or female. . . .

With respect to the bar, citizens of either sex have an undoubted right to plead their own cause there. Instances could be given of females being admitted to plead the cause of a friend, a husband, a son; and they have done it with energy and effect. I am assured that there is nothing in our laws or constitution to prohibit the licensure of female attornies; and surely our judges have too much gallantry to urge *prescription* in bar of their claim. . . .

[54]

Letters from Eliza Southgate to Her Cousin Moses Porter

September, 1800

. . . I wish not to alter the laws of nature—neither will I quarrel with the rules which custom has established and rendered indispensably necessary to the harmony of society. But every being who has contemplated human nature on a large scale will certainly justify me when I declare that the inequality of privilege between the sexes is very sensibly felt by us females, and in no instance is it greater than in the liberty of choosing a partner in marriage; true, we have the liberty of refusing those we don't like, but not of selecting those we do.

June, 1801

As to the qualities of mind peculiar to each sex, I agree with you that sprightliness is in favor of females and profundity of males. Their education, their pursuits, would create such a quality even tho' nature had not implanted it. The business and pursuits of men require deep thinking, judgment, and moderation, while, on the other hand, females are under no necessity of dipping deep, but merely

From Clarence Cook, ed., *A Girl's Life Eighty Years Ago: Letters of Eliza Southgate Bowne* (New York, 1887), pp. 37–41, 58–62, 101–2.

In her letters to her cousin, Eliza Southgate (Bowne) reveals the self-esteem and buried aspirations of girls in the new female academies during the early Federal period. Portrait by Malbone, in *A Girl's Life Eighty Years Ago* (1888), ed. Clarence Cook.

"skim the surface," and we too commonly spare ourselves the exertion which deep researches require. . . . Women who have no such incentives to action suffer all the strong energetic qualities of the mind to sleep in obscurity. . . . In this dormant state they become enervated and impaired, and at last die for *want of exercise.* . . . The cultivation of the powers we possess, I have ever thought a privilege (or I may say duty) that belonged to the human species, and not man's exclusive prerogative. Far from destroying the harmony that ought to subsist, it would fix it on a foundation that would not totter at every jar. Women would be under the same degree of subordination that they now are and they would perceive the necessity of such a regulation to preserve the order and happiness of society. . . . I know it is generally thought that in such a case women would assume the right of commanding. But I see no foundation for such supposition. . . . I had rather be the meanest reptile that creeps the earth, or cast upon the wide world to suffer all the ills "that flesh is heir to," than live a slave to the despotic will of another.

I am aware of the censure that will ever await the female that attempts the vindication of her sex, yet I dare to brave that censure that I know to be undeserved. . . .

May, 1802

. . . We all have a preference to some particular mode of life, and we surely ought to endeavor to arrive at that which will more probably ensure us most happiness. I have often thought what profession I should choose were I a man. . . . I have always thought if I felt conscious of possessing brilliant talents, the *law* would be my choice. . . . I should then hope to be a public character, respected and admired—but unless I was convinced I possessed the talents which would distinguish me as a speaker I would be anything rather than a lawyer. . . . But to be an eloquent speaker would be the delight of my heart. I thank Heaven I was *born* a woman. . . . But remember, I desire to be thankful I am not a man. I should not be content with moderate abilities—nay, I should not be content with mediocrity in anything, but as a woman I am equal to the generality of my sex, and I do not feel that great desire of fame I think I should if I was a man. . . .

UNIT 4

[*Crime and Deviance*]

A CRIME AGAINST THE STATE

In a society of true believers salvation bore directly on an individual's sense of self-worth and social and political status. Seventeenth-century Puritan rebels in England had denied the authority of priest, bishop, and king to mediate between the individual and God. They posited a priesthood of all believers and emphasized the private nature of each person's covenant with God. The voyage to Massachusetts had turned a dissenting movement into an established church and state and changed its character. The Massachusetts ministry modified the "covenant of grace" and stressed that the relationship of the individual to God had to be screened by the clergy, to insure that each private conscience was rightly informed; in practice this meant loyalty to the programs and policies of the civil establishment. To many settlers this resembled the repudiated "covenant of works" and the type of intervention that they had fought against in England.[22]

The *Trial of Anne Hutchinson* (1637) for the crime of breaking the law of God is an archetype of the political trial. Its purpose was not to assess the guilt or innocence of the defendant, but to demonstrate the power of the state and to secure conformity to its interpretation of the official view—in this case the Puritan Way.[23] The harmony of Massachusetts Bay colony was being disturbed by the spread of religious ideas that made the individual the judge of his or her state of grace and fueled opposition to a ruling oligarchy that tried to control all aspects of civil life.

The doctrines and practices of Anne Hutchinson had important implications for the relationship between men and women, because they put salvation beyond the control of men. If the prosecutors are to be believed, her views encouraged insubordination among women against the rule of their husbands. Although, before her trial, Hutchinson had never publicly stated any religious views for which she could be accused, she was associated in various ways with persons who were considered to be religious radicals. Her gatherings for religious instruction and discussion of sermons attracted many women and allowed her to influence popular opinion both for and against particular clergymen and doctrines.

The charges brought against Anne Hutchinson, and the interaction between her and the examiners during the trial, reveal basic attitudes toward women and the fear that Hutchinson might become a role model. In attributing social turmoil to the actions of a well-educated and independent woman, the prosecutors were not necessarily giving an accurate intepretation of the origins of the crisis: just as likely, they were showing their opposition to the participation of women in church governance. They were presenting a morality play about what happens when women step out of line and are not firmly controlled by their husbands.[24]

The trial was clearly unfair, by modern standards, but less so by those prevailing in the early seventeenth century. The defendant was not indicted and did not know the exact charges against her. Her lack of legal counsel is not so odd, considering that there were, as yet, no practicing lawyers in the tiny colony. The lack of a jury, too, was normal. Not until four years later, when the colony wrote its first law code, did it allow the accused in a criminal trial to choose a trial by jury instead of one by the bench.[25]

The undoubted drama of Hutchinson's trial arises from her skill at turning a ritual into a real, evidentiary hearing. She forced her accusers to choose between either finding legally acceptable evidence of the charges against her, or exposing themselves to the charges of having acted outside the law. Hutchinson herself had to decide whether to remain silent about her religious beliefs or to speak her conscience. Silence, which might have saved her and embarrassed her persecutors, would have implied acceptance of the policy that women had no role in formulating doctrine or in governing the church. Speaking her mind, on the other hand, would give the state the legal justification needed to banish her.[26]

After the trial many female supporters of Anne Hutchinson turned to the Society of Friends as their church. Quakers accepted the idea of inspiration by Divine Light and lay ministries that included women. Although the Quakers never became a major denomination, during the nineteenth century they produced a disproportionately large number of women leaders of the abolitionist and woman rights movements.

DOCUMENTS

A CRIME AGAINST THE STATE

[55]
Dicta of Saint Paul, Corinthians 14:34–35

As in all the churches of the saints, women are to remain quiet at meetings since they have no permission to speak; they must keep in the background as the Law itself lays it down. If they have any questions to ask, they should ask their husbands at home: it does not seem right for a woman to raise her voice at meetings.

From *The Jerusalem Bible: The Reader's Edition* (Garden City, New York: Doubleday, 1966).

[56]
The Trial of Mrs. Anne Hutchinson at the Court of Newton, Massachusetts (November 1637)

Language modernized.—Ed.

Mr. Winthrop, Governor: Mrs. Hutchinson, you are called here as one of those who have troubled the peace of the commonwealth and the churches here; you are known to be a woman that hath had a great share in the promoting and divulging of those

From Thomas Hutchinson, *The History of the Colony and Province of Massachusetts-Bay, edited from the Author's own copies of Volume I and II and his manuscript of Volume III*, with a memoir and additional notes, by Lawrence Shaw Mayop (Cambridge: Harvard University Press, 1936), Appendix II, pp. 366–91. Copyright © 1936 by the President and Fellows of Harvard College. Reprinted by permission of the President and Fellows of Harvard College.

opinions that are causes of this trouble; . . . you have spoken diverse things, as we have been informed, very prejudicial to the honor of the churches and ministers thereof; and you have maintained a meeting and an assembly in your house that hath been condemned by the general assembly as a thing not tolerable nor comely in the sight of God, nor fitting for your sex. Notwithstanding that was cried down, you have continued the same. Therefore, we have thought good to send for you to understand how things are, that if you be in an erroneous way we may reduce you, that so you may become a profitable member here among us. Otherwise, if you be obstinate in your course, then the court may take such course that you may trouble us no further. . . .

Mrs. H.: I do acknowledge no such thing, neither do I think that I ever put any dishonor upon you.

Gov.: Why do you keep such a meeting at your house as you do every week upon a set day?

Mrs. H.: It is lawful for me so to do, as it is all your practice; . . . can you find a warrant for yourself and condemn me for the same thing? . . .

Gov.: For this, that you appeal to our practice, you need no confutation. If your meeting had answered to the former it had not been offensive, but I will say that there was no meeting of women alone, but your meeting is of another sort, for there are sometimes men among you.

Mrs. H.: There was never any man with us.

Gov.: . . . By what warrant do you continue such a course?

Mrs. H.: I conceive there lies a clear rule in Titus, that the elder women should instruct the younger, and then I must have a time wherein I must do it.

Gov.: All this I grant you, I grant you a time for it, but what is this to the purpose that you, Mrs. Hutchinson, must call a company together from their callings to come to be taught of you? . . .

Mrs. H.: . . . If you look upon the rule in Titus, it is a rule to me. If you convince me that it is no rule, I shall yield.

Gov.: You know that there is no rule that crosses another, but this rule crosses that in the Corinthians. You must take it in this sense, that elder women must instruct the younger about their business, and to love their husbands and not make them to clash. . . . It will not well stand with the commonwealth that families should be neglected for so many neighbors and dames and so much time spent. We see no rule of God for this, we see not that any should have authority to set up any other exercises beside what authority hath already set up, and so what hurt comes of this you will be guilty of, and we for suffering you.

Dep. Gov.: . . . Mrs. Hutchinson hath so forestalled the minds of many by their resort to her meeting that now she hath a potent party in the country. . . . It being found that Mrs. Hutchinson . . . hath depraved [vilified] all the ministers and hath been the cause of what is fallen out. . . .

Hugh Peters, a Salem pastor, testifies about a previous interrogation of Ann Hutchinson, at a convocation of ministers.

Mr. Peters: . . . We thought it good to send for this gentlewoman, and she willingly came. At the very first we gave her notice that such reports there were that she did conceive our ministry different from the ministry of the Gospel. . . . I did then take upon me to ask her this question. What difference do you conceive to be between your teacher John Cotton and us? Briefly, she told me there was a wide and broad difference between our brother Mr. Cotton and our selves. I desired to know the difference. She answered that he preaches the covenant of grace and you the covenant of works, and that you are not able ministers of the new testament and know no more than the apostles did before the resurrection of Christ. . . .

The next morning

Mrs. H.: The ministers come in their own cause. Now the Lord hath said that an oath is the end of all controversy; though there be a sufficient number of witnesses, yet they are not according to the word, therefore I desire they make speak upon oath.

Gov.: Well, it is in the liberty of the court whether they will have an oath or no, and it is not in this case as in case of jury. . . .

Mrs. H.: But they are witnesses of their own cause.

Mr. Bradstreet: Mrs. Hutchinson, these are but circumstances and adjuncts to the cause. If they should mistake you in your speeches you would make them to sin if you urge them to swear.

Mrs. H.: That is not the thing. If they accuse me, I desire it may be upon oath.

Gov.: If the court be not satisfied, they may have an oath.

Debate follows about the ministers' speaking under oath, and about Mrs. Hutchinson bringing her own witnesses. The ministers do not take the oath.—Ed.

Gov.: Mr. Cotton, the court desires that you declare what you do remember of the conference . . . in question.

Mr. Cotton: I did not think I should be called to bear witness in this cause, and therefore did not labor to call to remembrance what was done. The elders . . . did first pray her to answer wherein she thought their ministry did differ from mine. . . . She told them to this purpose that they did not hold forth a covenant of grace as I did. But wherein did we differ? Why, she said, that they did not hold forth the seal of spirit as he doth. Where is the difference there? say they. Why, saith she, . . . you preach of the seal of the spirit upon a work, and he upon free grace . . . without respect to a work. . . . I told her I was very sorry that she put comparison between my ministry and theirs, for she had said more than I could myself. Rather I had that she had put us in fellowship with them and not have made that discrepancy. She said, she found the difference. . . . And I must say that I did not find her saying they were under a covenant of works, nor that she said they did preach a covenant of works. . . .

Mr. Peters: I humbly desire to remember our reverend teacher . . . she said we were not sealed with the spirit of grace, therefore could not preach a covenant of grace. . . .

Mr. Cotton: You do put me in remembrance that it was asked her why cannot we preach a covenant of grace? Why, saith she, because you can preach no more than you know. . . . Now, that she said you could not preach a covenant of grace, I do not remember such a thing. I remember well that she said you were not sealed with the seal of the spirit. . . .

Mrs. H.: If you please to give me leave, I shall give you the ground of what I know to be true. Being much troubled to see the falseness of the constitution of the Church of England, I had like to have turned separatist, whereupon I kept a day of solemn humiliation and pondering of the thing; . . . I bless the Lord, he hath let me see which was the clear ministry and which the wrong. Since that time, I confess . . . he hath left me to distinguish between the voice of my beloved and the voice of Moses, the voice of John Baptist and the voice of Antichrist, for all those voices are spoken of in scripture. Now if you do condemn me for speaking what in my conscience I know to be truth, I must commit myself unto the Lord.

Mr. Nowel: How do you know that that was the spirit?

Mrs. H.: How did Abraham know that it was God that bid him offer his son, being a breach of the sixth commandment?

Dep. Gov.: By an immediate voice.

Mrs. H.: So to me by an immediate revelation.

Dep. Gov.: How! An immediate revelation.

Mrs. H.: By the voice of his own spirit to my soul. . . .

Gov.: Daniel was delivered by miracle; do you think to be delivered so too?

Mrs. H.: I do here speak it before the court. I took that the Lord should deliver me by his providence. . . .

Dep. Gov.: I desire Mr. Cotton to tell us whether you do approve of Mrs. Hutchinson's revelations, as she hath laid them down.

Mr. Cotton: I know not whether I do understand her, but this I say, if she doth expect a deliverance in a way of providence—then I cannot deny it.

Dep. Gov.: No Sir, we did not speak of that.

Mr. Cotton: If it be by way of miracle, then I would suspect it.

Dep. Gov.: Do you believe that her revelations are true?

Mr. Cotton: That she may have some special providence of God to help her is a thing that I cannot witness against.

Dep. Gov. Good Sir, I do ask whether this revelation be of God, or no?

Mr. Cotton: I should desire to know whether the sentence of the court will bring her to any calamity, and then I would know of her whether she expects to be delivered from that calamity by a miracle or a providence of God.

Mrs. H.: By a providence of God I say I expect to be delivered from some calamity that shall come to me.

Gov.: The case is altered. . . . Now the mercy of God by a providence hath answered our desires and made her to lay open her self and the ground of all these disturbances to be by revelations. . . . They look for revelations and are not bound to the ministry of the word. . . . That hath been the root of all the mischief.

Dep. Gov.: These disturbances that have come among the Germans have been all grounded upon revelations. . . . They that have vented them have stirred up their hearers to take up arms against their prince and to cut the throats of one another. . . . Whether the devil may inspire the same into their hearts here I know not. . . . I am fully persuaded that Mrs. Hutchinson is deluded by the devil, because the spirit of God speaks truth in all his servants.

Gov.: I am persuaded that the revelation she brings forth is delusion.

All the court but some two or three ministers cry out: We all believe it—we all believe it.

Gov.: The court hath already declared themselves satisfied concerning the things you hear, and concerning the troublesomeness of her spirit and the danger of her course amongst us, which is not to be suffered. Therefore if it be the mind of the court that Mrs. Hutchinson, for these things that appear before us, is unfit for our society, and if it be the mind of the court that she shall be banished out of our liberties and imprisoned till she be sent away, let them hold up their hands.

All but three.

Gov.: Mrs. Hutchinson, the sentence of the court you hear is that you are banished from out of our jurisdiction, as being a woman not fit for our society, and are to be imprisoned till the court shall send you away.

Mrs. H.: I desire to know wherefore I am banished?

Gov.: Say no more, the court knows wherefore, and is satisfied.

NOTES

1. Mary P. Ryan, *Womanhood in America: From Colonial Times To The Present* (New York: New Viewpoints, 1975), pp. 1–41; Mary Beth Norton, *Liberty's Daughters: The Revolutionary Experience of American Women, 1750–1800* (Boston: Little, Brown, 1980), pp. 1–39.

2. Willard Hurst, *Law And The Conditions of Freedom in the Nineteenth-Century United States* (Madison: University of Wisconsin Press, 1956), pp. 8–9.

3. Mary Beth Norton, "Eighteenth-Century American Women in Peace and War: The Case of the Loyalists," *William and Mary Quarterly,* 3rd Series 33 (1976), 386–409.

4. Mary Lynn Salmon, "Life, Liberty & Dower: The Legal Status of Women after the American Revolution" in *Women, War and Revolution,* eds. Carol Ruth Berkin and Clara M. Lovett (New York: Holmes & Meier, 1980), pp. 85–106.

5. Morton J. Horwitz, *The Transformation of American Law, 1780–1860* (Cambridge, Mass.: Harvard University Press, 1977), pp. 56–58.

6. Lois Greene Carr and Lorena Walsh, "The Planter's Wife: The Experience of White Women in Seventeenth-Century Maryland," *William and Mary Quarterly,* 3rd Series 34 (1977), 542–71.

7. Marylynn Salmon, "The Property Rights of Women in Early America: A Comparative Study" (Ph.D. diss., Bryn Mawr College, 1980), 164, Table 7, p. 250. The chapter on South Carolina marriage settlements provides the only full description and analysis of who made settlements, their economic backgrounds, and the types of powers reserved by young women marrying for the first time and by

widows re-marrying for the period 1729–1830. In her sample of 495 agreements, the author found that only 25 percent of women marrying for the first time sought full control over their property.

8. Ibid. Table 7, p. 250. Full control over their property was sought by 58 percent of remarrying widows.

9. Marylynn Salmon, "'Equality or Submersion?' Feme Covert Status in Early Pennsylvania," in *Women of America: A History,* eds. Carol Ruth Berkin and Mary Beth Norton (Boston: Houghton Mifflin, 1979), pp. 98–100.

10. Norton, *Liberty's Daughters,* pp. 40–45, 56–59.

11. Kinvin Wroth and Hiller B. Zobel, eds., *Legal Papers of John Adams* (Cambridge, Mass.: The Belknap Press, 1965), vol. 2, pp. 48–52.

12. Nelson M. Blake, *The Road to Reno: A History of Divorce in the United States* (New York: Macmillan, 1962), pp. 31–33.

13. Ibid., pp. 34–40; Kelly D. Weisberg, "'Under Greet Temptations Heer' Women and Divorce in Puritan Massachusetts," *Feminist Studies* 2 (1975), 183–193; Henry S. Cohn, "Connecticut's Divorce Mechanism: 1636–1969," *The American Journal of Legal History* 14 (1970), 35–54.

14. Blake, *The Road to Reno,* pp. 41–47.

15. Norton, *Liberty's Daughters,* pp. 155–229.

16. Ibid., pp. 191–93.

17. Linda K. Kerber, *Women of the Republic: Intellect & Ideology in Revolutionary America* (Chapel Hill: University of North Carolina Press, 1980), pp. 189–231.

18. Daniel Scott Smith, "The Dating of the American Sexual Revolution: Evidence and Interpretation," in *The American Family in Social-Historical Perspective,* ed., Michael Gordon (New York: St. Martin's Press, 1973), pp. 321–335; Daniel Scott Smith and Michael S. Hindus, "Premarital Pregnancy in American 1640–1971: An Overview and Interpretation," *Journal of Interdisciplinary History* 4 (1975), 537–70.

19. Nancy Cott, "Divorce and the Changing Status of Women in Eighteenth-Century Massachusetts," *William and Mary Quarterly,* 3rd Series 33 (1976), 586–614.

20. Blake, *The Road to Reno,* pp. 48–63.

21. W. Elliot Brownlee and Mary M. Brownlee, eds., *Women in the American Economy: A Documentary History, 1625–1929* (New Haven: Yale University Press, 1976), pp. 72–73; Joan Hoff Wilson, "The Illusion of Change: Woman and the American Revolution," in *The American Revolution: Explorations in the History of American Radicalism,* ed. Alfred F. Young (DeKalb: Northern Illinois Press, 1976), pp. 395–97.

22. David Hall, "The Antinomian Controversy," in *Anne Hutchinson: Troubler of the Puritan Zion,* ed. Francis J. Bremer (New York, Robert E. Krieger, 1981), pp. 21–47. In the same volume: William K. B. Stover, "The Theological Dimension," pp. 28–37; Edward S. Morgan, "The Case Against Anne Hutchinson," pp. 51–57; and Kai T. Erikson, "Wayward Puritans," pp. 75–84.

23. Richard B. Morris, "Jezebel Before the Judges," in Bremer, *Anne Hutchinson,* pp. 58–59.

24. Ben Barker-Benfield, "Anne Hutchinson and the Puritan Attitude Toward Woman," in Bremer, *Anne Hutchinson,* pp. 99–111. In the same volume: Lyle Kohler, "The Case of the American Jezebels," pp. 112–123.

25. Morris, "Jezebel Before the Judges," pp. 58–64.

26. Anne F. Withington and Jack Schwartz, "The Political Trial," in Bremer, *Anne Hutchinson,* pp. 65–72.

CHAPTER 2

The Age of Jackson, Reconstruction, and the Gilded Age (1830–1890)

UNIT 1

[*Marriage and Property*]

THE PASSING OF THE OLD ORDER

The period between the War of 1812 and the Civil War was characterized by rapid economic growth punctuated by sudden financial crises. The depression that followed the Panic of 1819 aroused the hostility of farmers and artisans against banking corporations and other groups that had used political influence to gain economic privileges. The economic recovery was accompanied by a high rate of urbanization and rapid settlement of regions from New York State to the Ohio and Mississippi Rivers, the beginning of the transportation revolution, the extension of cotton cultivation in the old Southwest, and the rise of textile manufacturing in New England. Growth fed an appetite of growing expectations, risk taking, and a distrust of special interests. Increasing numbers of white men brought their aspirations and grievances into the political arena. Both Democrats and Whigs appealed to a broad constituency by attacking any clique or party that excluded the common people from equal access to the rewards of national growth. State constitutional conventions swept away the last property requirements for the vote for white men and made the judiciary subject to popular election.

The political debates over special privilege included a broad attack on "judge made law" and on the common law by those who sought to make the legislature the sole source of law making. The public debate helped educate the listening public, including women, about the way law shapes the boundaries of opportunity for individuals and groups. The portrayal of the common law as aristocratic and as a barrier to social change, by critics of the judicial law-making process, has obscured the dynamic role of the courts in

117

directing the course of legal change in the area of economic relations. Legal historians have argued that the enormous release of entrepreneurial energies that characterized Jacksonian society was underpinned by the transformation of common-law principles with regard to property, contract, and legal liability during the first half of the nineteenth century. Legal innovation moved largely toward laissez faire: judges, like legislators, identified the public interest with economic growth and concluded this could be best achieved by freeing entrepreneurs from the legal risks and restrictions associated with traditional concepts of fair exchange and communal responsibilities and by increasing individual discretion in the management of resources.[1]

The use of law by different groups of white males as an instrument to advance social change suggested the possibility of using it in the same way to advance the capacity of married women to determine their own role and to legitimize a new model of marriage. The *Marriage Agreement of Robert Owen and Mary Jane Robinson* (1832), the *Protest of Henry B. Blackwell and Lucy Stone* (1855), and the quotation from a *Critique of Marriage Agreements* (1844) illustrate the contrasting cultural visions that underlay the question of married women's property rights.

PIECEMEAL LEGAL REFORM

This section explores the process and substance of legal change, through a case study of New York. The documents raise the question whether the passage of the married woman's property act can be described as a revolution.[2] Mississippi passed the first women's property statute in 1839. By 1860 about seventeen states had introduced some form of legislation altering the common law on marital property. The powers granted by these statutes and subsequent amendments varied greatly, which meant that when married women moved from one state to another they often gained or lost rights.

Legislative Revision of Property Law

In New York, as in other states, it was the boom and bust nature of the economy that turned the attention of legislators to the issue of married women's property rights. Thomas Herttell, a 65-year-old Democratic assemblyman from New York City, introduced the first statute, during the Panic of 1837, with an impassioned speech in behalf of women's rights. He also advanced an economic argument appropriate for a year of rising bankruptcies, pointing to the consequences that ensued when a husband subjected his wife's property to the "hazards and vicissitudes of trade and speculation." This he combined with a picture of inept, morally degenerate, and improvident husbands wasting the patrimony of their wives on ill-chosen investments. The real villain, it would appear from his arguments, was the common law, which immobilized the wife in straitened circumstances, endangered the family in times of economic hardship, and created an exclusively male economy. Changing the marital property laws, he suggested, would give women economic opportunities and, by relieving pauperism, reduce public expenditures.

This was essentially the same argument found in the eighteenth-century statutes that had created exceptions to the marital property rule for certain classes of women. The New York legislature, in discussing debtor exemption laws, remarked on the frequency with which the family home was purchased by money from a wife's labor or endowment and the fatal effects of merging fortunes. The initial solution of the legislature was not to expand the wife's powers, as Herttell had suggested, but to find better ways to insulate family assets from creditors.

An additional stimulation for a property act was the movement for codification and legal reform. The codification movement emphasized that legislatures should be the sole source of legal change and that law should be spelled out comprehensively in written form. It attempted to do away with archaic, complex, and expensive legal forms, and found ready targets in the legal fiction of marital unity and the devices, such as antenuptial agreements and trusts, that were created to circumvent it.

The reform campaign centered on the faulty and expensive administration of equity in chancery courts. The abolition of the Court of Chancery by the 1846 New York State Constitution and the merger of law and equity procedures had the secondary effect of depriving married women of equity rights they had held since the eighteenth century. This moved the state legislature to act.

Meanwhile, the legal inequities in the wife's status at common law had begun to loom larger in the minds of women, who watched white men without property get the vote and slaves become the center of a great abolition crusade. In 1837, the year Herttell introduced his property bill, Sarah Grimké published *Letters on the Equality of the Sexes,* containing a harsh indictment of the common law. In the conservative columns of *Godey's Lady Book,* Sarah Hale wrote in favor of a property act, emphasizing how the common law relegated woman to the condition of a slave and impaired her influence with her husband and children. In the 1840s women active in the Abolitionist movement turned to woman rights. Paulina Wright Davis, Ernestine Rose, and Elizabeth Cady Stanton mounted petitioning campaigns to move out of the judiciary committee the various statutes that were introduced year after year. The quotations from the *Report of the Judiciary*

Committee on the Petitions to Extend and Protect the Rights of Property of Married Women (1842), and those from the *Albany Argus* (1848) on the final passage of such a bill, capture the anxiety politicians felt over the social ramifications of extending women's property rights in marriage.

The excerpts from *New York's Married Women's Property Statutes,* 1848–1887, presented here, which are representative of the national trend, depict a step-by-step legal reform that took more than a half-century to complete. If one compares the statutes with legal devices, such as antenuptial contracts and trusts, that were available to individual women in the late eighteenth century, what emerges is not a pattern of expanding rights but a piecemeal extension of some of the rights already available to the privileged. The traditional rationale for the existence of a wife's separate estate in equity, and the granting of control over its use, was to protect her from the coercive powers of her husband. The passage of the statutes indicates that marital problems had spread beyond the capacity of the courts to handle them on an individual basis. The eighteenth-century judicial solution—to enlarge the wife's capacity for self-protection—became the nineteenth-century legislative solution, in the form of the property acts.

It must be admitted that the Married Woman's Property Act was exactly the Pandora's box that its opponents had feared. Three months after the passage of the 1848 statute, the first women's rights convention met at Seneca Falls, New York, and issued the *Declaration of Sentiments.* In the following years a growing cadre of feminists, in conventions, on the lecture circuit, through articles, and before legislative committees, presented the grievances laid out in the *Declaration* and pursued its goals. The Earnings Act of 1860 reflects the demands of the organized women's rights movement, which emphasized the lack of protection for working wives.

Judicial Construction of the Statutes

The full effect of the Earnings Act, which radically altered the husband's common-law rights, would be determined in the courts. The judicial approach, illustrated by *Switzer* v. *Valentine* (1854), *Brooks* v. *Schwerin* (1873), and *Birkbeck* v. *Ackroyd* (1878) reflects particular attitudes toward marriage. As the cases here show, the judiciary chose to interpret the intent and spirit of the property acts as narrowly as possible. By establishing stringent requirements for determining what constituted a separate legal estate, judges could base many decisions on common-law principles. In practice, most married couples mingled their assets and the fruits of their labor, making it difficult for courts to determine who owned what. Moreover, the courts often treated intermingled assets as the property of the husband. As a result, the women least aided by the new statutes were working women who contributed to the financial support of their families:

women who managed family farms, ran boarding houses or stores, or worked at home manufacturing or in outside wage labor.

The first case, *Switzer v. Valentine* (1854), a Superior-Court decision, provides a good picture of an artisan family. Caroline Switzer, like many women in the rapidly growing cities, supplemented the family income by running a boarding house with the aid of her daughter. An entrepreneur, she leased several houses and contracted with boarders. She took out a loan to help expand her business and secured it with a chattel mortgage on the furniture thus purchased. When she could not repay the debt on time, the creditor, Mr. Valentine, foreclosed and took the furniture. Caroline's husband, Andrew Switzer, a carpenter, then sued for the return of the value of the furniture, claiming his wife had no authority to execute a mortgage. The court's decision clearly announced that a wife without a separate estate could not make a valid contract and that it was the creditor's responsibility to investigate whether the wife had a separate estate, before making the loan. The practical effect of this type of decision for other female entrepreneurs was to restrict their opportunity to get credit in their own name.

In *Brooks v. Schwerin* (1873) the court discussed the extent to which the Earnings Act affected a husband's right to his wife's services, labor, and earnings. Mrs. Brooks, a housewife who worked as a domestic servant while her children were in school, helped support the household. On her way home from work one evening she was injured and asserted her right under the Earnings Act to sue in her own name for damages for loss of wages. The defendant, Mr. Schwerin, tried to avoid payment by arguing, among other things, that she had lost nothing since her services belonged to her husband under common law. The judges hearing the case divided almost equally. The majority opinion is interesting because in granting Mrs. Brooks her right to her earnings, they upheld the husband's primary right to his wife's earnings and his concomitant right to sue for their recovery. The minority opinion was actually far more representative of the court's interpretation of the statutes in other cases. It applies to earnings the same standard of a separate estate used in *Switzer v. Valentine*. It does not deny restitution for loss to Mrs. Brooks, nor to any other woman who might find herself in this situation; it merely states that the husband is the person to sue, for he is the one who has suffered the real injury.

In *Birkbeck v. Ackroyd* (1878), a case involving the right of a husband to sue for the wages of his wife, the Court of Appeals clearly enunciated the principles that guided its decisions in subsequent cases. The court's interpretation of the purpose of the statute shows that the Earnings Act did represent an important advance in woman's legal capacity to protect herself from her husband, but it also suggests that from the point of view of the court, the time honored legal relationship between husband and wife had not been altered.

RECONSTRUCTION IN THE SOUTH
The Status of Freedwomen

Law and culture, which gave the husband and father the role of provider and protector, granted him extensive coercive powers over his household members. In the slave family, however, the coercive role was played by the white master. He encouraged marriages among slaves to increase the size of the labor force and to foster loyalty, and broke up slave families when it was economically advantageous. After the Civil War, when slaves eagerly sought to turn their self-marriages into formal, legal marriages, the former slave states enacted domestic relations statutes that legitimized existing marriages and children and prescribed legal responsibilities with enforcement procedures. One example is the *Act to Establish and Regulate The Domestic Relations of Persons of Color* (1866), of South Carolina, which established family support obligations for black married women. The obligations were different from those expected of white married women (but not unmarried mothers, who under common law were the legal guardians of their illegitimate children). The system of enforcing maintenance obligations seemed designed to secure a cheap labor force for plantations.

Freedwomen's Labor Contracts

Once blacks had entered into legal marriages, the economic privileges and obligations of family headship fell to black husbands and fathers. Black wives found themselves with two masters—their husbands, who had legal authority to control their services, and plantation owners. Black husbands negotiated labor contracts for their wives and families and guaranteed their performance. Typical examples are the agreements between E. J. Bowen and George Brown (1866); James Hays and Squire Brooks (1867), and B. P. Perry and Charles Boocher (1867). They became unnecessary after 1871, when Mississippi passed a statute freeing a wife's earnings from her husband's control.

Most black men found it difficult to control the labor of their wives, in the face of Southern whites who had little patience with the black man's legal privileges over his family. Planters made contracts with husbands when it was to their benefit or when they were unsure about the policy of the Freedman's Bureau. Bureau officials, although they believed that the black family should not be broken up, were unsympathetic to any disturbances to the free labor system.[3]

Reconstruction brought changes in the property rights of married women. In nine states, between 1867 and 1869, constitutional conventions dominated by radicals included a property clause. Six of the states—Alabama, Arkansas, Florida, Louisiana, Mississippi, and Texas—had already given some rights to married women before the Civil War. Virginia, however, did not budge on this issue until 1877. The clauses were passed largely in response to the widespread indebtedness of the postwar years; as had been true in the North, the married women's property acts were seen as a form of debtor relief. Whether the new title to property that women were allowed to acquire also carried the powers normally associated with property ownership was left to the legislatures and courts to decide.

Only three states—Georgia, North Carolina, and South Carolina—granted the wife new powers over her property. In *Huff* v. *Wright* (1869) the Georgia Supreme Court concluded that a wife could act as a free trader and bind her property for her own use. Nevertheless, her wages remained the absolute property of her husband, until 1943. The full potential of the 1868 constitutional provision in North Carolina was not realized until 1911. During the 1870s a married woman was allowed to become a free trader, with her husband's consent, or without it if she had been deserted. In 1911 the Martins Act gave her the full range of authority, except that she had to have her husband's agreement to the sale of her property.

South Carolina vacillated between liberal and conservative positions. Its 1870 statute, reflecting feminist influence, empowered the wife to make contracts as if single, and made her responsible for all debts she contracted except those for her necessary support; this remained the husband's full responsibility here and in all other states. During the 1880s the General Assembly and the courts trimmed the law in a protectionist direction, no longer allowing the wife to mortgage her property unless it was intended for her own benefit. Nor was she allowed to enter into business partnership, for this involved the obligation to contribute time and service, and these a wife had no legal authority to control (this was true in many Northern states as well). Moreover, the state supreme court ruled that since the South Carolina General Assembly had not expressly granted the wife authority over her wages, these belonged to the husband. This attempt to protect wives from economic exploitation created massive legal problems, and in 1895 the Assembly restored full rights to separate property. Protective legislation, here as elsewhere, had only clogged the courts and impeded the flow of capital. At the turn of the century, states increasingly let women fend for themselves, as feminists had suggested in the 1850s.[4]

DOCUMENTS

THE PASSING OF THE OLD ORDER

[57]
Marriage Agreement of Robert Dale Owen and Mary Jane Robinson (1832)

New York, Tuesday, April 12, 1832

This afternoon I enter into a matrimonial engagement with Mary Jane Robinson, a young person whose opinions on all important subjects, whose mode of thinking and feeling coincide more intimately with my own than do those of any other individual with whom I am acquainted. . . . We have selected the simplest ceremony which the laws of this State recognize. . . . This ceremony involves not the necessity of making promises regarding that over which we have no control, the state of human affections in the distant future, nor of repeating forms which we deem offensive, inasmuch as they outrage the principles of human liberty and equality, by conferring rights and imposing duties unequally on the sexes. The ceremony consists of a simply written contract in which we agree to take each other as husband and wife according to the laws of the State of New York, our signatures being attested by those friends who are present.

Of the unjust rights which in virtue of this ceremony an iniquitous law tacitly gives me over the person and property of another, I can not legally, but I can morally divest myself. And I hereby distinctly and emphatically declare that I consider myself, and earnestly desire to be considered by others, as utterly divested, now and during the rest of my life, of any such rights, the barbarous relics of a feudal,

From Elizabeth Cady Stanton et al., *History of Woman Suffrage* (New York, 1881), vol. 1, pp. 294–95.

despotic system, soon destined, in the onward course of improvement, to be wholly swept away; and the existence of which is a tacit insult to the good sense and good feeling of this comparatively civilized age.

I concur in this sentiment   Robert Dale Owen
Mary Jane Robinson

[58]
Protest of Henry B. Blackwell and Lucy Stone (1855)

While acknowledging our mutual affection by publicly assuming the relationship of husband and wife, yet in justice to ourselves and a great principle, we deem it a duty to declare that this act on our part implies no sanction of, nor promise of voluntary obedience to such of the present laws of marriage, as refuse to recognize the wife as an independent, rational being, while they confer upon the husband an injurious and unnatural superiority, investing him with legal powers which no honorable man would exercise, and which no man should possess. We protest especially against the laws which give to the husband:

1. The custody of the wife's person.

2. The exclusive control and guardianship of their children.

3. The sole ownership of her personal property, and use of her real estate, unless previously settled upon her, or placed in the hands of trustees, as in the case of minors, lunatics, and idiots.

4. The absolute right to the product of her industry.

5. Also against laws which give to the widower so much larger and more permanent an interest in the property of his deceased wife, than they give to the widow in that of the deceased husband.

6. Finally, against the whole system by which "the legal existence of the wife is suspended during marriage," so that in most states, she neither has a legal part in the choice of her residence, nor can she make a will, nor sue or be sued in her own name, nor inherit property.

We believe that personal independence and equal human rights can never be forfeited, except for crime; that marriage should be an equal and permanent partnership, and so recognized by law; that until it is so recognized, married partners should provide against the radical injustice of present laws by every means in their power.

We believe that where domestic difficulties arise, no appeal should be made to

From Elizabeth Cady Stanton et al., *History of Woman Suffrage* (New York, 1881), vol. 1, pp. 260–61.

Lucy Stone (1818–1893) broke the cultural barrier to women speaking before mixed audiences by establishing a career in public speaking. She publicly protested female submission in her marriage agreement with Henry Blackwell and by retaining her maiden name. Photograph courtesy the Sophia Smith Collection, Smith College, Northampton, Massachusetts.

legal tribunals under existing laws, but that all difficulties should be submitted to the equitable adjustment of arbitrators mutually chosen.

Thus reverencing law, we enter our protest against rules and customs which are unworthy of the name, since they violate justice, the essence of law.

(Signed) Henry B. Blackwell
Lucy Stone

[59]
Critique of Marriage Agreements in American Law Magazine (April 3, 1844)

[Marriage agreements obliterate] that just authority which nature and the laws give a man over his wife, as well as the obedience and subjection which the rules of the Gospel prescribe in the deportment of women.

Cited in Norma Basch, *In the Eyes of the Law: Women, Marriage and Property in Nineteenth-Century New York* (Ithaca: Cornell University Press, 1982), p. 79.

PIECEMEAL LEGAL REFORM
Legislative Revision of Property Law

[60]
Report of the Judiciary Committee of the New York State Assembly on the Petitions to Extend and Protect the Rights of Property of Married Women (April 12, 1842)

In a change so important and delicate in what may be regarded as the very fundamental institution of society, as is certainly the most sacred and precious, no degree of caution can be too great to guard against rash derangement of whatever may be good in the existing settled order of things.

Cited in Norma Basch, *In the Eyes of the Law: Women, Marriage and Property in Nineteenth-Century New York* (Ithaca: Cornell University Press, 1982), p. 145.

[61]
The Albany Argus *on the Passage of the New York Property Bill, April 7, 1848*

The bill giving to married women the separate control of their own property—a measure of great public moment, for good or for evil—passed the House yesterday, precisely in the shape in which it had passed the Senate, and requires only the Executive approval to become law.

Cited in Norma Basch, *In the Eyes of the Law: Women, Marriage and Property in Nineteenth-Century New York* (Ithaca: Cornell University Press, 1982), p. 136.

[62]
New York Married Women's Property Statutes (1848–1887)

AN ACT for the more effectual protection of the property of married women *(passed April 7, 1848):*
   . . . The real and personal property, and the rents issues and profits thereof of any female now married shall not be subject to the disposal of her husband; but shall be her sole and separate property as if she were a single female except so far as the same may be liable for the debts of her husband heretofore contracted.

   It shall be lawful for any married female to receive, by gift, grant devise or bequest, from any person other than her husband and hold to her sole and separate use, as if she were a single female, real and personal property, and the rents, issues and profits thereof, and the same shall not be subject to the disposal of her husband, nor be liable for his debts.

   AN ACT to amend the foregoing act *(passed April 11, 1849):*
   . . . Any married female may . . . convey and devise real and personal property, and any interest on estate therein, and the rents, issues and profits thereof in same manner and with like effect as if she were unmarried. . . .

   AN ACT concerning the rights and liabilities of husband and wife *(passed March 20, 1860):*

Cited in Susan Cary Nicholas, Alice M. Price, and Rachel Rubin, eds., *Rights and Wrongs: Women's Struggle for Legal Equality,* pp. 32–33. Reprinted with permission of The Feminist Press, Box 334, Old Westbury, New York 11568. Copyright © 1979 by The Feminist Press.

The property, both real and personal, which any married woman now owns, as her sole and separate property; that which comes to her by descent, devise, bequest, gift or grant; that which she acquires by her trade, business, labor or services, carried on or performed on her sole or separate account; that which a woman married in this state owns at the time of her marriage; and the rents, issues and proceeds of all such property, shall, notwithstanding her marriage, be and remain her sole and separate property, and may be sued, collected and invested by her in her own name, and shall not be subject to the interference or control of her husband, or liable for his debts, except such debts as may have been contracted for the support of herself or her children, by her as his agent.

Any married woman may, while married, sue and be sued in all matters having relation to her property, which may be her sole and separate property, or which may hereafter come to her by descent, devise, bequest, or the gift of any person except her husband, in the same manner as if she were sole. And any married woman may bring and maintain an action in her own name, for damages against any person or body corporate, for any injury to her person or character, the same as if she were sole; and the money received upon the settlement of any such action, or recovered upon a judgment, shall be her sole and separate property.

AN ACT to authorize and empower a husband to convey directly to his wife and a wife directly to her husband *(passed June 6, 1887):*

Any transfer or conveyance of real estate hereafter made by a married man directly to his wife, and every transfer or conveyance of real estate hereafter made directly by a married woman to her husband, shall not be invalid because such transfer or conveyance was made directly from one to the other without the intervention of a third person.

Judicial Construction of the Statutes

[63]
Switzer *v.* Valentine *(New York, 1854)*

The plaintiff, Andrew Switzer, sued to recover the value of the furniture taken from his home by the defendant Valentine. Mrs. Switzer, in the course of expanding her boarding house business, had signed a promissory note for $560.74 and secured it with a chattel mortgage on the furniture. When she failed to pay the debt, her creditor foreclosed and took the furniture. Her husband sued the creditor on the grounds that his wife had no legal authority to execute such a mortgage. The question before the court is whether the property statutes empowered a wife, engaged in business, to make contracts in the same way as a man or single woman.—Ed.

BY THE COURT: BOSWORTH J.

. . . . The evidence showed clearly that she and the plaintiff were husband and wife and that the defendant knew this when he took the note and mortgage. That they lived together as husband and wife, that he worked at his trade, and that she kept a boarding-house. That she made the purchases for the house, made contracts with the boarders, and received from them their board. All this was done with the husband's knowledge.

Prior to the acts of 1848 and 1849, allowing married women to take hold, and dispose of property as if they were single and unmarried, there is no doubt that for all purchases made by the wife with the knowledge and assent of the husband, and especially when the articles bought come to his possesesion, in the manner and to the extent that the articles in question did, he would be liable to the vendor for the price. They could be seized and sold on an execution against him. In judgment of law, they would be his property and not hers. . . .

Have the acts of 1848 and 1849 any bearing upon the question arising in this action? By these acts, she may take by gift or grant, from any person, except her husband, either real or personal property, and hold, convey, and devise it, or any interest in it, with like effect, as if she were unmarried. Does this do more than to capacitate a married woman to hold as her own a separate property, and to dispose of it, as effectually, as if she were unmarried? Does it authorize a married woman, even if she have a separate property, to become a general trader, and make valid contracts, in respect to any business which she may be disposed to undertake, or in respect to any speculations in which she may choose to engage? Is not the whole capacity which is given to her to purchase, limited to purchases which she may make on the credit of her separate estate, or for which she may pay, with such estate, or parts of it?. . . .

And is not all the new capacity, which is given to her to convey or devise, limited to a conveyance or devise of her separate property?

Can a married woman who has no separate estate make now any valid contract which she could not have made before these acts were passed?

In the present case, there is no pretence that Caroline Switzer ever had any separate estate. . . .

[The property] went to the plaintiff's house and possession, it was appropriated to his use, by being employed in a business prosecuted as a means of supporting his family. He is liable in law for its price, and it could be taken on execution to satisfy his debts. In judgment of law it was sold to him, and was his property, and the defendant is liable to him for its value. . . .

[64]
Brooks *v.* Schwerin *(New York, 1873)*

The plaintiff, Mrs. Brooks, while returning home from work, was run over by the defendant Schwerin's horse and wagon. She successfully sued him for recovery of damages. The defendant here is appealing on the grounds that her complaint should have been dismissed on the motion of his counsel since she could not prove negligence on his part. He further argued she could not use loss of wages as evidence of personal damage suffered as a result of the injury. To resolve the question of what evidence Mrs. Brooks can or cannot introduce, the Superior Court was compelled to address the issue of how far the 1860 earnings act had altered the common-law rule that all a wife's time and services belonged to her husband. The majority and dissenting opinions suggest the very different conclusions possible.—Ed.

BY THE COURT: C. EARLE. There was evidence tending to show that the plaintiff was returning home from her labor on the evening of April 13, 1865, between half-past seven and nine o'clock, passing along Thirty-second street . . . [W]hen she reached the corner of Thirty-second street and Broadway, she saw a street railway car coming up Broadway. The car was two or three lengths from the crossing. . . . As she approached the track, she . . . stopped and waited for the car to pass. While she was waiting, and just as the car had passed, the defendant came with his horse and wagon up Broadway at the rate of seven or eight miles an hour, and ran over her and injured her severely. She testified that, while waiting, she looked both up and down the street, but that she did not see the defendant's horse until she was knocked down. The defendant testified that it was quite dark at the time; that he was sitting in his wagon, about fifteen feet from his horse's head, and that he did not see the plaintiff until she was knocked down . . . and that standing in his wagon he could not see a person in front of his horse. . . .

The parties had equal rights in the street. He had the right to drive upon it and she had the right to cross it. Both were required to exercise that degree of care and prudence which the circumstances of the case demanded, she to avoid injury to herself, and he to avoid injury to another. . . . Whether she was negligent, whether she ought to have retreated to the sidewalk when she found she could not pass, whether it was prudent for her to stand in the street while the car passed, . . . and whether under all the circumstances she ought to have perceived the danger, were all questions fairly for the consideration of the jury. . . . Whether the defendant did drive so fast, . . . whether it was prudent to drive so fast over a street crossing, and whether the accident would have happened if he had driven slowly and prudently, were all questions for the jury. I am, therefore, of the opinion that the court did not err in refusing to nonsuit the plaintiff, and there only remains to be considered one other point to which our attention has been called.

At common law when a married woman was injured in her person, she was joined with her husband in an action for the injury. In such action nothing could be recovered for loss of service or for the expenses to which the husband had been subjected in taking care of and curing her. For such loss of service and expenses the husband alone could sue. It is now provided, by Section 2 of Chapter 90 of the Laws of 1860, that a married woman may "carry on any trade or business, and perform any labor of services on her sole and separate account, and the earnings of any married woman from her trade, business, labor or services shall be her sole and separate property, and may be used or invested in her own name." This statute effects a radical change of the common law which gave the husband the right to the labor, services and earnings of his wife. The services of the wife in the household in the discharge of her domestic duties still belong to the husband, and in rendering such service she still bears to him the common-law relation. So far as she is injured so as to be disabled to perform such service for her husband, the loss is his and not hers; and for such loss of service he, and not she, can recover of the wrong-doer. But when she labors for another, her services no longer belong to her husband, and whatever she earns in such service belongs to her as if she were a *feme sole.* So far as she is disabled to perform such service by an injury to her person, she can in her own name recover a compensation against the wrong-doer for such disability . . . under the seventh section of the same act, which provides that "any woman may bring and maintain an action in her own name, for damages against any person or body corporate for any injury to her person or character, the same as if she were sole," and the money recovered shall be her sole and separate property.

On the trial of this action it appeared that the plaintiff, before the injury, took charge of her family, and also that she was working out by the day, and earning ten shillings a day. . . . The defendant also excepted [objected] to the refusal of the court to charge [the jury] . . . "That the plaintiff cannot recover for the value of her time and services while she was disabled; such services and time belong, in law to the husband." The rulings of the court, in receiving the evidence and refusing to charge as requested, were proper within the principles of law above adverted to. If the defendant had requested the court to charge that the plaintiff could not recover for loss of service to her husband in his household in the discharge of her domestic duties, the request could not properly have been refused. But the request was broader, and proceeded upon the idea that all her time and services belonged to her husband, and that she could not recover anything for the value of her time or for the loss of any service while she was disabled. She was earning in an humble capacity ten shillings a day, and so far as she was disabled to earn this sum, the loss was hers, and the jury had the right to take it into account in estimating her damages. Suppose she had been a teacher in school, or a clerk in a store, earning a salary of $1,000 per year, and she had been disabled one whole year, could she not have shown the loss of her salary as one of the facts to be considered by the jury in estimating her damage? She certainly could if she had been a *feme sole,* and under the present statutes she had the same right being a married woman. . . .

JUDGMENT AFFIRMED

LOTT, *ch. C. (dissenting).* These provisions, [of the law of 1860] while securing to a married woman compensation for personal injuries as her sole and separate property, and giving to her the right to sue for it in her own name, do not give her a right to sue for her labor and services unless "performed on her sole and separate account"; and the earnings that are secured to her as her sole and separate property are such as arise and result from her labor and services performed on her sole and separate account; and it has recently been decided by the Court of Appeals that unless the wife is actually engaged in some business or service in which she would (but for the personal injury for which she is entitled to compensation) have earned something for her separate benefit, and which she has lost by reason of the injury, she has sustained no consequential damages, having lost nothing pecuniarily by reason of her inability to labor. This is placed distinctly on the ground that the services and earnings of the wife belong to the husband, and that he may maintain an action for them when she, at the time of the injury, was not carrying on any business, trade or labor upon or for her sole and separate account.

The facts disclosed in the present case do not entitle the plaintiff to a recovery for the value of the services lost while she was disabled.

It appeared by her own testimony that she resided at No. 104 West Thirty-second street, in the city of New York, and that she and her husband had resided there twelve years in one house, and that her husband was living at the time of the trial; that on the day of the accident she had been at work at Mrs. Scott's in Twenty-third street, for whom she was working by the day, and that her husband also worked out as a brass finisher; that she did all her own housework, that she took care of the children when at home; and that the children were at school when she was hurt. She testified in relation to her working at that time as follows: "I was able to go out and work by reason of their being at school, otherwise, I did my work and the work of my family, my own family washing; I did my own work and the family cooking; had the care and nursing of my children;" and she said that since the injury she could scarcely do any of her work.

This evidence did not show that the plaintiff was carrying on or conducting any business or trade, or performed any labor for her sole and separate use and benefit, on her own account, independent of and beyond the control of her husband, or that she herself kept what was received for her daily wages, or what disposition was made of them. Indeed, the fair inference is that she only worked out occasionally, and not as a general rule, and that at the time the injury occurred to her she was enabled to be absent and do what she did because her children were then at school, but that when they were at home she also remained there, taking care of them and doing the usual and ordinary household duties of the family. What she did was consistent with the practice of a husband and wife in moderate humble circumstances—to go out to work in the day-time and return in the evening—contributing their respective earnings to the general and common support and maintenance of themselves and their children. There is certainly nothing in such a fact, alone, which can characterize the work or labor thus done by the wife as performed for her sole and separate account, or that shows an intention that earnings resulting therefrom shall constitute or form part of her separate estate, and that the husband shall have no participation in or right to control and disposition thereof. The acts of the legislature above referred to are an innovation on the common-law rights of the husband, and it was incumbent on the plaintiff to show affirmatively and clearly that he (the husband) was divested thereby of those rights, and that she alone had become entitled to the benefits and privileges conferred by them on married women. Those facts do not appear.

I am, therefore, of opinion that the judgment should be reversed and a new trial ordered.

[65]
Birkbeck *v.* Ackroyd *(New York, 1878)*

APPEAL from judgment of the General Term of the Supreme Court, in the second judicial department, affirming a judgment in favor of plaintiff [Birkbeck].

This was an action to recover for work and labor.

Plaintiff claimed and recovered judgment for his own services as superintendent of defendant's [Ackroyd's] woolen mill, for the work and labor of his wife and several minor children; and also, as assignee of two adult sons, for their work and labor and that of their wives. . . .

ANDREWS, J. By the act Chap. 90 of the Laws of 1860, concerning "the rights and liabilities of married women," the common law doctrine that the husband is entitled to the services and earnings of his wife, was essentially modified.

The acts of 1848 and 1849 divested the title of the husband, *jure mariti,* during coverture, to the real and personal property of the wife, and enabled her to take from any person other than her husband and hold to her sole and separate use any property or estate and the rents, issues and profits thereof, in the same manner as if she were unmarried. Under these statutes it was held that she had, as incident to her right of property, the power of management and control, and that gains arising in the use of her separate estate or from business in which she engaged upon the credit of her separate estate, belonged to her and not to her husband. But the acts of 1848 and 1849 did not change the rule of the common law giving the husband the right to the services and earnings of the wife, in cases where she had no separate estate, and where her labor was not connected with the use of her separate property. This state of the law left a wife, who might be dependent upon her own labor for her support and the support of her children, without the legal power to control her earnings, and they were subject, as they were before these acts were passed, to be appropriated by the husband.

The hardship of this in cases where the husband was unable or unwilling to support his family, or was idle or dissolute, was apparent. The act of 1860 remedied this defect in the prior laws. By the second section a married woman is authorized "to carry on any trade or business, and perform any labor or services, on her sole and separate account." The section confers upon her the capacity of a *femme sole,* in respect to any business in which she may engage, and empowers her to labor on her own account. But it does not wholly abrogate the rule of the common law. She may still regard her interests and those of her husband as identical, and allow him to claim and appropriate the fruits of her labor. The bare fact that she performs labor for third persons, for which compensation is due, does not necessarily establish that she performed it, under the act of 1860, upon her separate account. The true construction of the statute is that she may elect to labor on her own account, and thereby entitles herself to her earnings, but in the absence of such an election or of circumstances showing that she intended to avail herself of the privilege and protection conferred by the statute, the husband's common law right to her earnings remains unaffected. . . .

When, therefore, the question arises as to the right of a husband to recover for the labor and services of the wife, it must be determined upon the facts and circumstances of the case. When the labor is performed under a contract with the wife, and by the contract payment is to be made to her, the inference would be strong, if not conclusive of her intention to avail herself of the protection of the statute. So where the wife is living apart from her husband, or is compelled to labor for her own support, or the conduct or habits of the husband are such as to make it necessary for her protection that she should control the proceeds of her labor, the jury might well infer that her labor was performed on her separate account. But where the husband and wife are living together, and mutually engaged in providing for the support of themselves and their family—each contributing by his or her labor to the promotion of the common purpose—and there is nothing to indicate an intention on the part of the wife to separate her earnings from those of her husband, her earnings, in that case, belong, we think, as at common law, to the husband, and he may maintain an action in his own right to recover them. Where the wife is engaged in a business, as that of a trader, and it is conducted in her name, there would be no room to question her right to the avails and profits. The duty still rests upon the husband to maintain and support the wife and their children, and it is not necessary in order to give the wife the protection intended by the statute to hold that, irrespective of her intention, her earnings in all cases, belong to her and not to the husband, and the language of the act does not admit of this interpretation.

The construction we have given to the statute supports the conclusion of the referee, that the plaintiff was entitled to recover the value of his wife's services. She worked with him and their minor children, in the mill, under no special contract, so far as appears, that she should receive the avails of her labor. The family were supported out of the joint earnings of the family, and the wife has never claimed her earnings as her separate property. Under these circumstances, the plaintiff was entitled to recover their value.

The same considerations apply to that part of the judgment founded upon the services rendered by the wives of the plaintiff's sons—the claim for which was assigned by them to the plaintiff.

There is no other question in the case requiring special consideration.

We think the judgment is right and should be affirmed.

RECONSTRUCTION IN THE SOUTH

The Status of Freedwomen

[66]
"An Act to Establish and Regulate the Domestic Relations of Persons of Color" (South Carolina, 1866)

I. The relation of husband and wife amongst persons of color is established.

II. Those who now live as such, are declared to be husband and wife.

III. In case of one man having two or more reputed wives, or one woman two or more reputed husbands, the man shall, by the first day of April next, select one of his reputed wives, or the woman one of her reputed husbands; and the ceremony of marriage, between this man or woman, and the person so selected, shall be performed.

IV. Every colored child, heretofore born, is declared to be the legitimate child of his mother, and also of his colored father, if he is acknowledged by such a father.

. . .

X. A husband shall not, for any cause, abandon or turn away his wife, nor a wife her husband. Either of them that abandons or turns away the other may be prosecuted for a misdemeanor; and upon conviction thereof, before a District Judge, may be punished by fine and corporal punishment, duly apportioned to the circumstances of aggravation or mitigation. A husband not disabled, who has been thus convicted of having abandoned or turned away his wife, or who has been shown to fail in maintaining his wife and children, may be bound to service by the District

Cited in Robert H. Bremner et al., eds., *Children and Youth in America: A Documentary History* (Cambridge, Mass.: Harvard University Press, 1971), vol. 2, pp. 39–40.

Judge from year to year, and so much of the profits of his labor as may be requisite, be applied to the maintenance of his wife and children; the distribution between them being made according to their respective merits and necessities. In like manner, a wife not disabled, who has been thus convicted, may be bound, and the proceeds of her labor applied to the maintenance of her children. In either case, any surplus profit shall go to the person bound. At the end of any year for which he was bound the husband shall have the right to return to, or receive back, his wife, and thereupon shall be discharged, upon condition of his afterwards maintaining his wife and children. A like right a wife shall have, at the end of a year for which she was bound, on condition of her making future exertions to maintain her family.

Freedwomen's Labor Contracts

[67]
Agreement between E. J. Bowen and George Brown (Mississippi, 1866)

Memorandum of an agreement made this . . . 4th day of January, 1866 between E. J. Bowen, party of the first part, and George Brown (Colored), party of the second part, all of Lawrence County, State of Mississippi. Witnesseth: that said party of the first part for the consideration hereinafter mentioned agrees to pay to the party of the second part eight dollars ($8.00) per month for the services of his wife "Malissa" during the year 1866. And further agrees to furnish comfortable quarters, wholesome food, and medical attendance when sick to the aforesaid Malissa and his child "Martha." Also to furnish the aforesaid child Martha with comfortable clothing and facilities for daily instructions in reading while living in his family.

And the said party of the second part for the consideration herein before mentioned agrees to see that his wife, the aforesaid "Malissa," works faithfully, that she is respectful in her manners, and obeys all reasonable orders that she may receive from her employers. And to claim no time as her own except public holidays and such time as may be granted her by her employers.

(Signed)
E. J. Bowen (Seal)
X (George Brown, his mark; seal)

Mississippi Freedman's Bureau Manuscripts, National Archives, R.G. 105.

[68]

Agreement between James Hays and Squire Brooks (Mississippi, 1867)

CONTRACT FOR HIRE

THIS AGREEMENT made in duplicate this 9th day of January, 1867 between James Hays of the first part and Squire Brooks, freedman of the second part, all of Holmes County, Mississippi.

Witnesseth: that the party of the second part hires his wife Marzella to work for the party of the first part for twelve (12) months, beginning on the 9th day of January, 1867 and ending on the first day of January, 1868, as a laborer, and Marzella to do all work necessary to carry on a farm, and the usual Sabbath work, and the work about the buildings, as and required by the party of the first part: and is to work the time each day she was accustomed to work before freed, and . . . pay her own taxes and medical bill, and account for all time lost by sickness at the rate of 50 cents per day, and for all time voluntarily lost to account for it at $1.00 per day, or the same for a part of a day. The party of the first part is to furnish Marzella with necessary working clothes.

. . . Squire is to receive for his wife's services for said time fifty-five ($55.00) dollars payable on the 24th day of December, 1867 in the then currency. . . . And, also [she is] to receive 3½ pounds of meat and one peck of meal per week while at work, and comfortable quarters.

Attested and read to the party of the   Witness our hands, having duly
second part by us, disinterested white   stamped the same
persons of said county
(signatures unclear)
                                                            James Hays
                                                            X (Squire Brooks, his mark)
                                              To be stamped when stamps can be se-
                                              cured.

Mississippi Freedman's Bureau Manuscripts, National Archives, R.G. 105.

[69]

Agreement between B. P. Perry and Charles Boocher (Mississippi, 1867)

Articles of agreement entered into by and between B. P. Perry of the first part and Charles Boocher, freedman, of the second part, both parties of the county and state aforesaid. Witnesseth, that I, B. P. Perry, on my part do agree to and with the said Charles Boocher to give him for his labor on my plantation one hundred and sixty dollars from the date hereof, until the 25th day of December of the present year. And I, Charles Boocher, do agree and bind myself to the said B. P. Perry to let him have my wife, Sharlot, as a cook, washer, and server and general house work, and her daughter Mariah as a general house servant, and Allen her son . . . as hand. And I, the said Perry, bind myself to pay him, the said Charles Boocher, for the services of his, Boocher's wife Sharlot, and her two children Mariah and Allen, the sum of two hundred and twenty dollars . . . provided that they work the entire present year. And I, the said Perry, do agree and bind myself to give him, Charles Boocher and his family . . . good and comfortable quarters and fashions. And I, Charles Boocher, on my part do agree and bind myself in consideration of the amount promised to be paid me by the said Perry at the end of the year, [and] promise to be [a] good and faithfull hand . . . and to cause my wife to perform her duty and her children also. And I further bind myself and family to obey all orders coming from our employer, B. P. Perry. And I, the said Charles Boocher, do agree to allow the said Perry . . . to deduct from the amount of my wages the sum of ninety eight dollars which he has now paid for our transportation. The said Perry is and shall be at liberty to discharge me or any one of my family, all of them at any time that we may fail to carry out fully our contract, without compensation for the time we had been in his service.

    In confirmation of which,

January 22, 1867   B. P. Perry (Seal)

                                                       X (Charles Boocher, his mark, seal)

Mississippi Freedman's Bureau Manuscripts, National Archives, R.G. 105.

UNIT 2

$$\left[\begin{array}{c} \textit{Family Roles} \end{array}\right]$$

WOMAN'S PLACE

In Anglo-American society the importance of the family for securing social stability was reinforced by an established church, a stable and homogeneous community, and a system of apprenticeship. During the nineteenth century, vast economic and political changes, along with massive shifts in population, altered the character of communities and the aspirations and opportunities of men and women. European commentators like Alexis de Tocqueville noted both an egalitarian spirit and a great anxiety about social disorder.

In this environment the family seemed the sole bulwark against anarchy. Between 1830 and 1870 a substantial literature emerged that presented the family as the mirror image of society and the home as a "utopian retreat" from the cares and moral compromises of competitive life. The cult of domesticity went beyond the earlier ideology of republican motherhood by imbuing all aspects of domestic life with social significance and identifying the home—woman's sphere—as the bastion of civilization. For the first time, womanhood became closely identified with what was delicate, spiritual, maternal. The conceptions of home and womanhood can be best understood as covert critiques of society and a means of reform.

The literature of the cult of domesticity is important not because it reflected reality but because it provided a model and guide for managing the home, rearing children, and civilizing society. The cultural model helps explain the emergence of the woman question and the nature of legal and political developments. A good example of the writing on woman's mission is the selection from *Mrs. A. J. Graves, Women in America* (1841).

One result of the separation of marital spheres and functions was that husbands and wives had different perceptions and experiences when they emigrated to the frontier. Diaries, letters, and songs illuminate outward behavior and reveal inner feelings. Hamlin Garland's song "Cheer Up, Brothers" may be compared with Esther Hanna's *Trail Diary*. The artificiality of the pervasive gender-related distinction between domestic and economic spheres is evident from *The Letter from Mary Ballou to Her Son Selden* (1852).

Often, memoirs indicate, the husband alone decided whether to emigrate, when, and to where. The consequences that a wife suffered under the law of domicile, if she refused to accompany her husband, are described in *Hair* v. *Hair*.

REPRODUCTIVE FREEDOM
Too Many Children

The safest and surest way of avoiding pregnancy was abstinence, but this ran counter to the husband's marital rights and what many perceived to be the law of God. The *Letter by an Anonymous "Lady" to Henry Wright* (circa 1845) and the *Letter to John Humphrey Noyes* (1872) speak of the sacrifices and tragedies that came with involuntary motherhood. Some historians have suggested that the Victorian image of woman as passionless and delicate, which reversed the colonial image, became a device to increase the control by women over their own bodies.[5]

Family Planning Advertisements

By the middle of the nineteenth century, changes in the economy and in patterns of education had made a large family of young children into an economic liability. There was, in fact, a continuous decline in family size during the century. Women relied on more than one method to reduce the incidence of childbirth. Contraception, the least secure means, was the one least likely to exacerbate marital tensions. Newspapers abounded with advertisements for pills and mechanical devices, such as *Dr. Cameron's Patent Family Regulator, or, Wife's Protector* (1847), which treated contraception as a form of health protection.

Another method, used as a last resort, was abortion. The advertisements of *Madam Costello's Medical Remedies* (1846) and for *Madame Restell's Pills, in the New York Herald* (1870) indicate how openly this activity was conducted. The slender historical evidence suggests that during the colonial and early federal periods, abortion was used mainly by single women, for whom it was socially tolerated.

On the eve of the Civil War, physicians associated with the American Medical Association (AMA), which represented only a small portion of the profession, led a crusade against abortion that pushed legislators beyond a concern for possible excesses to straightforward opposition. The leaders of the AMA were disturbed by the increase in the number of married women, mostly native-born Americans, taking advantage of abortion. They saw declining family size as a threat to the future of the Anglo-Saxon race. The AMA code of medical ethics, which barred members from performing abortions, placed them at a competitive disadvantage.

Antiabortion literature in medical journals between 1860 and 1880 also indicated an antagonism toward changing sex roles. These articles show that the chief purpose of women was to produce children; anything that interfered with that or allowed them to "indulge" in less important activities seemed to threaten marriage, the family, and society itself. Horatio Storer, the leader of the medical crusade against abortion, wrote: "I would not transplant them, from their proper and God given sphere, to the pulpit, the forum, or the cares of state, nor would I repeat the experiment . . . of females attempting the practice of the medical profession."[6]

The Criminalization of Birth Control

English and early American common law, following traditional religious doctrine as to when a fetus became a "person," that is infused with a "soul" or "animated," did not make abortion before "quickening" a crime. (Quickening refers to the stage of pregnancy when the fetus can be felt to move. This usually occurs between the fourth and fifth month.) The effect of this approach was to allow women to decide their future privately, without interference from the state. In the mid-nineteenth century, judicial policy began to change in the direction of making all abortions illegal. Two cases, *Commonwealth* v. *Bangs*, Mass. (1812) and *Mills* v. *Commonwealth*, Pa. (1850), illustrate the changing interpretation of the common-law rule. While improvements in medical science made revision of the legal code possible, they do not by themselves explain the change in social policy. The Mills decision, which occurs after the proliferation of commercial advertising on abortion and conception, suggests that the new restrictions on women were related to a policy of encouraging population growth among traditional American stock.

The same shift can be seen in statutory law. The first statutes, appearing as part of the effort to create uniform criminal law, were aimed primarily at medical abuses associated with abortion. *The Connecticut Statute of 1821*, which became a model for other states, and the *Illinois Statute of 1827* are examples. Neither proscribe abortion, only one particular method which was as likely to end a woman's life as to end her pregnancy. And neither makes the woman guilty of anything. The Connectict Statute, in fact, takes care to preserve the woman's common-law right to attempt to rid herself of a suspected pregnancy. The law specifically did not make it a crime to give a woman an abortificent before quickening. The Illinois law appears to be broader since it makes the administration of a poisonous substance illegal at any stage of gestation. In practice, however, it was almost impossible to convict a physician or pharmacist of murder since a conviction required proof of intent and until the quickening of the fetus there was no accurate way of knowing if the woman was pregnant or merely ill.

The statutes passed in the post-Civil War era have a different goal, which becomes apparent when these early laws are compared with the *Comstock Act of 1873*. This act made the dissemination to the general public of knowledge about both contraception and abortion along with devices a criminal offense. State laws passed between 1860 and 1880 made the use of artificial methods to prevent pregnancy illegal except to preserve health. The decision as to what constituted a valid health need resided in the hands of licensed physicians.

Such legislation to discourage all family-planning methods except abstinence was ill-suited to limiting malpractices and fraud, since by limiting the size of the legal market it directed business into the unregulated black markets. It was more appropriate to a policy of encouraging population growth and of discouraging sexual relations outside of marriage. What was new was not the goals, which have characterized American policy since the colonial era, but the legal approach. Since population growth was not in fact a problem, some historians have suggested that these acts were inspired by racial considerations. The more basic question is: why did judges and legislatures fear allowing women to choose when to bear children and how many?[7]

THE WOMEN'S RIGHTS MOVEMENT
Woman's Rage

The selections in this section depict a social reality that often made the authority of the husband and father a personal tragedy for the wife and mother. As documents for the colonial and early federal period show, wife battering, drunken husbands, and mothers driven by necessity to support their families were not peculiar to the nineteenth century. The incidence of family violence did increase, owing perhaps to the enormous pressure on men to succeed and to the breakdown of community control accompanying the geographical mobility. With the idealization of womanhood and the home, once culturally accepted forms of patriarchal discipline came to be seen as male abuse of power. Large numbers of women joined reform associations of various kinds, where they learned that their private grievances were shared by other women. An association such as the New York Female Moral Reform Society, created in the late 1830s to reclaim prostitutes, was transformed into an institution attacking male dominance. The "brutal cruelty of self-styled lords and masters" over "pure minded gentle women" became a constant refrain.[8] Abolitionist posters of black babies being torn from their mothers' breasts, and stories of sexual violence by planters, paralleled stories of seduction and abandonment of trusting girls who subsequently fell into prostitution. Joining a movement to protect the helpless or the civil rights of blacks conformed to the image of female selflessness. In the abolitionist movement women learned how to turn their perception of female oppression into a political movement.[9]

Seneca Falls

In 1848 Elizabeth Cady Stanton and Lucretia Mott put out a call for a women's rights convention to be held at Seneca Falls, New York. Many of those who attended were involved in the abolitionist movement and in temperance, and some had worked in the petitioning campaign for the Married Women's Property Act. Those who later became leaders of the organized women's rights movmement were married women and mothers who did not question the suitability of their sex for domestic activities. What they sought was the right to decide for themselves as individuals what activities and behavior were appropriate. Their focus on the legal status of wives was both a social and political commentary about men as protectors of the family and the extent of democracy in the United States. The *Declaration of Sentiments,* which recited the grievances of women, was patterned on the Declaration of Independence to emphasize that the absolute power of men was no more derived from the consent of the governed than it earlier had been from the king of England. It was a logical step in the evolution of ideas on women's rights: it linked the absolute authority of men at home—the primary source of women's rage—with control over the political process, which few had questioned before.

Expanding the Grounds for Divorce

The most vivid reminder of a married woman's slave-like status was her inability to get a legal divorce from a brutal or irresponsible husband. Between 1830 and 1870 many states liberalized their statutes by including extreme cruelty and desertion as grounds for absolute divorce. The proposed statute presented here, *An Act in Regard to Divorces Dissolving the Marriage Contract* (1861), reflects this trend. Its purpose was to provide a measure of justice for women and help preserve the family as an institution.

The premise underlying these statutes was that the court had an obligation to intervene on behalf of an injured wife when the husband withdrew his protection by deserting her or treating her cruelly. Separation with alimony was not a sufficient remedy because it prevented a wife from remarrying and living within a proper family setting—a position reminiscent of the Puritan argument for divorce that was promoted by women's rights and temperance groups. An extraordinary analysis of how the laws of marriage and divorce defeated their own ends is provided by Elizabeth Cady Stanton's "Address on the Divorce Bill" (1861), on behalf of a women's rights convention resolution. In the clearest possible way she describes the way the marriage contract itself diverges from both eighteenth- and nineteenth-century principles of contract. The statutory changes of the nineteenth century, which involved moving the grounds for separation into the category of divorce, didn't produce an increase in the divorce rate until the end of the century, when they were used in ways never envisioned by their makers.

In New York, divorce reform had been under consideration since the 1840s but did not receive serious attention until the 1850s, when the organized women's movement increased the pressure. The selection from Horace Greeley, "On Freedom of Divorce" (1853), presents the view of the opposition—the prevailing view—and reflects the outlook of the judiciary. Both the proponents and opponents of liberalized divorce believed in the importance of marriage as an institution. The opponents, however, clearly had less faith that women would stay married under the existing structure of authority. Horace Greeley, the editor of the *New York Tribune* and a leader of the Republican party, consistently thwarted passage of divorce reform in the 1850s. The Civil War drew everyone's attention to the national struggle and helped undermine any chance of reintroducing the divorce issue.[10]

TRENDS IN FAMILY LAW

Divorce and Alimony

It was up to the courts to decide what type of behavior on the part of a husband constituted cruelty or desertion. The selection from a *Supreme Court of Alabama Opinion* (1870) reflects the judicial approach elsewhere and shows how far a husband could go before a court would deem he had broken his contract. If we compare the standards here with those prevailing

in eighteenth- and nineteenth-century cases involving separation and separate maintenance, it becomes clear that the standards had not changed much.

The judicial outlook that helped produce liberalized divorce and a new
approach to alimony may be seen in *Prince* v. *Prince* (1845). Although South
Carolina did not permit divorce, it resolved the problem of marital dissolution by developing standards to provide a wife with separate maintenance,
where cohabitation was impossible. As the court observes, prior to this case
alimony had been a payment to the wife out of the husband's property. It
was designed to allow the maltreated wife to live separately and to assure the
financial security of all wives, particularly those who owned property. In
granting alimony out of a husband's income, the court extended the protecting arm of alimony to a broader segment of women. This accorded with the
general inclination of Jacksonian democracy to extend broadly what had
been the privilege of a few. Underpinning judicial and legislative innovation
in the area of divorce and alimony was an image of the husband as the strong
protector that was essentially hostile to the egalitarian principles that inspired the emerging women's rights movement.

Custody and Guardianship

Barry v. *Mercein* (New York, 1842), illustrates the court's attitude toward
the idea that married women should have the same right as men to determine
their own destiny; it also touches on the notion that couples who choose to
separate should be free to work out their own child custody arrangements
which the court will enforce.

John A. Barry, finding his economic opportunities restricted by the
Panic of 1837, decided to move his wife and two children to Nova Scotia.
His wife did not want to leave New York and her family of origin, and
unlike most women, she was not compelled by economic circumstances to
act against her own wishes. The couple made an agreement to separate. He
would take the infant son and she would keep the infant daughter. John
Barry later decided not to carry out their agreement and entered a suit in the
Chancery Court for custody of their daughter, hoping through this action to
lead his wife to join him. The Chancery Court, following the "tender years
doctrine" developed in *Commonwealth* v. *Addicks* (1813), affirmed the primary right of the father to the child, while giving temporary custody to the
mother. In four subsequent hearings, John Barry failed in his attempt to
assert his right.

Finally he entered a plea of habeas corpus in the common law court
against his wife's father. In deciding the question of who should get custody,
the court faced the more basic issue of breaking with tradition and giving
recognition to an agreement between husband and wife. This was theoreti-

cally possible if the court chose to apply to family issues the "will theory of contract," a nineteenth-century innovation in common law used in economic relations. This concept assumed that it was in the best interests of society to allow individuals the greatest freedom to work out their own arrangements and that the court should not impose community values on private moral decisions. How the court resolves this basic question determines who has the power to make child custody decisions in this type of situation.

If the court concludes there was no valid contract, then it must decide itself who should receive custody. In making this decision the court could apply either the traditional common-law principle, giving the father automatic custody, or the newer precedent that placed the best interest of the child above the father's primary right.

Under this principle either outcome was possible, depending on which theory of child rearing the judge subscribed to. In this case, how is the court's view of the best interest of the child affected by its view of where authority in the family should rest?

The concept that the best interest of the child should prevail did not become accepted judicial policy among the states until the late nineteenth century. Rhode Island first adopted the doctrine in *McKim* v. *McKim* (1879). A comparison of this case with *Barry* v. *Mercein* will show how the law develops over time in response to new cultural conditions. Anna B. McKim, like Eliza Anna Barry, lived apart from her husband with her father and daughter, without bothering to get a legal separation. In this case, however, there was no written agreement, only tacit acceptance of the situation. Charles McKim, who later became one of New York's most prominent architects, entered a writ of habeas corpus for the custody of the daughter. As in *Barry* v. *Mercein*, the real purpose of the suit was probably to persuade his wife to return, and here, too, there is no legal evidence that the husband had acted improperly. Thus both cases involve women following their personal desires rather than their legal duty. In both cases the superior right of the father is affirmed, but the outcome is different.

In the thirty-five years that separated the two cases, the theory that only a mother could provide the type of emotional nurture a child needs had evolved into an ideology. Thus in *McKim* v. *McKim* the judge rejected the idea of a substitute mother. In addition, the evolving ideology of the home was making it increasingly difficult to believe that a proper environment for child rearing could be created where the mother was compelled to return to her husband in order to be with her child. The wife is seen by the court as a separate person. This is symbolized here by the fact that the legal action was taken by the husband against the wife and not, as in *Barry* v. *Mercein* against the wife's father, who was providing the protection.

Because *McKim* v. *McKim* was setting a new precedent in Rhode Island, the judge took pains to show that the doctrine being applied had well-established roots in both English and American common law. In his reference to *Commonwealth* v. *Addicks* (1813), he observed in passing that the father eventually won his suit. He also referred to *Barry* vs. *Mercein* and mistakenly used it to show a development in behalf of the mother. Here, as in the previous cases, the mother's claim to custody was not as yet treated as a legal right, but based on cultural theories about children's needs. One is left to wonder what would have happened if Charles McKim, whose superior legal right was affirmed here, had persisted as long as Addicks and Barry.

After the Civil War, the trend toward recognizing a mother's personal, but not legal, right to her children appears in the matter of guardianship as well. Under common law, a father could, in his will, appoint a person other than the mother as guardian of his children after his death. The testamentary guardian was subject to the supervision of the Court of Chancery and could be removed for good cause. An example of the change is *The California Law on Guardianship* (1870), which restricts the right of the father. It accepts the mother's right as guardian to make independent decisions regarding her children, even if they are contrary to her husband's wishes as expressed in his will.

EQUALITY AS THE
BEST FORM OF PROTECTION
The Political Strategy of Suffrage

The passage of the first Married Women's Property Act in 1848 encouraged women's rights activists to pursue legislative action, but also demonstrated how slow and limited reform would be if women did not have the vote. In her "Address to the New York State Legislature" (1854), Elizabeth Cady Stanton spoke on behalf of equal rights and established the intellectual foundation of the suffrage movement. She raised two fundamental questions: Is there an identity of interests between men and women under the prevailing social arrangements; and what is the best form of protection for women?

The process of petitioning in individual states, on behalf of specific property legislation, brought suffrage to the top of the women's rights agenda at the close of the Civil War. In addition, many of the women who served in civilian capacities during the war had been politicized by their relations with public servants, many of whom were incompetent or corrupt. The general flowering of ambitions for radical social change, together with the constant political flux, made the time seem ripe for women to push for greater participation in the new democratic order.

Feminists like Stanton and her ally, Susan B. Anthony, among others, wanted a constitutional amendment to enfranchise both freedmen and also women. The leaders of the Republican party needed the black vote, however, to solidify their position. They regarded the inclusion of women in an omnibus equal rights bill as a distraction to the passage of the black franchise, and therefore the Fourteenth Amendment, which gave freedmen the vote, became the first part of the federal constitution ever to associate the word male with suffrage and citizenship. Many abolitionists, including Frederick Douglass, who had staunchly defended women's rights, refused to withhold support from either the Fourteenth or the Fifteenth Amendments. Stanton and Anthony, who had organized petition campaigns for suffrage in New York during the 1850s, believed that the Fourteenth Amendment would set back the cause of suffrage to what it had been a century earlier. One of the few black women who supported Stanton and Anthony in their opposition to a constitutional amendment excluding women, was Sojourner Truth. Her 1867 speech, *"Keeping the Thing Going while Things are Stirring,"* at the Convention of the American Equal Rights Association, in New York, was based on her experience as both a slave and a free woman.

Stanton and Anthony left the Equal Rights Association, which they had founded during the Civil War, to start an all-female suffrage association, the National Woman Suffrage Association (NWSA). Lucy Stone, one of the earliest publicists of women's rights, formed the competing American Woman Suffrage Association (AWSA).[11] One of the most effective organizations for promoting women's rights was the Women's Christian Temperance Union (WCTU), whose president, Frances E. Willard, turned women's concerns about the home into political channels. The selection from the WCTU *Home Protection Manual* (1879) is an example of her approach.

The Male Response to Female Suffrage

Politicians and professional men were the most vocal in their opposition to woman suffrage, constantly predicting the downfall of home, church, and state. The great passion and rhetoric generated by the suffrage issue suggest that men were translating the controversy into personal, family terms: they assumed that suffrage would make women equal and lead them to behave like men. Perhaps this explains the recurring imagery of family breakdown, mannish maidens, and aproned husbands, such as appears even today in literature opposing the Equal Rights Amendment. An example is the editorial, *"The Woman's Rights Convention—The Last Act of the Drama,"* from the *New York Herald* (1852) and the selection by a Catholic leader, *Orestes Brownson,* on *"The Woman Question,"* (1869).

The Litigation Strategy for Suffrage

In 1869 leaders of the National Woman Suffrage Association formed a plan to test the Fourteenth Amendment by bringing a case before the U.S. Supreme Court. Supporters of the litigation strategy, although not expecting a favorable decision, urged that criminal trials for women attempting to register as voters would put the issue into public attention. The idea originated with a lawyer, Francis Minor, the husband of Virginia Minor, president of the Missouri Woman Suffrage Association. He argued that the Fourteenth Amendment could be construed so as to give women the vote, and received support in this approach from some lawyers and judges. The idea languished, however, until the unconventional Victoria Woodhull presented a "Memorial" to Congress in 1871, for passage of enabling legislation to allow woman suffrage under existing provisions of the Fourteenth Amendment.

The notion of asserting a right, rather than petitioning for it, appealed to Susan B. Anthony, who in the 1850s had canvassed on behalf of the New York Earnings Act, suffrage, and divorce reform. During 1871 and 1872 attempts by women to vote in Missouri, New Hampshire, Connecticut, New York, Ohio, Illinois, California, and Michigan produced only a few court cases. One of them involved Anthony, who along with thirteen other women in Rochester, New York, actually voted in an election on November 5, 1872. They were arrested on federal criminal charges of unlawful voting, carrying a possible three-year jail term.

The original purpose of the statute under which they were arrested and tried had been to prevent Southern whites from voting more than once in the same election. The case was perfect for Anthony's purpose, and generated much publicity, but the actions of Anthony's lawyer and the judge prevented it from going to the U.S. Supreme Court. She had been imprisoned briefly before her trial. Her counsel, acting against her wishes and without her knowledge, paid her bail because, as a gentleman, he could not bear to see a respectable woman behind bars. This prevented her from taking the case immediately to the Supreme Court on a writ of habeas corpus. Again, although Anthony refused to pay the fine after the trial, hoping this would send her back to jail, the judge refused to enforce the judgment.[12]

United States of America v. *Susan B. Anthony* (1873) captures the essence of the argument long made by women about their lack of civil rights. The judge refused to let the defendant testify on her own behalf. After the attornies completed their presentations, he drew from his pocket a written opinion prepared before the trial that instructed the jury to bring in a guilty verdict. When Anthony's counsel protested this unconstitutional procedure and requested that the jury be polled, the judge summarily discharged the jurors. Judge Hunt's actions were indiscreet, but made sense within a particular legal and political perspective. Anthony did not contest the basic fact that she had voted. Her defense was that the Fourteenth Amendment's Privileges and Immunities Clause gave all citizens, including women, the right to vote regardless of state law. If the jury were allowed to make their own decision on guilt or innocence, they would in practice be making a judgment on an issue of law and this was the domain of the judiciary. Although the judge ruled that the Fourteenth Amendment was inapplicable, he probably feared, on the basis of experience, that the jurors might decide the case on the basis of their own feelings about right and wrong, rather than in terms of strictly legal points. The judge's own behavior lends support to the argument of legal realists that the decision as to the outcome of a case or the policy to be advanced often precedes recourse to and the elaboration of formal legal principles.

The trial of Susan B. Anthony had the characteristics of the political trial. Its purpose was not to assess the guilt or innocence of the defendant, but to secure conformity to the established order. The harmony of the nation was being undermined by the proliferating demands for social change. Anthony was using the case to promote woman suffrage through judicial action. Judge Hunt was not only signaling the public that judicial policy on woman suffrage was settled, but using the case to broadcast what the consequences would be for women who pursued a tactic of direct action. The case was being closely followed by the press. Judge Hunt probably thought firmness would lead Anthony to capitulate to reality and allowed her to speak for the first time just before sentencing. The selection presented here is the interchange that occurred at this time.

Two years after the Anthony trial, another case became the test for whether the privileges and immunities of citizenship include the right to vote. In *Minor* v. *Happersett* (1875) note how the court uses a narrow construction of its own authority to throw the issue back to the legislative arena.

The first state or territory to extend the right to vote to women was the new territory of Wyoming, noted for its violent and hard-drinking men and its scarcity of women. The man who introduced the suffrage bill, Colonel William H. Bright, believed that mothers and wives were capable of exercising full citizen rights better than blacks and most white male inhabitants of the undeveloped territory. He was supported by a Democratic legislature and a Republican governor. Wyoming also had liberal property acts and divorce laws, all of which made sense in a region trying to attract women and develop a stable family order. The selection given here is Colonel Bright's bill, "An Act to Grant to the Women of Wyoming Territory the Right of Suffrage and to Hold Office" (1869).

Jury Service

Wyoming was also the first state or territory to give women the right to serve on juries. It did so in order to solve a major problem: the transient males who served on juries were unable or unwilling to convict lawbreakers. However, the experiment of calling women to juries, described by Grace Raymond Hebard in *The First Woman Jury*, did not last long.

Washington Territory, like Wyoming, initially assumed that suffrage carried with it the right and obligation of jury duty. In *Rosencrantz* v. *Washington Territory* (1884), a woman, trying to get a conviction set aside on technical grounds, raised the issue of whether married women living with their husbands were legally competent to sit as jurors. The selection from Judge Turner's dissenting opinion contains arguments similar to those used to deny women the right to practice law. These later were used by the same court to restrict jury service to male citizens. Underlying Turner's argument that women cannot be jurors is the general theory that a person deciding the fate of a defendant must be at least equal in status and capable of making independent decisions. Turner explores the issue of whether the advances in woman's property and political rights had placed her in a position of equality in relationship to her husband.

DOCUMENTS

WOMAN'S PLACE

[70]

Mrs. A. J. Graves, on Women's Sphere (1841)

. . . Our chief aim throughout these pages is to prove that her domestic duties have a paramount claim over everything else upon her attention—that *home* is her appropriate sphere of action, and that whenever she neglects these duties, or goes out of this sphere of action to mingle in any of the great public movements of the day, she is deserting the station which God and nature have assigned to her. She can operate far more efficiently in promoting the great interests of humanity by supervising her own household than in any other way. Home, if we may so speak, is the cradle of the human race; and it is here the human character is fashioned either for good or for evil. It is the "nursery of the future man and of the undying spirit"; and woman is the nurse and the educator. Over infancy she has almost unlimited sway; and in maturer years she may powerfully counteract the evil influences of the world by the talisman of her strong, enduring love, by her devotedness to those intrusted to her charge, and by those lessons of virtue and wisdom which are not of the world.

And is not this a sphere wide enough and exalted enough to satisfy her every wish? Whatever may be her gifts or acquirements, here is ample scope for their highest and noblest exercise. If her bosom burns with ardent piety, here she will find hearts to be kindled into devotion and souls to be saved. Is she a patriot? It is here she can best serve her country by training up good citizens, just, humane, and enlightened legislators. Has she a highly cultivated intellect? Let her employ it,

From Mrs. A. J. Graves, *Woman in American: Being an Examination into the Moral and Intellectual Condition of American Female Society* (New York, 1841), pp. 155–58.

then, in leading those young, inquiring minds, which look up to her for guidance, along the pleasant paths of knowledge. . . . Oh! that the mind of woman were enlightened fully to discern the extent and the importance of her domestic duties— to appreciate her true position in society; for she would be in no danger of wandering from her proper sphere, or of mistaking the design of her being.

That woman should regard home as her appropriate domain is not only the dictate of religion, but of enlightened human reason. Well-ordered families are the chief security for the permanent peace and prosperity of the state, and such families must be trained up by enlightened female influence acting within its legitimate sphere. If man's duties lie abroad, woman's duties are within the quiet seclusion of home. . . . If his greatness and power are most strikingly exhibited in associated action upon associated masses, her true greatness and her highest efficiency consists in individual efforts upon individual beings. The religion and the politics of man have their widest sphere in the world without; but the religious zeal and the patriotism of woman are most beneficially and powerfully exerted upon the members of her household. It is in her home that her strength lies; it is here that the gentle influence, which is the secret of her might, is most successfully employed; and this she loses as soon as she descends from her calm height into the world's arena. . . .

In this age of excitement, it is specially incumbent upon woman to exert her utmost influence to maintain unimpaired the sacredness and the power of the family institution. . . .

[71]
"Westward Ho" for Husbands

Cheer up, brothers, as we go
O'er the mountains, westward ho,
Where herds of deer and buffalo
Furnish the fare.

CHORUS: Then o'er the hills in legions, boys
Fair freedom's star
Points to the sunset regions, boys
ha, ha, ha-ha!

Hamlin Garland's song, *"Cheer up Brothers,"* cited in John Mack Faragher, *Women and Men on the Overland Trail* (New Haven: Yale University Press, 1979), p. 166.

When we've wood and prairie land,
Won by our toil
We'll reign like kings in fairy land,
Lords of the soil!

[72]
"Westward Ho" for Wives

I think of home and the dear ones there; each day I am getting farther from them. I feel a sadness steal over me at times when I think that I shall see them no more on earth, but it is all for the best. It is better that my affections should be more turned from earth. Oh, that I could set them upon 'things heavenly and divine'. . . . Will try to be calm and submissive.

From Esther Hanna's Trail Diary cited in John Mack Faragher, *Women and Men on the Overland Trail* (New Haven: Yale University Press, 1979) p. 175.

[73]
Mary Ballou on Life in a California Mining Camp (1852)

This letter was written as a journal, rather than at one sitting. While preserving Mary Ballou's use of capital letters for words inside sentences, a form reminiscent of pre-nineteenth century writing, the editors have introduced capital letters to start new sentences and have also altered punctuation and spelling.—Ed.

Negrobar, California (1852)

My Dear Selden,

We are about as usual in health. Well, I suppose you would like to know what I am doing in this gold region. Well, I will try to tell you what my work is here in this muddy Place. All the kitchen that I have is four posts stuck down into the ground and covered over the top with factory cloth, no floor but the ground. This is a Boarding House kitchen. There is a floor in the dining room, and my sleeping room is covered with nothing but cloth. We are at work in a Boarding House.

This letter is quoted from Christine Fischer, ed., *Let Them Speak for Themselves: Women in the American West, 1849–1900* (Hamden, Conn.: Archon Books, 1977), pp. 42–46.

Oct. 27

Now I will try to tell you what my work is in this Boarding House. Well, sometimes I am washing and Ironing, sometimes I am making mince pie and Apple pie and squash pies. Sometimes frying mince turnovers and Donuts. I make Biscuit and now and then Indian johnny cake, and then again I am making minute pudding filled with raisins . . . and I am stuffing a ham of pork that cost forty cents a pound. Sometimes . . . I am making gruel for the sick, now and then cooking oysters, sometimes making coffee for the French people strong enough for any man to walk on that has Faith as Peter had. . . . Sometimes I am feeding my chickens and then again I am scaring the Hogs out out of my kitchen and Driving the mules out of my Dining room. . . . Sometimes I am up all times a night, scaring the Hogs and mules out of the house. Last night, there, a large rat came down [and] pounced onto our bed in the night. . . . Sometimes I am taking care of Babies and nursing at the rate of Fifty dollars a week, but I would not advise any Lady to come out here and suffer the toil and fatigue that I have suffered for the sake of a little gold; neither do I advise any one to come. . . . Occasionally I run in and have a chat with Jane and Mrs. Durphy, and I often have a hearty cry. No one but my maker knows my feelings. And then I run into my little cellar, which is about four feet square, as I have no other place to run that is cool. . . .

November 2

. . . I will tell . . . you a little of my bad feelings. On the 9 day of September there was a little fight took place in the store. I saw them strike each other through the window in the store. One went and got a pistol and started towards the other man. I never go into the store, but your mother's tender heart could not stand that, so I ran into the store and Begged and pleaded with him not to kill him, for eight or ten minutes, not to take his life for the sake of his wife and three little children, to spare his life. And then I ran through the Dining room into my sleeping room and Buried my Face in my bed so as not to hear the sound of the pistol, and wept Bitterly. Oh! I thought if I had wings how quick I would fly to the States. That night at supper table he told the Boarders if it had not been for what that Lady said to him, Scheles would have been a dead man. After he got his passion over he said that he was glad that he did not kill him; so you see that your mother saved one Human being's life. You see that I am trying to relieve all that suffering and trying to do all the good that I can. . . .

October 11

I washed in the forenoon and made a Democrat flag; in the afternoon sewed twenty yards of splendid worsted fringe around it, and I made Whig flag. They are both swinging across the road, but the Whig Flag is the richest. I had twelve Dollars for making them, so you see that I am making Flags with all the rest of the various kinds of work that I am doing; and then again I am scouring candle sticks and washing the floor and making soft soap. The People tell me that it is the first Soft Soap they knew made in California. Sometimes I am making mattresses and sheets. I have no windows in my room. All the light that I have shines through canvas that covers the House, and my eyes are so dim that I can hardly see to make a mark, so I think you will excuse me for not writing any better. I have three Lights burning now, but I am so tired and Blind that I can scarcely see and hear. I am among French and Dutch and Scotch and Jews and Italians and Swedes and Chinese and Indians and all manner of tongues and nations, but am treated with due respect by them all. . . .

Oh, my dear Selden, I am so homesick, I will say to you once more to see that Augustus has every thing that he needs to make him comfortable; and by all means have him Dressed warm this cold winter. I worry a great deal about my Dear children. It seems as though my heart would break when I realize how far I am from Dear Loved ones. This from your affectionate mother.

Mary B. Ballou

[74]
Hair *v.* Hair *(South Carolina, 1858)*

The opinion of the Court was delivered by DARGAN, CH.

The plaintiff charges in her bill that her husband, the defendant . . . before the solemnnization of their nuptials, entered into a solemn engagement, that if she would marry him he would never remove her, without her consent, from the neighborhood of her mother, or to a place where she could not enjoy her mother's society and that of her friends. On this condition she married him. . . . Her mother (Mrs. Matheney,) also obtained from him . . . a similar promise, as the condition of her assent to the marriage. The marriage was celebrated on the 13th October, 1853. From that time the young pair lived with the plaintiff's mother until the 9th December, 1854, during which period the plaintiff bore to her husband a daughter, who is the only issue of the marriage. At the last mentioned date, the defendant with his wife and child went to live at a place which he had bought, about a half mile distant from that of his mother-in-law, where, as the plaintiff herself says, they "lived in comfort, peace, and harmony, up to the twenty-seventh day of September, 1857." This statement appears to be in strict conformity with the truth, except as relates to some immoralities on his part which had come to her knowledge, and which were condoned on her part by their subsequent cohabitation.

After the plaintiff and defendant had gone to live at their own home, he became

10 Rich. (S.C.) 163 (1858).

restless and dissatisfied, and anxious to remove to Louisiana, to which state some of his near relatives had emigrated. His land was poor, and he wished, as he says in his answer, to better his condition by moving to a country where lands were fertile and cheap. But his wife was unwilling to go, positively refused, and pleaded his solemn engagement and promise made previous to their marriage. . . . They had frequent and intemperate altercations on the subject, he insisting that she should accompany him in his move to the west, and she pertinaciously refusing and declaring that she never would leave the place near her mother's, where she then lived.

Perceiving that he could make no impression upon her mind, nor effect any change of her will, he announced to her his determination to go without her, unless she should choose to accompany him. She said he might go and leave her, provided he would leave her the negroes (three in number, the only ones he had, which he had acquired by his marriage with her). She says in her bill that he consented to this arrangement about leaving the negroes. In his answer he denies it, and there is no further proof. Under these circumstances, and at this stage of the controversy, he commenced making preparations for his departure. He rented his land, sold his crop in the field, some hogs, etc., with the view of raising the necessary funds.

Whether his preparations were made secretly, as charged in the bill, or not, he did not communicate to *her* the fact that he was making his preparation, nor his design *then* to go. She had no reason to believe that he was going at that particular time. It took her by surprise. In fact, it would seem that she did not believe that he would go at all, unless she consented to accompany him. Having completed his preparations, on Sunday, the 27th September, 1857, about the hour of midnight, he called his two negro women to the field, under the pretence of driving out the hogs, but in fact, with the view of securing and carrying them off. He seized them both. They made a great outcry, which reached the ear of the plaintiff at the house. The negroes were unwilling to go; one of them (Hagar) made her escape; the other one (Ann) he tied, went to the house and got her young child. He put them both in a conveyance which he had ready, carried them to Blackville, where he put them on the cars that same night, and carried them off to Louisiana, where they yet remain.

The plaintiff continued to reside, and still resides, at the same house. . . . (She has with her Hagar, . . . the furniture that was in the house, some provisions, wheat, flour, etc., and three horses, said by one of the witnesses to be old and of little value. On the eleventh day after the defendant's departure, the plaintiff filed this bill, setting forth the facts that have been recited, and asking an injunction to restrain him from disturbing her in the possession of the property in her possession, or from selling or disposing of the same, until some adequate provision shall be made by the defendant, under the order of this Court, for the support of the plaintiff and her child.

The defendant, on learning that his wife had filed a bill against him for alimony, immediately returned to South Carolina, filed his answer, and has submitted himself to the judgment of the Court. On his return the defendant visited his wife and made earnest overtures to her to accompany him to his new home in the

Parish of Bienville, in Louisiana, promising to treat her with the kindness and affection due to her as his wife. These overtures were rejected by her with firmness and with passionate disdain. . . . She intimated that she would live with him if he would come back to the place which he had left. She said she would not go with him to the west to save his life, and that she intended to live and die where she was. The defendant, in his answer, repeats his proposals to take his wife and child with him to his home in the west, and to provide for them to the best of his ability.

These are the undisputed facts of the case, and the question for the court to decide is whether under these circumstances the plaintiff is entitled to a decree for alimony. We are of opinion that the decree cannot be sustained upon the principles which prevail in this Court on the subject. . . .

. . . In South Carolina alimony is granted for bodily injury inflicted or threatened and impending . . . and affecting life or health. Alimony is also granted in South Carolina for the desertion of the wife by the husband. To these may be added a third class of cases, in which, though the husband has inflicted or threatened no bodily injury upon the wife, yet practices such obscene and revolting indecencies in the family circle, and so outrages all the sentiments of delicacy and refinement characteristic of the sex, that a modest and pure minded woman would find these grievances more dreadful and intolerable to be borne, than the most cruel inflictions upon her person, she would be held justifiable in fleeing from the polluting presence of that monster, with whom in an evil hour she had united her destinies. . . .

Except in cases embraced within the three classes above commented on, I am not aware that a suit for alimony has been sustained in South Carolina. The plaintiff has sought to bring her case within the principles of the second class. She charges desertion. . . .

. . . No divorce has ever been granted in South Carolina. As no jurisdiction in the state is authorized to grant divorces for any cause, and the Legislature has ever refused to exercise its supreme power for such a purpose, it became necessary for the Court of Equity to interpose, to afford relief for a great wrong which would otherwise be without a remedy. Thus it is that our Courts of Equity have, from an early period, exercised the power of granting relief in cases of desertion of the wife by the husband. The relief granted is a decree for alimony, which is an allowance out of the estate of the husband proportional to its value, to be paid to the wife at stated periods, during the separation.

The question is whether the plaintiff has made out a case of desertion. That the defendant left her and removed to another state, is beyond controversy and not denied. But did he leave her in an unjustifiable manner? He most earnestly solicited her for years, to accompany him. At length, upon her persistent, I may well say, obstinate, refusal, he went alone—without his wife and child. Certainly the husband, by our laws, is lord of his own household and sole arbiter on the question as to where himself and family shall reside. But she complains that before the marriage he entered into a solemn engagement, without which the marriage would never have been solemnized. . . . My opinion is that he made the promises in the manner charged in the bill. But they created a moral obligation only. It may be conceded to be very dishonorable to him to commit a breach of the promises he made, in order to obtain the hand of his wife in marriage. . . . Such a promise is nullity. The contract of matrimony has its well understood and its well defined legal duties, relations and obligations, and it is not competent for the parties to interpolate into the marriage compact any condition in abridgment of the husband's lawful authority over her person, or his claim to her obedience. . . .

Stripped of all extraneous matters, the simple question is, did the defendant desert his wife, the plaintiff? It must be a legal desertion. It is not every withdrawal of himself by the husband from the society of the wife that constitutes desertion in legal contemplation. The conduct of the wife must be blameless. If she elopes, or commits adultery or violates or omits to discharge any of the important hymeneal obligations which she has assumed upon herself, the husband may abandon her without providing for her support; and this Court would sustain him in such a course of conduct.

The husband has the right, without consent of the wife, to establish his domicile in any part of the world, and it is the legal duty of the wife to follow his fortunes, wheresoever he may go. The defendant, in the exercise of his undoubted prerogative, had determined to make his domicile . . . in the State of Louisiana, and wished his wife to accompany him. *She,* preferring the society of her mother and her relatives, refused to go—in opposition to his wishes. . . . Considering the relative duties and obligations of husband and wife, as defined by the law, who, under these circumstances, is guilty of desertion? The wife assuredly.

What I have said would constitute a sufficient ground for refusing the prayer of the bill. Yet, there is another additional and sufficient ground of defense on the part of the husband. Within a very short period after the filing of the bill, he returned to the state for the purpose, I must believe, of inviting his wife to his new home which he had established in the west. He twice visited her for this purpose. To these invitations she gave a stern, angry, and insulting refusal. To the Court, in his answer, he renews these overtures and offers to receive his wife in his new home, and to treat her with conjugal affection and tenderness. Under these circumstances the Court could not give alimony, even if he was wrong in the beginning. Though alimony has been decreed, if the husband makes a *bona fide* offer to take back the wife whom he has deserted, and to treat her with conjugal kindness and affection, and the wife refuses, on application by the husband the Court will, if satisfied of the sincerity of the husband's offers, rescind the decree for alimony. . . .

It is ordered and decreed, that the Circuit decree be reversed, and that the bill [for alimony] be dismissed.

REPRODUCTIVE FREEDOM

Too Many Children

[75]

Letter from an Anonymous Lady to Henry Wright (circa 1845)

Before we married, I informed him (the husband) of my dread of having children. I told him I was not yet prepared to meet the sufferings and responsibilities of maternity. He entered into an agreement to prevent it for a specified time. This agreement was disregarded. After the legal form was over and he felt that he could now indulge his passion without loss of reputation, and under legal and religious sanctions, he insisted on the surrender of my person to his will. He violated his promise at the beginning of our united life. That fatal bridal night!. . . . I can never forget it. It sealed the doom of our union, as it does of thousands.

He was in feeble health, so was I; and both of us mentally depressed. But the sickly germ was implanted and conception took place. We were poor. . . . In September, 1838, we came to and settled in a new country. In the March following my child . . . was born. After three months' struggle, I became reconciled to my, at first, unwelcome child. . . .

In one year I found I was again to be a mother. I was in a state of frightful despair. My first-born was sickly and troublesome, needing constant care and nursing. My husband chopped wood for our support. . . . I felt that death would be preferable to maternity under such circumstances. A desire and determination to get rid of my child entered into my heart. I consulted a lady friend, and by her persuasion and assistance killed it. Within less than a year, maternity was again imposed upon me, with no better prospect of doing justice to my child. It was a most painful conviction to me; I felt that I could not have another child at the time. . . .

I consulted a physician, and told him of my unhappy state of mind. . . . He told me how to destroy it. After experimenting on myself three months, I was successful. . . .

[A fourth unwanted pregnancy followed, and the baby was carried to term.]

Such had been my false religious and social education, that, in submitting my person to his passion, I did it with the honest conviction that, in marriage my body became the property of my husband. He said so; all women to whom I applied for

Cited in Gerda Lerner, ed., *The Female Experience: An American Documentary* (Indianapolis: Bobbs-Merrill, 1977), pp. 425–27.

counsel said it was my duty to submit; that husbands expected it, had a right to it, and must have this indulgence whenever they were excited, or suffer; and that in this way alone could wives retain the love ocounsel said it was my duty to submit; that husbands expected it, had a right to it, and must have this indulgence whenever they were excited, or suffer; and that in this way alone could wives retain the love of their husbands. I had no alternative but silent suffering submission to his passion, and then procure abortion or leave him, and thus resign my children to the tender mercies of one with whom I could not live myself. Abortion was most repulsive to every feeling of my nature. It seemed degrading, and at times rendered me an object of loathing to myself. . . .

But even then I saw and argued the justice of my personal rights in regard to maternity. . . . I insisted on my right to say when and under what circumstances I would accept of him the office of maternity, and become the mother of his child. I insisted that it was for me to say when and how often I should subject myself to the liability of becoming a mother. But he became angry with me; claimed ownership over me; insisted that I, as a wife, was to submit to my husband *"in all things;"* threatened to leave me and my children, and declared I was not fit to be a wife. Fearing some fatal consequences to my child or to myself—being alone, destitute, and far from helpful friends, in the far West, and fearing that my little one would be left to want—I stifled all expression of my honest convictions, and ever after kept my aversion and painful struggles in my own bosom. . . .

[76]
Letter to a Member of the Oneida Community (1872)

May 12, 1872

I must tell you a sad story. Two years ago last September my daughter was married, the next June she had a son born. The next year in July she had a daughter born; and if nothing happens to prevent she will be confined for the third time in the coming June; that is three times is less than two years. Her children are sickly, and she is sick and discouraged. When she first found she was in the family way, this last time, she acted like a crazy person; went to her family physician, and talked with him about having an operation performed. He encouraged her in it, and performed it before she left the office, but without success. She was in such distress that she thought she could not live to get home. I was frightened at her looks, and soon learned what she had done. I tried to reason with her, but found her reason had left

From the book *Primers for Prudery: Sexual Advice to Victorian America* edited by Ronald Walters. © 1974 by Prentice-Hall, Inc., Englewood Cliffs, N.J. 07632, pp. 168–69. By permission.

her on that subject. She said she never would have this child if it cost her life to get rid of it. After a week she went to the doctor again. He did not accomplish his purpose, but told her to come again in three months. She went at the time appointed in spite of my tears and entreaties. I told her that I should pray that Christ would discourage her; and sure enough she had not courage to try the operation, and came home, but cannot be reconciled to her condition. She does not appear like the same person she was three years ago, and is looking forward with sorrow instead of joy to the birth of her child. I often think if the young women of the [Oneida] Community could have a realizing sense of the miseries of married life as it is in the world, they would ever be thankful for their home.

Your sincere friend, ———

Family Planning Advertisements

[77]
Dr. Cameron's Patent Family Regulator, or, Wife's Protector (1847)

STRICTLY CONFIDENTIAL

A new invention, at once safe, sure and [of] easy application.

In introducing this novel invention, the writer feels he is broaching a delicate subject. These few explanatory remarks are not, therefore, designed for the public eye, but addressed to those only who have entered the married state, who I trust would not be likely to misconstrue the motives of the author, or convert his invention to an evil purpose; and but for that class of females is this invention particularly designed, who have entered the married state with such enfeebled constitutions, inherited either from their ancestors, by sickness, or by having indulged so far in the fashionable follies of our age, as to render them incapable of becoming mothers without endangering their own lives, or imparting to their offspring imbecility of mind or sickly constitution, which would render existence anything but a blessing.

There are those also whose families are already too numerous for their means of support, and to this class the writer thinks his invention cannot but prove a welcome

Cited in John Paul Harper, "Be Fruitful and Multiply: Planned Parenthood in Nineteenth-Century America," in Carol Ruth Berkin and Mary Beth Norton, eds., *Women in America: A History* (Boston: Houghton Mifflin, 1979), pp. 266–67. Copyright © 1979 by Houghton Mifflin Company.

agent in exonerating them from some of the most cruel sufferings of life, and thus smooth the future pathway of their present existence.

Besides these, there are too those in the bloom of womanhood, the very picture of health, who having just entered the married state tremble in constant fear of the awful wreck so often produced by the first born, when,

> *If not her life upon the altar sacrifice expire,*
> *The rosy cheek, the ruby lip it will require.*

The above instrument is for sale by Dr. W. Scott, Agent for the inventor, at No. 6 Endicott Street, Boston. Price $5.00. Any one wishing for one of these instruments, by addressing a letter, post paid, through the Post Office, to Dr. Scott, and enclosing $5.00 in it, the instrument will be immediately forwarded.

[78]
Madame Costello's Medical Remedies (1846)

MADAME COSTELLO

FEMALE PERIODICAL PILLS—GUARANTEED in every case where the monthly periods have become irregular from cold. Their certainty of action has been long acknowledged by the medical profession and hundreds that have uselessly tried various boasted remedies. Care is sometimes necessary to their use, though they contain no medicine detrimental to the constitution. Advice gratis to all those who use the pills, by Madame Costello, 34 Lispenard Street, between Walker and Canal, where the pills are sold. Price $1 per box.

MADAME COSTELLO

FEMALE PHYSICIAN AND GRADUATE AS MIDWIFE—offers her professional services to the ladies of this city and country. Having had long experience and surprising success in the treatment of diseases incident to her sex, or those suffering from irregularity, that she will be happy to afford a comfortable temporary home at her residence, where they can always have the best medical treatment and the matronly care and nursing, or, if preferred, will wait on and attend them at their own homes until perfectly recovered. Madame C. particularly begs to impress on the minds of the delicate that she officiates personally in every case, so that hesitation or dread need never to be apprehended.

New York Sun, February 26, 1846, cited in James C. Mohr, *Abortion in America: the Origins and Evolution of National Policy* (New York: Oxford University Press, 1978), p. 126.

N. B.—Madame Costello would inform ladies residing out of the city, whose health would not permit them of travelling, that she would devote her personal attendance upon them in any part of the United States, within reasonable distance.

Madame C. can be consulted at her residence, 34 Lispenard Street, at all times, and with the strictest regard to the wishes of her patients.

[79]
Madame Restell's Pills (1870)

A CERTAIN CURE FOR MARRIED LADIES, with or without medicines, by Madame Restell, Professor of Midwifery; over 30 years practice. Her infallible French Female Pills, No. 1, price $1, or No. 2, specially prepared for married ladies, price $5, which can never fail, are safe and healthy. Sold only at her office, No. 1 Fifty-Second street, first door from Fifth Avenue, and at druggists, 152 Greenwich Street, or sent by mail. Caution—All others are counterfeit.

New York Herald, May 16, 1870, cited in John Paul Harper, "Be Fruitful and Multiply: Planned Parenthood in Nineteenth-Century America," in Carol Berkin and Mary Norton, eds., *Women of America: A History,* p. 267. Copyright © 1979 by Houghton Mifflin Company.

The Criminalization of Birth Control

[80]
Commonwealth *v.* Bangs *(Massachusetts, 1812)*

The defendant was indicted October term, 1810, for assaulting and beating one *Lucy Holman,* and administering to her a certain dangerous and deleterious draught or potion, against her will, with intent to procure the abortion or premature birth of a bastard child, of which she was then pregnant, and which the defendant had before that time begotten of her body, to the great damage of the said *Lucy,* against good morals and good manners, in evil example to others in like case to offend.

The *Solictor-General,* at the trial, entered a *noli prosequi* [an order to withdraw prosecution] as to the assault and battery charged in the indictment.

9 Mass. 386 (1812).

A verdict was found at the same term, that the defendant was guilty of all the several matters charged in the indictment, excepting that the said potion was taken by the said *Lucy* voluntarily.

After the verdict was returned, the defendant moved the court to arrest the judgment, on the ground that no indictable offense was described in the indictment except the part non-pros'd [not prosecuted] by the *Solicitor-General;* and the cause stood over to this term for the consideration of that motion.

Fay [Bangs's lawyer] in support of the motion, contended that the principal charge in the indictment amounting to no more than an aggravated assault and battery, as to which the *Solicitor-General* had entered a *noli prosequi,* and of which there was no evidence at the trial, there remained nothing against the defendant but the administering with the patient's consent some potion with intent that the same should produce an abortion. No abortion was produced; and if there had been, there is no averment that the woman was quick with child; both which circumstances are necessary ingredients in the offense intended to be charged in the indictment.

An indictment for administering a potion, with intent to procure an abortion, must contain an allegation that an abortion ensued and that the woman was quick with child.

The *Solicitor-General* argued that any overt act, perpetrated with the intent to procure a misdeameanor to be committed, was itself a misdemeanor; and the patient's consent to take a deleterious draught did not make the administering of it lawful.

BY THE COURT. There can be no sentence upon this verdict. The assault and battery are out of the case, and no abortion is alleged to have followed the taking of the potion; and if any had been alleged and proved to have ensued, the averment that the woman was quick with child at the time is a necessary part of the indictment.

[81]

Mills *v.* Commonwealth *(Pennsylvania, 1850)*

Jonathan Gibbons Mills, a dentist, was convicted of seducing Mary Elizabeth Lutz, but the Supreme Court set this aside on a procedural technicality. He was then charged and convicted of "wilfully, maliciously, unlawfully, and wickedly" administering to and causing to be administered to this girl he had made pregnant, "dangerous, unwholesome and pernicuous pills, herbs, drugs, potions, teas, liquids, powders, and mixtures," with the intent to cause and procure a "miscarriage and abortion" and "the premature birth and destruction" of her child. Mills sought to have this conviction set aside as well on the grounds that the offense for which he

13 Pa. 627–635 (1850).

was indicted did not exist in either the common or statutory law of Pennsylvania. He argued that it was not an indictable offence to attempt to procure an abortion, where the mother is not quick with child and the indictment did not state that the mother had quickened. A jury convicted Mills of the same crime against Catharine Ann Lutz, but cleared him of the charge she had brought as well, of assault. Note the question of whether the woman wanted or did not want to end an unwanted pregnancy is not considered in the opinion of the court delivered by Judge J. Coulter—Ed.

COULTER J. . . . It is a flagrant crime at common law to attempt to procure the miscarriage or abortion of the woman. Because it interferes with and violates the mysteries of nature in that process by which the human race is propagated and continued. It is a crime against nature which obstructs the fountain of life, and therefore it is punished. The next error assigned is, that it ought to have been charged in the count that the woman had become *quick*. But, although it has been so held in Massachusetts and some other States, it is not, I apprehend, the law in Pennsylvania, and never ought to have been the law anywhere. It is not the murder of a living child which constitutes the offence, but the destruction of gestation by wicked means and against nature. The moment the womb is instinct with embryo life, and gestation has begun, the crime may be perpetrated. The allegation in this indictment was therefore sufficient, to wit: "that she was then and there pregnant and big with child." By the well settled and established doctrine of the common law, the civil rights of an infant *in ventre sa mere* are fully protected at all periods after conception. A count charging a wicked intent to procure a miscarriage of a woman "then and there being pregnant," by administering potions, etc., was held good by the Supreme Court of this state, January 1846. There was therefore a crime at common law sufficiently set forth and charged in the indictment. . . .

[82]
Connecticut Statute on Abortion (1821)

Every person who shall wilfully and maliciously administer to or cause to be administered to, or taken by, any person or persons, any deadly poison or other noxious and destructive substance, with an intention him, her or them thereby to murder, or thereby to cause or procure the miscarriage of any woman then being quick with child, and shall be thereof duly convicted, shall suffer imprisonment in Newgate Prison during his natural life or for such other term as the court having cognizance of the offence shall determine.

Cited in James C. Mohr, *Abortion in America: The Origins and Evolution of National Policy* (New York: Oxford University Press, 1978), p. 21.

[83]
Illinois Statute on Abortion (1827)

XLV. If any woman shall endeavor privately, either by herself or the procurement of others, to conceal the death of any issue of her body, male or female, which if born alive would by law be a bastard, so that it may not come to light, whether it shall have been murdered or not, every such mother being convicted thereof, shall suffer imprisonment in the county jail, for a term not exceeding one year: *Provided however,* that nothing herein contained shall be so construed as to prevent such mothers from being indicted and punished for the murder of such bastard child.

XLVI. Every person who shall willfully and maliciously administer, or cause to be administered to, or taken by any person, any poison or other noxious or destrictive substance or liquid, with the intention to cause the death of such person, and being thereof duly convicted, shall be punished by confinement in the penitentiary for a term not less than one year, and not more than seven years. And every person who shall administer, or cause to be administered or taken, any such poison, substance or liquid, with the intention to procure the miscarriage of any woman then being with child, and shall thereof be duly convicted, shall be imprisoned for a term not exceeding three years in the penitentiary, and fined in a sum not exceeding one thousand dollars.

From N. H. Purple, ed., *Statutes of Illinois . . . in Force January 1, 1857,* Part I (2nd ed. Chicago, 1857), pp. 364–65.

[84]
Federal Statute on Contraception and Abortion: The Comstock Act (1873)

Be it enacted by the Senate and House of Representatives of the United States of America in Congress assembled, That whoever, within . . . the exclusive jurisdiction of the United States, shall sell, . . . or offer to sell, or to lend, or to give away, or in any manner to exhibit, or shall otherwise publish or offer to publish in any manner, or shall have in his possession, for any such purpose or purposes, any obscene book,

"An Act of the Suppression of Trade in, and Circulation of, Obscene Literature and Articles of Immoral Use," in Acts and Resolutions of the United States of America Passed at the Third Session of the Forty-Second Congress, December 2, 1872—March 3, 1873 (Washington, D.C., Government Printing Office, 1873), pp. 234–36.

pamphlet, paper, writing, advertisement, circular . . . or other article of an immoral nature, or any drug or medicine, or any article, whatever, for the prevention of conception, or for causing unlawful abortion, or shall advertise the same for sale, or shall write or print, or cause to be written or printed, any card, circular, book, pamphlet, advertisement, or notice of any kind, stating when, where, how, or of whom, or by what means, any of these articles in this section hereinbefore mentioned, can be purchased or obtained, or shall manufacture, draw, or print, or in any wise make any of such articles, shall be deemed guilty of a misdemeanor, and, on conviction thereof . . . shall be imprisoned at hard labor in the penitentiary for not less than six months nor more than five years for each offense, or fined not less than one hundred dollars nor more than two thousand dollars, with costs of court.

SEC. 148. That no obscene, lewd or lascivious book, pamphlet, picture, paper, print, or other publication of an indecent character, or any article or thing designed or intended for the prevention of conception or procuring of abortion, nor any article or thing intended or adapted for any indecent or immoral use . . . shall be carried in the mail, and any person who shall knowingly deposit, for mailing any of the hereinbefore-mentioned articles or things, or any notice, or paper containing any advertisement relating to the aforesaid articles or things, and any person who, in pursuance of any plan or scheme for disposing of any of the hereinbefore-mentioned articles or things, shall take, or cause to be taken, from the mail any such letter or package, shall be deemed guilty of a misdemeanor, and, on conviction shall, be fined not less than one hundred dollars nor more than five thousand dollars, or imprisoned at hard labor not less than one year nor more than ten years, or both, in the discretion of the judge.

SEC. 3. That all persons are prohibited from importing into the United States, from any foreign country, any of the herein-before-mentioned articles or things, except the drugs herein-before-mentioned when imported in bulk, and not put up for any of the purposes before mentioned; . . .

THE WOMEN'S RIGHTS MOVEMENT
Women's Rage

[85]
Iowa Folksong: "Single Girl"

When I was single, I went dressed so fine,
Now I am married, go ragged all the time.
Chorus: Lord, how I wish I was a single girl again.

Dishes to wash and spring to go to,
Now I am married I've everything to do.
Two little children, lyin' in the bed,
Both of them so hungry, Lord, they can't hold up their heads.
Wash um and dress um and send um to school,
Long comes that drunkard and calls them a fool.

When I was single, marryin' was my crave,
Now I am married, I'm troubled to my grave.

Cited in John Mack Faragher, *Women and Men On the Overland Trail* (New Haven: Yale University Press, 1979), pp. 152–153.

[86]
Recollections from a Rural District in Upstate New York (before 1848)

In those early days a husband's supremacy was often enforced in rural districts by corporeal chastisement, and it was considered by most people as quite right and proper—as much so as the correction of refractory children in like manner. I remember in my own neighborhood a . . . Methodist class leader and exhorter . . . esteemed a worthy citizen, who every few weeks gave his wife a beating with his horsewhip. He said it was necessary, in order to keep her in subjection and because she scolded so much. Now this wife, surrounded by six or seven little children . . . was obliged

From Elizabeth Cady Stanton et al., *History of Woman Suffrage* (New York, 1881), vol 1, pp. 88–89.

to spin and weave cloth for all the garments of the family . . . to milk . . . to make butter and cheese, and do all the cooking, washing, making, and mending . . . and, with the pains of maternity forced upon her every eighteen months, was whipped by her pious husband, "because she scolded."

[87]
Recollections from a New England Mill Town (1830s)

The laws relating to women were such, that a husband could claim his wife wherever he found her, and also the children she was trying to shield from his influence, and I have seen more than one poor woman skulk behind her loom or her frame when visitors were approaching the end of the aisle where she worked. Some of these [women] were known under assumed names, to prevent their husbands from trusteeing their wages. It was a very common thing for a male person of a certain kind to do this, thus depriving his wife of all her wages, perhaps, month after month.

From Harriet Robinson, *Loom and Spindle, or Life Among the Early Mill Girls* (Boston, 1898), pp. 66–68.

Seneca Falls

[88]
The Declaration of Sentiments, Seneca Falls Convention (1848)

When, in the course of human events, it becomes necessary for one portion of the family of man to assume among the people of the earth a position different from that which they have hitherto occupied, but one to which the laws of nature and of nature's God entitle them, a decent respect to the opinions of mankind requires that they should declare the causes that impel them to such a course.

We hold these truths to be self-evident: that all men and women are created equal, that they are endowed by their Creator with certain inalienable rights: that among these are life, liberty, and the pursuit of happiness; that to secure these rights governments are instituted, deriving their just powers from the consent of the

From Elizabeth Cady Stanton et al., *History of Woman Suffrage* (New York, 1881), vol. 1, pp. 70–72.

governed. Whenever any form of government becomes destructive of these ends, it is the right of those who suffer from it to refuse allegiance to it, and to insist upon the institution of a new government, laying its foundations on such principles, and organizing its powers in such form, as to them shall seem most likely to effect their safety and happiness. Prudence, indeed, will dictate that governments long established should not be changed for light and transient causes; and accordingly all experience hath shown that mankind are more disposed to suffer, while evils are sufferable, than to right themselves by abolishing the forms to which they were accustomed. But when a long train of abuses and usurpations, pursuing invariably the same object, evinces a design to reduce them under absolute despotism, it is their duty to throw off such government, and to provide new guards for their future security. Such had been the patient sufferance of the women under this government, and such is now the necessity which constrains them to demand the equal station to which they are entitled.

The history of mankind is a history of repeated injuries and usurpations on the part of man toward woman, having in direct object the establishment of an absolute tyranny over her. To prove this, let facts be submitted to a candid world.

He has never permitted her to exercise her inalienable right to the elective franchise.

He has compelled her to submit to laws, in the formation of which she had no voice.

He has withheld from her rights which are given to the most ignorant and degraded men—both natives and foreigners.

Having deprived her of this first right of a citizen, the elective franchise, thereby leaving her without representation in the halls of legislation, he has oppressed her on all sides.

He has made her, if married, in the eye of the law, civilly dead.

He has taken from her all right to property, even to the wages she earns.

He has made her, morally, an irresponsible being, as she can commit many crimes with impunity, provided they be done in the presence of her husband. In the covenant of marriage, she is compelled to promise obedience to her husband, he becoming, to all intents and purposes, her master—the law giving him power to deprive her of her liberty, and to administer chastisement.

He has so framed the laws of divorce, as to what shall be the proper causes, and in case of separation, to whom the guardianship of the children shall be given, as to be wholly regardless of the happiness of women—the law, in all cases, going upon the false supposition of the supremacy of man, and giving all power into his hands.

After depriving her of all rights as a married woman, if single, and the owner of property, he has taxed her to support a government which recognizes her only when her property can be made profitable to it.

He has monopolized nearly all the profitable employments, and from those she is permitted to follow she receives but a scanty remuneration. He closes against her all the avenues to wealth and distinction which he considers most honorable to himself. As a teacher of theology, medicine, or law, she is not known.

He has denied her the facilities for obtaining a thorough education, all colleges being closed against her.

He allows her in Church, as well as State, but a subordinate position, claiming Apostolic authority for her exclusion from the ministry, and, with some exceptions, from any public participation in the affairs of the Church.

He has created a false public sentiment by giving to the world a different code of morals for men and women, by which moral delinquencies which exclude women from society are not only tolerated but deemed of little account in man.

He has usurped the prerogative of Jehovah himself, claiming it is his right to assign for her a sphere of action, when that belongs to her conscience and to her God.

He has endeavored, in every way that he could, to destroy her confidence in her own powers, to lessen her self-respect, and to make her willing to lead a dependent and abject life.

Now, in view of this entire disfranchisement of one-half the people of this country, their social and religious degradation—in view of the unjust laws above mentioned, and because women do feel themselves aggrieved, oppressed, and fraudulently deprived of their most sacred rights, we insist that they have immediate admission to all the rights and privileges which belong to them as citizens of the United States.

In entering upon the great work before us, we anticipate no small amount of misconception, misrepresentation, and ridicule; but we shall use every instrumentality within our power to effect our object. We shall employ agents, circulate tracts, petition the State and National legislatures, and endeavor to enlist the pulpit and the press in our behalf. We hope this Convention will be followed by a series of Conventions embracing every part of the country.

Expanding the Grounds for Divorce

[89]
"An Act in Regard to Divorces" (New York, 1861)

Section 1. In addition to the cases in which a divorce, dissolving the marriage contract, may now be decreed by the supreme court, such a divorce may be decreed by said court in either of the cases following:

1. Where either party to the marriage shall, for the period of three years next

From *Address of Elizabeth Cady Stanton on the Divorce Bill before the Judiciary Committee of the New York State Senate in the Assembly Chamber, February 8, 1861* (Albany, 1861).

preceding the application for such divorce, have willfully deserted the other party to the marriage, and neglected to perform to such party the duties imposed by their relation.

2. Where there is and shall have been for the period of one year next preceding the application for such divorce, continuous and repeated instances of cruel and inhuman treatment by either party, so as greatly to impair the health or endanger the life of the other party, thereby rendering it unsafe to live with the party guilty of such cruelty or inhumanity.

The foregoing sections shall not apply to any person who shall not have been an actual resident of this state for the period of five years next preceding such application for such divorce.

[90]
Elizabeth Cady Stanton on Behalf of the Divorce Bill (1861)

GENTLEMEN OF THE JUDICIARY—In speaking to you, gentlemen, on such delicate subjects as marriage and divorce, in the revision of laws which are found in your statute books, I must use the language I find there.

May I not, without the charge of indelicacy, speak in a mixed assembly of Christian men and women, of wrongs which my daughter may tomorrow suffer in your courts, where there is no woman's heart to pity, and no woman's presence to protect?

I come not before you, gentlemen, at this time, to plead simply the importance of divorce in cases specified in your bill, but the justice of an entire revision of your whole code of laws on marriage and divorce. . . . If civilly and politically man must stand supreme, let us at least be equals in our nearest and most sacred relations. . . .

The contract of marriage is by no means equal. From Coke down to Kent, who can cite one law under the marriage contract where woman has the advantage? The law permits the girl to marry at twelve years of age, while it requires several more years of experience on the part of the boy. In entering this compact, the *man* gives up nothing that he before possessed; he is a *man* still: while the legal existence of the woman is suspended during marriage and is known but in and through the husband. She is nameless, purseless, childless; though a woman, an heiress, and a mother. . . .

The laws on divorce are quite as unequal as those on marriage; yes, far more so. The advantages seem to be all on one side, and the penalties on the other. In case of

From *Address of Elizabeth Cady Stanton on the Divorce Bill before the Judiciary Committee of the New York State Senate in the Assembly Chamber, February 8, 1861* (Albany, 1961).

divorce, if the husband be the guilty party he still retains a greater part of the property! If the wife be the guilty party she goes out of the partnership penniless (*Kent,* vol. 2, p. 33; *Bishop on Divorce,* p. 489). In New York and some other states the wife of the guilty husband can now sue for a divorce in her own name, and the costs come out of the husband's estate; but in a majority of the states she is still compelled to sue in the name of another, as she has no means of paying costs, even though she may have brought her thousands into the partnership. "The allowance to the innocent wife of *ad interim,* alimony, and money to sustain the suit, is not regarded as strict right in her, but of sound discretion in the court" (*Bishop on Divorce,* p. 581). "Many jurists," says *Kent* (vol. 2, p. 88), "are of opinion that the adultery of the husband ought not be noticed or made subject to the same animadversions as that of the wife, because it is not evidence of such entire depravity, nor equally injurious in its effects upon the morals and good order and happiness of domestic life". . . .

Say you, these are but the opinions of men? On what else, I ask, are the hundreds of women depending who this hour demand in our courts a release from burdensome contracts? Are not these delicate matters left wholly to the discretion of the courts? Are not young women, from our first families, dragged into your public courts—into assemblies of men exclusively? The judges all men, the jurors all men! No true woman there to shield them by her presence from gross and impertinent questionings, to pity their misfortunes or to protect against their wrongs! The administration of justice depends far more on the opinions of eminent jurists than on law alone, for law is powerless when at variance with public sentiments. . . .

If marriage is a human institution, about which man may legislate, it seems but just that he should treat this branch of his legislation with the same common sense that he applies to all others. If it is a mere legal contract, then it should be subject to the restraints and privileges of all other contracts. A contract, to be valid in law, must be formed between parties of mature age, with an honest intention in said parties to do what they agree. The least concealment, fraud or intention to deceive, if proved, annuls the contract. . . . But in marriage, no matter how much fraud and deception are practiced, nor how cruelly one or both parties have been misled; no matter how young or inexperienced or thoughtless the parties, nor how unequal their condition and position in life, the contract cannot be annulled. Think of a husband telling a young and trusting girl, but one short month his wife, that he married her for her money; that those letters, so precious to her, that she read and re-read, and kissed and cherished, were written by another; that their splendid home, of which, on their wedding day, her father gave to him the deed, is already in the hands of his creditors; that she must give up the elegance and luxury that now surround her, unless she can draw fresh supplies of money to meet their wants. . . .

Do wise Christian legislators need any arguments to convince them that the sacredness of the family relation should be protected at all hazards? The family—that great conservator of national virtue and strength—how can you hope to build it up in the midst of violence, debauchery and excess. . . . Call that sacred, where innocent children trembling with fear fly to the corners and dark places of the house, to hide from the wrath of drunken, brutal fathers, but forgetting their past sufferings rush out again at their mother's frantic screams, "Help! oh, help!" Behold the agonies of those young hearts as they see the only being on earth they love, dragged about the room by the hair of her head, kicked and pounded and left half dead and bleeding on the floor! Call that sacred, where fathers like these have the power and legal right to hand down their natures to other beings, to curse other generations with such moral deformity and death! . . .

Fathers! do you say, let your daughters pay a life-long penalty for one unfortunate step? How could they, on the threshold of life, full of joy and hope, believing all things to be as they seemed on the surface, judge of the dark windings of the human soul? How could they foresee that the young man, today so noble, so generous, would in a few short years be transformed into a cowardly, mean tyrant or a foul-mouthed, bloated drunkard? What father could rest at his home by night, knowing that his lovely daughter was at the mercy of a strong man, drunk with wine and passion, and that, do what he might, he was backed up by law and public sentiment? The best interests of the individual, the family, the state, the nation, cry out against these legalized marriages of force and endurance.

There can be no heaven without love; and nothing is sacred in the family and home, but just so far as it is built up and anchored in purity and peace. Our newspapers teem with startling accounts of husbands and wives having shot or poisoned each other, or committed suicide, choosing death rather than the indissoluble tie, and still worse, the living death of faithless men and women, from the first families in the land, dragged from the privacy of home into the public prints and courts, with all the painful details of sad, false lives.

Now, do you believe, honorable gentlemen, that all these wretched matches were made in heaven? That all these sad, miserable people are bound together by God? But, say you, does not separation cover all these difficulties? No one objects to separation, when the parties are so disposed. . . . Now, if a noble girl of seventeen marries, and is unfortunate in her choice, because the cruelty of her husband compels separation, in her dreary isolation, would you drive her to a nunnery, and shall she be a nun indeed? She, innocent child, perchance the victim of a father's pride, or a mother's ambition. . . . Henceforth, do you doom this fair young being . . . to a joyless, loveless, solitude? By your present laws you say, though separated, she is married still; indissolubly bound to one she never loved; by whom she was never wooed or won; but by false guardians sold. And now, no matter though in the coming time her soul should for the first time wake to love, and one of God's own noblemen should echo back her choice, the gushing fountains of her young affections must all be stayed. Because some man still lives who once called her wife, no other man may give her his love; and if she love not the tyrant to whom she is legally bound, she shall not love at all. . . .

What do our present divorce laws amount to? Those who wish to evade them have only to go into another state to accomplish what they desire. If any of our citizens cannot secure their inalienable rights in New York state, they may, in Connecticut and Indiana.

Why is it that all contracts, convenants, agreements and partnerships are left wholly at the discretion of the parties, except that which of all others, is considered most holy and important, both for the individual and the race?

But, say you, what a condition we should soon have in social life, with no restrictive laws. I ask you, what have we now? . . . In this state, are over forty thousand drunkards' wives, earnestly imploring you to grant them deliverances from their fearful bondage. Thousands of sad mothers, too, with helpless children, deserted by faithless husbands, some in California, some in insane asylums, and some in the gutter, all pleading to be released. They ask nothing but a quit-claim deed to themselves.

Thus far, we have had the man-marriage, and nothing more. From the beginning, man has had the whole and sole regulation of the matter. He has spoken in Scripture, and he has spoken in law. As an individual, he has decided the time and cause for putting away a wife; and as a judge and legislator he still holds the entire control.

[91]
Horace Greeley on Freedom of Divorce (1852–1853)

Marriage indissoluble may be an imperfect test of honorable and pure affection—as all things human are imperfect—but it is the best the State can devise; . . . its overthrow would result in a general profligacy and corruption, such as this country has never known and few of our people can adequately imagine. [If] marriage may be dissolved whenever the parties are tired of each other . . . more false than true marriages would be contracted; because libertines would resort to marriage as a cloak for lecherous designs, which the legal penalties of bigamy and adultery now compel to pursue a more circuitous and less shaded path. . . . I utterly abhor what you term "the right of woman to choose the father of her child" . . . seeing that it conflicts directly and fatally with the paramount right of each child through minority to protection, guardianship, and initimate daily counsel and training from both parents. Your sovereignty of the individual is in palpable collision with the purity of society and the sovereignty of God.

From *The New York Tribune,* Dec. 18, 1852, and Jan. 28, 1853, as cited in Nelson Blake, *The Road to Reno: A History of Divorce in the United States* (New York: Macmillan, 1962), pp. 84–86.

TRENDS IN FAMILY LAW
Divorce and Alimony

[92]
What Constitutes Legal Cruelty
(Alabama Supreme Court, 1870)

PETERS, J.—The Christian interpretation of the contract of marriage requires that the husband shall love the wife, that he shall "delight in her as in himself," and when the proofs show that he habitually fails to do this, the courts will interpose upon very slight indications of peril to her body or health, for her protection by divorce.

WHAT CONSTITUTES LEGAL CRUELTY

2. If the conduct of the husband is shown to be habitually cold, indifferent, rude, harsh, vulgar, obscene, and profane towards the wife, and she is seen shortly after being with him, in the privity of the marital relation in tears, with bruises on her face and on her lips, and on her side, of ruinous character, and the husband admits, when complained of, that these indications of bad treatment were produced by him, his explanation that they were given in playfulness and jest, and not in anger or in earnest, will not be sufficient to rescue his conduct from the construction that these appearances are evidence of legal cruelty sufficient to justify a divorce in favor of the wife for that cause.

WHEN CHILDREN WILL NOT BE TAKEN FROM MOTHER

3. Upon a dissolution of the marriage by divorce in favor of the wife, if she has possession of the children of the marriage, who are of tender years, and two of them are girls and one a boy, and it appears that the mother is a woman of polite education and of amiable disposition and virtuous; and if it appears that the father, the husband, is habitually rude, profane, vulgar, obscene, hypocritical in his conduct and insulting in his language to females in his household, with some evidence of a tendency to drunkenness, and cold and indifferent to his children and disposed to sell them to their grandmother "for cash," and denounces them as "damned nasty babies," of whom he is tired; in such a case the children will not be separated or taken from the care and tuition of the mother.

From *Chicago Legal News,* June 25, 1870.

INJUNCTION AGAINST HUSBAND'S CLAIM

4. If during marriage the husband conveys or causes to be conveyed to the wife, by deed, a house and lot in which they are then residing, for the purpose of securing it from confiscation on account of the husband's treason against the government, and he received and holds possession of the deed for her, and if he is insolvent or likely to become insolvent and has received moneys or estate belonging to the wife as her separate property, of considerable value, under the laws of this State for their protection, upon a dissolution of the marriage by divorce in the wife's favor, she will be protected in her possession of such house and lot, and the furniture therein, by injunction against the husband's claim.

[93]
Sarah Prince *v.* George Prince
(South Carolina, 1845)

This case illustrates, not only the long and complicated legal process involved in determining alimony, but also a new approach to the idea of support. The plaintiff, Sarah Prince, claiming desertion, petitioned the court for alimony. The defendant, George Prince, denied the marriage and claims about his income. Before the court could make a decision about alimony, it first had to ascertain the true facts. The case came to trial in 1841. Chancellor Dunkin, after taking testimony about whether the ceremony that had taken place under Jewish law constituted a marriage, delivered a decree sustaining the charge of desertion. The court, however, felt it needed additional information about the financial position of the defendant. The Chancellor appointed a Master (a court assistant), to find out the facts and make recommendations. In 1844 Chancellor Johnston issued a decree based on the Master's report. The defendant appealed the decision on the grounds that alimony cannot be decreed out of the profits of daily labor. The court, after reviewing the history of the case and the evidence, addresses the question of whether it has the authority to issue an alimony decree when a husband has no capital or fixed income.—Ed.

By the CHANCELLOR. From the testimony of Mr. Poznanskie, the court has come to the conclusion that a ceremony took place between the parties, which, according to the Hebrew law, constituted a valid marriage; but it was very informal, such, according to Mr. Poznanskie's evidence, as he had never before known.

The ceremony took place at Portsmouth, England, on the 2d March, 1835. . . . This court can only interfere for the purpose of giving alimony. . . . The com-

1 Rich (S.C.) 282 (1845).

plainant alleges that she has a child by the defendant, and that the income of the
defendant from his occupation as an apothecary . . . was not less than four or five
thousand dollars.

Let it be referred to the Master to enquire and report what is the pecuniary
condition of the defendant, and that the Master have leave to report any special
matter.

In February, 1844 this case again came up, on exceptions to the Master's report,
before Johnston, Ch., who pronounced the following decree:

The bill states that the parties, who are Jews, were married in England several
years ago, and that after a short period of cohabitation, the defendant deserted his
wife, who has a child by him, came to this State and took another woman to his bed,
and now lives with her in comfortable circumstances, [on] the fruits of his income as
a druggist.

The answer denies the alleged marriage with the plaintiff, although it admits
that the defendant cohabited with her; and repudiates the child, although born after
the cohabitation. It evades the charge of illicit intercourse and cohabitation with
another woman; but admits that the defendant is living comfortably and in the
enjoyment of a reasonable income from his employment of a druggist.

The case was heard by Chancellor Dunkin, who delivered a decree on the merits
in February, 1841. This decree establishes a marriage between the parties on the 2d
of March, 1835. This fact being established, the answer sufficiently sustains the
charge of desertion. Proceeding upon this assumption, as I suppose, the Chancellor
regarded the case as having been made out by the plaintiff; the only remaining
question before the court was as to the remedy to be administered. . . .

The report which now comes up states that "the Master does not find any proof
that the defendant is in possession of any estate, either real or personal; but from the
testimony submitted he finds that he is in the receipt of money; that he lives
comfortably and well; and that in the Master's own mind there is little doubt that he
is in possession of funds sufficient to meet any decree that may be awarded against
him."

Every question raised in the exceptions is expressly, or by necessary implication,
concluded by the decree, except the single one whether alimony can be decreed in
respect to the income of the husband arising not from capital, but from his daily
labor and diligence; and if it can, then what should be the amount of it in this case.

The evidence reported shows the existence of considerable income. The answer
admits it. It appears that the defendant has been in the habit of taking boarders; that
he vends medicines and occasionally administers them; that he lives in a hired house,
for which he regularly pays a considerable rent; and that he supports a woman who
lives with him. And one of the witnesses, who collects for him, leaves the impression
that his income may reasonably be estimated at not less than $1800 per annum. The
question is whether a husband, in these circumstances, is not bound to contribute to
the support of his wife whom he has deserted.

Let us look into this question with a view to principle, as well as to authority. It is one of most serious import, especially to the humbler and more defenseless classes of the community. If the wealthy man denies to his wife the duties of the marriage relation, there is no difficulty in compelling him to sustain her out of his property. But it seems to be doubted whether the poor may not desert their duties with impunity. Is this so? And if so, upon what principle can the distinction be sustained?

By marriage the husband becomes entitled to whatever personalty the wife may possess, and to all her earnings. She is reduced to a state of comparative servitude. She cannot change her situation by another marriage, more agreeable and more beneficial to her. She is deprived of the power of making contracts; and, of course, of the means of accumulating property, or laying by the means of subsistence in sickness or old age. Will it do to say that the husband, entitling himself to all these advantages, and subjecting the wife to all these disabilities, by the marriage, is not bound, by all the means in his power, to sustain her? And if he deserts her, shall his desertion, which is itself a wrong, excuse him from the performance of this obligation? Certainly not. It would be a reproach to the law if it were so. God knows, the condition of all women, but especially of married women, is bad enough by the common law of England, and advancing civilization loudly demands its amelioration. But that law, which almost enslaves the wife, makes the husband liable for her support. It is a duty he has undertaken with her aid, if he chooses to avail himself of it; and for which he is bound, if he rejects that assistance.

No doubt, circumstances must have their influence in determining the amount which should be decreed to an abandoned wife. If the parties are laboring people, the wife needs less. If she is in bad health, however, the amount should be increased. If the labor of the husband is of a comparatively unprofitable character, or if he is sickly, allowance should be made for these circumstances. If, on the other hand, he is in good health, and skilful, and is actually realizing considerable profits, the partner of his fortunes should not be refused a reasonable participation in them. Every case must be governed by its circumstances.

Certainly most of the reported cases show that alimony has been decreed out of visible property, or fixed and permanent income. But the visible property is only evidence of the income: and permanent and fixed income, such as annuities, and the like, is only resorted to because of its greater certainty, and as furnishing a surer means of administering redress. But when income is proved to exist, although not fixed, but dependent upon the daily exertions of the husband, this shall not be exempt; and he, in respect to it, will be compelled to do what law and moral duty require of him.

The principle in fact is that in all cases you are to look to the means of affording a remedy; and if you can find them, the remedy should be administered.

In this case it is vain to deny that the defendant has the means of supporting his wife. The fact stares us in the face, that he does support another woman, and lives in comfort.

It is said, however, that casualties may hereafter reduce his means. The same argument would apply if he were in the possession of tangible property. The act of God may strip him of that. If this were a suit for debt, we should feel no hesitation in decreeing it, without reference to any contingency. Is the right of a wife of a less sacred character than a creditor's demand? We only refer to the means of the husband in the one case, and not in the other, because the wife has embarked with her husband in a common bottom, and is bound to share in his fortune, whether good or bad. But another answer is that a decree for alimony is not unchangeable. Under a change of circumstances, the amount may be either increased or diminished: though this is seldom done, and never for light or trivial causes. . . .

I will close what I have to say on this head, by repeating that the allowance is a matter of sound discretion, and that in making it, all the circumstances must be considered: with this further observation, that more is to be allowed to the wife when, by a decree on the merits the husband is decided to be in the wrong, than *pendente lite,* when this must necessarily be unascertained; and by adverting to the general rule, that a greater proportion is to be allowed out of a small than a large income. . . . Having now determined the general principles, by way of direction to the Master, I shall recommit the report; that he may, upon the evidence already before him, or which shall be offered, report a reasonable estimate of the defendant's income, and a specific sum to be allowed out of it, for alimony.

Something is said in one of the exceptions, with respect to the child, as if it were disputed that this child is the child of the plaintiff, or born within wedlock. The Master will bear evidence on this point, if offered, and report accordingly; and if the child shall from the evidence appear to be defendant's its support and education will also be considered and reported upon. . . .

Curia, per [Decision by] JOHNSTON, Ch. The court sees no reason to differ from the decree as to the fact of marriage, nor from the instructions under which the report was recommitted to the Master. . . .

It is ordered that the appeal be dismissed and the decree affirmed.

Custody and Guardianship

[94]
People ex rel. Barry *v.* Mercein *(New York, 1842)*

John A. Barry and Eliza Anna Mercein were married in 1835 in New York, and shortly thereafter moved to Nova Scotia where they lived for about one year. They returned to New York and Mr. Barry went into a business which failed in the winter of 1837, by which time they had two children, a son and a daughter. It was agreed that Eliza Anna and the children would stay in New York at her father's house while John went back to Nova Scotia to reestablish himself in business. When John returned several weeks later, Eliza Anna refused to go to Nova Scotia with him, and an agreement was worked out between them and her father.—Ed.

"Agreement made this 7th day of June, 1838, between John A. Barry of the first part, Eliza Anna Barry of the second part, and Thomas R. Mercein of the third part. *Whereas certain differences have existed* between John A. Barry and Eliza Anna, which it is their *mutual desire shall be amicably and peacefully arranged and reconciled;* and John A. Barry's business requiring him to be *absent from New York for a time;* and *neither individual at present wishing a final separation.* It is AGREED . . . that the said John A. Barry *shall leave in the care and keeping of his wife, until the first day of May next ensuing,* their daughter Mary Mercein, and that on that day or soon thereafter *he shall relinquish* to Eliza Anna, his wife, *all his right existing at that or accruing at any then future period to their said daughter, provided his said wife shall then require him so to do.* The aforesaid parties also *covenant* and *agree* that Mercein, the son of the said John A. and Eliza Anna, shall be left in the care and keeping of his said mother until she shall be required by his father to deliver him, the said Mercein, to him the said John A. Barry; the mother having at such time, the option to accompany him. *Finally,* it is agreed between the aforesaid parties, that this document may be *cancelled, annulled and destroyed at any moment by the mutual consent of John A. Barry and Eliza Anna his wife.* In witness" etc.

In the latter part of June, 1838, the relator again embarked for Nova Scotia, and returned on the 8th of September following. At this time he proposed to his wife that he would remain in New York until spring, provided she would positively promise then to retun with him to Nova Scotia. She refused; and, in the course of the interview, he spoke of taking their son from her in case she persisted in her refusal. She acknowledged his power of doing so, but admonished him that such a step would *seal their fate.* The son was afterward given up to the relator, and has since remained with him.

> Between May, 1839 and July, 1842 John Barry brought five actions in the courts of New York to gain custody of his daughter. Each time he brought a writ of habeas corpus, demanding that his father-in-law, Thomas Mercein, relinquish custody of the daughter. In the first four instances the court refused, each time finding that the child needed the care and nurture of her mother. Only in this last instance did the court change its mind. The "relator" in this case is John Barry and the "respondent" his father-in-law, Thomas Mercein.—Ed.

COWEN, J. This is a proceeding by writ of *habeas corpus* instituted by Mr. Barry for the purpose of enforcing his rights as the father of his infant child, detained by his wife, with the sanction of her father, in the house of the latter.

The relator's claim, in different aspects, has been examined and decided on several previous writs before different commissioners; . . .

Another objection is, that Mr. Mercein should not have been made a party; the child not being detained by him. The detention is by his daughter, at his house, with his countenance and consent. If that be wrong on her part, it is equally so on his; for in respect to a civil injury, the law regards every one who participates in and promotes it, as a principal wrong-doer and severally responsible to the party whose rights have been invaded. It is impossible to avoid seeing that, if Mr. Barry is entitled to the custody of his child, Mr. Mercein is, in fact, the principal offender. Had his hand been withdrawn, it is morally certain that the relator would have been put to encounter no serious difficulty in reclaiming the custody of his child without a law-suit. . . .

The defendant [Thomas Mercein] claims that Mrs. Barry was lawfully at his house; and that, in her right, he is properly accessory to the detention of the child. This brings us to a consideration of the legal rights and powers of the relator and his wife in respect to their offspring. These rights and powers, like nearly all others when the claims of husband and wife come in conflict, depend upon a rule too elementary to require the adduction of authority; and too obvious to have been denied in the whole course of this particular controversy, from the hearing before the chancellor in the summer of 1839, through the several hearings before commissioners in this court, and the court for the correction of errors. The principle is thus stated in 1 {*Blackstone Commentaries*} 468: "The very being or legal existence of the woman is suspended during the marriage, or at least is incorporated and consolidated into that of the husband." Their relative power over the person of the child follows as a consequence, and is stated in the same book, to the following effect: the legal power of the father over his child is sufficient to keep the latter in order and obedience. The father is entitled to the benefit of his child's labor while it lives with and is maintained by him; while the mother, as such, is entitled to no power over it, but only to reverence and respect. The father's legal power ceases at the age of twenty-one. The extent of the rule is shown by the exceptions which the book mentions at p. 471. They are such as to shield the wife from corporal abuse, though "the courts of law will still permit the husband to restrain the wife of her liberty in case of any gross misbehavior."

One consequence necessarily resulting from the legal identity of husband and wife answers Mrs. Barry's claim to the custody of the child; which, as counsel have insisted, arises out of the relator's written agreement that she should retain it. That upon a proper construction of its words, she could derive any such right as is now claimed for her, I do not admit. But, for the purposes of the argument, suppose it an agreement for permanent separation—a complete relinquishment by the relator of all claim whatever, and a transfer of his right to Mrs. Barry. A single passage from the law shows its futility: "A man cannot grant any thing to his wife, or enter into covenant with her, for the grant would be to suppose her separate existence, and to covenant with her would be only to covenant with himself" (1 *Black. Com.* 468). As an agreement, therefore, the writing was void. As a delegation of power, it was revocable in its own nature, and in this instance has been actually revoked. Whatever latitude may have occasionally been allowed for the framing of bargains between husband and wife through trustees, I must be allowed to deny that it stands on any principle which can with propriety be applied to the case in question. I am aware that a separate maintenance may be settled by the husband on the wife, and that . . . they may covenant for the separation of their persons; that this may, if you please, be done under such pretexts as the parties shall choose to allege, whether in consonance or not with the law of divorce; and that courts both of law and equity have sanctioned such arrangements, by carrying them into effect. The practice probably started on the principle I have mentioned, of protection against corporal abuse, without its being sought with sufficient care to distinguish the fact from the mere declaration of the parties.

The courts do not seem to have foreseen that, in doing so much, they empowered the parties to be their own judges in a matter which may vitally affect the interests of society. The practice is by no means entitled to favor; and the courts are beginning to regret that they ever allowed it to any extent. It is at best letting into our system the doctrine of conventional divorce in its worst form. The advocates of that doctrine carry out their system to its proportional consequences. They would leave the parties at liberty to marry again; thus fulfilling the supposed law of nature with comparative decency. Our law still proclaims the obligation of the marriage contract, while it aids the parties in measures to evade that obligation and thus to defraud both the law and one another. The whole is indeed a matter of agreement between persons who are immediately interested; and the consequences, if confined to them, might be regarded as of little moment. The discouragement to enterprise in business, the wreck of private fortune, and loss of character, might be placed to the account of retribution for such wickedness or weakness as cannot endure the trouble of becoming respectable. But the evil does not stop here. An innocent family and a wide circle of connections are perhaps brought to share in the misfortune and disgrace, with more or less intensity as they may be more nearly or remotely related. The sentiments of filial reverence are subverted, and the conjugal relation itself distrusted and traduced. Husbands and wives with feelings and appetites already too violent for the restraints of duty or of shame, are thrown into the highway of temptation. It is said that the husband's common law right to correct the wife began to be doubted in the politer reign of Charles the Second (1 *Black. Com.* 471). It has since ceased to exist. In asserting the principle on which the barbarous practice of correction was abolished, the courts should beware of the opposite extreme that characterized the same reign. Much as we may congratulate ourselves on the abolition of unreasonable severity, such an achievement would but poorly compensate for the general corruption of domestic morals.

I make these remarks because they come into the argument that the doctrine of separate maintenance cannot be made to bear on the agreement in question; which, as it seems to me, is neither within the original principle of the rule, nor the sphere of its most extended practice. If the husband has a right to transfer the marriage bed to his wife, I deny that he has, therefore, the right still farther to violate his duty by selling his children, with or without it. These he holds under the duty of a personal trust, inalienable even to another who is . . . his wife, with whom he can make no contract whatever. . . .

 . . . . Admitting that an agreement for present separation is valid as between the parties, (and I have supposed it to be a kind of divorce which the courts cannot very well gainsay at this day), I am yet unable to see that, as a consequence, the husband may contract away the custody of his children. It need not be denied that a father may, even at common law, bind out his child to an apprenticeship, as this court seem to have thought in *The Matter of M'Dowles*. Here again is a narrow exception, the principle of which should never be extended to any other case. The exception itself was so very doubtful that a statute was deemed necessary for conferring a right on the parent even to this extent. Those countries in which the father has a general power to dispose of his children, have always been considered barbarous. Our own law never has allowed the exercise of such power except for some specific and temporary purpose, such as apprenticeship during the father's life, or guardianship after his death. But was it ever heard that during this lifetime, he could bind out his child to his own wife, even as an apprentice? The case of the M'Dowles was of persons competent to contract. The disability of husband and wife was not in question. In the language of Lord Kenyon, applied by Chancellor Walworth to the agreement in question, I ask "how can it be in the power of any persons by their private agreement to alter the character and condition which by law results from the state of marriage while it subsists?"

 The rights of the relator being clearly unimpaired by the alleged bargain between him and his wife, the case is, on its merits, brought down to the single point on which it was considered before the chancellor, *viz.* whether, assuming that the wife resolves to continue in her state of separation, a due regard to the welfare of the child will warrant an order for its delivery to the relator; or whether we shall allow her and her father longer to oppose the supposed necessities of nurture to the demands of law. I say, demands of law, because the defendant's case was presented to the chancellor in its strongest possible aspect; and no doubt was entertained by him of the relator's right in legal strictness. This was in the summer of 1839, and could not have been long after the child was weaned. The chancellor then said, if delivered to its father, he had no apprehension it would be treated with unkindness, adding, "I have no doubt that his elder daughters, to whose good characters and amiable dispositions Mrs. Barry herself bears full and ample testimony, would endeavor faithfully to discharge the duties of a mother to their infant sister, as far as they were able to do so, as they have already done to the brother." After considerable hesitation, he refused an order in favor of the relator, on the sole ground of the child's then tender age. The case was again investigated before Judge Inglis, before this court, the court of errors, and finally on a *habeas corpus* issued in October, 1840, returnable before Mr. Justice Oakley. It is now three years since it was examined by the chancellor, and more than a year and a half since the suit was commenced before Mr. Justice Oakley. The case has at no stage appeared to be any stronger against the relator than it was when before the chancellor; and the inquiry seems to come with scarcely a plausible answer—why should his child be longer withheld? It is at present nearly five years old. The father's claim, if not stronger, is at least more apparent, for it is by no means unimportant that he has a right to train up this child as he has his other daughters, with dispositions to serve him affectionately in the business of his household, should its health become sufficiently stable. This may indeed be essential to the child's welfare, and, I am strongly inclined to believe, will be better attended to by the relator than by the wife. It is equally his right and his duty to see that the child shall also be properly educated in other respects.

The general allegation that a daughter may be well in the hands of a mother who chooses to leave her husband, would, if allowed, work an entire subversion of his right. When we are told in Mr. Mercein's return, that this child is still in such delicate health as to require a mother's care, the first answer which strikes the mind is the generality and unsatisfactory nature of the allegation—an allegation by which, if allowed, the relator may still be baffled till his child is twenty-one. Let it be taken, however, that evidence of a propensity on his part wilfully to withdraw his child beyond the reach of maternal care should form a ground for our refusing to interfere in his favor: the attempt to make out such a case is a very extraordinary one. We have seen this man for years soliciting the woman to go with the child, and aid him in its nurture. Barring some matrimonial bickering, the state of his affections was not at all impeached before the chancellor; and there is now nothing left to impugn the sincerity of his attachment both to the mother and child. He has manifested an anxiety which nothing could repress, that they should both come to the home he has prepared and the table he has spread for them; or, if his wife's better feelings should revive and she were to follow after him and his child, he would no doubt joyfully receive her at any time, and strive to forget that she had ever left him. The argument has been urged as if there were, in the abstract, such an unfitness in a woman returning to the bed and board of her husband as can not be endured consistently with a proper sense of duty. I have listened in vain for a single lisp, even in argument, that there would be more danger in this woman returning to the relator than in the return of any wife to any husband in christendom. From all we can collect, I am inclined to think she would stand in as little danger from his temper as from his morals. That the former has been well balanced and regulated in his intercourse with society at large, it is not necessary either to affirm or deny. Its general amenity in his family was expressly conceded by Chancellor Walworth, after a severe scrutiny. Before us there has been no attempt to impeach it.

The chancellor was also of opinion that, as between him and his wife, nothing had occurred which was legally sufficient to authorize a decree of separation; and the promise of the relator during courtship, that she should continue near her parents, is not now interposed as a reason for her voluntary separation. To everything else that was attempted in proof before the chancellor, we may well apply the remarks of Sr. William Scott, in *Evans* v. *Evans,* "Mere turbulence of temper, petulance of manners, infirmity of mind, are not to be numbered among the causes" of voluntary separation. No corporal violence or menace of corporal violence has at any stage of the controversy . . . been pretended; and looking at some disclosures in the course of it—the pecuniary embarrassment of the relator, the cause of that embarrassment, the manner in which it was met by the wife, and the irritating disputes which ensued concerning the rights and duties of the parties—it is rather a matter of surprise that we have not witnessed much greater displays of ill temper on his side than have as yet been charged. His affections have been unwarrantably trifled with; and it is by no means the least evidence in his favor that during the course of a tedious litigation he has been the more unwavering in his suit, from entertaining the hope that success would be tributary to a restoration of his conjugal rights. That he was habitually unfeeling or even rude in language towards his wife during the time when they cohabited together, is now scarcely pretended. The utmost that can be imputed are occasional ebullitions of anger and vexation, arising from momentary excitement operating upon a temper naturally hasty, but by no means unrelenting. The children of his first marriage are intelligent and amiable, and have uniformly demeaned themselves towards Mrs. Barry with great attention and respect.

I entertain no fears, therefore, on what has seemed to me the whole stress of the argument upon the merits against the relator—the alternative between Mrs. Barry's returning to her husband, and abandoning the care of her child. I see nothing to furnish either a legal or moral excuse on her part for hesitating upon such an alternative.

Clearly, however, it should be enough for this part of the argument that the conduct of the relator has been such as to leave her without excuse. If she still continue in a state of separation, the consideration of a few facts will be sufficient to remove all objection against the child being restored to the husband; indeed, dispel all fear of its welfare in his hands. That he now commands a comfortable home with adequate means for supporting the child, is no longer denied. He is at the head of an interesting family, mostly I believe daughters, who have been bred under his care in the best manner; some of them from childhood to age. That he is qualified, and eminently so, for the moral and mental instruction of this child is clear. That in his family the child can and will derive, from his daughters and other means, care and attention fully proportioned to its physical wants, we have reason to be confident. Besides, the next oldest child of the marriage with Mrs. Barry has, with her consent and that of her relatives, been left in the exclusive charge of the relator, from an age still younger than that of the child whose custody she claims to withhold. The condition of the older child has been open to enquiry, and yet we hear not a pretence that its custody could have been more properly bestowed. In short, we know that the relator ranks well as a man of intellect and education. We have evidence that, though not affluent, he is yet a man of business and enterprise, in the prime of life and health, of sound morals and estimable character, with a comfortable home and every means and disposition to take proper care of the child whose custody he sues for. . . .

On the right of the matter now before us, there never has been even an issue. That the relator is the husband and father was never denied. The only issue was, on the expediency of leaving the child for nurture with a mother who had withdrawn from her husband and bade him defiance. Whether the same morbid excuse for desertion may continue, it is not necessary to enquire; but only whether the wrong should, under new circumstances, be allowed longer to suspend the assertion of right. The claim of the husband has throughout been allowed to be paramount by everybody except the wife. It has not been denied that he is the legal head of the whole family, wife and children inclusive; and I have heard it urged from no quarter that he should be brought under subjection to a household democracy. All will agree that such a measure would extend the right of suffrage quite too far. Yet I do not see how this defense can be sustained unless we are prepared to go that length. Marriage is indeed regarded by our law as a mere civil contract; but not such an one as is capable of repudiation by a majority of the family, or even the assent of the whole. [Barring] some slight amelioration, its obligations should be maintained in all their ancient rigor. There is scarcely a doubt that matrimony in the severe form of monogamy, with the prerogatives of the husband as they are announced by the common law, are no less according to the order of nature and providence than of positive institution.

Where the child is of such tender years as to be incapable of election, it should be delivered to the father on his attending to receive it. That is this case.

NELSON, *Ch. J. dissenting:* It is quite certain that the facts and circumstances which appeared before Judge Oakley, and which were by him held insufficient to entitle the relator to the custody of his child, should be so regarded by us also, that decision, while unreversed, being conclusive upon the parties and subject matter. I am of opinion that the case has not been materially varied on the present occasion. The circumstance of a year and a half having been added to the age of the child since the former hearing, seems to me too unimportant to afford ground for changing the legal judgment of a court. It appears affirmatively, moreover, that the personal care and nurture of the mother were as necessary to the well being of the child at the period of the former hearing as they are now. The subject matter therefore remains essentially the same, and if so, the same result should follow. My brethren, however, have arrived at a different conclusion, and an order must therefore be entered that the child be delivered to the relator.

[95]
McKim *v.* McKim *(Rhode Island, 1879)*

November 1, 1879, DURFEE C. J. In this case a writ of *habeas corpus* issued at the request of Charles F. McKim to his wife, Anne B. McKim, for the production of their infant daughter. The child was produced in obedience to the writ. She was four years old in August last and is in appearance delicate and frail. The physician who attended her for two years testifies that she is afflicted with a bronchial affection, and with another trouble which impairs her health; that she is better now than formerly, but is still delicate, requiring constant watchfulness and care by some person who is familiar with her character and constitution, and that, in his opinion, she would suffer if taken from her mother, who is devoted in attention to her. Charles F. McKim, the father, lives in New York, where he pursues the profession of an architect. Anne B. McKim, the mother, lives with her parents in Newport, having left the house of her husband in the spring of 1877. The child has always been with the mother. The object of the proceeding is to have her transferred to the custody of the father.

Charles F. McKim, according to the testimony of men who know him well, is a gentleman of excellent character. He married his wife in October, 1874. She lived with him in New York until May, 1875. She then lived with him in Newport, until January, 1876. . . . In January, 1876, they returned to New York, where they resided in a house which was provided and partly furnished for them by Mrs. McKim's father, until May, 1877. Since then she has lived apart from him, and, for the most part, in her father's house at Newport. The petitioner represents that their married life was perfectly happy until after the birth of their child, when one Rose Wagner came to live with them as nurse and friend of Mrs. McKim, and too completely monopolized her. He attributes to her presence and influence the estrangement which has led to their separation.

Mrs. McKim denies that the estrangement is attributable to Rose Wagner; and we think the charge that is attributable to her has not been sustained. Mrs. McKim attributes it to her husband's character and conduct. She accuses him of harshness, untruthfulness, and a low standard of moral sentiment. Her charges, however, except in a single instance, are vague and indefinite, though she intimates that he has been guilty of misconduct, as yet undisclosed, by which he has forfeited her respect, and which renders it impossible for her to live with him again as his wife. No testimony has been submitted to show any misconduct on his part which *legally* justifies her desertion of him.

We think the petitioner is morally fit to have the custody of his child and that he is entirely competent to provide for her education and physical wants. But, on the other hand, the child will doubtless enjoy equally good advantages where she now is, in the house of her maternal grandfather, who is a man of means, and she will have, in addition to them, the affectionate care of a mother who, whatever her idiosyncrasies, is evidently a lady of superior moral and mental endowments; whereas with her father she will probably have to be confided to a hired nurse or servant. The welfare of the child, considering her tender age, her sex, and the delicacy of her constitution, will in our opinion be best subserved by leaving her for the present with her mother. Indeed we think that, for the present, to take her from her mother is too hazardous an experiment for us to try, unless the law, in deference to the superior right of the father, requires it of us. The question is, then, does the law require it?

The law as laid down in England in *Rex* v. *Greenhill,* decided in 1836, favored the father at the expense of the mother to such an extent that it shocked the moral sentiment of the nation and led to a modification by act of Parliment. The doctrine of *Rex* v. *Greenhill,* however, was a relapse from the more reasonable doctrine of earlier cases. In *Rex* v. *Delaval,* decided in 1763, and again in *Blissett's case,* a few years later, Lord Mansfield, while recognizing the preferable right of the father, held that the court had a discretion for the good of the child, to decide each particular case according to its circumstances.

In this country the earlier English doctrine has generally been adopted. In the *Commonwealth* v. *Briggs,* Chief Justice Shaw said that "in the case of a child of tender years, the good of the child is to be regarded as the prominent consideration." It is true that in that case the court decided that the father was entitled to the custody of his child; but the child, though he was only between three and four years old, was a boy, and it does not appear that his health was such as to demand a mother's anxious care. There are American cases—several of them—in which the mother was allowed to retain the custody, solely because of the sex and tender years, or of the tender years, without regard to sex, of the child. In *Ex parte Shumpart,* the child was a girl between four and five years old, and the court refused to take her from her mother and deliver her to the father. In *The Commonwealth* v. *Addicks,* there were two female children aged respectively seven and ten, and the court at first refused to transfer them from the mother to the father; though the transfer was made three years later upon a second application. In *The State* v. *Paine,* there were three children, a girl aged five, and two boys, aged seven and three. The court transferred the eldest boy to the father, but left the girl and the youngest boy with the mother, solely on the ground that they were of too tender an age to be removed from the protecting care of the mother. In *The State* v. *King,* the child, a girl two and a half years old, was transferred from father to mother, because at her tender age she needed a mother's care. In *The People* v. *Mercein,* there were several efforts by writ of *habeas corpus* to obtain for a father from the mother the custody of their infant daughter, all which were unavailing. On the authority of these cases we think there can be no doubt that it is the well-being of the child, rather than the right of either parent, which ought to control the court in its decision, and that, even where the father is of good character and the mother not free from fault, it may yet be the duty of the court, out of regard for the tender age, the sex, or the delicate constitution of the child, to leave the child in the wakeful custody of the mother.

The petitioner presses on our consideration the remark of Chief Justice Shaw in *Commonwealth* v. *Briggs,* that "the unauthorized separation of the wife from the husband without any apparent *justifiable* cause, is a strong reason why the child should not be restored to her." We are sensible of the weight of this remark: and if the child here, instead of being a girl, were a boy of somewhat riper age, in good health, we might deem it our duty under the law to restore him to his father, even at the risk of tearing the mother's heartstrings asunder. We are led in this case to leave the child with the mother, not for the mother's sake, but for the good of the child.

The petitioner argues that it will be no detriment to the child to allow him to carry her with him to New York, because the mother will follow. Perhaps she will, but we cannot be sure of it. As we have said, the evidence before me does not show any legal cause of separation. But the evidence does show a strong repugnance on the part of the wife to a renewal of her marital relations, and does also show that the last year she lived with her husband her health mysteriously gave way as if it were sapped by secret troubles. Now, in view of this evidence we see no reason to believe that the mother, even if she should follow her child, would consent to live with her husband again as his wife, and we very much doubt the wisdom of coercing her to live with him in any other manner. A home so constituted could hardly be a happy home, even for a child.

Our decision is that for the present at least the child be allowed to remain with the mother. We wish to add, however, a single monitory remark. The mother should remember that this decision is not necessarily definitive, and that while the custody of the child is confided to her, the father's right has not been forfeited. It will be her duty to respect his right and to allow him every proper opportunity to cultivate the affection of the child. Especially will it be her duty to refrain from any attempt to alienate the child from the father, or to instil into her mind any thought or feeling which a daughter ought not to cherish for her father. A failure to observe this monition may be good ground for another application on the part of the petitioner for the custody of his child. But we are confident that the respondent, knowing the wishes of the court, will conform to them.

Let an order be entered recommitting the child to the mother.

[96]
California Law on Guardianship (1870)

GUARDIANS BY THE STATUTE

6. *Of this State.*—Under the statute of this State the power to appoint guardians is vested, first, in the father; second in the mother; and third in the Probate Court.

7. Under the statute of this State, a testamentary guardian has only the powers of a probate guardian, and cannot therefore take the personal custody of the ward so long as there is a mother who is competent, willing and worthy to have the custody and tuition of her child.

PERSONAL CUSTODY OF CHILDREN

8. *Rights and Powers of Father and Mother in regard to.*—If the father dies, having appointed a guardian for his children by his last will and testament, but leaving a

From *Chicago Legal News,* April 16, 1870.

widow who is a qualified and fit person to have the personal custody of her children, such widow is entitled, if she so desires, to the personal care and custody of the children. In such case the power of the testamentary guardian only extends to such special directions as the father may have given in his will with reference to the education and settlement of his children, and the care and management of their property, and does not include the personal custody of the children, if objection thereto be made by the mother.

EQUALITY AS THE BEST FORM OF PROTECTION

The Political Strategy for Suffrage

[97]

Address by Elizabeth Cady Stanton to the State Legislature (New York, 1854)

. . . . Yes, gentlemen, in republican America, in the nineteenth century, we, the daughters of the revolutionary heroes of '76, demand at your hands the redress of our grievances—a revision of your State Constitution—a new code of laws. Permit us then, as briefly as possible, to call your attention to the legal disabilities under which we labor.

1st. Look at the position of woman as woman. It is not enough for us that by your laws we are permitted to live and breathe, to claim the necessaries of life from our legal protectors—to pay the penalty of our crimes; we demand the full recognition of all our rights as citizens of the Empire State. We are persons; native, free-born citizens; property-holders, tax-payers; yet are we denied the exercise of our right to the elective franchise. We support ourselves, and, in part, your schools, colleges, churches, your poor-houses, jails, prisons, the army, the navy, the whole machinery of government, and yet we have no voice in your councils. We have every qualification required by the Constitution, necessary to the legal voter, but the one of sex. . . .

Again we demand in criminal cases that most sacred of all rights, trial by a jury of our own peers. The establishment of trial by jury is of so early a date that its beginning is lost in antiquity; but the right of trial by a jury of one's own peers is a great progressive step of advanced civilization. No rank of men have ever been

Cited in Miriam Schneir, ed., *Feminism: The Essential Historical Writings* (New York: Vintage Books, 1972), pp. 111–16. Courtesy Random House, Inc.

After the Civil War, the leaders of the women's rights movement concluded that radical change in the conditions of women's lives could be achieved only through direct participation in public decision making. *Harper's Bazar* (sic), June 12, 1869.

satisfied with being tried by jurors higher or lower in the civil or political scale than themselves; for jealousy on the one hand, and contempt on the other, has ever effectually blinded the eyes of justice. Hence, all along the pages of history, we find the king, the noble, the peasant, the cardinal, the priest, the layman, each in turn protesting against the authority of the tribunal before which they were summoned to appear. . . . And shall woman here consent to be tried by her liege lord, who has dubbed himself law-maker, judge, juror, and sheriff too?—whose power, though sanctioned by Church and State, has no foundation in justice and equity, and is a bold assumption of our inalienable rights. . . . It is not to be denied that the interests of man and woman in the present undeveloped state of the race, and under the existing social arrangements, are and must be antagonistic. The nobleman can not make just laws for the peasant; the slaveholder for the slave; neither can man make and execute just laws for woman, because in each case, the one in power fails to apply the immutable principles of right to any grade but his own. . . . Listen to our just demands and make such a change in your laws as will secure to every woman tried in your courts, an impartial jury. At this moment among the hundreds of women who are shut up in prisons in this State, not one has enjoyed that most sacred of all rights—that right which you would die to defend for yourselves—trial by a jury of one's peers.

2d. Look at the position of woman as wife. Your laws relating to marriage—founded as they are on the old common law of England, a compound of barbarous usages, but partially modified by progressive civilization—are in open violation of our enlightened ideas of justice, and of the holiest feelings of our nature. . . .

It is impossible to make the Southern planter believe that his slave feels and reasons just as he does—that injustice and subjection are as galling as to him—that the degradation of living by the will of another, the mere dependence on his caprice, at the mercy of his passions, is as keenly felt by him as his master. . . .

If you, too, are thus deluded, what avails it that we show by your statute books that your laws are unjust—that woman is the victim of avarice and power? What avails it that we point out the wrongs of woman in social life; the victim of passion and lust? You scorn the thought that she has any natural love of freedom burning in her breast, any clear perception of justice urging her on to demand her rights.

Would to God you could know the burning indignation that fills woman's soul when she turns over the pages of your statute books, and sees there how like feudal barons you freemen hold your women. Would that you could know the humiliation she feels for [her] sex, when she thinks of all the beardless boys in your law offices, learning these ideas of one-sided justice—taking their first lessons in contempt for womankind—being indoctrinated into the incapacities of their mothers, and the lordly, absolute rights of man over all women, children, and property, and to know that these are to be our future presidents, judges, husbands, and fathers. . . .

In conclusion, then, let us say, in behalf of the women of this State, we ask for all that you have asked for yourselves in the progress of your development, since the *Mayflower* cast anchor beside Plymouth rock; and simply on the ground that the rights of every human being are the same and identical. You may say that the mass of the women of this State do not make the demand; it comes from a few sour, disappointed old maids and childless women.

You are mistaken; the mass speak through us . . . the laboring women who are loudly demanding remuneration for their unending toil; those women who teach in our seminaries, academies, and public schools for a miserable pittance; the widows who are taxed without mercy; the unfortunate ones in our work-houses, poor-houses, and prisons. . . .

[98]
Sojourner Truth: "Keeping the Thing Going while Things Are Stirring" (1867)

. . . . There is a great stir about colored men getting their rights, but not a word about the colored women; and if colored men get their rights, and not colored women theirs, you see the colored men will be masters over the women, and it will be just as bad as it was before. So I am for keeping the thing going while things are stirring; because if we wait till it is still, it will take a great while to get it going again. White women are a great deal smarter, and know more than colored women, while colored women do not know scarcely anything. They go out washing, which is about as high as a colored woman gets, and their men go about idle strutting up and down; and when the women come home, they ask for their money and take it all, and then scold because there is no food. I want you to consider on that, chil'n. I call you chil'n; you are somebody's chil'n, and I am old enough to be mother of all that is here. I want women to have their rights. In the courts women have no right, no voice; nobody speaks for them. I wish woman to have her voice there among the pettifoggers. If it is not a fit place for women, it is unfit for men to be there.

I am above eighty years old; it is about time for me to be going. I have been forty years a slave and forty years free, and would be here forty years more to have equal rights for all. . . . I have done a great deal of work; as much as a man, but did not get so much pay. I used to work in the field and bind grain, keeping with the cradler; but men doing no more, got twice as much pay. . . . We do as much, we eat as much, we want as much. . . . I suppose I am about the only colored woman that goes about to speak for the rights of the colored women. I want to keep the thing stirring, now that the ice is cracked.

From Elizabeth Cady Stanton et al., *History of Woman Suffrage* (New York, 1881), vol. 2, pp. 193–94.

Sojourner Truth (c. 1797–1873) was a slave in New York state until 1827. Religious mysticism turned her into a reformer. She traveled around the country speaking out on abolition and women's rights. Photograph courtesy the Sophia Smith Collection, Smith College, Northampton, Massachusetts.

[99]
Frances E. Willard: The Home Protection Manual (1879)

In many towns the municipal authorities could, if they would, adopt a special ordinance, by which women might vote on the question of license. A petititon asking for this should be thoroughly circulated, every person of legal age being given the opportunity to sign, and should be presented to the council by a strong delegation, after having first been read and expounded at a great public meeting of the people.

. . . If they will not grant this, do not say, in dolorous accents, "It was of no use, and we'll not try again"; but faithfully use your two best weapons, the printed and spoken word seasoned with prayer. Throng the primaries where the fathers are again chosen; work up the sentiment; toil on the election day; and place men in their stead who will grant what your petition asked. Or, if not successful the first year, try again the second. With the motto "The W.C.T.U. never surrenders," success is sure.

From Francis E. Willard, *Home Protection Manual, A Guide for Local and State Women's Christian Temperance Union Chapters on Political Work,* in Ann Chapman, ed., *Approaches to Women's History* (Washington D.C.: American Historical Association, 1979), p. 64.

The Male Response to Female Suffrage

[100]
"The Woman's Rights Convention— The Last Act of the Drama" (New York Herald, *September 12, 1852*)

The farce at Syracuse has been played out. . . .

Who are these women? What do they want? What are the motives that impel them to this course of action? The *dramatis personae* of the farce enacted at Syracuse present a curious conglomeration of both sexes. Some of them are old maids, whose personal charms were never very attractive, and who have been sadly slighted by the masculine gender in general; some of them women who have been badly mated,

From Elizabeth Cady Stanton et al., *History of Woman Suffrage* (New York, 1981), vol. 1, pp. 853–54.

Frances Willard (1839–
1898), president of the
Women's Christian Tem-
perance Union, 1879–1898.
Frances Willard and Mary
A. Livermore, eds., *A
Woman of the Century*
(1893).

whose own temper, or their husbands', has made life anything but agreeable to
them, and they are therefore down upon the whole of the opposite sex; some, having
so much of the virago in their disposition, that nature appears to have made a
mistake in their gender—mannish women, like hens that crow; some of boundless
vanity and egotism, who believe that they are superior in intellectual ability to "all
the world and the rest of mankind," and delight to see their speeches and address in
print; and man shall be consigned to his proper sphere—nursing the babies, washing
the dishes, mending stockings, and sweeping the house. This is "the good time
coming." . . . Of the male sex who attend these conventions for the purpose of
taking part in them, the majority are hen-pecked husbands, and all of them ought to
wear petticoats. . . .

The World without Suffrage

Queen of the Family: The Most Important Office in the World

Looking into the Future: The World with Suffrage

The Wife and Mother at a Primary

The Father Stays at Home,
Attending to the Children

The Supreme Court as Re-Organized

Illustrations from L. P. Brockett, M.D., *Woman: Her Rights, Wrongs, Privileges, and Responsibilities* (1869).

How did woman first become subject to man as she now is all over the world? By her nature, her sex, just as the Negro is and always will be, to the end of time, inferior to the white race and therefore doomed to subjection; but happier than she would be in any other condition, just because it is the law of her nature. The women themselves would not have this law reversed. . . .

[101]
Orestes A. Brownson on "The Woman Question" (1869)

The conclusive objection to the political enfranchisement of women is, that it would weaken and finally break up and destroy the Christian family. The social unit is the family, not the individual; and the greatest danger to American society is that we are rapidly becoming a nation of isolated individuals, without famly ties or affections. . . .

Extend now to women suffrage and eligibility; give them the political right to vote and to be voted for; render it feasible for them to enter the arena of political strife, to become canvassers in elections and candidates for office, and what remains of family union will soon be dissolved. The wife may espouse one political party, and the husband another, and it may well happen that the husband and wife may be rival candidates for the same office, and one or the other doomed to the mortification of defeat. Will the husband like to see his wife enter the lists against him, and triumph over him? Will the wife, fired with political ambition for place or power, be pleased to see her own husband enter the lists against her, and succeed at her expense? Will political rivalry and the passions it never fails to engender increase the mutual affection of husband and wife for each other, and promote domestic union and peace, or will it not carry into the bosom of the family all the strife, discord, anger, and division of the political canvass? . . .

From *Catholic World*, May 1869. Cited in Aileen S. Kraditor, ed., *Up from the Pedestal: Selected Writings in the History of American Feminism* (New York: Quadrangle/New York Times Books, 1968), pp. 192–93. Reprinted by permission of *Times* Books, a division of Quadrangle/The New York Times Book Co., Inc. © 1968 by Aileen S. Kraditor.

The Litigation Strategy for Suffrage (1869–1875)

[102]
United States of America *v.* Susan B. Anthony
(1873)

Judge Hunt: (Ordering the defendant to stand up) Has the prisoner anything to say why sentence shall not be pronounced?

Miss Anthony: Yes, your honor, I have many things to say; for in your ordered verdict of guilty, you have trampled under foot every vital principle of our government. My natural rights, my civil rights, my political rights, my judicial rights, are all alike ignored. Robbed of the fundamental privilege of citizenship, I am degraded from the status of a citizen to that of a subject; and not only myself individually, but all of my sex, are, by your honor's verdict, doomed to political subjection under this, so-called, form of government.

Judge Hunt: The Court cannot listen to a rehearsal of arguments the prisoner's counsel has already consumed three hours in presenting.

Miss Anthony: May it please your honor, I am not arguing the question, but simply stating the reasons why sentence cannot, in justice, be pronounced against me. Your denial of my citizen's right to vote is the denial of my right of consent as one of the governed, the denial of my right of representation as one of the taxed, the denial of my right to a trial by a jury of my peers as an offender against law, therefore, the denial of my sacred rights to life, liberty, property and—

Judge Hunt: The Court cannot allow the prisoner to go on.

Miss Anthony: But your honor will not deny me this one and only poor privilege of protest against this high-handed outrage upon my citizen's rights. May it please the Court to remember that since the day of my arrest last November, this is the first time that either myself or any person of my disfranchised class has been allowed a word of defense before judge or jury—

Judge Hunt: The prisoner must sit down—the Court cannot allow it.

Miss Anthony: All of my prosecutors, from the 8th ward corner grocery politician, who entered the complaint, to the United States Marshal, Commissioner, District Attorney, District Judge, your honor on the bench, not one is my peer, but each and all are my political sovereigns; and had your honor submitted my case to the jury, as was clearly your duty, even then I should have had just cause of protest, for not one of those men was my peer; but, native or foreign born, white or black,

24 F. Cas. 829 (N.D.N.Y.) 1873, in Barbara A. Babcock, Ann E. Freedman, Eleanor Holmes Norton, and Susan Ross, eds., *Sex Discrimination and the Law: Causes and Remedies* (Boston: Little Brown, 1973), p. 9–10.

rich or poor, educated or ignorant, awake or asleep, sober or drunk, each and every man of them was my political superior; hence, in no sense, my peer. Even, under such circumstances, a commoner of England, tried before a jury of Lords, would have far less cause to complain than should I, a woman, tried before a jury of men. Even my counsel, the Hon. Henry R. Selden, who has argued my cause so ably, so earnestly, so unanswerably before your honor, is my political sovereign. Precisely as no disfranchised person is entitled to sit upon a jury, and no woman is entitled to the franchise, so, none but but a regularly admitted lawyer is allowed to practice in the courts and no woman can gain admission to the bar—hence, jury, judge, counsel, must all be of the superior class.

Judge Hunt: The Court must insist—the prisoner has been tried according to the established forms of law.

Miss Anthony: Yes, your honor, but by forms of law all made by men, interpreted by men, administered by men, in favor of men, and against women; and hence, your honor's ordered verdict of guilty, against a United States citizen for the exercise of *"that citizen's right to vote,"* simply because that citizen was a woman and not a man. But yesterday, the same man-made forms of law declared it a crime punishable with a $1,000 fine and six months' imprisonment, for you and me, or any of us, to give a cup of cold water, a crust of bread, or a night's shelter to a panting fugitive as he was tracking his way to Canada. And every man or woman in whose veins coursed a drop of human sympathy violated that wicked law, reckless of consequences, and was justified in so doing. As then, the slaves who got their freedom must take it over, or under, or through the unjust forms of law, precisely so, now, must women, to get their right to a voice in this government, take it; and I have taken mine, and mean to take it at every possible opportunity.

Judge Hunt: The Court orders the prisoner to sit down. It will not allow another word.

Miss Anthony: When I was brought before your honor for trial, I hoped for a broad and liberal interpretation of the Constitution and its recent amendments, that should declare all United States citizens under its protecting aegis—that should declare equality of rights the national guarantee to all persons born or naturalized in the United States. But failing to get this justice—failing even to get a trial by a jury not of my peers—I ask not leniency at your hands but rather the full rigors of the law.

Judge Hunt: The Court must insist (here the prisoner sat down).

Judge Hunt: The prisoner will stand up (here Miss Anthony arose again). The sentence of the Court is that you pay a fine of one thousand dollars and the costs of the prosecution.

Miss Anthony: May it please your honor, I shall never pay a dollar of your unjust penalty. All the stock in trade I possess is a $10,000 debt, incurred by publishing my paper—The Revolution—four years ago, the sole object of which was to educate all women to do precisely as I have done: rebel against your man-made, unjust, unconstitutional forms of law, that tax, fine, imprison, and hang women, while they deny them the right of representation in the government; and I shall work on with might and main to pay every dollar of that honest debt, but not a penny shall go to this unjust claim. And I shall earnestly and persistently continue to urge all women to the practical recognition of the old revolutionary maxim, that "Resistance to tyranny is obedience to God."

Judge Hunt: Madam, the Court will not order you committed until the fine is paid.

[103]
Minor *v.* Happersett, *U.S. Supreme Court (1875)*

Mr. Chief Justice WAITE delivered the opinion of the Court:

This was an action brought in the Circuit Court of St. Louis County, Missouri, by the plaintiffs in error, against the defendant, a registering officer, for refusing to register Virginia L. Minor as a lawful voter. . . .

It is admitted by the pleadings that the defendant refused to register the plaintiff, solely for the reason that she is a female; and that she possesses the qualifications of an elector in all respects, except as to the matter of sex as before stated. . . .

. . . The direct question is, therefore, presented whether all citizens are necessarily voters.

The Constitution does not define the privileges and immunities of citizens. For that definition we must look elsewhere. In this case we need not determine what they are, but only whether suffrage is necessarily one of them. . . .

The amendment did not add to the privileges and immunities of a citizen. It simply furnished an additional guaranty for the protection of such as he already had. No new voters were necessarily made by it. . . .

In this condition of the law in respect to suffrage in the several States it cannot for a moment be doubted that if it had been intended to make all citizens of the United States voters, the framers of the Constitution would not have left it to implication. So important a change in the condition of citizenship as it actually existed, if intended, would have been expressly declared. . . .

And still again, after the adoption of the fourteenth amendment, it was deemed necessary to adopt a fifteenth, as follows: "The right of citizens of the United States to vote shall not be denied or abridged by the United States, or by any State, on account of race, color, or previous condition of servitude." The fourteenth amendment had already provided that no State should make or enforce any law which should abridge the privileges or immunities of citizens of the United States. If

88 U.S. 162 (1875).

suffrage was one of these privileges or immunities, why amend the Constitution to prevent its being denied on account of race, etc.? . . .

If suffrage was intended to be included within [the obligations of the amendment which declares that no person shall be deprived of life, liberty, or property without due process of law], language better adapted to express that intent would most certainly have been employed. The right of suffrage, when granted, will be protected. He who has it can only be deprived of it by due process of law, but in order to claim protection he must first show that he has the right.

But we have already sufficiently considered the proof found upon the inside of the Constitution. That upon the outside is equally effective.

The Constitution was submitted to the States for adoption in 1787, and was ratified by nine States in 1788, and finally by the thirteen original States in 1790. Vermont was the first new State admitted to the Union, and it came in under a constitution which conferred the right of suffrage only upon men of the full age of twenty-one years, having resided in the State for the space of one whole year next before the election, and who were of quiet and peaceable behavior. This was in 1791. The next year, 1792, Kentucky followed with a constitution confining the right of suffrage to free male citizens of the age of twenty-one years who had resided in the State two years or in the county in which they offered to vote one year next before the election. Then followed Tennessee, in 1796, with voters of freemen of the age of twenty-one years and upwards, possessing a freehold in the county wherein they may vote, and being inhabitants of the State or freemen being inhabitants of any one county in the State six months immediately preceding the day of election. But we need not particularize further. No new State has ever been admitted to the Union which has conferred the right of suffrage upon women, and this has never been considered a valid objection to her admission. On the contrary, as is claimed in the argument, the right of suffrage was withdrawn from women as early as 1807 in the State of New Jersey, without any attempt to obtain the interference of the United States to prevent it. Since then the governments of the insurgent States have been reorganized under a requirement that before their representatives could be admitted to seats in Congress they must have adopted new constitutions, republican in form. In no one of these constitutions was suffrage conferred upon women, and yet the States have all been restored to their original position as States in the Union. . . .

Certainly, if the courts can consider any question settled, this is one. For nearly ninety years the people have acted upon the idea that the Constitution, when it conferred citizenship, did not necessarily confer the right of suffrage. If uniform practice long continued can settle the construction of so important an instrument as the Constitution of the United States confessedly is, most certainly it has been done here. Our province is to decide what the law is, not to declare what it should be.

We have given this case the careful consideration its importance demands. If the law is wrong, it ought to be changed; but the power for that is not with us. The arguments addressed to us bearing upon such a view of the subject may perhaps be sufficient to induce those having the power, to make the alteration, but they ought not to be permitted to influence our judgment in determining the present rights of the parties now litigating before us. No argument as to woman's need of suffrage can be considered. We can only act upon her rights as they exist.

[104]

Myra Bradwell on "An Act to Grant to the Women of Wyoming Territory the Right of Suffrage and to Hold Office"

Be it enacted by the Council and House of Representatives of Wyoming Territory:

Section 1. That every woman of the age of 21 years, residing in this Territory, may at every election to be holden under the laws thereof to cast her vote. And her rights to the elective franchise and to hold office shall be the same under the election laws of the Territory as those of electors.

Sec. 2. This Act shall take effect and be in force from and after its passage.

. . . . We congratulate this young Territory of the West upon the liberal and just spirit it has manifested in passing this law, and predict that although it is the first, it will not long be the only territory where such a law may be found. We believe that when women vote in the future elections of Wyoming, and hold office as some of them will, and it is found that the influence and power of the mass of women is exercised on the side of law, order and temperance, that other States will wish for this very influence and power, to reform many of the existing abuses in the exercise of political power. To all well-educated, ambitious females, who have no local ties to bind them, we would say, emigrate to Wyoming, but engage in no business unless you understand it thoroughly, and under no circumstances take any office unless you are able to perform its duties with credit to yourself and honor to the Territory.

From *Chicago Legal News*, December 25, 1869.

Esther Morris, of South Pass, Wyoming, is credited with persuading Colonel Bright to introduce suffrage. She later became the first woman to be elected a justice of the peace. Frances Willard and Mary Livermore, eds., *A Woman of the Century* (1893).

Jury Service

[105]
Grace Raymond Hebard, "The First Woman Jury" (Wyoming Territory, 1870)

When the Grand Jury was empanelled in March, 1870, for the regular term of court of the First Judicial District of Wyoming, it brought in indictments to be tried in the first court to be held under the jurisdiction of Wyoming Territory to be presided over by Hon. John H. Howe. . . . Among other names for this Grand Jury appeared those of . . . Miss Eliza Stewart (a school teacher), Mrs. Amelia Hatcher (a widow), Mrs. G.F. Hilton (wife of a physician), Mrs. Mary Mackel (wife of one of the clerks at Fort Sanders), Mrs. Agnes Baker (wife of a merchant), and Mrs. Sarah W. Pease (wife of the Deputy Clerk of the court).

In a dignified and clear voice, for the first time in criminal court history the following words were spoken, ringing in the ears of the assembly which packed the temporary court house: "Ladies and Gentlemen of the Grand Jury." Among other things which Justice Howe told the women of the jury, was that the eyes of the world were upon them as pioneers serving in a movement that was to test the power of being able to protect and defend themselves from the evils of which women were victims. He further assured them that there was no impropriety of women serving as jurors and that he would see that they received the fullest protection of his court; that "you shall not be driven by the sneers, jeers and insults of a laughing crowd from the temple of justice, as your sisters have from some of the medical colleges of the land. The strong hand of the law shall protect you."

The first mixed grand jury was in session for three weeks, during which time bills were brought for consideration for several murder cases, cattle and horse stealing and illegal branding. . . . The women . . . were a target for the artists who, not being able to take a photograph of the women because they were heavily veiled, produced them in caricature and forwarded them to the Eastern papers. . . . Some of these caricatures represented the women holding their babies in their laps while doing jury service, and couplets of all sorts were invented, of which the following is characteristic:

> Baby, baby, don't get in a fury;
> Your mama's gone to sit on the jury.

The Grand Jury insisted that all laws should be enforced that related to the suppression of gambling, the regulation of saloons and the observance of Sunday. So persis-

Journal of American History 7 (1913), pp. 1302–4, 1313, 1325.

Wyoming's experiment with female jurists made news across the country and inspired sketches such as this one. Dee Brown, *The Gentle Tamers: Women of the Old West* (Lincoln: University of Nebraska Press, 1958).

tent were they in the rigid enforcement of these special laws that the next legislature, with zeal worthy of a better cause, lost no time in repealing the law (i.e., Sunday closing of saloons). . . .

There were three terms of court at which women served as jurors. . . . Being in poor health, Justice Howe resigned from the bench, presiding for the last time in court September 20, 1871. A Judge from the South was appointed to take his place as Chief Justice. The new Judge was opposed to woman suffrage and prohibited the selection of women as jurors, Associate Justice W. S. Jones concurring with him. Another factor contributing to the discontinuing of women doing jury service was the fact that in an important murder trial in Cheyenne two women served on a jury, one of whom, the wife of the first mayor of that city, was taken seriously ill during the long drawn out and tedious case, necessitating the waiting of the court until such time as she was able again to sit on the case. This delay created a prejudice among some of the lawyers in regard to women juries, and they used their influence to have the court decide against further service by mixed juries. The practice of a mixed jury has never been resumed in Wyoming.

[106]
Rosencrantz *v.* Territory of Washington *(1884)*

Mollie Rosencrantz, indicted by a mixed grand jury for the crime of keeping a house of "ill-fame," moved to have the indictment set aside because the grand jury was selected in a manner not prescribed by law since it included married women. Her motion was overruled. She was then tried, found guilty, and sentenced to pay a fine of $400 and the costs of the action. She appealed on the grounds that the overruling of her objection was in error. The Code of 1881 provided that all electors and householders should be competent grand jurors. In deciding whether married women living with their husbands belonged to this class, the territorial supreme court first had to deal with the question of whether the legislature, in extending suffrage to women had also meant to make them jurors. Then it had to decide whether married women could be considered householders. The majority opinion rested on a broad construction of legislative purpose. It concluded that the Code of 1881, in prescribing the qualifications of grand jurors, had reference not only to the class of persons who at the time of its enactment possessed the qualifications, but also to all other persons who should become possessed of the qualifications. It went on to argue that the common law disabilities of a wife as a member of the family had been removed and that she now was in a position of equality with her husband. Judge Turner in his dissent relied on a narrow construction. The selection presented here focuses on his description of gender characteristics and whether the common-law relationship between husband and wife had been changed.—*Ed.*

JUDGE TURNER'S DISSENT:

. . . I do not believe that females are competent under the law, as grand or petit jurors, nor do I believe that females who are married and living with their husbands are "householders," within the meaning of. . . . 2078 of the Code which provides, "all qualified electors shall be competent to serve as petit jurors, and all qualified electors and householders shall be competent to serve as grand jurors, etc." . . . Who shall be qualified electors, and what classes of citizens shall be subject to jury duty, are entirely different questions having no proper relation to each other. . . . It is said that the rights of the weaker sex, if I may now call them so, are more regarded than in the days of Blackstone; and that the theory of that day, that women are unfitted by physical Constitution and mental characteristics to assume and perform the civil and political duties and obligations of citizenship, has been exploded by the advanced ideas of the nineteenth century. This may be true. No man honors the sex more than I. None has witnessed more cheerfully the improvement in the laws of the States, and particularly in the laws of this Territory, whereby many of the disabilities of that day are removed from them, and their just personal and property rights put upon an equal footing with those of men. I cannot say, however, that I wish to see them

2 (Wash. T.) 267 (1884).

perform the duties of jurors. The liability to perform jury duty is an obligation, not a right. In the case of woman, it is not necessary that she should accept the obligation to secure or maintain her rights. If it were, I should stifle all expression of the repugnance that I feel at seeing her introduced into associations and exposed to influences which, however others regard it, must, in my opinion, shock and blunt those fine sensibilities, the possession of which is her chiefest charm, and the protection of which, under the religion and laws of all countries, civilized or semi-civilized, is her most sacred right. . . .

. . . As to the meaning of the word "householder," in the statute. Householder means, according to all the definitions, "the head of a family." I think that in all cases where there is a husband living with his family, that he is in contemplation of law the head, and the only head, of the family. It has been said, "the term house-holder has no reference to a holding of property. It is understood to mean the head, master, or person who has the charge of, and provides for a family," etc. . . .

The husband was not only the head of the family at common law, because under that law he had the right to be obeyed by all the family, including the wife, but because of inherent and acquired differences between himself and wife, in mental and physical constitution. He was better fitted to wage the war for present subsistence, and to accumulate the competence that was to make provision against want in the future.

The experience gained by him in prosecuting this branch of the partnership matured his judgment, strengthened his will, and made him confident and self-reliant. I believe that the facts I have mentioned obtain to this day, and that they operate and will continue to operate, to give the husband paramount authority in the household, as that term is understood at common law, until an upheaval of nature has reversed the position of man and woman in the world. Legislative enactment would not make white black, nor can it provide the female form with bone and sinew equal in strength to that with which nature has provided man. No more can it reverse the law of cause and effect, and clothe a timid, shrinking woman, whose life theater is, and will continue to be, and ought to continue to be, primarily the home circle, with the masculine will and self-reliant judgment of a man.

The law has not attempted to do any such thing. . . . It cannot be truthfully said that changes in the property or civil rights of women in this Territory, such as are found in the statutes, has had or has begun to have such an effect. . . . The control of the husband over community personal property, extending to the right to dispose of such property as he pleases, without accounting to the wife, is another particular in which the legal rights of the husband are superior to those of the wife.

The right of the husband over the wife is again recognized in the provision giving him the preference right to select the homestead for the family, from the community real property.

This right of a selection of the family homestead suggests another matter in which the right of the husband is paramount. His domicile is the domicile of the wife, and she may not abandon it for one year without giving him legal ground for the divorce. The converse proposition is not true. The wife cannot say to her husband, "You must live here, if you wish to live with me"; but the husband may so say to the wife, if he offers her a home suitable to her condition. . . .

There is an exception in the law in favor of the wife from responsibility for criminal acts done in the presence of her husband, which it is believed the statutes of this Territory have not wiped out.

How can the wife be considered an entirely free agent in matters of only civil concern, and of but little moment, when it is the policy of the law to consider that she is so much under the influence of the husband, that it will not hold her responsible for crimes committed in his presence?

UNIT 3

$$\Big[\textit{Occupational Choice}\Big]$$

OPPORTUNITY AND REALITY IN URBAN AMERICA

The documents in the section on Women and Family Roles explored the question of society's preoccupation with keeping women out of public life. The documents in this section explore the question of why the power of the state was used to bar women from legal, but not mechanical, occupations.

The Factory

The cotton mills at Lowell, Massachusetts, in the 1820s and 1830s drew on rural girls and widows in the surrounding region for unskilled labor. In the selection *Yankee Girls Troop to the Mills*, Harriet Robinson describes the motivation of these girls. There was a high turnover in the female labor force, partly because of cultural sanctions against married women working. In addition, the mills provided women no opportunity to move into other skilled labor or the managerial class. When, as a result of growing competition, the pace of work was accelerated and wages fell, skilled workers such as Sarah G. Bagley organized the Lowell Female Labor Reform Association and joined union men in demanding ten-hour day legislation for factory workers. In response to petitions, the Massachusetts House of Representatives made the first governmental investigation of labor conditions. A special committee visited Lowell and other mill towns to collect information; their findings and recommendations are contained in the *Investigation of Labor*

Conditions (1845). Their reasons for rejecting maximum-hour legislation show how the Jacksonian concepts of equality and freedom of contract were used increasingly to protect employers and limit the opportunities of workers. The report lacks the usual reference to women's delicacy and makes no comment that women needed special protection. The repeated failure of movements for a ten-hour day that would cover both men and women is important for understanding why the women's movement, including trade union women in the Progressive era, turned to the ideology of womanhood to achieve maximum hours legislation.

Most working women were employed in domestic service and garment trades, performed either in their own homes or in small shops. The plight of these women, later government investigation showed, was in many ways much worse than that of factory girls. Between 1830 and 1890, women's share of the labor force increased from 7.4 percent to 17 percent. Census figures underrepresented their presence for many reasons, including the fact that one of the largest female industries was not listed in the census.[13]

Prostitution

The selections from William Sanger's *A History of Prostitution* (1858) suggest the size of this industry and the motivations of women who entered it. Sanger, a resident physician at Blackwell's Island Women's Prison in New York City, interviewed 2,000 prostitutes on what led them into the trade and collected statistics on their background. According to Table 1, which lists "The Previous Trade or Calling of Women Who Became Prostitutes," most came directly from home. Sanger's finding confirmed the views of female reformers that seduction and abandonment led single girls to ruin, while drunkenness, desertion, and a husband's adultery forced married women into the trade to support their families.

Victorians saw white women as victims of men's uncontrolled appetites, but seldom, except during slavery, showed the same concern for women of color. The exposure of a white slave trade in the early twentieth century led to the passage of the Mann Act, while the exposure of the same activity during a California Senate hearing on Chinese immigration became part of the evidence to restrict immigration. Chinese men were brought here to build the railroad, Chinese women to supply the houses of prostitution that were a central institution of the heavily male frontier cities and towns. The selections from the California Senate Committee, on the *"Social, Moral and Political Effect of Chinese Immigration"* (1876), include an example of a *Labor Contract* (1873) entered into by a Chinese immigrant to help pay her passage to this country.

ACCESS TO PRIVILEGE AND AUTHORITY
Educational Barriers

The image of republican motherhood promoted by the American revolution provided a cultural impetus for educating girls. In the early nineteenth century, the Northeast saw a proliferation of female academies designed to prepare women for their new civic role. Women hoped that teaching school would open opportunities for single women and free them from dependence on the marriage market. The expansion of public education provided jobs, but not professional opportunity. Women, paid half the rate of men, were expected to leave teaching when they married. The larger school systems replicated the patriarchal model, with male superintendents and principals preparing the curriculum for teachers to follow, and inspecting their work. Other professions, which carried a greater measure of prestige and economic return, remained closed.[14] Colleges and professional schools refused to admit women, barring the path to opportunity. Although it is true that as yet few professionals received their training in college, higher education offered the quickest route to breaking down customary distrust. In her *Speech at The National Woman's Rights Convention in Cincinnati* (1855) Lucy Stone draws on her own experience to describe the social impact of these barriers on women. Not until the 1840s were women allowed into a liberal arts program—at Oberlin College, a school founded on antislavery principles. In the Midwest and West after the Civil War, state universities needed human bodies and admitted women, but private colleges did not follow Oberlin's example, and women had to develop their own college system.[15]

Medicine became the first profession to provide women with career opportunities. Medicine offered real opportunities because many women, brought up in Victorian delicacy, shrank from being treated by male physicians. Elizabeth Blackwell (1821–1910), the first woman to be admitted to a regular medical college, decided on a medical career after many years of teaching. In 1847, the year she began knocking on the doors of medical schools, Samuel Gregory of Boston began soliciting funds for what was to become the first woman's medical school, the New England Female Medical College (1849). In 1850 the Woman's Medical College of Pennsylvania opened.

When Elizabeth Blackwell applied to medical schools, she was well prepared, having studied in the offices of a number of liberal doctors, who provided her with letters of recommendation. After the major medical schools rejected her, she turned to country schools and was accepted by Geneva Medical College in western New York. In *"The Medical Co-education of the Sexes,"* Stephen Smith, then a student at Geneva and later a nationally prominent public health physician, relates how the barrier came down and describes the impact of a woman's presence. The story is funny, but the tale of how Blackwell gained admission captures the essence of women's continuing problems. Although Elizabeth Blackwell proved to be a superior student and her presence improved the educational environment, neither Geneva nor other medical colleges admitted more women. Harvard considered admitting Harriet Hunt, a successful Boston physician, but bowed to student opposition: they claimed it would lower the value of their degrees. After the Civil War, Blackwell, who did not believe in separate education, organized a woman's medical school and hospital that had higher standards than those at the elite schools. Customarily barred from internships at regular hospitals, most women in the nineteenth century received their degrees and postgraduate training at women's medical colleges and women's hospitals. The next breakthrough came in the 1870s, when a number of medical colleges admitted women. By 1893 women comprised 12 to 18 percent of the doctors practicing in large cities.[16]

The letter from *George Palmer Putnam to Mary Corinna Putnam* (1861) illustrates the pressures arising from sex-role expectations. The cultural contradiction between the early training of women and their adult role expectations produced great resentment, but not necessarily any action. However, a special fervor by the first generation who dared not to conform smoothed the way, somewhat, for the next generation. Mary Putnam (Jacobi), the first prominent female research doctor and the first woman to be admitted to a medical association, was, like so many of her generation, reared permissively and rewarded as a child for successful competitive achievement. When she reached adolescence, however, she was expected to place family before her other interests.

By the time Mary Putnam made her decision, the previous generation of professional women had produced an alternative model, which spread with the women's movement. Those women who sought the very best educational credentials went abroad to study. Mary Putnam was the first woman admitted to the Sorbonne Medical College of the University of Paris.[17]

New Cultural Barriers

As more women sought higher education and entrance into the professions, doctors felt a professional obligation to their clients and the public to speak out on the women's issue and describe the consequences to women and society of disregarding biological differences. Science replaced religion as an explanatory model for the existing division of social responsibility and in some ways was more devastating because it linked progress and evolution to biologically determined sex roles. Carl Vogt's *Lectures on Man, His Place in*

Creation, and in the History of the Earth (1864) is an example of this literature based on studies of the difference in the brain and physiology between women and men. Evolution, in its popularized form, meant the survival of the fittest and the propagation of a superior race through selection and a knowledge of physiology.[18]

An example of the medical literature describing the physiological hazards of intense intellectual activity for adolescent girls is Dr. Edward Clarke's *Sex in Education: or, A Fair Chance for the Girls* (1873), which, through many editions, terrorized a generation of parents with girls who had professional aspirations. The good doctor gained credence for his generalizations by virtue of his professional standing and by his use of detailed case histories. Although science and medicine did not create the image of the delicate female, through their elaboration of such an image they made it difficult to formulate social and legal policy decisions on nongender-related grounds. In the late nineteenth century, judges increasingly invoked physiology along with legal principles, on behalf of decisions that preserved the status quo.

ENTERING THE LEGAL PROFESSION, 1869–1894

Why did women first seek admission to the bar in 1869 and not earlier? The answer must begin with the observation that a professional, more particularly a lawyer, was a person vested with the right to command, direct, and advise others. Before a woman could realistically entertain the idea of a legal career, women had to have the right to own and use property and had to see themselves as separate persons with interests different from those of men. The struggle for married woman's property rights had advanced this perspective. Women then had to move to the next stage, of thinking of themselves as persons exercising authority. The suffrage movement speeded this process. The right to become lawyers, officers of the court, some suffragists believed would enhance women's status and claims to the franchise.

Occupational Freedom and the State Courts

The first two women to test the possibility of being admitted to practice before the courts appeared to be concerned primarily with advancing the status of their sex. Once the idea entered the public mind, many others were inspired to become lawyers to advance women's rights and their own careers. In addition to being associated with the suffrage movement, the pioneers often had supportive families and sometimes gained training from a brother, husband, father, or family friend.

Arabella Babb Mansfield (1846–1911), who applied for admission to the bar in Iowa in 1869, had a close attachment to her brother, who was a lawyer. After graduating from Iowa Wesleyan in 1866, she taught English at Simpson College for a year and a half before returning home and marrying John Mansfield, a professor of natural history at Iowa Wesleyan. She and her husband studied law together and applied for admission to the bar together. The Iowa Court accepted her application without difficulty and she became the first woman regularly admitted to the practice of law in the United States. Without ever practicing law, however, she went for a Master of Arts degree and formed the Iowa Woman's Suffrage Association. After moving with her husband to Depauw, Iowa, she became a professor and administrator.[19]

Like Arabella Mansfield, Myra Colby Bradwell (1831–1894) was encouraged by her family and friends to pursue a career in law. Bradwell's background had given her a deep appreciation of the importance and social leverage of the legal profession. She had grown up in an abolitionist family and at eighteen had married the son of a poor farmer, who used the law as a vehicle to achieve rapid financial and political success. Bradwell studied law with her husband while bearing four children, running a private school, and doing civic work with the Sanitary Commission during and after the Civil War. In 1868 she established a weekly newspaper, *The Chicago Legal News*, and a legal publishing firm. Her journal soon became the most widely read and influential law publication in the Midwest. Any lawyer who wanted to keep abreast of the latest decisions read the paper, including Bradwell's editorials, in which she covered topics that ranged from courtroom decorum and railroad regulation to women's rights. Interested in influencing the law, but not in practicing it, Bradwell applied for a license in order to establish women's rights and open the profession for others. If anyone was the perfect candidate, she was, yet the Illinois Supreme Court rejected the application. Her case gained national attention when she took the issue to the United States Supreme Court.[20]

A comparison of the response of the Iowa, Illinois, and U.S. Supreme Courts illustrates how views about gender were related to whether the court construed its powers in a broad or a narrow way. The Iowa Court clearly had liberal views about women and wanted to establish a precedent. The committee appointed by the court to review Mansfield's qualification wrote:

> Your committee takes unusual pleasure in recommending the admission of Mrs. Mansfield, not only because she is the first lady who has applied for this authority in this state, but because, in her examination, she has given the very best rebuke possible to the imputation that ladies cannot qualify for the practice of law. And we feel confident from the intimation of the

court given on the application made, that we speak not only of the sentiments of the court, and of your committee, but the entire members of the bar, when we say that we heartily welcome Mrs. Mansfield as one of our members, and most cordially recommend her admission.[21]

The legal problem the court faced was the fact that the Iowa Statute regulating admission to the bar clearly limited this privilege to "white male citizens." The committee, however, suggested that the Iowa Construction statute, a law describing how to establish the meaning of certain legal terms, changed the language of the law on admission. Judge Springer accepted this interpretation and added that "when restrictive words of a statute treated individuals unfairly the court could construe that statute as extending to others not expressly included in it."[22]

The Illinois court took a different tack. Initially, the State Supreme Court denied Bradwell admission to the bar on the grounds that the relationship between attorney and client is contractual and she, as a married woman, was not bound by her contracts. This did not apply to Bradwell, however, who had obtained a special legislative act enabling her to make binding contracts, so that she could own and manage *The Chicago Legal News*.

When Bradwell appealed this decision she did not use her own special charter as reason to admit her to the bar because this would not have achieved her broad purpose. She argued instead that two pieces of legislation combined to give all women the right to contract: She had helped to write the Married Woman's Property Act of 1861 and the Earnings Act of 1868.

The Illinois State Supreme Court once again denied Bradwell a license (*In re Bradwell*, 1869), but this time on the grounds of sex. Justice Lawrence, who presented the court's opinion, first discussed the meaning of the married woman's property act. He stated that giving women control over their own property and earnings did not by implication "invite them to enter, equally with men, upon those fields of trade and speculation by which property is acquired through the agency of contracts."

Since the issue of whether married women could make contracts was not the basis of the court's decision this time, it did not have to state an opinion on the subject. This raises the question of whether this dictum (an unnecessary statement in passing) was the court's way of letting women know the continuing limitations on their rights.

Justice Lawrence then went on to explain the grounds for denying Bradwell, and all women, admission to the bar. The state legislature had set two limitations on the court's discretion in granting admission to the bar: (1) the court had to set terms of admission that would promote the proper administration of justice; (2) the court "should not admit any persons or class of persons who are not intended by the legislature to be admitted even though their exclusion is not expressly required by statute." It was this second limitation on the court's discretion that Justice Lawrence used as the reason to exclude women.

How did the Court know that the state legislature meant to exclude women through this injunction? Justice Lawrence explained that it could not have been the intent of the legislature, when setting down the terms of admission, to include women because at the time the state passed this statute, it had adopted the common law of England "so far as it was applicable to its (Illinois') condition." The admission of women to the bar would violate the common law, that ancient body of unwritten laws and customs developed in England.

In this statement the Illinois court effectively defined common law as an unchanging body of rules applied to judicial decision making. This was the view of common law held by eighteenth-century American judges. It was not the only possible definition, however, and Justice Park in Connecticut in 1881 defined it this way:

> [I]f we hold that the construction of the statute is to be determined by the admitted fact that its application to women was not in the minds of the legislators when it was passed, where shall we draw the line? All progress in social matters is gradual. We pass imperceptibly from a state of public opinion that utterly condemns some course of action to one that strongly approves it. . . . When the statute we are now considering was passed it probably never entered the mind of a single member of the Legislature that black men would ever be seeking for admission under it.[23]

By defining the common law as essentially an unchanging body of rules, the Illinois court was denying itself the power to interpret the principles set down by the state legislature for admission to the bar, in a way inconsistent with past practices.

The court then set forth another reason for narrowly defining its power. In "declining to exercise our discretion in their (women's) favor until the propriety of their participating in the offices of the state and the administration of public affairs shall be recognized by the law-making department of the government," Judge Lawrence argued that the Illinois court was only upholding a basic principle of the American constitutional system—the division of powers among the three branches of government. He also stressed that the court was protecting liberty.

Having clearly stated that the court did not have the power to substitute the personal opinions of judges for the intent of the legislature, the question remained, had the legislature passed any statute that might have permitted the court to assume that it wanted all statutes to apply equally to men and women? The court recognized that there was such a statute and proceeded to show why the 1845 Construction Statute excluded women and that the admission of women to the bar would be "repugnant" to the state legislature at the time.

What we have, then, is a court in one state narrowly defining its power, which resulted in women being barred from the practice of law, and a court in a neighboring state broadly interpreting its power. The result was contrary decisions on the same issue.

Yet, the question arises, was the Illinois court *really* following the principles of strict interpretation when it linked the right to practice law to the right of suffrage? Why must a court, unless told otherwise by the state legislature, assume there is a linkage? We gain some insight into the thinking of the Illinois judges and why they went to such great lengths to deny Myra Bradwell admission to the bar if we view the occupation of attorney as a form of public office. An attorney, by definition, is an officer of the court.

Another question arises out of the reasoning of the Illinois court. When the court said, "God designed the sexes to occupy different spheres of action," was it talking about common law or about some notion of "natural law"—that is, a law, ordained by God or by the forces of nature, outside the power of the courts to change? What are the consequences of tampering with nature or God's decision? Judge Lawrence did not discuss this issue, but by looking at a decision of the Wisconsin Supreme Court, *In re Goodell, 1875* that denied R. Lavinia Goodell permission to practice before it, we get an idea of what some judges thought were the social implications of altering the relationship between the different spheres traditionally filled by men and women.

In examining this opinion, which apparently barred women from practicing law in Wisconsin on the grounds that they were by physiology and character unsuited for the nastiness of the courts, it is important to know that Lavinia Goodell had been practicing in the district courts of Wisconsin for two years. The court was denying her application to practice before the Supreme Court of Wisconsin, the highest appellate court in the state.

Each of the courts, applying the notion of judicial precedent, treated the cases not on the individual merits of the persons involved but with an eye to larger implications. Not all courts assumed, however, that admission to the bar carried with it the implication of suffrage. Ironically, perhaps, Myra Bradwell and Arabella Mansfield may also have believed, with these judges, that entrance into the legal profession would bring the right of suffrage and the demise of the ideas about separate spheres.

Occupational Freedom and the U.S. Supreme Court

When the Illinois Supreme Court denied Bradwell's petition, it gave her a chance to test the applicability of the Fourteenth Amendment to extending women's rights. If she won her case in the U.S. Supreme Court, women would not have to fight the issue state by state. Her arguments based on

Section I, "the privileges and immunities clause" of *The Fourteenth Amendment*, was presented before the Supreme Court by her counsel, the politically influential Senator Matthew Carpenter of Wisconsin. The selection from the *Argument of Hon. Matt H. Carpenter, January 18, 1872, Upon the Application of Myra Bradwell to Be Admitted to the Bar* describes the strategy she and Carpenter used. In arguing that the privileges and immunities clause applied to occupational freedom, but not to suffrage, his brief helped to undercut the forthcoming litigation efforts of the National Woman Suffrage Association. Bradwell was active in The American Woman's Suffrage Association.

At the time Carpenter presented this brief he presented another one in behalf of the state of Louisiana against the applicability of the Fourteenth Amendment to occupational freedom of butchers. The U.S. Supreme Court linked its decision in *Bradwell* v. *Illinois* (1873) to the Slaughter-House Cases, in which a group of butchers challenged a Louisiana law requiring that all livestock in a large geographic area be slaughtered by a single New Orleans firm. They argued that this monopoly denied a livelihood to all other butchers in the region.

Before the passage of the Fourteenth Amendment, states were free to treat different groups, including women, as unequally as they pleased. Some of the constitutional questions raised by the passage of this amendment revolved around (1) whether the privileges and immunities clause simply reaffirmed existing individual rights against the national government and states, or created new ones; and (2) whether it altered the allocation of governmental power. The position of the Supreme Court on these crucial issues appeared first in the Slaughter-House Cases. The majority chose to interpret the privileges and immunities clause very narrowly, arguing that it pertained only to rights peculiar to national citizenship such as the right to travel to the seat of government, the right to move freely from one state to another, and the right to claim diplomatic protection when out of the country.

By linking the decision in *Bradwell* v. *Illinois* to the controlling one in Slaughter-House, the majority opinion, presented by Justice Miller, avoided the issue of gender. The concurring opinion, presented by Justice Bradley, which agreed with the outcome but not the reasoning, showed more clearly the Supreme Court's view on the issue of equal rights. Myra Bradwell's editorial, *"The XIVth Amendment and Our Case"* (1873), asks how Justice Bradley and two other justices who agreed with him could conclude on one day that the Fourteenth Amendment did guarantee occupational freedom, but state on the next day that it made no such guarantee to women.

Usually, when state courts refused to admit women to the bar, state legislatures then passed acts granting them that right, but not the right to suffrage. The process was time consuming, however, and not completed nationally until the end of the century. One person's experience is captured by Belva Lockwood in *"My Efforts to Become a Lawyer"* (1888). The first hurdle was in getting an education. Most lawyers and judges still received their training in law offices, a route that was not practicable for women because it did not provide the professional standing they needed to overcome distrust.

With great humor, Lockwood describes her effort to gain admission to law school and then to the District of Columbia courts, and to the U.S. Supreme Court. Her story continues with *In re Lockwood* (1893), when she petitioned the U.S. Supreme Court to compel the Virginia Supreme Court of Appeals to admit her to practice before it. Although Lockwood was involved in the woman's rights movement and even ran for the U.S. presidency in 1884, she wanted to practice law primarily to enjoy a financially rewarding occupation. Other women were admitted to practice, but were isolated from the rest of the profession: the American Bar Association, for example, did not accept women as members until 1918.[24]

DOCUMENTS

OPPORTUNITY AND REALITY
IN URBAN AMERICA

The Factory

[107]

"Yankee Girls Troop to the Mills," by Harriet Robinson (1830s)

The law took no cognizance of woman as a money-spender. She was a ward, an appendage, a relict. Thus it happened, that if a woman did not choose to marry, or, when left a widow, to re-marry, she had no choice but to enter one of the few employments open to her, or to become a burden on the charity of some relative.

In almost every New England home could be found one or more of these women, sometimes welcome, more often unwelcome, and leading joyless, and in many instances unsatisfactory, lives. The cotton factory was a great opening to these lonely and dependent women. From a condition approaching pauperism they were at once placed above want, they could earn money, and spend it as they pleased. . . .

Some of the mill-girls helped maintain widowed mothers, or drunken, incompetent, or invalid fathers. Many of them educated the younger children of the family, and young men were sent to college with the money furnished by the untiring industry of their women relatives.

Indeed, the most prevailing incentive to our labor was to secure the means of education for some *male* member of the family. To make a *gentleman* of a brother or a son, to give him a college education, was the dominant thought in the minds of a

From Harriet Robinson, *Loom and Spindle*, or *Life Among the Early Mills Girls* (Boston, 1898), pp. 76–77.

great many of these provident mill-girls. I have known more than one to give every cent of her wages, month after month, to her brother, that he might get the education necessary to enter some profession.

[108]

Investigation of Labor Conditions, Massachusetts House of Representatives (March 12, 1845)

The Special Committee to which was referred sundry petitions relating to the hours of labor have considered the same and submit the following report:

REPORT

The first petition which was referred to your committee came from the city of Lowell, and was signed by Mr. John Quincy Adams Thayer and eight hundred and fifty others, "peaceable, industrious, hard working men and women of Lowell." The petitioners declare that they are confined "from thirteen to fourteen hours per day in unhealthy apartments," and are thereby "hastening through pain, disease and privation, down to a premature grave." They therefore ask the legislature "to pass a law providing that ten hours shall constitute a day's work," and that no corporation or private citizen "shall be allowed, except in cases of emergency, to employ one set of hands more than ten hours a day." . . .

The whole number of names on the several petitions is 2,139, of which 1,151 are from Lowell. A very large proportion of the Lowell petitioners are females. Nearly one half of the Andover petitioners are females. The petition from Fall River is signed exclusively by males.

In view of the number and respectability of the petitioners who had brought their grievances before the legislature, the Committee asked for and obtained leave of the House to send for "persons and papers." . . .

On the 13th of February, the Committee held a session to hear the petitioners from the city of Lowell. Six of the female and three of the male petitioners were present and gave in their testimony.

The first petitioner who testified was *Eliza R. Hemmingway*. She had worked 2 years and 9 months in the Lowell Factories; 2 years in the Middlesex, and 9 months in the Hamilton Corporations. Her employment is weaving—works by the piece. The Hamilton Mill manufactures cotton fabrics. The Middlesex, woollen fabrics. She is now at work in the Middlesex Mills and attends one loom. . . . She complained of the hours for labor being too many, and the time for meals too limited. In

From Massachusetts *House Document*, no. 50 (March 1845), pp. 1–15.

Victorian images of women both in literature and in judicial decisions contrasted sharply with the reality of women's lives in rural, frontier, and urban areas. This picture and the two that follow illustrate the structure of opportunity and authority in the work place.

A cotton factory in the early nineteenth century.

Cotton pickers waiting to have their day's collection weighed. Courtesy National Archives, Washington, DC.

Female Slaves of New York—Sweaters and Their Victims. Frank Leslie's *Illustrated Newspaper*, November 8, 1888 (Library of Congress, Washington, DC).

the summer season, the work is commenced at 5 o'clock, A.M. and continued till 7 o'clock, P.M., with half an hour for breakfast and three quarters of an hour for dinner. During eight months of the year, but half an hour is allowed for dinner. The air in the room she considered not to be wholesome. There were 293 small lamps and 61 large lamps lighted in the room in which she worked, when evening work is required. These lamps are also lighted sometimes in the morning. About 130 females, 11 men, and 12 children (between the ages of 11 and 14) work in the room with her. She thought the children enjoyed about as good health as children generally do. The children work but 9 months out of 12. The other 3 months they must attend school. [She] thinks that there is no day when there are less than six of the females out of the mill from sickness. There was more sickness in the Summer than in the Winter months, though in the summer lamps are not lighted. She thought there was a general desire among the females to work but ten hours, regardless of pay. Most of the girls are from the country, who work in the Lowell Mills. The average time which they remain there is about three years.

She knew of one girl who last winter went into the mill at half past 4 o'clock, A.M., and worked till half past 7 o'clock, P.M. She did so to make more money. She earned $25 to $30 per month. There is always a large number of girls at the gate wishing to get in before the bell rings. . . .

Of the Middlesex Corporation one-fourth part of the females go into the mill before they are obliged to. They do this to make more wages. A large number come to Lowell to make money to aid their parents who are poor. She knew of many cases where married women came to Lowell and worked in the mills to assist their husbands to pay for their farms. The moral character of the operatives is good. There was only one American female in the room with her who could not write her name.

Miss Sarah G. Bagley said she had worked in the Lowell Mills eight years and a half—six years and a half on the Hamilton Corporation, and two years on the Middlesex. She is a weaver and works by the piece. She worked in the mills three years before her health began to fail. She is a native of New Hampshire and went home six weeks during the summer. Last year she was out of the mill a third of the time. She thinks the health of the operatives is not so good as the health of the females who do housework or millinery business. The chief evil, so far as health is concerned, is the shortness of time allowed for meals. The next evil is the length of time employed—not giving them time to cultivate their minds. She spoke of the high moral and intellectual character of the girls. That many were engaged as teachers in the Sunday schools. That many attended the lectures of the Lowell Institute. She thought that the girls generally were favorable to the ten hour system. She had presented a petition, same as the one before the Committee, to 132 girls, most of whom said that they would prefer to work but ten hours. In a pecuniary point of view, it would be better, as their health would be improved. They would have more time for sewing. The intellectual, moral and religious habits would also be benefited by the change. Miss Bagley said, in addition to her labor in the mills, she had kept evening school during the winter months, for four years, and thought that this extra labor must have injured her health.

Miss Judith Payne testified that she came to Lowell 16 years ago, and worked a year and a half in the Merrimack Cotton Mills, left there on account of ill health, and remained out over seven years. She was sick most of the time she was out. Seven years ago she went to work in the Boott Mills, and has remained there ever since; works by the piece. She has lost, during the last seven years, about one year from ill health. She is a weaver and attends three looms. Last payday she drew $14.66 for five weeks' work; this was exclusive of board. She was absent during the five weeks but half a day. She says there is a very general feeling in favor of the ten hour day among the operatives. She attributes her ill health to the long hours of labor, the shortness of time for meals, and the bad air of the mills. . . .

Miss Olive J. Clark . . . is employed on the Lawrence Corporation; has been there five years; makes about $1.62½ per week, exclusive of board. . . . Her health never was good. The work is not laborious; [she] can sit down about a quarter of the time. About 50 girls work in the spinning room with her, three of whom signed the petition. She is in favor of the ten hour system, and thinks that the long hours had an affect upon her health. She is kindly treated by her employers. There is hardly a week in which there is not someone out on account of sickness. Thinks the air is bad, on account of the small particles of cotton which fly about. . . .

Mr. Herman Abbott had worked in the Lawrence Corporation 13 years. Never heard much complaint among the girls about the long hours; never heard the subject spoken of in the mills. Does not think it would be satisfactory to the girls to work only ten hours, if their wages were to be reduced in proportion. Forty-two girls work in the room with him. The girls often get back to the gate before the bell rings.

Mr. John Quincy Adams Thayer has lived in Lowell four years, "works at physical labor in the summer season and mental labor in the winter." Has worked in the big machine shop 24 months, off and on; never worked in a cotton or woolen mill. Thinks that the mechanics in the machine shop are not so healthy as in other shops; nor so intelligent as the other classes in Lowell. He drafted the petition; has heard of many complain of the long hours.

Mr. S. P. Adams, a member of the House from Lowell, said he worked in the machine shop, and the men were as intelligent as any other class and enjoyed as good health as any persons who work indoors. The air in the shop is as good as in any shop. About 350 hands work there, about half a dozen of whom are what is called ten-hour men. They all would be ten-hour men if they could get as good pay.

The only witnesses whom the Committee examined, whose names were not on the petition, were Mr. Adams and Mr. Isaac Cooper, a member of the House from Lowell who also has worked as an overseer in the Lawrence Cotton Mills for nine years. His evidence was very full. He gave it as his opinion that the girls in the mills enjoy the best health, for the reason that they rise early, go to bed early, and have three meals regular. In his room there are 60 girls, and since 1837 he has known of only one girl who went home from Lowell and died. He does not find that those who stay the longest in the mill grow sickly and weak. The rooms are heated by steam-pipes, and the temperature of the rooms is regulated by a thermometer. It is so, he believes, in all the mills. The heat of the room varies from 62 to 68 degrees.

The above testimony embraces all the important facts which were elicited from the persons who appeared before the Committee.

On Saturday, the 1st of March, a portion of the Committee went to Lowell to examine the mills. . . . They first proceeded to the Merrimack Cotton Mills, in which are employed usually 1,200 females and 300 males. They were permitted to visit every part of the works and to make whatever inquiries they pleased of the persons employed. They found every apartment neat and clean, and the girls, so far as personal appearance went, healthy and robust, as girls are in our country towns. . . . Your Committee returned fully satisfied that the order, decorum, and general appearance of things in and about the mills could not be improved by any suggestion of theirs, or by any act of the Legislature.

During our short stay in Lowell we gathered many facts, which we deem of sufficient importance to state in this report, and first, in relation to the Hours of Labor. . . .   . . .

The following table shows the average hours of work day, throughout the year, in the Lowell Mills:

	HOURS	MIN.		HOURS	MIN.
January	11	24	July	12	45
February	12	—	August	12	45
March	11	52	September	12	23
April	13	31	October	12	10
May	12	45	November	11	56
June	12	45	December	11	24

THE GENERAL HEALTH OF THE OPERATIVES

In regard to the health of the operatives employed in the mills, your Committee believe it to be good. The testimony of the female petitioners does not controvert this position, in general, though it does in particular instances. The population of the city of Lowell is now rising to 26,000, of which number about 7,000 are females employed in the mills. It is the opinion of Dr. Kimball, an eminent physician of Lowell, with whom the Committee had an interview, that there is less sickness among the persons at work in the mills, than there is among those who do not work in the mills; . . .

The petitioners thought that the statements made by our city physician, as to the number of deaths, were delusive, inasmuch as many of the females when taken sick in Lowell do not stay there, but return to their homes in the country and die. Dr. Kimball thought that the number who return home when seized with sickness was small. Mr. Cooper, who is a gentleman of great experience, says that he has known but one girl who, during the last eight years, went home from Lowell and died. We have no doubt, however, that many of the operatives do leave Lowell and return to their homes when their health is feeble, but the proportion is not large. Certainly it has created no alarm, for the sisters and acquaintances of those who have gone home return to Lowell to supply the vacancies which their absence had created.

Your Committee . . . [has] come to the conclusion, *unanimously,* that legislation is not necessary at the present time, and for the following reasons:

1st. That a law limiting the hours of labor, if enacted at all, should be of a general nature. That it should apply to individuals or copartnerships as well as to corporations. Because, if it is wrong to labor more than ten hours in a corporation, it is also wrong when applied to individual employers. . . . But it will be said in reply to this, that corporations are the creatures of the Legislature, and therefore the Legislature can control them in this, as in other matters. This is to a certain extent true, but your Committee would go farther than this, and say, that not only are corporations subject to the control of the Legislature but individuals are also, and if it should ever appear that the public morals, the physical condition, or the social well-being of society were endangered, from this cause or from any cause, then it would be in the power and it would be the duty of the Legislature to interpose its prerogative to avert the evil.

2d. Your Committee believe that the factory system, as it is called, is not more injurious to health than other kinds of indoor labor. That a law which would compel all of the factories in Massachusetts to run their machinery but ten hours out of the 24, while those in Maine, New Hampshire, Rhode Island and other states in the Union were not restricted at all, the effect would be to close the gate of every mill in the State. It would be the same as closing our mills one day in every week. . . . We could not compete with our sister States, much less with foreign countries, if a restriction of this nature was put upon our manufactories.

3d. It would be impossible to legislate to restrict the hours of labor, without affecting very materially the question of wages; and that is a matter which experience has taught us can be much better regulated by the parties themselves than by the Legislature. Labor in Massachusetts . . . is on an equality with capital, and indeed controls it, and so it ever will be while free education and free constitutions exist. And although we may find fault, and say, that labor works too many hours, and labor is too severely tasked, yet if we attempt by legislation to enter within its orbit and interfere with its plans, we will be told to keep clear and to mind our own business. Labor is intelligent enough to make its own bargains, and look out for its own interests, without any interference from us; . . . Massachusetts men and Massachusetts women, are equal to this, and will take care of themselves better than we can take care of them. . . .

4th. The Committee do not wish to be understood as conveying the impression, that there are no abuses in the present system of labor; we think there are abuses; we think that many improvements may be made, and we believe will be made, by which labor will not be so severely tasked as it now is. We think that it would be better if the hours for labor were less, if more time was allowed for meals, if more attention was paid to ventilation and pure air in our manufactories and workshops, and many other matters. We acknowledge all this, but we say, the remedy is not with us. We look for it in the progressive improvment in art and science, in a higher appreciation of man's destiny, in a less love for money and a more ardent love for social happiness and intellectual superiority. Your Committee, therefore, while they agree with the petitioners in their desire to lessen the burdens imposed upon labor, differ only as to the means by which these burdens are sought to be removed. . . .

Wm. Schouler, Chairman

Prostitution

[109]
Survey of the Extent and Causes of Prostitution, by Dr. William Sanger (1858)

TABLE 1
Previous Trade or Calling of Women at Blackwell Island Women's Prison Who Became Prostitutes

OCCUPATIONS	NUMBERS
Artist	1
Nurse in Bellevue Hospital, N.Y.	1
School teachers	3
Fruit-hawkers	4
Paperbox makers	5
Tobacco-packers	7
Attended stores or bars	8
Attended school	8
Embroiderers	8
Fur-sewers	8
Hat-trimmers	8
Umbrella makers	8
Flower-makers	9
Shoe-binders	16
Vest-makers	21
Cap-makers	24
Book-folders	27
Factory girls	37
Housekeepers	39
Milliners	41
Seamstresses	59
Tailoresses	105
Dress-makers	121
Servants	933
Lived with parents or friends	499
Total	2000

From William Sanger, M.D., *The History of Prostitution: Its Extents, Causes, and Effects Throughout the World* (New York, 1858), pp. 506–11, 524, 614.

INTERVIEWS OF MARRIED WOMEN AT BLACKWELL ISLAND
WHO BECAME PROSTITUTES

C.C.: My husband deserted me and four children. I had no means to live. . . .

J.S.: My husband committed adultery. I caught him with another woman, and then he left me. . . .

A.G.: My husband eloped with another woman. I support the child.

A.B.: My husband accused me of infidelity, which was not true. I only lived with him five months. I was pregnant by him, and after my child was born I went on the town to support it.

C.H.: My husband was a drunkard and beat me.

P.T.: My husband was intemperate and turned out to be a thief. He was sent to prison.

TABLE 2
The Proportion of Prostitutes to Men in Large Cities

New York	1	prostitute to every 57 men
Buffalo	1	" " " 57 "
Louisville	1	" " " 56 "
New Haven	1	" " " 76 "
Norfolk	1	" " " 26 "
Savannah	1	" " " 39 "
and the mean of the whole is	1	" " " 52 "

[110]
California Senate Investigation of Chinese Immigrants (1876)

Testimony of Rev. A. W. Loomis: These Chinawomen that you see on the streets here were brought for the accommodation of white people, not for the accommodation of Chinese; and if you pass along the streets where they are to be found you will see that they are visited not so much by Chinese as by others—sailors and low people. The women are in a condition of servitude. Some of them are inveigled away from home under promises of marriage to men here, and some to be secondary wives, while some are stolen. They are sold here. Many women are taken from the Chinese owners, and are living as wives and as secondary wives. Some have children, and these children are legitimate.

Cited in Rosalyn Baxandall et al., eds., *America's Working Women: A Documentary History, 1600 to the Present* (New York: Vintage Books, 1976), p. 98. Courtesy Random House, Inc.

[111]
Chinese Labor Contract (1873)

An agreement to assist the woman Ah Ho, because coming from China to San Francisco she became indebted to her mistress for passage. Ah Ho herself asks Mr. Yee Kwan to advance her six hundred and thirty dollars, for which Ah Ho distinctly agrees to give her body to Mr. Yee for service of prostitution for a term of four years. There shall be no interest on the money. Ah Ho shall receive no wages. At the expiration of four years Ah Ho shall be her own master. Mr. Yee Kwan shall not hinder or trouble her. If Ah Ho runs away before her time is out, her mistress shall find her and return her, and whatever expense is incurred in finding and returning her Ah Ho shall pay. On this day of agreement Ah Ho, with her own hands, has received from Mr. Yee Kwan six hundred and thirty dollars. If Ah Ho shall be sick at any time for more than ten days, she shall make up by an extra month of service for every ten days sickness. Now, this agreement has proof—this paper received by Ah Ho is witness.

Cited in Rosalyn Baxandall et al., eds., *America's Working Women: A Documentary History, 1600 to the Present* (New York: Vintage Books, 1978), p. 99. Courtesy Random House, Inc.

Tung Chee

Twelfth year, ninth month, and fourteenth day
(about middle of October, eighteen hundred and seventy-three)

ACCESS TO PRIVILEGE AND AUTHORITY
Educational Barriers

[112]
Lucy Stone's Speech at the National Woman's Rights Convention, Cincinnati (1855)

The last speaker alluded to this movement as being that of a few disappointed women. From the first years to which my memory stretches, I have been reproved

Cited in Ann Chapman, ed., *Approaches to Women's History* (Washington, D.C.: American Historical Association, 1979), p. 62.

with "It isn't fit for you; it doesn't belong to women." Then there was but one college in the world where women were admitted, and that was in Brazil. I would have found my way there, but by the time I was prepared to go, one was opened in the young State of Ohio—the first in the United States where women and Negroes could enjoy opportunities with white men. I was disappointed when I came to seek a profession worthy an immortal being—every employment was closed to me, except those of the teacher, the seamstress, and the housekeeper. . . .

. . . We are told woman has all the rights she wants; and even women, I am ashamed to say, tell us so. They mistake the politeness of men for rights—seats while men stand in this hall tonight, and their adulations; but these are mere courtesies. We want rights. The flour-merchant, the house-builder, and the post-man charge us no less on account of our sex; but when we endeavor to earn money to pay all these, then, indeed, we find the difference. Man, if he have energy, may hew out for himself a path where no mortal has ever trod, held back by nothing but what is in himself; the world is all before him, where to choose; and we are glad for you, brothers, men, that it is so. But the same society that drives forth the young man, keeps woman at home—a dependent—working little cats on worsted, and little dogs on punctured paper; but if she goes heartily and bravely to give herself to some worthy purpose, she is out of her sphere and she loses caste. Women working in tailor-shops are paid one-third as much as men. Some one in Philadelphia has stated that women make fine shirts for twelve and a half cents apiece; that no woman can make more than nine a week, and the sum thus earned, after deducting rent, fuel, etc., leaves her just three and a half cents a day for bread. Is it a wonder that women are driven to prostitution?

[113]
Stephen Smith, M.D. on The Admission of the First Woman to a Male Medical College (1847)

Medical circles were recently entertained by a symposium of prominent physicians discussing the propriety of the medical co-education of the sexes. All of the writers were opposed to the suggestion; some, notably Dr. Weir Mitchell, of Philadelphia, expressed the utmost disgust at the proposition. It happened to me to have witnessed the first instance of the co-education of medical students of both sexes in this country, and the results quite upset the theories of these gentlemen.

The first course of medical lectures which I attended was in a medical college in the interior of this State in 1847–48. The class, numbering about 150 students, was

From "The Medical Co-education of the Sexes" (1892), cited in *Pioneer Work in Opening the Medical Profession to Women: Autobiographical Sketches by Dr. Elizabeth Blackwell,* intro. by Dr. Mary Roth Walsh (New York: Schocken, 1977), pp. 255–59.

composed largely of young men from the neighbouring towns. They were rude, boisterous, and riotous beyond comparison. . . .

Some weeks after the course began the dean appeared before the class with a letter in his hand, which he craved the indulgence of the students to be allowed to read. Anticipation was extreme when he announced that it contained the most extraordinary request which had ever been made to the faculty. The letter was written by a physician of Philadelphia, who requested the faculty to admit as a student a lady who was studying medicine in his office. He stated that she had been refused admission by several medical colleges, but, as this institution was in the country, he thought it more likely to be free from prejudice against a woman medical student. The dean stated that the faculty had taken action on the communication, and directed him to report their conclusion to the class. The faculty decided to leave the matter in the hands of the class, with this understanding—that if any single student objected to her admission, a negative reply would be returned. It subsequently appeared that the faculty did not intend to admit her, but wished to escape direct refusal by referring the question to the class, with a proviso which, it was believed, would necessarily exclude her.

But the whole affair assumed the most ludicrous aspect to the class, and the announcement was received with the most uproarious demonstrations of favour. A meeting was called for the evening, which was attended by every member. The resolution approving the admission of the lady was sustained by a number of the most extravagant speeches, which were enthusiastically cheered. The vote was finally taken, with what seemed to be one unanimous yell, 'Yea!' When the negative vote was called, a single voice was heard uttering a timid 'No.' The scene that followed passes description. A general rush was made for the corner of the room which emitted the voice, and the recalcitrant member was only too glad to acknowledge his error and record his voice in the affirmative. The faculty received the decision of the class with evident disfavour, and returned an answer admitting the lady student. Two weeks or more elapsed, and as the lady student did not appear, the incident of her application was quite forgotten, and the class continued in its riotous career. One morning, all unexpectedly, a lady entered the lecture-room with the professor; she was quite small of stature, plainly dressed, appeared diffident and retiring, but had a firm and determined expression of face. Her entrance into that Bedlam of confusion acted like magic upon every student. Each hurriedly sought his seat, and the most absolute silence prevailed. For the first time a lecture was given without the slightest interruption, and every word could be heard as distinctly as it would if there had been but a single person in the room. The sudden transformation of this class from a band of lawless desperadoes to gentlemen, by the mere presence of a lady, proved to be permanent in its effects. A more orderly class of medical students was never seen than this, and it continued to be to the close of the term. . . .

At the close of the term our lady student came up for examination for graduation, and took rank with the best students of the class. As this was the first instance of the granting of a medical diploma to a woman in this country, so far as the faculty had information, there was at first some hesitation about conferring the degree. But it was finally determined to take the novel step, and in the honour list of the roll of graduates for that year appears the name, Dr. Elizabeth Blackwell.

[114]
George Palmer Putnam to Mary Corinna Putnam (February 13, 1861)

My Dear Minnie,
I want you to think over one or two questions. . . .

1. Whether the claims of home and your mother are not at present *superior,* even to those disinterested and worthy plans, and—

2. What possible evil can result from your *suspending* those medical studies entirely, except general reading at home, for the space of two years? Or rather—why would it not be *better* for *you* as well as *us* that you should do so?

I will not stop to write out all the reasons and pros and cons which are suggested in this connection. "A word to the wise"(?)—I only want you carefully, deliberately, and conscientiously to consider and *weigh* all you know I *might* say, to *persuade* you to this postponement. I have no idea of exercising any authority or imposing any command. *You* don't need any—and you *ought* not to need any. . . . I think it highly desirable that you should be at home *chiefly* during the next two years and especially during this present year. I really and deliberately think that you owe more to your mother and the younger children than you do to anyone else or to any other plans of enterprise, however worthy and important. I think you may be of *immense* use in relieving and cheering your mother, and that she will *need* your aid at home—and that you may benefit the young children and aid generally in *systematizing* home and rendering it cheerful and happy—and that, for the next two years, this is quite as important and *more* obligatory than any other claims.

I don't ask you to give up your plans—or lose the advantage of all you have done—but only to *suspend them* for this time, so far as they take you from home. You would, of course, continue at Miss Gibson's and you could doubtless do a good deal of studying at home.

Your affectionate Father.

From Ruth Putnam, ed., *Life and Letters of Mary Putnam Jacobi* (New York: G. P. Putnam's Sons, 1925), pp. 60–61.

New Cultural Barriers

[115]
Carl Vogt, Lectures on Man, His Place in Creation, and in the History of the Earth *(1864)*

It has long been observed that among peoples progressing in civilization, the men are in advance of women, whilst among those which are retrograding, the contrary is the case. Just as, in respect of morals, woman is the conservator of old customs and uses, of traditions, legends, and religion; so in the material world she preserves primitive forms, which but slowly yield to the influence of civilization. . . . In the same manner woman preserves, in the formation of the head, the earliest stage from which the race or tribe has been developed, or into which it has relapsed. Hence, then, is partly explained the fact that the inequality of sexes increases with the progress of civilization.

Cited in John S. Haller and Robin M. Haller, *The Physician and Sexuality in Victorian America* (New York: W. W. Norton, 1974), p. 56. Courtesy University of Illinois Press.

[116]
Dr. Edward H. Clarke on the Physical and Social Ramifications of Female Higher Education (1873)

I. INTRODUCTION

It has just been said that the educational methods of our schools and colleges for girls are, to a large extent, the cause of "the thousand ills" that beset American women. . . . Those grievous maladies which torture a woman's earthly existence, called leucorrhoea, amenorrhoea, dysmenorrhoea, chronic and acute ovaritis, prolapsus uteri, hysteria, neuralgia . . . arise from a neglect of the peculiarities of a woman's organization. The regimen of our schools fosters this neglect. The regimen of a college arranged for boys, if imposed on girls, would foster it still more.

From Edward H. Clarke, M.D., *Sex in Education; or, a Fair Chance for the Girls* (Boston, 1873), pp. 22–24, 61–67, 79–82, 87, 91, 104–15, 131–33, 139–41.

II. CLINICAL EVIDENCE

Clinical observation confirms the teachings of physiology . . . It is not asserted here . . . that all the female graduates of our schools and colleges are pathological specimens. But it is asserted that the number of these graduates who have been permanently disabled to a greater or less degree by these causes is so great, as to excite the gravest alarm, and to demand the serious attention of the community. If these causes should continue for the next half-century, and increase in the same ratio as they have for the last fifty years, it requires no prophet to foretell that the wives who are to be mothers in our republic must be drawn from trans-Atlantic homes. The sons of the New World will have to re-act, on a magnificent scale, the old story of unwived Rome and the Sabines.

Miss D_____ entered Vassar College at the age of fourteen. Up to that age, she had been a healthy girl, judged by the standard of American girls. Her parents were apparently strong enough to yield her a fair dower of force. The catamenial menstrual function first showed signs of activity in her Sophomore Year, when she was fifteen years old. Its appearance at this age is confirmatory evidence of the normal state of her health at that period of her college career. Its commencement was normal, without pain or excess. She performed all her college duties regularly and steadily. She studied, recited, stood at the blackboard, walked, and went through her gymnastic exercises, from the beginning to the end of the term, just as boys do. Her account of her regimen there was so nearly that of a boy's regimen, that it would puzzle a physiologist to determine, from the account alone, whether the subject of it was male or female. She was an average scholar, who maintained a fair position in her class, not one of the anxious sort, that are ambitious of leading all the rest. Her first warning was fainting away, while exercising in the gymnasium, at a time when she should have been comparatively quiet, both mentally and physically. This warning was repeated several times, under the same circumstances. Finally she was compelled to renounce gymnastic exercise altogether. In her Junior Year the organism's periodical function began to be performed with pain, moderate at first but more and more severe with each returning month. When between seventeen and eighteen years old, dysmenorrhoea was established as the order of that function. Coincident with the appearance of pain there was a diminution of excretion; and as the former increased the latter became more marked. In other respects she was well; and in all respects she appeared to be well to her companions and to the faculty of the college. She graduated before nineteen, with fair honors and a poor physique. The year succeeding her graduation was one of steadily advancing invalidism. She was tortured for two or three days out of every month; and for two or three days after each season of torture was weak and miserable, so that about one sixth or fifth of her time was consumed in this way. The excretion from the blood, which had been gradually lessening, after a time substantially stopped, though a periodical effort to keep it up was made. She now suffered from what is called amenorrhoea. At the same time she became pale, hysterical, nervous in the ordinary sense, and almost continually complained of headache. Physicians were applied to for aid: drugs were administered; travelling, with consequent change of air and scene, was undertaken; and all with little apparent avail. . . . The evidence was altogether in favor of an arrest of the development of the reproductive apparatus, at a stage when the development was nearly complete. Confirmatory proof of such an arrest was found in examining her breast, where the milliner had supplied the organs nature should have grown. It is unnecessary for our present purpose to detail what treatment was advised. It is sufficient to say that she probably never will become physically what she would have been had her education been physiologically guided.

The arrest of development of the reproductive system is most obvious to the superficial observer in that part of it which the milliner is called upon to cover up with pads, and which was alluded to in the case of Miss D_____. This, however, is too important a matter to be dismissed with a bare allusion. ". . . If only here and there an individual were found with such an organization, not much harm comparatively would result; but when a majority or nearly all have it, the evil becomes one of no small magnitude." . . .

These clinical observations are sufficient to illustrate the fact that our modern methods of education do not give the female organization a fair chance, but that they check development and invite weakness. It would be easy to multiply such observations from the writer's own notes alone, and, by doing so, to swell this essay into a portly volume; but the reader is spared the needless infliction. Other observers have noticed similar facts and have urgently called attention to them.

Dr. Fisher, in a recent excellent monograph on insanity, says, "A few examples of injury from *continued* study will show how mental strain affects the health of young girls particularly. Every physician could, no doubt, furnish many similar ones."

"Miss A_____ graduated with honor at the normal school after several years of close study, much of the time out of school; never attended balls or parties; sank into a low state of health at once with depression. Was very absurdly allowed to marry while in this state, and soon after became violently insane, and is likely to remain so."

III. REASONS WHY WORKINGCLASS WOMEN SUFFER LESS

There are two reasons why female operatives of all sorts are likely to suffer less, and actually do suffer less, from such persistent work, than female students; why Jane in the factory can work more steadily with the loom than Jane in college with the dictionary; why the girl who makes the bed can safely work more steadily the whole year through than her little mistress of sixteen who goes to school. The first reason is that the female operative, of whatever sort, has, as a rule, passed through the first critical epoch of woman's life: she has got fairly by it. In her case, as a rule, unfortunately there are too many exceptions to it, the catamenia have been established; the function is in good running order; the reproductive apparatus—the engine within an engine—has been constructed, and she will not be called upon to furnish force for building it again. The female student, on the contrary, has got these tasks before her, and must perform them while getting her education; for the period of female sexual development coincides with the educational period. The same five years of life must be given to both tasks. After the function is normally established and the apparatus made, woman can labor mentally or physically, or both, with very much greater persistence and intensity than during the age of development. . . .

. . . The second reason why female operatives are less likely to suffer, and actually do suffer less, than school girls, from persistent work straight through the year, is because the former work their brains less. To use the language of Herbert Spencer, "That antagonism between body and brain which we see in those, who, pushing brain-activity to an extreme, enfeeble their bodies," does not often exist in female operatives, any more than in the male. On the contrary, they belong to the class of those who, in the words of the same author, by "pushing bodily activity to an extreme, make their brains inert." . . .

IV. CONCLUSION

". . . . How should the race *not* deteriorate, when those who morally and physically are fitted to perpetuate it are (relatively), by a law of physiology, those least likely to do so?" The answer to Mr. Greg's inquiry is obvious. If the culture of the race moves on into the future in the same rut and by the same methods that limit and direct it now; if the education of the sexes remains identical, instead of being appropriate and special; and especially if the intense and passionate stimulus of the identical co-education of the sexes is added to their identical education—then the sterilizing influence of such training, acting with tenfold more force upon the female than upon the male, will go on, and the race will be propagated from its inferior classes.

(It is a fact not to be lost sight of, says Dr. J. C. Toner of Washington, that the proportion between the number of American children under fifteen years of age, and the number of American women between the child-bearing ages of fifteen and fifty, is declining steadily. In 1830 there were to every 1,000 marriageable women 1,952 children under fifteen years of age. Ten years later there were 1,863, or 89 less children to every thousand women than in 1830. In 1850 this number had declined to 1,720; in 1860 to 1,666; and in 1870 to 1,568. The total decline in the forty years was 384, or about 20 percent of the whole proportional number in 1830, a generation ago. The United States census of 1870 shows that there is, in the city of New York, but one child under fifteen years of age, to each thousand nubile women, when there ought to be three; and the same is true of our other large cities.—(*The Nation,* August 28, 1873, p. 145.)

The stream of life that is to flow into the future will be Celtic rather than

American: it will come from the collieries, and not from the peerage. Fortunately, the reverse of this picture is equally plausible. The race holds its destinies in its own hands. The highest wisdom will secure the survival and propagation of the fittest. Physiology teaches that this result, the attainment of which our hopes prophesy, is to be secured, not by an identical education, or an identical co-education of the sexes, but by *a special and appropriate education, that shall produce a just and harmonious development of every part.*

Let one remark be made here. It has been asserted that the chief reason why the higher and educated classes have smaller families than the lower and uneducated is that the former criminally prevent or destroy increase. The pulpit, as well as the medical press, has cried out against this enormity. That a disposition to do this thing exists and is often carried into effect, is not to be denied and cannot be too strongly condemned. On the other hand, it should be proclaimed, to the credit and honor of our cultivated women, and as a reproach to the identical education of the sexes, that many of them bear in silence the accusation of self-tampering, who are denied the oft-prayed-for trial, blessing, and responsibility of offspring. . . .

ENTERING THE LEGAL PROFESSION
Occupational Freedom and the State Courts

[117]
In re Bradwell *(Illinois, 1869)*

Mr. Justice LAWRENCE delivered the opinion of the Court:

At the last term of the court, Mrs. Myra Bradwell applied for a license as an attorney at law, presenting the ordinary certificates of character and qualifications. The license was refused, and it was stated, as a sufficient reason, that under the decisions of this court, the applicant, as a married woman, would be bound neither by her express contracts, nor by those implied contracts, which it is the policy of the law to create between attorney and client.

Since the announcement of our decision, the applicant has filed a printed argument, in which her right to a license is earnestly and ably maintained. Of the qualifications of the applicant we have no doubt, and we put our decision in writing in order that she, or other persons interested, may bring the question before the next legislature.

The applicant, in her printed argument, combats the decision of this court in

55 (Ill.) 535 (1869).

the case of *Carpenter* v. *Mitchell*, 50 Ill. 470, in which we held a married woman was not bound by contracts having no relation to her own property. We are not inclined to go over again the grounds of that decision. It was the result of a good deal of deliberation and discussion in our council chamber, and the confidence of the present members of this court in its correctness cannot easily be shaken. We are in accord with all the courts in this country which have had occasion to pass upon a similar question, the Supreme Court of Wisconsin, in *Conway* v. *Smith,* 13 Wis. 125, differing from us only on the minor point, as to whether, in regard to contracts concerning the separate property of married women, the law side of the court would take jurisdiction.

As to the main question, the right of married women to make contracts not affecting their separate property, the position of those who assert such right is, that because the legislature has expressly removed the common law disabilities of married women in regard to holding property not derived from their husbands, it has, therefore, by necessary implication, also removed all their common law disabilities in regard to making contracts, and invited them to enter, equally with men, upon those fields of trade and speculation by which property is acquired through the agency of contracts. The hiatus between the premise and conclusion is too wide for us to bridge. It may be desirable that the legislature should relieve married women from all their common law disabilities. But to say that it has done so, in the act of 1861, the language of which is carefully guarded, and which makes no allusion to contracts, and does not use that or any equivalent term, would be simple misinterpretation. It would be going as far beyond the meaning of that act as that act goes beyond the common law in changing the legal status of women. The act itself is wise and just, and therefore entitled to a liberal interpretation. This we have endeavored to give it in the cases that have come before us, but we do not intend to decide that the legislature has gone to a length in its measure of reform for which the language it has carefully used furnishes no warrant.

It is urged, however, that the law of the last session of the legislature, which gives to married women the separate control of their earnings, must be construed as giving to them the right to contract in regard to their personal services. This act had no application to the case of *Carpenter* v. *Mitchell,* having been passed after that suit was commenced, and we were unmindful of it when considering this application at the last term. Neither do we now propose to consider how far it extends the power of a married woman to contract, since, after further consultation in regard to this application, we find ourselves constrained to hold that the sex of the applicant, independently of coverture, is as our law now stands, a sufficient reason for not granting this license.

Although an attorney at law is an agent, as is claimed by the applicant's argument, when he has been retained to act for another, yet he is also much more than an agent. He is an officer of the court, holding his commission, in this State, from two of the members of this court, and subject to be disbarred by this court for what our statute calls "mal-conduct in his office." He is appointed to assist in the

Myra Colby Bradwell (1831–1894). Frances Willard and Mary Livermore, eds., *A Woman of the Century* (1853).

administration of justice, is required to take an oath of office, and is privileged from arrest while attending courts.

Our statute provides that no person shall be permitted to practice as an attorney or counsellor at law without having previously obtained a license for that purpose from two of the justices of the Supreme Court. By the second section of the act, it is provided that no person shall be entitled to receive a license, until he shall have obtained a certificate from the court of some county of his good moral character, and this is the only express limitation upon the exercise of the power thus entrusted to this court. In all other respects it is left to our discretion to establish the rules by which admission to this office shall be determined. But this discretion is not an arbitrary one, and must be exercised subject to at least two limitations. One is, that the court should establish such terms of admission as will promote the proper administration of justice; the second, that it should not admit any persons or class of persons who are not intended by the legislature to be admitted, even though their exclusion is not expressly required by the statute.

The substance of the last limitation is simply that this important trust reposed in us should be exercised in conformity with the designs of the power creating it. Whether, in the existing social relations between men and women, it would promote the proper administration of justice, and the general well being of society, to permit women to engage in the trial of cases in court, is a question opening a wide field of discussion upon which it is not necessary for us to enter.

It is sufficient to say that, in our opinion, the other implied limitation upon our power, to which we have above referred, must operate to prevent our admitting women to the office of attorney at law.

If we were to admit them, we should be exercising the authority conferred upon us in a manner which, we are fully satisfied, was never contemplated by the legislature. Upon this question, it seems to us neither this applicant herself, nor any unprejudiced and intelligent person, can entertain the slightest doubt.

It is to be remembered that at the time this statute was enacted, we had, by express provision, adopted the common law of England, and, with three exceptions, the statutes of that country passed prior to the fourth year of James the First, so far as they were applicable to our condition.

It is to be also remembered that female attorneys at law were unknown in England, and a proposition that a woman should enter the courts of Westminster Hall in that capacity, or as a barrister, would have created hardly less astonishment than one that she should ascend the bench of Bishops, or be elected to a seat in the House of Commons.

It is to be further remembered that when our act was passed, that school of reform, which claims for women participation in the making and administering of the laws had not then arisen, or, if here and there a writer had advanced such theories, they were regarded rather as abstract speculations than as an actual basis for action. That God designed the sexes to occupy different spheres of action, and that it belonged to men to make, apply, and execute the laws, was regarded as an almost axiomatic truth.

It may have been a radical error, but that this was the universal belief certainly admits of no denial. A direct participation in the affairs of government, in even the most elementary form, namely, the right of suffrage, was not then claimed, and has not yet been conceded, unless recently, in one of the newly settled territories of the West.

In view of these facts, we are certainly warranted in saying, that when the legislature gave to this court the power of granting licenses to practice law, it was with not the slightest expectation that this privilege would be extended equally to men and women. Neither has there been any legislation since that period, which would justify us in presuming a change in the legislative intent. Our laws, today, in regard to women, are substantially what they have always been, except in the change wrought by the acts of 1861 and 1869, giving to married women the right to control their own property and earnings.

Whatever, then, may be our individual opinions as to the admission of women to the bar, we do not deem ourselves at liberty to exercise our power in a mode never contemplated by the legislature, and inconsistent with the usages of courts of the common law, from the origin of the system to the present day.

But it is not merely an immense innovation in our own usages, as a court, that we are asked to make. This step, if taken by us, would mean that, in the opinion of this tribunal, every civil office in this State may be filled by women; that is in harmony with the spirit of our constitution and laws that women should be made governors, judges, and sheriffs. This we are not yet prepared to hold.

In our opinion, it is not the province of a court to attempt, by giving a new interpretation to an ancient statute, to introduce so important a change in the legal position of one-half the people. Courts of justice were not intended to be made the instruments of pushing forward measures of popular reform. If it be desirable that those offices which we have borrowed from the English law, and which, from their origin, some centuries ago, down to the present time, have been filled exclusively by men, should also be made accessible to women, then let the change be made, but let it be made by that department of the government to which the constitution has entrusted the power of changing the laws.

The great body of our law rests merely upon ancient usage. The right of a husband in this State to the personal property of his wife, before the act of 1861, rested simply upon such usage, yet who would have justified this court, if prior to the passage of that act, it had solemnly decided that it was unreasonable that the property of the wife should vest in the husband, and this usage should no longer be recognized? Yet was it not as unreasonable that a woman by marriage should lose the title of her personal property, as it is that she should not receive from us a license to practice law? The rule in both cases, until the law of 1861, rested upon the same common law usage, and could have pleaded the same antiquity.

In the one case it was never pretended that this court could properly overturn the rule, and we do not see how we could be justified should we disregard it in the other.

The principle can not be too strictly and conscientiously observed, that each of the three departments of the government should avoid encroachment upon the other, and that it does not belong to the judiciary to attempt to inaugurate great social or political reforms. The mere fact that women have never been licensed as attorneys at law is, in a tribunal where immemorial usage is as much respected as it is and ought to be in courts of justice, a sufficient reason for declining to exercise our discretion in their favor, until the propriety of their participating in the offices of State and the administration of public affairs shall have been recognized by the law-making department of the government,—that department to which the initiative in great measures of reform properly belongs.

For us to attempt, in a matter of this importance, to inaugurate a practice at variance with all the precedents of the law we are sworn to administer, would be an act of judicial usurpation, deserving of the gravest censure. If we could disregard, in this matter, the authority of those unwritten usages which make the great body of our law, we might do so in any other, and the dearest rights of person and property would become a matter of mere judicial discretion.

But it is said the twenty-eighth section of chapter 90 of the revised statutes of 1845 provides that, whenever any person is referred to in the statute by words importing the masculine gender, females, as well as males, shall be deemed to be included.

But the thirty-sixth section of the same chapter provides that this rule of construction shall not apply when there is anything in the subject or context repugnant to such construction. This is the case in the present instance.

In the view we have taken of this question, the argument drawn by the applicant from the constitution of the United States has no pertinency.

In conclusion, we would add that, while we are constrained to refuse this application, we respect the motive which prompts it, and we entertain a profound sympathy with those efforts which are being so widely made to reasonably enlarge the field for the exercise of woman's industry and talent. While those theories which are popularly known as "woman's rights" can not be expected to meet with a very cordial acceptance among the members of a profession, which, more than any other, inclines its followers, if not to stand immovable upon the ancient ways, at least to make no hot haste in measures of reform, still, all right minded men must gladly see new spheres of action opened to woman, and greater inducements offered her to seek the highest and widest culture.

There are some departments of the legal profession in which she can appropriately labor. Whether, on the other hand, to engage in the hot strifes of the bar, in the presence of the public, and with momentous verdicts the prizes of the struggle, would not tend to destroy the deference and delicacy with which it is the pride of our ruder sex to treat her, it is a matter certainly worthy of her consideration.

But the important question is, what effect the presence of women as barristers in our courts would have upon the administration of justice, and the question can be satisfactorily answered only in the light of experience. If the legislature shall choose to remove the existing barriers, and authorize us to issue licenses equally to men and women, we shall cheerfully obey, trusting to the good sense and sound judgment of women themselves, to seek those departments of the practice in which they can labor without reasonable objection.

Application denied

[118]
In re Goodell *(Wisconsin, 1875)*

RYAN C. J.: In courts proceeding according to the course of the common law, a bar is almost as essential as a bench. And a good bar may be said to be a necessity of a good court. This is not always understood, perhaps not fully by the bar itself. On the bench, the lesson is soon learned that the facility and accuracy of judicial labor are largely dependent on the learning and ability of the bar. And it well becomes every court to be careful of its bar and jealous of the rule of admission to it, with the view of fostering in it the highest order of professional excellence.

The constitution makes no express provision for the bar. But it establishes courts, amongst which it distributes all the jurisdiction of all the courts of Westminister Hall, in equity and at common law. And it vests in the courts all the judicial power of the state. The constitutional establishment of such courts appears to carry with it the power to establish a bar to practice in them. And admission to the bar appears to be a judicial power. It may therefore become a very grave question for adjudication here, whether the constitution does not entrust the rule of admissions to the bar, as well as of expulsion from it, exclusively to the discretion of the courts.

The legislature has, indeed, from time to time, assumed power to prescribe rules for the admission of attorneys to practice. When these have seemed reasonable and just, it has generally, we think, been the pleasure of the courts to act upon such statutes, in deference to the wishes of a coordinate branch of the government, without considering the question of power. We do not understand that the circuit courts generally yielded to the unwise and unseemly act of 1849, which assumed to force upon the courts as attorneys, any persons of good moral character, however unlearned or even illiterate; however disqualified, by nature, education or habit, for the important trusts of the profession. We learn from the clerk of this court that no application under that statute was ever made here. The good sense of the legislature has long since led to its repeal. And we have too much reliance on the judgment of the legislature to apprehend another such attempt to degrade the courts. The state suffers essentially by every such assault of one branch of the government upon another; and it is the duty of all the coordinate branches scrupulously to avoid even all seeming of such. If, unfortunately, such an attack upon the dignity of the courts should again be made, it will be time for them to inquire whether the rule of admission be within the legislative or the judicial power. But we will not anticipate such an unwise and unbecoming interference in what so peculiarly concerns the courts, whether the power to make it exists or not. In the meantime, it is a pleasure

39 (Wisc.) 232 (1875).

to defer to all reasonable statutes on the subject. And we will decide this motion on the present statutes, without passing on their binding force.

This is the first application for admission of a female to the bar of this court. And it is just matter for congratulation that it is made in favor of a lady whose character raises no personal objection: something perhaps not always to be looked for in women who forsake the ways of their sex for the ways of ours.

The statute provides for admission of attorneys in a circuit court upon examination to the satisfaction of the judge, and for the right of persons so admitted to practice in all the courts here except this; but that to entitle any one to practice in this court he shall be licensed by order of this court. While these sections give a rule to the circuit courts, they avoid giving any to this court, leaving admission here, as it ought to be, in the discretion of the court. This is, perhaps, sufficient answer to the present application, which is not addressed to our discretion, but proceeds on assumed right founded on admission in a circuit court. But the novel positions on which the motion was pressed appear to call for a broader answer.

The language of the statute, of itself, confessedly applies to males only. But it is insisted that the rule of construction necessarily extends the terms of the statute to females. The rule is that words in the singular number may be construed plural, and in the plural, singular; and that words of the masculine gender may be applied to females; unless, in either case, such construction would be inconsistent with the manifest intention of the legislature. . . .

And the argument for this motion simply is this: that the application of this permissive rule of construction to a provision applicable in terms to males only, has effect, without other sign of legislative intent, to admit females to the bar from which the common law has excluded them ever since courts have administered the common law. This is sufficiently startling. But the argument cannot stop there. Its logic goes far beyond the bar. The same pre-emptory rule of construction would reach all or nearly all the functions of the state government, would obliterate almost all distinction of sex in our statutory *corpus juris,* and make females eligible to almost all offices under our statutes, municipal and state, executive, legislative and judicial, except so far as the constitution may interpose a virile qualification. Indeed the argument appears to overrule even this exception. For we were referred to a case in Iowa, which unfortunately we do not find in the reports of that state, holding a woman not excluded by the statutory description of "any white male person." If we should follow that authority in ignoring the distinction of sex, we do not perceive why it should not emasculate the constitution itself and include females in the constitutional right of male suffrage and male qualification. Such a rule would be one of judicial revolution, not of judicial construction. There is nor sign nor symptom in our statute law of any legislative imagination of such a radical change in the economy of the state government. There are many the other way; an irresistible presumption that the legislature never contemplated such confusion of functions between the sexes. The application of the permissive rule of construction here would not be in aid of the legislative intention, but in open defiance of it. We cannot stultify the court by holding that the legislature intended to bring about a sweeping revolution of social order, by adopting a very innocent rule of statutory construction.

Some attempt was made to give plausibility to the particular construction urged upon us, founded on . . . [two other statutes.] It was represented that one admits women to every department of the university, excepting the military only, and so necessarily including the law department; that the other directs admission to the bar of the graduates of the law department; that the legislature had thus provided for the admission of female graduates of the law school, and ought therefore to be understood as intending the admission of women under the general statute. If the legislature had so provided for the admission of female graduates, we do not perceive how that could aid the construction of the general statute, or this lady, who does not appear to be a graduate. But, unfortunately for the position, the statutes were not stated with the fair accuracy which becomes counsel, and do not support it. . . .

So we find no statutory authority for the admission of females to the bar of any court of this state. And, with all the respect and sympathy for this lady which all men owe to all good women, we cannot regret that we do not. We cannot but think the common law wise in excluding women from the profession of the law. The profession enters largely into the well being of society; and, to be honorably filled and safely to society, exacts the devotion of life. The law of nature destines and qualifies the female sex for the bearing and nurture of the children of our race and for the custody of the homes of the world and their maintenance in love and honor. And all life-long callings of women, inconsistent with these radical and sacred duties of their sex, as is the profession of the law, are departures from the order of nature; and when voluntary, treason against it. The cruel chances of life sometimes baffle both sexes, and may leave women free from the peculiar duties of their sex. These may need employment, and should be welcome to any not derogatory to their sex and its proprieties, or inconsistent with the good order of society. But it is public policy to provide for the sex, not for its superfluous members and not to tempt women from the proper duties of their sex by opening to them duties peculiar to ours. There are many employments in life not unfit for female character. The profession of the law is surely not one of these. The peculiar qualities of womanhood, its gentle graces, its quick sensibility, its tender susceptibility, its purity, its delicacy, its emotional impulses, its subordination of hard reason to sympathetic feeling, are surely not qualifications for forensic strife. Nature has tempered woman as little for the juridical conflicts of the court room, as for the physical conflicts of the battle field. Womanhood is moulded for gentler and better things. And it is not the saints of the world who chiefly give employment to our profession. It has essentially and habitually to do with all that is selfish and malicious, knavish and criminal, coarse and brutal, repulsive and obscene, in human life. It would be revolting to all female sense of the innocence and sanctity of their sex, shocking to man's reverence for womanhood and faith in woman, on which hinge all the better affections and humanities of life, that woman should be permitted to mix professionally in all the nastiness of the world which finds its way into courts of justice; all the unclean issues, all the collateral questions of sodomy, incest, rape, seduction, fornication, adultery, pregnancy, bastardy, legitimacy, prostitution, lascivious cohabition, abortion, infanticide, obscene publications, libel and slander of sex, impotence, divorce: all the nameless catalogue of indecencies, *la chronique scandaleuse* of all the vices and all the infirmities of all society, with which the profession has to deal, and which go towards filling judicial reports which must be read for accurate knowledge of the law. This is bad enough for men. We hold in too high reverence the sex without which, as is truly and beautifully written, *la commencement de la vie est sans secours, le milieu sans plaisir, et la fin sans consolation* [the beginning of life is without help, the middle without pleasure, and the end without consolation], voluntarily to commit it to such studies and such occupations. *Non tali auxilio nec defensoribus istis* [not by such aid nor by those defenders], should juridical contests be upheld. Reverence for all womanhood would suffer in the public spectacle of woman so instructed and so engaged. This motion gives appropriate evidence of this truth. No modest woman could read without pain and self abasement, no woman could so overcome the instincts of sex as publicly to discuss, the case which we had occasion to cite *supra, King* v. *Wiseman.* And when counsel was arguing for this lady that the word, person, in sec. 32, ch. 119, necessarily includes females, her presence made it impossible to suggest to him as *reductio ad absurdum* of his position, that the same construction of the word in sec. 1, ch. 37, would subject woman to prosecution for rape. Discussions are habitually necessary in courts of justice which are unfit for female ears. The habitual presence of women at these would tend to relax the public sense of decency and propriety. If, as counsel threatened, these things are to come, we will take no voluntary part in bringing them about.

BY THE COURT—The motion is denied.

Occupational Freedom and the U.S. Supreme Court

[119]

The Fourteenth Amendment, United States Constitution (1868)

Section 1. All persons born or naturalized in the United States, and subject to the jurisdiction thereof, are citizens of the United States and of the State wherein they reside. No State shall make or enforce any law which shall abridge the privileges or immunities of citizens of the United States; nor shall any State deprive any person of life, liberty, or property, without due process of law; nor deny any person within its jurisdiction the equal protection of the laws.

[120]

Argument of the Hon. Matt. H. Carpenter before the U.S. Supreme Court, January 18, 1872, upon the Application of Myra Bradwell to be Admitted to the Bar

This is a writ of error to the supreme court of the State of Illinois, to review the proceedings of that court, denying the petition of the plaintiff in error to be admitted to practice as an attorney and counsellor of that court under the XIVth amendment of the Constitution of the United States. . . .

This record presents the broad question, whether a married woman, being a citizen of the United States and of a State, and possessing the necessary qualifications, is entitled by the Constitution of the United States to be admitted to practice as an attorney and counsellor at law in the courts of the State in which she resides. This is a question not of taste, propriety, or politeness, but of civil right.

Before proceeding to discuss this question, it may be well to distinguish it from the question of the right of female citizens to participate in the exercise of the elective franchise.

The great problem of female suffrage draws to itself, in prejudiced minds, every question relating to the civil rights of women; and it seems to be feared that doing justice to woman's rights in any particular would probably be followed by the establishment of the right of female suffrage, which it is assumed, would overthrow Christianity, defeat the ends of modern civilization, and upturn the world.

While I do not believe that female suffrage has been secured by the existing amendments to the Constitution of the United States, neither do I look upon that result as at all to be dreaded. It is not, in my opinion, a question of *woman's rights* merely, but, in a far greater degree, a question of man's rights. When God created man, he announced the law of his being, that it was not well for him to be alone, and so he created woman to be his helpmate and companion. . . . Where women are received on an equality with men, we find good order and good manners prevailing. Because women frequent railroad cars and steamboats, markets, shops, and post offices, those places must be, and are, conducted with order and decency. The only

From *Chicago Legal News*, January 20, 1872.

great resorts from which woman is excluded by law are the election places; and the violence, rowdyism, profanity, and obscenity of the gathering there in our largest cities are sufficient to drive decent men even away from the polls. If our wives, sisters and daughters were going to the polls, we should go with them, and good order would be observed. . . .

I have more faith in female suffrage to reform the abuses of our election system in the large cities than I have in the penal election laws to be enforced by soldiers and marines. Who believes that, if ladies were admitted to seats in Congress, or upon the bench, or were participating in discussions at the bar, such proceedings would thereby be rendered less refined, or that less regard would be paid to the rights of all?

But whether women should be admitted to the right of suffrage is one thing; whether this end has already been accomplished is quite another. . . . The XIVth and XVth amendments seem to settle this question against the right of female suffrage. These amendments seem to recognize the distinction at first pointed out between *"privileges and immunities,"* and *the right* to vote.

The XIVth amendment declares, "all persons born and naturalized in the United States and of the State wherein they reside." Of course, women, as well as men, are included in this provision, and recognized as citizens. This amendment further declares, "No State shall make or enforce any law which shall abridge the privileges of immunities of citizens of the United States." If the privileges and immunities of a citizen cannot be abridged, then, of course, the privileges and immunities of all citizens must be the same. The second section of this amendment provides that "representatives shall be apportioned among the several States according to their respective numbers, counting the whole number of persons in each State, excluding Indians, not taxed. But when the *right to vote* at any election, etc. is denied to any of the *male inhabitants,* being twenty-one years of age, etc., the basis of representation therein shall be reduced in the proportion which the number of such *male citizens* twenty-one years of age in such State."

It cannot be denied, that the right or power of a State to exclude a portion of its male citizens from the right to vote, is recognized by this second section; from which it follows that the *right to vote* is not one of the "privileges or immunities" which the first section declares shall not be abridged by any State. The right of female suffrage is also inferentially denied by that provision of the second section, above quoted, which provides, that when a State shall deny the right to vote to any *male citizen,* "the basis of representation therein shall be reduced in the proportion which the number of such *male citizens* shall bear to the whole number of *male citizens* in such State."

. . .

The XVth amendment is equally decisive. It recognizes the right—that is, power—of any State to exclude a portion of its citizens from the right to vote, and only narrows this right in favor of a particular class. Its language is: "The right of citizens of the United States to vote shall not be denied or abridged, etc., on account of race, color, or previous condition of servitude." This amendment was wholly unnecessary upon the theory that the XIVth amendment had established or recognized the right of every citizen to vote. It recognizes the right of a State to exclude a portion of its citizens, and only restrains that power so far as to provide that citizens shall not be excluded on account of race, color, or previous condition of servitude. In every other case, the power of exclusion recognized by the XIVth amendment is untouched by the XVth amendment.

. . .

I come now to the narrower and precise question before the court: Can a female citizen, duly qualified in respect of age, character and learning, claim, under the XIVth amendment, [the] privilege of earning [a] livelihood by practicing at the bar of a judicial court?

. . .

We have already seen that the right to vote is not one of those privileges which are declared to be common to all citizens and which no State may abridge meant that it is a political right, which any State may deny to a citizen, except on account of race, color or previous condition of servitude. It therefore only remains to determine whether admission to the bar belongs to that class of privileges which a State may not abridge, or that class of political rights as to which a State may discriminate between its citizens. . . .

In *Cummings* v. *Missouri,* 4 Wall., 321, this court says:

> . . . The theory upon which our political institutions rest is, that all men have certain inalienable rights—that among these are life, liberty, and the pursuit of happiness; and that in the pursuit of happiness all avocations, all honors, all positions, are alike open to every one, and that in the protection of these rights all are equal before the law. Any deprivation or extension of any of these rights for past conduct is punishment, and can be in no otherwise defined.

No broader or better enumeration of the privileges which pertain to American citizenship could be given. "Life, liberty, and the pursuit of happiness, and, in the pursuit of happiness, all avocations, all honors, all positions, are alike open to every one; and in the protection of these rights all are equal before the law."

In *Ex Parte Garland* (4 Wall., 378), this court says:

> . . . . Attorneys and counselors are officers of the court, admitted as such by its order, *upon evidence of their possessing sufficient legal learning and fair private character.* . . . The order of admission is the judgment of the court, that the parties possess the requisite qualifications as attorneys and counselors, and are entitled to appear as such and conduct causes therein. From its entry the parties become officers of the court, and are responsible to it for professional misconduct. They hold their office during good behavior, *and can only be deprived of it for misconduct, ascertained by the judgment of the court, after opportunity to be heard has been offered.* Their admission or their exclusion is the exercise of judicial power, and has been so held in numerous cases. . . . The attorney and counselor being, by the solemn judicial act of the court, clothed with his office, does not hold it as a matter of grace and favor. The right which it confers upon him is a *right* of which he can only be deprived by the judgment of the court, for moral or professional delinquency. The legislature may

undoubtedly prescribe qualifications for the office, to which he must conform, as it may, where it has exclusive jurisdiction, prescribe qualifications for the pursuit of the ordinary avocations of life.

From these cases the conclusion is irresistible, that the profession of the law, like the clerical profession and that of medicine, is an avocation open to every citizen of the United States. And while the Legislature may prescribe qualifications for entering upon this pursuit, they cannot, under the guise of fixing qualifications, exclude a class of citizens from admission to the bar. The Legislature may say at what age candidates shall be admitted; may elevate or depress the standard of learning required. But a qualification, to which a whole class of citizens never can attain, is not a regulation of admission to the bar, but is, as to such citizens, a prohibition. For instance, a State Legislature could not, in enumerating the qualifications, require the candidate to be a white citizen. This would be the exclusion of all colored citizens, without regard to age, character, or learning. Such an act would abridge the rights of all colored citizens by denying them admission into one of the avocations which this court has declared is alike open to every one. I am certain this court would declare it void. And I challenge the most astute mind to draw any distinction between such an act and a custom which denies this privilege to all female citizens, without regard to age, character or learning. If the Legislature may, under pretense of fixing qualifications, declare that no female citizen shall be permitted to practice law, they may as well declare that no colored citizen shall practice law. . . .

Why may a colored citizen buy, hold, and sell land in any State of the Union? Because he is a citizen, and that is one of the privileges of a citizen. Why may a colored citizen be admitted to the bar? Because he is a citizen and that is one of the avocations open to every citizen; and no State can abridge his right to pursue it. Certainly no other reason can be given.

Now, let us come to the case of Myra Bradwell. She is a citizen of the United States, and of the State of Illinois. She has been judicially ascertained to be of full age, and to possess the requisite character and learning. Indeed, the court below, in their opinion, found in the record, page 9, say: "Of the ample qualifications of the applicant we have no doubt."

Still, admission to the bar was denied the petitioner, not upon the ground that she was not a citizen; not for want of age or qualifications; not because the profession of the law is not one of those avocations which are open to every American citizen as matter of right, upon complying with the reasonable regulations prescribed by the legislature; but upon the sole ground that inconvenience would result from permitting her to enjoy her legal rights in this, to wit, that her clients might have difficulty in enforcing the contracts they might make with her, as their attorney, because of her being a married woman. . . .

Concede, for argument, that the XIVth amendment ought to have read thus: "No State shall make or enforce any law which shall abridge the privileges or immunities of any citizens except married women"; yet that exception is not found in the sweeping provision of this amendment. . . . If this court shall approve this exception, in the very teeth of the unambiguous language of the Constitution, where may we expect judicial legislation to stop? Can this court say that married women have no rights that are to be respected? Can this court say, that when the XIVth amendment speaks of all persons, etc., and declares them to be citizens, it means all male persons and unmarried females? Or can this court say that, when the XIVth amendment declares "the privileges of no citizen shall be abridged" it means that the privileges of no male citizen or unmarried female citizen shall be abridged? This would be bold dealing with the constitutional provision. It would be excluding a large proportion of the citizens of the United States from privileges which the Constitution declares shall be the inheritance of every citizen alike. . . .

But again: Mrs. Bradwell, admitted to the bar, becomes an officer of the court, subject to its summary jurisdiction. Any malpractice or unprofessional conduct towards her client would be punishable by fine, imprisonment, or expulsion from the bar, or by all three. Her clients would, therefore, not be compelled to resort to actions at law against her. . . .

But let it not be supposed that, in trying to answer as to the inconveniences imagined by the court below, I am at all departing from the broad ground of constitutional right upon which I rest this cause. I maintain that the XIVth amendment opens to every citizen of the United States, male or female, black or white, married or single, the honorable professions as well as the servile employments of life; and that no citizen can be excluded from any one of them. Intelligence, integrity, and honor are the only qualifications that can be prescribed as conditions precedent to any entry upon any honorable pursuit or profitable avocation, and all the privileges and immunities which I vindicate to a colored citizen, I vindicate to our mothers, our sisters, and our daughters. The inequalities of sex will undoubtedly have their influence, and be considered by every client desiring to employ counsel.

There may be cases in which a client's right can only be rescued by an exercise of the rough qualities possessed by men. There are many cases in which the telling sympathy and the silver voice of woman would accomplish more than the severity and sternness of man could achieve. Of a bar composed of men and women of equal integrity and learning, women might be more or less frequently retained, as the taste of judgment of clients might dictate. But the broad shield of the Constitution is over them all, and protects each in that measure of success which his or her individual merits may secure.

[121]

Bradwell *v.* Illinois, *U.S. Supreme Court (1873)*

Concurring Opinion of Mr. Justice BRADLEY joined by Justices FIELD and SWAYNE:

I concur in the judgment of the court in this case . . . but not for the reasons specified in the opinion just read.

The claim that, under the Fourteenth Amendment of the Constitution, which declares that no State shall make or enforce any law which shall abridge the privileges and immunities of citizens of the United States, the statute law of Illinois, or the common law prevailing in that State, can no longer be set up as a barrier against the right of females to pursue any lawful employment for a livelihood (the practice of law included), assumes that it is one of the privileges and immunities of women as citizens to engage in any and every profession, occupation, or employment in civil life.

It certainly cannot be affirmed as an historical fact, that this has ever been established as one of the fundamental privileges and immunities of the sex. On the contrary, the civil law as well as nature herself has always recognized a wide difference in the respective spheres and destinies of man and woman. Man is, or should be, women's protector and defender. The natural and proper timidity and delicacy which belongs to the female sex evidently unfits it for many of the occupations of civil life. The constitution of the family organization, which is founded in the divine ordinance, as well as in the nature of things, indicates the domestic sphere as that which properly belongs to the domain and functions of womanhood. The harmony, not to say identity, of interests and views which belong, or should belong, to the family institution is repugnant to the idea of a woman adopting a distinct and independent career from that of her husband. So firmly fixed was this sentiment in the founders of the common law that it became a maxim of that system of jurisprudence that a woman had no legal existence separate from her husband, who was regarded as her head and representative in the social state; and, notwithstanding some recent modifications of this civil status, many of the special rules of law flowing from the dependent upon this cardinal principle still exist in full force in most States. One of these is, that a married woman is incapable, without her husband's consent, of making contracts which shall be binding on her or him. This very incapacity was one circumstance which the Supreme Court of Illinois deemed important in rendering a married woman incompetent fully to perform the duties and trusts that belong to the office of an attorney and counselor.

It is true that many women are unmarried and not affected by any of the duties, complications, and incapacities arising out of the married state, but these are exceptions to the general rule. The paramount destiny and mission of woman are to fulfill the noble and benign offices of wife and mother. This is the law of the Creator. And the rules of civil society must be adapted to the general constitution of things, and cannot be based upon exceptional cases.

The humane movements of modern society, which have for their object the multiplication of avenues of woman's advancement, and of occupations adapted to her condition and sex, have my heartiest concurrence. But I am not prepared to say that it is one of her fundamental rights and privileges to be admitted into every office and position, including those which require highly special qualifications and demanding special responsibilities.

[122]

Myra Bradwell, "The XIVth Amendment and Our Case" (1873)

We have heretofore published a telegraphic report of the opinion of a majority of the Judges of the Supreme Court of the United States, delivered by Miller, J., affirming the judgment of the Supreme Court of Illinois, refusing to grant us a license to practice law, upon the sole ground that we were a woman. We have since received an official copy of the opinion of the court, also the opinion of Bradley, J., concurred in by Field, J., and an official notification that the late lamented Chief Justice Chase, for whose opinion we always had the greatest respect, dissented entirely from the opinion of the court. . . . Although we do not believe the construction of the XIV amendment, as given by a majority of the court, and their definition of the privileges and immunities of citizens of the United States are sound, we take great pleasure in saying that the opinion delivered by Judge Miller is confined strictly to the points at issue, and is just such a one as might be expected from an able and experienced jurist entertaining the views that Judge Miller does upon these constitutional questions. He does not for a moment lower the dignity of the judge by traveling out of the record to give his individual views upon what we commonly term *"Women's Rights."*

We regard the opinion of Judge Bradley as in conflict with his opinion delivered in what are known as the New Orleans Slaughter-house Cases, . . . In that case Judge Bradley said: *"There is no more sacred right of citizenship than the right to pursue unmolested a lawful employment in a lawful manner. It is nothing more or less than the sacred right of labor."* In speaking of pursuits that required the granting of licenses, the judge said:

> Public policy may require that these pursuits should be regulated and supervised by
> the local authorities in order to promote the public health, the public order and the
> general well being, but they are open to all proper applicants, and none are *rejected*

Editorial in *Chicago Legal News,* May 10, 1873.

except those who fail to exhibit the requisite qualifications. . . . All these systems of regulation are useful and entirely competent to the governing power, and are not at all inconsistent with the great rights of LIBERTY OF PURSUIT, which is one of the *fundamental* principles of a free government as well as one of the fundamental privileges of an American citizen.

If as Judge BRADLEY says, the *liberty of pursuit* is one of the fundamental privileges of an American citizen, how can he then, and be consistent, deprive an American citizen of the right to follow any calling or profession under laws, rules and regulations that shall operate equally upon all, simply because such citizen is a woman?

[123]
Belva Lockwood, "My Efforts to Become a Lawyer" (1888)

[To] *Mrs. Belva A. Lockwood:*

Madam,

The Faculty of Columbian College have considered your request to be admitted to the Law Department of this institution, and after due consultation, have considered that such admission would not be expedient, as it would be likely to distract the attention of the young men.

Respectfully,
Geo. W. Samson, Pres.

I was much chagrined by this slap in the face, and the inference to be drawn from it, that my rights and privileges were not to be considered a moment whenever they came in conflict with those of the opposite sex. My husband counselled that I should keep silence about it, as his relations with Dr. Samson, as ministers and co-laborers in the same church, had hitherto been friendly. But the truth would out. The newspaper men got hold of it, as newspaper men will, and came to me and demanded to see the letter, declaring that the action of Dr. Samson was a matter of public interest. My husband protested; but I read them the letter, retaining the original, which I still have.

Next year the National University Law School was opened, and, ostensibly as part of its plan to admit women to membership on the same terms as young men, I was invited, with other ladies, to attend the classes, and gladly accepted. . . . It was not long before there commenced to be a growl by the young men, some of them

From *Lippincotts Monthly Magazine,* February 1888. Cited in W. Elliot Brownlee and Mary M. Brownlee, eds., *Women in the American Economy: A Documentary History, 1625–1929* (New Haven: Yale University Press, 1976), pp. 297–307. Reprinted by permission.

Belva Ann Bennett McNall
Lockwood (1830–1917).
Frances Willard and Mary
Livermore, eds., *A Woman
of the Century* (1893).

declaring openly that they would not graduate with women. The women were notified that they could no longer attend the lectures, but would be permitted to complete the course of studies. As Commencement day approached, it became very evident that we were not to receive our diplomas, nor be permitted to appear on the stage with the young men at graduation. This was a heavy blow to my aspirations, as the diploma would have been the entering wedge into the court and saved me the weary contest which followed.

For a time I yielded quite ungracefully to the inevitable, while Lydia S. Hall solaced herself by marrying a man named Grafan and leaving the city. She was not a young woman at that time, but a staid matron past forty; and after her departure I entirely lost sight of her, and suppose she became "merged," as Blackstone says, in her husband. I was not to be squelched so easily.

I asked a member of the bar, Frances Miller, Esq., to move my admission to the bar of the Supreme Court, D.C., which he did some time in the latter part of July, 1872, and I was referred to the examining committee for report. I at once hunted up the committee and asked for the examination. It was with evident reluctance that the committee came together for the examination, which was quite rigid and lasted for three days. I waited for weeks after this, but the committee did not report. Thereupon I entered complaint of their action to the Supreme Justice, David K. Cartter, and another committee was appointed. It was Judge Cartter who one year before, in the revision of the Laws of the District of Columbia, knowing that some women in the District were preparing for admission to the bar, had asked that the rule of court be so amended as to strike out the word "male," and it had been done, so that this disability no longer stood in my way. The new committee, like the old one, examined me for three days, but would not report. . . .

After the political sky had cleared, I made my appearance at a course of lectures in the Georgetown College Law Class, but when a call was made by the Chancellor for the settlement of dues my money was declined, and I was informed by a note from the Chancellor, a few days later, that I could not become a member of the class. . . .

I now grew a little bolder, and to a certain extent desperate, and addressed the following letter to President Grant, then President ex officio of the National University Law School.

No. 432 Ninth Street, N.W.
Washington, D.C., September 3, 1873

To His Excellency U.S. Grant, President U.S.A.:
Sir,
    You are, or you are not, President of the National University Law School. If you are its President, I desire to say to you that I have passed through the curriculum of study in this school, and am entitled to, and demand, my diploma. If you are not its President, then I ask that you take your name from its papers, and not hold out to the world to be what you are not.

Very respectfully,
Belva A. Lockwood

This letter contained about as much bottled-up indignation as it was possible for one short missive to conceal under a respectful guise. I received no direct answer, but next week I was presented by the Chancellor of the University, W. B. Wedgewood, with my diploma duly signed, and a few days after I was admitted to the bar.

On my admission, the clerk remarked, "You went through to-day, Mrs. Lockwood, like a knife. You see the world moves in our day." Justice Cartter said, "Madam, if you come into this court we shall treat you like a man." Justice Arthur McArthur remarked "Bring on as many women lawyers as you choose: I do not believe they will be a success." These comments did not affect me, as I already had my hands full of work, and cases ready to file in anticipation of my admission. My friends had confidence in my ability; and the attention that had been called to me in the novel contest I had made not only gave me a wide advertising, but drew towards me a great deal of substantial sympathy in the way of work. Besides this, I had

already booked a large number of government claims, in which I had been recognized by the heads of the different Departments as attorney. . . . There is a good
opening at the bar for the class of women who have taste and tact for it.

But neither my ambitions nor my troubles ceased with my admission to the
District bar. On or about the 1st of April, 1874, having an important case to file in
the Court of Claims, I asked one A. A. Hosmer, a reputable member of the bar of
that court, to move my admission thereto, having previously filed with the clerk my
power of attorney in the case, and certificate from the clerk of the District Court of
my good standing therein, as required by the rule of that court.

At precisely twelve o'clock the five justices of that dignified court marched in,
made their solemn bows, and sat down. Without ceremony, after the formal opening
of the court by the clerk, and the reading of the minutes of the last session, my
gracious attorney moved my admission. There was a painful pause. Every eye in the
court-room was fixed first upon me, and then upon the court, when Justice Drake, in
measured words, announced, "Mistress Lockwood, you are a woman." For the first
time in my life I began to realize that it was a crime to be a woman; but it was too
late to put in a denial, and I at once pleaded guilty to the charge of the court. Then
the chief justice announced, "This case will be continued for one week." I retired in
good order, but my counsel who had only been employed for that occasion, deserted
me, and seemed never afterwards to have backbone enough to keep up the fight.

On the following week, duly as the hand of the clock approached the hour of
twelve, I again marched into the court-room, but this time almost with as much
solemnity as the judges, and accompanied by my husband and several friends. When
the case of Lockwood was reached, and I again stood up before that august body, the
solemn tones of the chief justice announced, "Mistress Lockwood, you are a married
woman!" Here was a new and quite unexpected arraignment, that almost took my
breath away for the moment; but I collected myself, and responded, with a wave of
my hand towards my husband, "Yes, may it please the court, but I am here with the
consent of my husband," Dr. Lockwood at the same time bowing to the court. My
pleading and distressed look was of no avail. The solemn chief justice responded,
"This cause will be continued for another week."

Three weeks later, I was again present on the solemn assembling of that court.
It took Judge Nott one hour and a half to deliver his opinion, which closed as
follows:

> The position which this court assumes is that under the laws and Constitution
> of the United States a court is without power to grant such an application, and that
> a woman is without legal capacity to take the office of attorney.

Of course this was a squelcher, and with the ordinary female mind would have
ended the matter; for it was concurred in without a dissenting voice by the other four
judges on that august bench. But I was at this time not only thoroughly interested in

the law, but devoted to my clients, anxious that their business should not suffer, and determined to support my family by the profession I had chosen. My cases and my powers of attorney were filed in the court, and there was nothing to prevent me from taking the testimony, which I did, and preparing the notices and motions which my clients filed. Nevertheless I found that I was working continuously at a disadvantage, and that my clients lacked the confidence in me that I would have commanded had I stood fairly with the court. . . .

. . . I at once appealed it to the United States Supreme Court, hoping that before the case would be reached in that court I should have had the three years of good standing in the court below, and thus become entitled to admission thereto under the rule, which reads, "Any attorney in good standing before the highest court of any State or Territory for the space of three years shall be admitted to this court when presented by a member of this bar." I read the rule over carefully and repeatedly, to make sure that it included me, and asked myself, Why not? Was not I a member of the bar of the Supreme Court of the District of Columbia in good standing? Had I not been such for three years? The law did not say "any man," or "any male citizen," but "any attorney."

Patiently, hopefully, I waited. At last, in October, 1876, full of hope and expectations, and in company with the Hon. A. G. Riddle, whom I asked to introduce me, I presented myself before the bar of the United States Supreme Court for admission thereto. Again I had reckoned without my host. My attorney made the presentation, holding my credentials in his hand. Those nine gowned judges looked at me in amazement and dismay. The case was taken under advisement, and on the following Monday an opinion rendered, of which the following is the substance: "As the court knows no English precedent for the admission of women to the bar, it declines to admit, unless there shall be a more extended public opinion, or special legislation." No pen can portray the utter astonishment and surprise with which I listened to this decision. My reverence for the ermine vanished into thin air. I was dazed, and kept repeating to myself, "No English precedent! How about Queen Eleanor and Elizabeth, who sat in the *aula regia* and dispensed the duties of chief chancellor of the English realm in person? How about Anne, Countess of Pembroke, who was hereditary sheriff of Westmoreland, and who at the assizes at Appleby sat with the judges on the bench?" "A more extended public opinion,"—how was I to make it? "Special legislation,"—how was I to obtain it, with a family to support, and a sick husband on my hands? I went home, and again took up the thread of my law cases before the District bar, but determined not to let this matter rest.

What next? When Congress assembled in December, I appealed to the Hon. Benjamin F. Butler to draft and introduce in that body a bill for the admission of women to the bar of the United States Supreme Court. This was my first bid for the special legislation. The bill was carefully drawn, introduced, recommended by the House Judiciary for passage, debated, and ingloriously lost on its third reading.

The following year a second bill, drafted, at my suggestion, by Hon. Wm. G. Lawrence, fared even worse than the first, and died almost before it was born.

During all these years of discouragement I was indefatigable in the prosecution of my cases before the bar of the District, and had won some reputation as a lawyer. My husband, after three years of total prostration, died, April 23, 1877. In the autumn of 1877 some of the newspaper men of Washington, who had begun to be interested in the long and unequal contest that I had waged, asked me what I intended to do next. "Get up a fight all along the line," I replied. "I shall ask again to be admitted to the bar of the Supreme Court, I shall myself draft a bill and ask its introduction into both Houses of Congress; and, as I have now a case to be brought in the Federal court in Baltimore, *Royuello* v. *Attoché*, I shall ask admission to the bar of the Federal court at Baltimore." This latter claim had been sent to me from the city of Mexico, and was for fifty thousand dollars, "Very well," said they: "we are going to help you out this time." And they did.

I prepared and asked the Hon. John M. Glover to introduce into the House of Representatives, in December, 1877, the following bill:

> Be it enacted by the Senate and House of Representatives of the United States of America in Congress assembled:
>
> That any woman duly qualified who shall have been a member of the highest court of any State or Territory, or of the Supreme Court of the District of Columbia, for the space of three years, and shall have maintained a good standing before such Court, and who shall be a person of good moral character, shall, on motion, and the production of such record, be admitted to practise before the Supreme Court of the United State.

I was soon called to make an argument before the House Committee on the Judiciary after which the bill was favorably reported without a dissenting voice, and passed the House early in the session by two-thirds majority.

On reaching the Senate, it was referred to the Senate Judiciary and committed to the Hon. Aaron A. Sargent, of California. Conceiving that the bill as it passed the House was not broad enough, he amended it, but his amendment was lost, and the Judiciary Committee made an adverse report on the bill. I had done a great deal of lobbying and had used a great many arguments to get the bill through, but all to no avail. With consummate tact, Mr. Sargent had the bill recommitted, but it went over to the next session. I worked diligently through the second series of the Forty-fifth Congress for the passage of my bill, but the Judiciary Committee made a second adverse report on the bill, and this time Mr. Sargent had the forethought to have the bill calendared, so that it might come up on its merits.

But another misfortune overtook me: Mr. Sargent was taken ill before my bill was reached, and compelled to go to Florida for his health. What was I to do now? Here was my work for years about to be wrecked for want of a foster-mother in the Senate to take charge of it. I knew pretty well the status of every member of that body, for I had conversed with all of them, both at this and at the previous session, and in this extremity I went to the Hon. Joseph E. McDonald, of Indiana, and besought him to take charge of the bill. . . . From the time he assumed this responsibility Senator McDonald was vigilant in the interest of the bill, and, as the Forty-fifth Congress drew to a close, used what influence he could to get the bill up. It was in a precarious position. A single objection would carry it over. . . .

I have been interested in many bills in Congress, and have often appeared before committees of Senate and House, but this was by far the strongest lobbying that I ever performed. Nothing was too daring for me to attempt. I addressed Senators as though they were old familiar friends, and with an earnestness that carried with it conviction. Before the shadows of night had gathered, the victory had been won. The bill admitting women to the bar of the United States Supreme Court passed the Senate on the 7th of February, 1879. It was signed by the President, Rutherford B. Hayes, some days later.

On the 3rd of March, 1879, on motion of the Hon. A. G. Riddle, I was admitted to the bar of the United States Supreme Court. The passage of that bill virtually opened the doors of all the Federal Courts in the country to the women of the land, whenever qualified for such admission. I was readily admitted to the District Courts of Maryland and Massachusetts after this admission to the Supreme Court.

On the 6th of March, 1879, on motion of the Hon. Thomas J. Durant, I was admitted to the bar of the United States Court of Claims. Thus ended the great struggle for the admission of women to the bar. Most of the States in the Union have since recognized her right thereto, and notably the State of Pennsylvania, as in the case of Carrie B. Kilgore, who has recently been admitted to the Supreme Court of the State.

[124]
In re Lockwood, *U.S. Supreme Court (1893)*

Mr. Chief Justice FULLER delivered the opinion of the court:

This is an application by Belva A. Lockwood for leave to file a petition for a mandamus requiring the Supreme Court of Appeals of Virginia to admit her to practice law in that court. Mrs. Lockwood has been for many years a member of the bar of this court and of the Supreme Court of the District of Columbia, and also she avers, of the bars of several States of the Union. Her complaint is that she recently applied to the Supreme Court of Appeals of Virginia to be admitted to the practice of law in that court, and the court denied her application, notwithstanding it is provided by a statute of that State that "any person duly authorized and practising as counsel or attorney at law in any State or Territory of the United States, or in the District of Columbia, may practise as such in the courts of this State." Code Va.

154 (U.S.) 116 (1893).

1887, §3192; and she alleges that the only reason for the rejection of her application was that she is a woman. . . . Our interposition seems to be invoked upon the ground that petitioner has been denied a privilege or immunity belonging to her as a citizen of the United States, and enjoyed by the women of Virginia, in contravention of the second section of Article IV of the Constitution and of the Fourteenth Amendment.

In *Minor* v. *Happersett,* 21 Wall. 162, this court held that the word "citizen" is often used to convey the idea of membership in a nation, and in that sense, women, if born of citizen parents within the jurisdiction of the United States, have always been considered citizens of the United States, as much so before the adoption of the Fourteenth Amendment of the Constitution as since; but that the right of suffrage was not necessarily one of the privileges or immunities of citizenship before the adoption of the Fourteenth Amendment, and that amendment did not add to these privileges and immunities. Hence, that a provision in a state constitution which confined the right of voting to male citizens of the United States was no violation of the Federal Constitution.

In *Bradwell* v. *The State,* 16 Wall. 130, it was held that the right to practise law in the state courts was not a privilege or immunity of a citizen of the United States; that the right to control and regulate the granting of license to practise law in the courts of a State is one of those powers that was not transferred for its protection to the Federal government, and its exercise is in no manner governed or controlled by citizenship of the United States in the party seeking such license.

Section 3192 of the Code of Virginia quoted in this application is one of twelve sections constituting chap. 154 of that Code, entitled, "Of Attorneys-at-Law Generally." Section 3193 reads: "Every such person shall produce, before each court in which he intends to practise, satisfactory evidence of his being so licensed or authorized, and take an oath that he will honestly demean himself in the practise of the law, and to the best of his ability execute his office of attorney-at-law; and also, when he is licensed in this State, take the oath of fidelity to the Commonwealth."

It was for the Supreme Court of Appeals to construe the statute of Virginia in question, and to determine whether the word "person" as therein used is confined to males, and whether women are admitted to practise law in that Commonwealth.

UNIT 4

$$\Big[\textit{Crime and Deviance}\Big]$$

INSANITY

The Jacksonian Era saw a vast increase in the number of mental asylums. It used to be thought that asylums, like prisons, developed to contain disruptive males but recent studies show that most inmates were women. In some institutions such as The New York State Lunatic Asylum at Utica, opened in 1843, and the Willard Asylum, opened in 1869, the female inmate population was composed largely of immigrants and Catholics; in others, like The New Jersey State Lunatic Asylum at Trenton, opened in 1848, the female population was largely white, middle class, Presbyterian and Methodist.

Commitment records provided valuable information about community perceptions of what constituted "insane" behavior in women. Curable mental illness for women seems to have been defined as deviance from the model of true womanhood and domesticity. Women were often institutionalized for the type of loud and violent behavior considered acceptable, if not desirable, in men. Among women the cause of stress leading to antisocial behavior was likely to be family conflict, often wife-beating. The asylum was used largely for private family ends, and most women were committed for acts that embarrassed or disrupted the household and taxed the patience of those around them. Many women manifested their rage with outbursts against domesticity, violating dress and etiquette codes, or revealed their frustrations in delusions of power and authority.[25]

The Trial of Elizabeth Packard (1864) attracted much public attention. It dramatized the conflict within individual families over assertions of personal autonomy by married women and exposed the use of mental asylums to sustain cultural norms—in this case a wife's submission to her husband. White middle class women absorbed into their popular consciousness the larger culture's passion for liberty and equality. They were most likely to express their yearning for self-determination indirectly through religious activity. This pitted the norm of obedience to a husband's authority against freedom of conscience and freedom of speech.

Elizabeth Packard (1817–1897), a model housewife with six children, was married to the pastor of the Presbyterian church in Manteno, Illinois. Independent religious inquiry led her away from the orthodox Calvinism preached by her husband towards religious views that affirmed female worth and capacity. Her conviction that the Holy Ghost was the female counterpart to God the Father and acted through spiritual women emboldened her to discuss more openly her own views on theology and slavery. Her husband responded to this rejection of his authority by denouncing her before his congregation. When this failed to reduce her, Theophilus Packard had her committed to the state mental institution for the curably insane at Jacksonville.

Illinois law at that time permitted a husband to institutionalize a wife without prior notice. It provided no legal procedure by which she could challenge charges of insanity before incarceration. The law required the agreement of the superintendent, who was a doctor. Normally a husband had to present two medical opinions and evidence of disruptive behavior. Once hospitalized a wife could only be discharged into her husband's custody. Mrs. Packard regularly refused to return home on his terms since this would be voluntary slavery. For three years Dr. McFarland, the Superintendent, tried to get her to recognize that her actions were the product of a "wilfull spirit," rather than the "spirit of God within her."

Unable to change her mind, the hospital finally discharged her into her husband's custody on the technical grounds that she was incurably insane. To prevent his wife from seeing their children and teaching them subversive ideas, Theophilus Packard shipped her to distant relatives. She escaped and returned home. He locked her in her room while making arrangements to commit her to a Massachusetts hospital for the incurably insane. Neighbors came to her aid and obtained a writ of habeas corpus. In this way Elizabeth Packard gained the jury trial and vindication she had long sought. Her husband then sold the family property and absconded with the money and their minor children. This transformed Elizabeth Packard into an advocate for married women's right to retain their own earnings, to control their own property and to the custody of their children. She did not, however, see the need for suffrage.

Elizabeth Packard is better known for lobbying in behalf of laws requiring jury trials for commitment and for other forms of protection against

The Trial of Mrs Packard. Mrs. E. P. W. Packard, *Modern Persecution, or, Married Woman's Liabilities, as Demonstrated by the Action of the Illinois Legislature* (New York, 1873).

abuse of power by mental asylums. She published and sold personally enough copies of her books to support herself and her children in comfort. Her claims that other women were institutionalized for the same reason, that torture was used in hospitals and that patients were employed for private gain were confirmed through legislative investigation.

Psychiatrists and reformers, striving for recognition of insanity as an illness that might be cured with proper treatment then and now oppose jury trials as inappropriate and inhumane. Hospitalization and treatment should be a medical matter and left in the hands of experts.[26] The question raised by the transcript of *The Trial of Mrs. Elizabeth Packard* continues to be important. Can medical and social conceptions of normality be separated?

INFANTICIDE

In 1868, while investigating and publicizing the living and working conditions of women wage earners in different industries, reporters for Susan B. Anthony's short-lived suffragist newspaper, *The Revolution*, uncovered the case of Hester Vaughan, a young English immigrant and domestic servant. Abandoned by her unfaithful husband, and seduced and made pregnant by her employer, Vaughan went to Philadelphia where, alone in a rooming house, she gave birth to her illegitimate child. The baby was found dead in bed with her, its head crushed, and she was ·subsequently convicted of murder. Anthony used the case to bring attention to the double standard and to the connection between the powerlessness of working women and the need for suffrage.

The case illustrates the way poverty and the lack of legal knowledge and legal aid circumscribed the rights of poor women more than women in other classes. Hester Vaughan did not know how to avoid having a child and she did not know how to use the law to help her support the child. If legal aid had been available, she could have brought an action for "fornication and bastardy" against the father. Although this action had the form of a criminal complaint, it was in substance a civil suit, usually brought before the birth of the child. Court-ordered settlements, providing a hospital fee and child support (but not damages) to the women, were much less common, given the reluctance of courts to convict, than out-of-court settlements.

Infanticide was the unmentionable and most covered up crime in the Victorian era. To gain some idea of its frequency, Roger Lane has pointed out, one needs to look at the annual death register. The cause of death of infants found on streets was generally listed there as "unknown." In Philadelphia, between 1861–1901, this averaged around fifty-five a year. On the other hand, between 1839–1901 only fifty-nine cases of infanticide came to a verdict and only one, that of Hester Vaughan, led to a first-degree murder verdict. Most indictments never came to trial. The lack of trials and convictions was closely related to the fact, in situations such as that of Hester Vaughan, that it was difficult to distinguish between a natural and an unnatural death.[27]

A search of Philadelphia court records turned up no trial transcript of the Vaughan case, only a transcript of jury selection and a record of conviction. Thus the only evidence available about this case comes from the information collected by a defense committee organized while Hester Vaughan awaited execution. The documents in this section illustrate the type of defense that feminist lawyers would have made to a jury of peers if either of these existed at the time; they reveal the type of investigation that should have been made before indictment for a crime. To interview Vaughan, the Working Woman's Association sent a committee to Moyamensing Prison that included a specialist in female disorders, Dr. Clemence Lozier (1813–1888), who was known for organizing the New York Medical College and Hospital for Women in 1863.[28]

After receiving the report of the committee, the Working Woman's Association held a well-publicized public meeting at Cooper Institute, December 31, 1868, and sent a memorial to the Governor of Pennsylvania asking for a retrial or pardon. Without fanfare Vaughan was pardoned several months later. She was shipped back to England, not to New York where the representatives of the Working Woman's Association awaited her arrival at the train station. The excerpts from the *Report to the Working Woman's Association on The Case of Hester Vaughan* and the *Petition to the Governor of Pennsylvania* raise a legal and social issue: Was Hester Vaughan a victim or criminal?

DIFFERENTIAL TREATMENT OF MEN AND WOMEN

The 1879 and 1880 Massachusetts statutes on commitments and parole of those convicted of drunkenness show the impact of gender on how the law treated the same offense. Like the selection on commitments to mental asylums, it reveals not a legal, but a social standard in sentencing and the use of reformatory prisons to sustain cultural norms. The acts prescribe differences in the number of times young men and women may commit the same offense before incarceration, as well as different terms of imprisonment and parole. The acts reflect a general trend in the nineteenth century, toward shifting the discretionary powers of a judge to superintendents of prisons and asylums. The penal model that emerged in the Jacksonian era and developed through the rest of the century involved a conception of the prison as a place for reforming behavior. The document raises the question of why a drunken woman seemed more dangerous to society than a besotted man.

DOCUMENTS

INSANITY

[125]

"The Great Trial of Mrs. Elizabeth Packard—A Full Report of the Trial, Incidents, etc.," by Stephen R. Moore, Attorney at Law (1864)

In the winter of 1859 and 1860 there were differences of opinion between Mr. Packard and Mrs. Packard upon matters of religion, which resulted in prolonged and vigorous debate in the home circle. The heresies maintained by Packard were carried by the husband from the fireside to the pulpit and made a matter of inquiry by the church, and which soon resulted in open warfare; and her views and propositions were misrepresented . . . from the pulpit, and herself made the subject of unjust criticism. In the Bible Class and in the Sabbath School she maintained her religious tenets, and among her kindred and friends defended herself from the obloquy of her husband.

To make the case fully understood, I will here remark that Mr. Packard was educated in the Calvinistic faith, and for twenty-nine years has been a preacher of that creed, and would in no wise depart from the religion of his fathers. . . .

Mrs. Packard is a lady of fine mental endowments and blest with a liberal education. She is an original, vigorous, masculine thinker, and were it not for her superior judgment, combined with native modesty, she would rank as a "strong-minded woman." As it is, her conduct comports strictly with the sphere usually occupied by woman. She dislikes parade or show of any kind. Her confidence that Right will prevail, leads her to too tamely submit to wrongs. She was educated in

From E. P. W. Packard, *Great Disclosure of Spiritual Wickedness in High Places, with an Appeal to the Government to Protect the Inalienable Rights of Married Women* (Boston, 1865: Arno Press reprint, 1974), pp. 122–24, 127–31, 135–37, 147–49.

the same religious belief with her husband, and during the first twenty years of married life his labors in the parish and in the pulpit were greatly relieved by the willing hand and able intellect of his wife. . . .

. . . . They have been married twenty-five years, and have six children, the youngest of whom was eighteen months old when she was kidnapped and transferred to Jacksonville. The older children have maintained a firm position against the abuse and persecutions of their father toward their mother, but were of too tender age to render her any material assistance.

Her views of religion are more in accordance with the liberal views of the age in which we live. . . . She stands fully on the platform of man's free agency and accountability to God for his actions. She believes that man, and nations, are progressive; and that in His own good time, and in accordance with His great purposes, Right will prevail over Wrong, and the oppressed will be freed from the oppressor. She believes slavery to be a national sin, and the church and the pulpit a proper place to combat this sin. These, in brief, are the points in her religious creed which were combatted by Mr. Packard, and were denominated by him as "emanations from the devil" or "the vagaries of a crazed brain."

For maintaining such ideas as above indicated, Mr. Packard denounced her from the pulpit, denied her the privilege of family prayer in the home circle, expelled her from the Bible Class, and refused to let her be heard in the Sabbath School. He excluded her from her friends and made her a prisoner in her own house.

Her reasoning and her logic appeared to him as the ravings of a mad woman— her religion was the religion of the Devil. To justify his conduct, he gave out that she was insane and found a few willing believers among his family connections. . . .

Christopher W. Knott was the first witness sworn by the respondent to maintain the issue on his part, that she was insane; who being sworn, deposed and said:

I am a practicing physician in Kankakee City. Have been in practice fifteen years. Have seen Mrs. Packard; saw her three or four years ago. Am not much acquainted with her. Had never seen her until I was called to see her at that time. I was called to visit her by Theophilus Packard. I thought her partially deranged on religious matters, and gave a certificate to that effect. I certified that she was insane upon the subject of religion. I have never seen her since.

Cross-examination.—This visit I made her was three or four years ago. I was there twice, one-half hour each time. I visited her on request of Mr. Packard, to determine if she was insane. I learned from him that he designed to convey her to the State Asylum. Do not know whether she was aware of my object, or not. Her mind appeared to be excited on the subject of religion; on all other subjects she was perfectly rational. It was probably caused by overtaxing the mental faculties. She was what might be called a monomaniac. Monomania is insanity on one subject. Three-fourths of the religious community are insane in the same manner, in my opinion. Her insanity was such that with a little rest she would readily have recovered from it.

The female mind is more excitable than the male. I saw her perhaps one-half hour each time I visited her. I formed my judgment as to her insanity wholly from conversing with her. I could see nothing except an unusual zealousness and warmth upon religious topics. Nothing was said, in my conversation with her, about disagreeing with Mr. Packard on religious topics. Mr. Packard introduced the subject of religion the first time I was there. The second time, I introduced the subject. Mr. Packard and Mr. Comstock were present. The subject was pressed on her for the purpose of drawing her out. Mrs. Packard would manifest more zeal than most of people upon any subject that interested her. I take her to be a lady of fine mental abilities, possessing more ability than ordinarily found. She is possessed of nervous temperament, easily excited, and has a strong will. I would say that she was insane, the same as I would say Henry Ward Beecher, Spurgeon, Horace Greeley and like persons, are insane. Probably three weeks intervened between visits I made Mrs. Packard. This was in June, 1860.

Re-examined.—She is a woman of large, active brain, and nervous temperament. I take her to be a woman of good intellect. There is no subject which excites people so much as religion. Insanity produces, oftimes, ill-feelings towards the best friends, and particularly the family or those more nearly related to the insane person—but not so with monomania. She told me in the conversation that the Calvinistic doctrines were wrong, and that she had been compelled to withdraw from the church. She said that Mr. Packard was more insane than she was, and that people would find it out. I had no doubt that she was insane. I only considered her insane on that subject, and she was not bad at all. I could not judge whether it was hereditary. I thought if she was withdrawn from conversation and excitement, she could have got well in a short time. Confinement in any shape, or restraint, would have made her worse. I did not think it was a bad case: it only required rest.

J. W. Brown, being sworn said:

I am a physician; live in this city; have no extensive acquaintance with Mrs. Packard. Saw her three or four weeks ago. I examined her as to her sanity or insanity. I was requested to make a visit, and had an extended conference with her. I spent some three hours with her. I had no difficulty in arriving at the conclusion, in my mind, that she was insane.

Cross-examination.—I visited her by request of Mr. Packard, at her house. The children were in and out of the room; no one else was present. I concealed my object in visiting her. She asked me if I was a physician, I told her no; that I was an agent, selling sewing machines, and had come to her to sell her one.

The first subject we conversed about was sewing machines. She showed no signs of insanity on that subject.

The next subject discussed, was the social condition of the female sex. She exhibited no special marks of insanity on that subject, although she had many ideas quite at variance with mine on the subject.

The subject of politics was introduced. She spoke of the condition of the North and the South. She illustrated her difficulties with Mr. Packard by the difficulties between the North and South. She said the South was wrong, and was waging war for two wicked purposes: first, to overthrow a good government, and second, to establish a despotism on the inhuman principle of human slavery. But that the North, having Right on their side, would prevail. So Mr. Packard was opposing her, to overthrow free thought in woman; that the despotism of man may prevail over the wife; but that she had Right and Truth on her side, and that she would prevail.

During the conversation I did not fully conclude that she was insane.

I brought up the subject of religion. We discussed that subject for a long time, and then I had not the slightest difficulty in concluding that she was hopelessly insane.

Question: Dr., what particular idea did she advance on the subject of religion that led you to the conclusion that she was hopelessly insane?

Answer: She advanced many of them. I formed my opinion not so much on any one idea advanced, as upon her whole conversation. She then said that she was the "Personification of the Holy Ghost." I did not know what she meant by that.

Question: Was not this the idea conveyed to you in that conversation: that there are three attributes of the Deity—the Father, the Son, and the Holy Ghost? Now, did she not say that the attributes of the Father were represented in mankind, in man; that the attributes of the Holy Ghost were represented in woman; and that the Son was the fruit of these two attributes of the Deity?

Answer: Well, I am not sure but that was the idea conveyed, though I did not fully get her idea at the time.

Question: Was not that a new idea to you in theology?

Answer: It was.

Question: Are you much of a theologian?

Answer: No.

Question: Then because the idea was a novel one to you, you pronounce her insane.

Answer: Well, I pronounced her insane on that and other things that exhibited themselves in this conversation.

Question: Did she not show more familiarity with the subject of religion and the questions of theology, than you had with these subjects?

Answer: I do not pretend much knowledge on these subjects.

Question: What else did she say or do there, that showed marks of insanity?

Answer: She claimed to be better than her husband—that she was right—and that he was wrong—and that all she did was good, and all he did was bad; that she was farther advanced than other people, and more nearly perfection. She found fault particularly that Mr. Packard would not discuss their points of difference on religion in an open, manly way, instead of going around denouncing her as crazy to her friends and to the church.

She had a great aversion to being called insane. Before I got through the conversation she exhibited a great dislike to me and almost treated me in a contemptuous manner. She appeared quite ladylike. She had a great reverence for God and a regard for religion and pious people.

Re-examined—

Question: Dr., you may now state all the reasons you have for pronouncing her insane.

Answer: I have written down, in order, the reasons which I had, to found my opinion on, that she was insane. I will read them.

1. That she claimed to be in advance of the age thirty or forty years.
2. That she disliked to be called insane.
3. That she pronounced me a Copperhead, and did not prove the fact.
4. An incoherency of thought. That she failed to illuminate me and fill me with light.
5. Her aversion to the doctrine of the total depravity of man.
6. Her claim to perfection or nearer perfection in action and conduct.
7. Her aversion to being called insane.
8. Her feelings towards her husband.
9. Her belief that to call her insane and abuse her was blasphemy against the Holy Ghost.
10. Her explanation of this idea.
11. Incoherency of thought and ideas.
12. Her extreme aversion to the doctrine of the total depravity of mankind, and in the same conversation saying her husband was a specimen of man's total depravity.
13. The general history of the case.
14. Her belief that some calamity would befall her, owing to my being there, and her refusal to shake hands with me when I went away. . . .

Sybil Dole, sworn, and says—

I am Mr. Packard's sister; have known her twenty-five years. Her natural disposition is very kind and sweet. Her education is very good; her morals without a stain or blemish. I first observed a change in her after we came to Manteno. . . . She talked in a wild excited manner; the subject was partly religion. She spoke of her own attainments; she said she had advanced in spiritual affairs. This was two or three years before she went to the Asylum.

The next time was when she was preparing to go to New York State. She was weeping and sick. Her trunk was packed and ready to go, but Mr. Packard was sick. From her voice, and the manner she talked, I formed an opinion of her insanity. She talked on various points; the conversation distressed me very much; I could not sleep. She was going alone; we tried to persuade her not to go alone. She accused Mr. Packard very strongly of depriving her of her rights of conscience—that he would not allow her to think for herself on religious questions, because they disagreed on these topics. She made her visit to New York. The first time I met her after her return her health was much improved; she appeared much better. . . .

At another time, at the table, she was talking about religion. When Mr. Packard remonstrated with her, she became angry and told him she would talk what and when she had a mind to. She rose up from the table and took her tea-cup and left the room in great violence.

Cross-examined.—I am a member of Mr. Packard's church, and am his sister. He and I have often consulted together about Mrs. Packard. Mr. Packard was the first to ever suggest that she was insane; after that, I would more carefully watch her actions to find out if she was insane. The religious doctrines she advanced were at variance with those entertained by our church. She was a good, neat, thrifty, and careful housekeeper. She was economical, kept the children clean and neatly dressed. She was sane on all subjects except religion. I do not think she would have entertained these ideas, if she had not been insane. I do not think she would have wanted to have withdrawn from our church and unite with another church if she had not been insane. She said she would worship with the Methodists. They were the only other Protestant denomination that held service at Manteno at the time. I knew when she was taken to Jacksonville Hospital: she was taken away in the morning; she did not want to go; we thought it advisable for her to go. . . .

{Mrs. Packard's defense called several witnesses, including physicians, neighbors and a local justice of the peace, all of whom testified that they believed her to be sane. The final witness gave the following testimony}

Dr. Duncanson, sworn, and said:

I live here; am a physician; have been a clergyman; have been a practicing physician twenty-one years. Have known Mrs. Packard since this trial commenced. Have known her by general report for three years and upwards. I visited her at Mr. Orr's. I was requested to go there and have a conversation with her and determine if she was sane or insane. Talked three hours with her, on political, religious and scientific subjects, and on mental and moral philosophy. I was educated at and received diplomas from the University of Glasgow, and Anerson University of Glasgow. I went there to see her and prove or disprove her insanity. I think not only that she is sane, but the most intelligent lady I have talked with in many years. We talked religion very thoroughly. I find her an expert in both departments, Old School and New School theology. There are thousands of persons who believe just as she does. Many of her ideas and doctrines are embraced in Swedenborgianism, and many are found only in the New School theology. The best and most learned men of both Europe and this country are advocates of these doctrines, in one shape or the other; and some bigots and men with minds of small caliber may call these great minds insane; but that does not make them insane. An insane mind is a diseased mind. These minds are the perfection of intellectual powers, healthy, strong, vigorous, and just the reverse of diseased minds, or insane. Her explanation of woman representing the Holy Ghost, and man representing the male attributes of the Father, and that the Son is the fruit of the Father and the Holy Ghost, is a very ancient theological dogma and entertained by many of our most eminent men. On every topic I introduced, she was perfectly familiar, and discussed them with an intelligence that at once showed she was possessed of a good education and a strong and vigorous mind. I did not agree with her in sentiment on many things, but I do not call people insane because they differ from me, nor from a majority, even, of people. . . . You might with as much propriety call Christ insane, because he taught the people many new and strange things; or Galileo; or Newton; or Luther; or Robert Fulton; or Morse, who electrified the world; or Watts or a thousand others I might name. . . .

So with Mrs. Packard; there is wanting every indication of insanity that is laid down in the books. I pronounce her a sane woman, and wish we had a nation of such women.

This witness was cross-examined at some length, which elicited nothing new, when he retired. . . .

On the 18th day of January, 1864, at 10 o'clock, p.m., the jury retired for consultation, under the charge of the sheriff. After an absence of seven minutes, they returned into court, and gave the following verdict:

We the undersigned, jurors in the case of Mrs. Elizabeth P.W. Packard, alleged to be insane, having heard the evidence in the case, are satisfied that said Elizabeth P.W. Packard is sane. . . .

Cheers rose from every part of the house; the ladies waved their handkerchiefs and pressed around Mrs. Packard and extended her their congratulations. It was some time before the outburst of applause could be checked. When order was restored, the counsel for Mrs. Packard moved the court that she be discharged. Thereupon the court ordered the clerk to enter the following order:

It is hereby ordered that Mrs. Elizabeth P.W. Packard be relieved from all restraint incompatible with her condition as a sane woman.

C. R. Starr,
*Judge of the 20th Judicial Circuit of
the State of Illinois*

January 18, 1864

INFANTICIDE

[126]

Report to the Working Woman's Association on the Case of Hester Vaughan (1868)

. . . Imagine, if you please, a girlish figure; a sweet, intelligent face, soft brown eyes, broad forehead, warm earnest mouth, and you have a slight idea of Hester Vaughan. Her story is quickly told. She was born in Glouchestershire, England; well reared by respectable parents; married a man, a native of Wales, and came to this country full of hope and enthusiasm for the future. A few weeks, and Hester was deserted. Some other woman had a prior claim, it is supposed, and the scamp has never since been heard of. Then came the tug of war for Hester Vaughan, as for every other woman who finds herself compelled to fight the battle of life alone. Think of this young girl, a stranger in a strange land, with neither friend or relative to advise or comfort. For several weeks she lived out as a servant in a family at Jenkintown; was then recommended as a dairy maid to another family, and here misfortune befell her. Overcome, not in a moment of weakness and passion, but by superior strength—brute force—Hester Vaughan fell a victim to lust—and the gallows. That man also went his way. Three months after this terrible occurrence, Hester removed to Philadelphia and hired a room there. She supported herself by little odd jobs of work from different families, always giving the most perfect satisfaction. During one of the fiercest storms of last winter she was without food or fire or comfortable apparel. She had been ill and partially unconscious for three days before her confinement, and a child was born to Hester Vaughan. Hours passed before she could drag herself to the door and cry out for assistance, and when she did it was to be dragged to a prison where she now lies with the near prospect of a halter. Is it not terrible that this victim of a man's craven lust should be thus foully dealt with, while her seducer walks the earth free and unmolested? In this connection let me say that no amount of coaxing or entreaty will induce Hester Vaughan to name the man who thus cruelly wronged her. Since that time he was married. "If he were alone," said Hester, "I would ring his name through the whole country, but nothing will induce me to send terror and disgrace into the heart of an innocent, trusting woman." . . .

I had an interview with Judge Ludlow, the man who pronounced the sentence of death upon poor Hester. "I do not think her a bad woman, naturally," said the Judge; "she has an excellent face, but there was no course open for me but the broad course of condemnation; she was, in the opinion of the jury, guilty of the murder of her child." "Mrs. Kirk," he continued, quite earnestly, "you have no idea how rapidly the crime of infanticide is increasing. Some women must be made an exam-

From *The Revolution* (December 10, 1868), 357–58.

Clemence Lozier (1813–1888), physician and reformer, founder of New York Medical College and Hospital for Women, 1863. She helped finance the newspaper *The Revolution,* was a member of the Working Woman's Associations and president of the National Woman Suffrage Association, 1877–1978). James Parton et al., *Eminent Women of the Age)* Hartford, Conn., 1868).

ple of. It is for the establishment of a principle, ma'am." "Establishment of principle" indeed. I suggested to the Judge that he inaugurate the good work by hanging a few men, but, strange to relate, he has not been able to see it in that light. . . . The very day that poor Hester was sentenced to be hung by the neck until she was dead, Oxford Alexander, a colored man, was also sentenced for the murder of his wife. Hester imprisoned for a man's diabolical lust, is so heinously guilty that she may not walk out on to the corridor near by the side of her cell, while Oxford Alexander can . . . have the benefit of out-door air and exercise; and more than this, 20,000 of the most respectable citizens of Pennsylvania have petitioned Governor Geary for the man's pardon; and not one woman in Philadelphia, so far as we could learn with the exception of Dr. Smith, has said a good word for Hester Vaughan.

MRS. DOCTOR LOZIER'S REPORT

Mrs. Doctor Lozier said: I freely corroborate all that has been said by Mrs. Kirk. As a physician I was cordially invited to accompany her to Philadelphia, and had authority, not only to question this poor woman in regard to her own condition, but also in regard to all that occurred. I judged for myself, from her own honest and ingenuous answers to the questions; but I also consulted with Mrs. Doctor Smith, who has been a practicing physician for fifteen years, a woman of large influence and a neighbor of the judge who condemned Hester Vaughan. Doctor Smith had not heard of the case till she read of the sentence the next morning, and she concluded to call on Judge Ludlow and ask him the particulars. He gave her a permit to visit Hester Vaughan at her pleasure. She has done so once or twice a week, for five months. She told me she had questioned and cross-questioned the girl, had taken her by surprise; and had come to the conclusion that she was innocent of the crime of infanticide.

It appears that the plea of puerperal fever and puerperal blindness was never used on her behalf. *{Puerperal fever, caused by blood poisoning due to infection in the birth passages, was the major cause of maternal deaths in the nineteenth century.}* Her lawyer, after visiting her once, never came near her again. He paid her a visit and took her money, and promised to defend her; but he never saw her again until she was brought to court. He never inquired into any of the particulars of her former history, or of her present condition. When Mrs. Dr. Smith went to see him he said, "Oh, yes; it is now too late; she has been condemned, and is to be hung". . . . "Well," said Mrs. Smith, "you took her last thirty dollars and promised to defend her; and have you called on her?" He replied, ". . . Was that all the money she had?" Well, then he remembered that he had not called on her; consequently when her case came up he was unprepared to give her any defense. Dr. Smith . . . has sent to Governor Geary ten letters, praying for her immediate release on the ground of her innocence. . . . For three months, [Dr. Smith] thinks, [Hester] was irresponsible for her acts—the victim of puerperal mania. When she is spoken of about her condition at the time, she says: "It was so dark"—she seems hardly to have recognized a ray of light—and she adds: "I never saw my child." I have had large experience in obstetric practice. My record shows over two thousand cases; and I have had several cases of puerperal blindness—in one case lasting over four days and four nights; for four days and nights the patient did not see. And I believe what this poor girl says when she says, "I did not see." I asked her how the skull could have been injured, for it seems the skull was indented, and she said "I must have lain on it; when I waked up, the child lay under me." She might have swooned or fainted in her agony. I have no doubt that she suffered from puerperal mania for at least three months. Her sight is still very weak. But there is another point. The child was never examined. No one can prove that it ever lived. The lungs should have been examined. If the child had lived, the lungs would float; but if the air had never permeated those vessels, the lungs would sink. So, I repeat, it has never been proved that the child was alive. Now it was a premature birth; it was an eight months' child, and the children of that period very seldom live. . . . It has been said in some of our papers, today, that the marks on the head prove that the child was destroyed. I do not see that it is proved. That poor woman, in her agony, alone, without fire, without light, may have injured the child but not wilfully. I said to her: "Hester, do you love children?" She replied "No one ever loved children more than I do—no one, I dearly love them. I wish I had my poor little babe. It would be some comfort to me." . . . .

[127]

Petition to the Governor of Pennsylvania in Behalf of Hester Vaughan (1868)

To His Excellency the Governor of the State of Pennsylvania:

The Working Woman's National Association, through their Committee, whose names are here appended, after careful investigation of the cases of Hester Vaughan, now confined in a Pennsylvania prison for the alleged crime of INFANTICIDE, would respectfully represent that, as they believe she was condemned on insufficient evidence and with inadequate defense, justice demands a stay of proceedings and a new trial; or, if that be impracticable, they most earnestly pray your Excellency to grant her an unconditional pardon.

Whereas the right of trial by a jury of one's peers is recognized by the governments of all civilized nations as the great palladium of rights, of justice, and equality to citizen: therefore,

Resolved, that this Association demand that in all civil and criminal cases woman shall be tried by a jury of her peers; shall have a voice in making the law, in electing the judge who pronounces her sentence, and the sheriff who, in case of execution, performs for her that last dread act.

Resolved, that the existence of the death penalty, odious as it is when a man is the victim, is doubly so to a case like this of Hester Vaughan—a young, artless, and inexperienced girl—a consideration that should startle every mother into a sense of her responsibility in making and executing the laws under which her daughters are to live or perish.

Resolved, that as capital punishment is opposed to the genius of our institutions and the civilization of the age, we demand that the gallows—that horrible relic of barbarism—be banished from the land; for human life should be held alike sacred by the individual and the state.

From *The Revolution* (December 10, 1868), p. 358.

DIFFERENTIAL TREATMENT OF
MEN AND WOMEN

[128]

Massachusetts Statutes on The Crime of Drunkenness
(1879–1880)

1. An Act Relating to Commitments To The Reformatory Prison For Women.
Chap. 229 (1879)

Section 1. Any woman convicted of the offence of drunkenness by the voluntary
use of intoxicating liquor, who has been before convicted of that offence, may be
punished by imprisonment in the reformatory prison for women for not less than
four months and not more than two years.

Section 2. The commissioners of prisons, whenever they shall judge that there
is good cause so to do, may, by an order in writing, transfer any woman from the
reformatory prison for women to the state workhouse at Bridgewater, or to the state
almshouse at Tewksbury, there to be detained until the expiration of the term of
time for which such woman was ordered to be imprisoned in the reformatory prison
for women.

Section 3. The commissioners of prisons, whenever they shall judge that there
is good cause to do, may, with the consent of any woman who may be imprisoned in
the reformatory prison for women, contract to have such woman employed in domestic service upon such terms as shall seem to said commissioners fit, having regard to
her welfare and reformation, for a term of time, not exceeding the term of imprisonment, as they shall approve. And if after such contracting for domestic service the
conduct of such woman during the term of imprisonment shall not, in the opinion of
said commissioners, be good, they may order the return of such women to the
reformatory prison for women, there to be detained to the end of the original term of
imprisonment.

2. An Act Relative To The Punishment for Drunkenness. Chap. 221 (1880)

Section 2. When a male person is convicted of the offence of drunkenness as
aforesaid, and it is proved that he has been convicted of a like offence twice before
within the next preceding twelve months, he may be punished by a fine not exceeding ten dollars, or by imprisonment in any place now provided by law for common
drunkards, for a term not exceeding one year. It shall not be necessary in complaints
under this act to allege such previous convictions.

From *Massachusetts Acts and Resolves Passed by the General Court in Years 1879 and 1880,* pp. 563 and 171
    respectively.

Section 3. When it shall appear to the county commissioners of any county, or in Suffolk county to the board of directors of public institutions, that a person imprisoned under the provisions of section two of this act, in any jail, house of correction, or other place of punishment in their respective jurisdictions, has reformed, they may issue to him a permit to be at liberty during the remainder of his term of sentence; and the board that has issued such permit may revoke the same at any time previous to the expiration of the original term of sentence. The state board of health, lunacy and charity may issue to persons confined in the state workhouse the permits authorized by this section.

NOTES

1. Willard Hurst, *Law And The Conditions of Freedom in the Nineteenth-Century United States* (Madison: University of Wisconsin Press, 1956), pp. 3–70; Morton J. Horwitz, *The Transformation of American Law, 1780–1860* (Cambridge, Mass.: Harvard University Press, 1977), pp. 1–252; Lawrence M. Friedman, *A History of American Law* (New York: Simon & Schuster, 1973), pp. 91–265.

2. The discussion in this section follows that of Norma Basch, *In the Eyes of the Law: Women, Marriage and Property in Nineteenth-Century New York* (Ithaca: Cornell University Press, 1982).

3. Noralee Frankel, "Federal and State Policy in Mississippi, 1862–70: Legal Patriarchy and Rural Black Women" (Paper delivered at Annual Meeting of the American Historical Association Convention, Washington, D.C., December 1980).

4. Suzanne D. Lebsock, "Radical Reconstruction and the Property Rights of Southern Women," *Journal of Southern History* 43 (May 1977), 195–216.

5. Daniel Scott Smith, "Family Limitation, Sexual Control, and Domestic Feminism in Victorian America," in *Clio's Consciousness Raised: New Perspectives on the History of Women*, ed. Mary Hartman and Lois W. Banner (New York: Harper Colophon Books, 1974), pp. 119–36; Linda Gordon, *Woman's Body, Woman's Right: A Social History of Birth Control in America* (New York: Penguin, 1977), p. 102; Nancy F. Cott, "Passionless: An Interpretation of Victorian Sexual Ideology, 1790–1850," in *A Heritage of Her Own: Toward A New Social History of Women*, ed. Nancy Cott and Elizabeth Pleck (New York: Simon & Schuster, 1979), pp. 162–81.

6. James C. Mohr, *Abortion in America: The Origins and Evolution of National Policy, 1800–1900* (New York: Oxford University Press, 1978), pp. 168–69.

7. Gordon, *Woman's Body, Woman's Right*, pp. 3–158.

8. Carroll Smith-Rosenberg, "Beauty, The Beast, and the Militant Woman: A Case Study in Sex Roles and Social Stress in Jacksonian America," in Cott and Pleck, *A Heritage of Her Own*, pp. 197–221.

9. Ellen Carol DuBois, *Feminism and Suffrage: The Emergence of An Independent Women's Movement in America* (Ithaca: Cornell University Press, 1978), pp. 31–32; Keith E. Melder, *Beginnings of Sisterhood: The American Woman's Rights Movement, 1800–1850* (New York: Schocken Books, 1977); Lois W. Banner, *Elizabeth Cady Stanton: A Radical for Women's Rights* (Boston: Little, Brown, 1980).

10. Blake, *The Road to Reno*, pp. 61–79.

11. DuBois, *Feminism and Suffrage*, pp. 53–202.

12. Karen O'Conner, *Women's Organizations' Use of the Courts* (New York: Lexington Books, 1980), pp. 33–37; Barbara Allen Babcock et al., *Sex Discrimination and the Law Causes and Remedies* (Boston: Little, Brown, 1975), pp. 7–9.

13. W. Elliot Brownlee and Mary M. Brownlee, eds., *Women in the American Economy: A Documentary History, 1625–1929* (New Haven: Yale University Press, 1976), pp. 13–17.

14. David B. Tyack, *The One Best System: A History of American Urban Education* (Cambridge, Mass.: Harvard University Press, 1974), pp. 59–64.

15. Adele Simmons, "Education and Ideology in Nineteenth-Century America: The Response of Educational Institutions to the Changing Role of Women," in *Liberating Women's History: Theoretical and Critical Essays,* ed. Berenice A. Carroll (Urbana: University of Illinois Press, 1976), pp. 115–26.

16. Mary Roth Walsh, *'Doctors Wanted: No Women Need Apply': Sexual Barriers in the Medical Profession, 1835–1975* (New Haven: Yale University Press, 1977), pp. 1–186; Dr. Elizabeth Blackwell, *Pioneer Work in Opening the Medical Profession to Women: Autobiographical Sketches* (New York: Schocken Books, 1977).

17. Edward T. James et al., eds., *Notable American Women: A Biographical Dictionary* (Cambridge, Mass.: Harvard University Press, 1971), vol. 2, pp. 263–65; Ruth Putnam, ed. *Life and Letters of Mary Putnam Jacobi* (New York: G. P. Putnam's Sons, 1925).

18. John S. Haller and Robin M. Haller, *The Physician and Sexuality in Victorian America* (New York: W. W. Norton, 1974), pp. 47–87.

19. James, *Notable American Women*, vol. 2, pp. 492–93.

20. James, *Notable American Women*, vol. 1, pp. 223–25.

21. *Chicago Legal News,* October 16, 1869.

22. Kathleen E. Lazarou, "Fettered Portias: Obstacles Facing Nineteenth-Century Women Lawyers," *Women Lawyers Journal* 64 (Winter 1978), 22.

23. Lazarou, "Fettered Portias," p. 29.

24. Lazarou, "Fettered Portias," pp. 21–30; D. Kelly Weisberg, "Barred From the Bar: Woman and Legal Education in the United States 1870–1890," *Journal of Legal Education* 28 (1977), 485–507.

25. Ellen Dwyer, "Female Insanity In Nineteenth Century New York: An Analysis of Asylum Casebooks" (Paper delivered at The Quantitative History and Women's History Conference, Chicago: Newberry Library, July 1979); Joel Schwartz, "Women and the Mental Asylum in Nineteenth-Century America: The Case of The Trenton State Asylum" (Paper delivered at The Quantitative History and Women's History Conference, Chicago: Newberry Library, July 1979).

26. *Notable American Women*, vol. 3, pp. 1–2; Mrs. E. P. W. Packard, *Modern Persecution; or, Married Woman's Liabilities, as Demonstrated by the Action of the Illinois Legislature* (New York, 1873); Myra Himmelhoch, with Arthur H. Shaffer, "Elizabeth Packard: Nineteenth-Century Crusader for the Rights of Mental Patients," *Journal of American Studies* 13 (December 1979), 343–75; Barbara Leslie Epstein, *The Politics of Domesticity: Women, Evangelism, and Temperance in Nineteenth-Century America* (Middletown: Wesleyan University Press, 1981) pp. 45–88.

27. Roger Lane, *Violent Death in the City: Suicide, Accident and Murder in Nineteenth Century Philadelphia* (Cambridge, Mass.: Harvard University Press, 1979) pp. 94–101.

28. *Notable American Women*, vol. 2, pp. 440–42.

CHAPTER 3

[
*From the Progressive
Era to the New Deal,
1890–1937*
]

UNIT 1

[*Family Roles*]

WOMAN'S NATURE

Changing Models of Womanhood

During the Progressive era, a growing interest in science and scientific thought brought a new perspective to childbearing and childrearing. Underlying public policy discussions were a set of beliefs that linked social progress with natural science and psychology. The scientific and popular thought concerning women came out of the Victorian tradition; the evolutionary and medical model defined women as mothers. The excerpts from a sociologist, William Thomas, *"On a Difference in the Metabolism of the Sexes"* (1897), and from a psychologist, G. Stanley Hall, *Physiology and Adolescent Education* (1904), illustrate the scientific model. The popular song, *"Mother, Queen of Home"* (1899) and the excerpt from a speech by a labor leader, Edward O. Donnell, *"Women as Bread Winners"* (1897), show the same vision in popular thought.

The 1920s model used Freudian psychology to extend the medical view of woman's nature, but altered conceptions about female sexuality. The wife-companion model, which de-emphasized mothering and stressed sexual love and happiness in marriage, is illustrated by the excerpts from Margaret Sanger, *"Happiness in Marriage"* (1926), and the selection by Dr. Douglas A. Thom on *"Child Management"* (1930).[1]

289

The New Feminist Perspective

At the turn of the century there emerged a new view of womanhood that rejected the progressive feminist assumption that women were naturally different, although equal. The women who broke with the separate but equal doctrine worked not in the traditional centers of female activity, but in academia. Their empirical research in psychology and social theory, carried on through the 1920s, helped develop the idea that both men and women possessed the same basic mental apparatus and emotional impulses, but differed in their behavior as a result of environment and social training. *The Mental Traits of Men and Women* (1903) by Helen Thompson (Woolley) was the pathbreaking study. Although the new feminists differed with the active women reformers over the separate but equal issue, they shared a belief in women's rights and a concern over the importance of environment and socialization.[2]

MARRIAGE AND DIVORCE

At the height of the Victorian era the divorce rate began mounting sharply and by the late 1920s more than one in every six marriages terminated in divorce. Between 1889 and 1906 state legislatures responded by enacting a host of procedural reforms to make divorce more difficult, and Easterners waged an unsuccessful crusade for uniform divorce laws to close the escape hatches. In the early twentieth century, the new profession of sociology turned its attention to the problem of marriage and divorce, and many questioned the idea that making divorce more difficult would produce more stable marriages. George Elliott Howard's *"Is the Freer Granting of Divorce an Evil?"* is an example of the new professional perspective that affected judicial attitudes.[3]

Many sociologists, and later historians, linked the growing rate of marital dissolution to changing expectations arising from the women's rights movement. As more women entered the economy, they reasoned, fewer felt compelled to tolerate unsatisfactory unions for the sake of economic security. Elaine Tyler May has found little evidence to support this common interpretation in the divorce statistics and case records of Los Angeles and New Jersey for 1880 and 1920. In 1880, divorce was most likely to result from the failure of husband and wife to live up to Victorian expectations about responsibilities and behavior. In the 1880 Los Angeles sample of divorced wives, an unusually large number, one-third, worked. Divorce petitions showed that these women worked, however, not because they wanted to, but because their husbands failed to carry out their marital obligations of support; that was part of their complaint.

In 1920, divorce was greatly affected by social ideals about marriage and happiness. Because of bureaucratization and routinization, jobs provided less personal satisfaction. The period saw a new emphasis on the cultivation of feminine charms, on romance as depicted in Hollywood films, and on a consumer lifestyle. In this culture, divorce was more likely to result from frustrations growing out of "great expectations."

The grounds for divorce remained largely those established in the Jacksonian era. The most important changes arose not from legal categories, but from the attitudes of both wives and judges. More wives petitioned for divorce, and judges granted a higher percentage of requests. There was a more significant change towards alimony. In 1920, a considerably larger percentage of wives seeking divorce requested alimony, and a large percentage of those requesting it were likely to receive it. On the whole, however, alimony was still rarely asked for and rarely granted. The fact that a wife worked was not likely in 1920 to affect her ability to get alimony. The most important factors affecting alimony, in both periods, were the presence of children and the issue of fault. Considerably more wives without children in 1920 were being granted alimony; this judicial approach reflected not only reality, but the affirmation of the traditional model of marital responsibilities. In 1880 few husbands sought custody of their children, but if they did they were more likely to succeed than in 1920.

The pattern of divorce statistics suggests that judges were less likely to believe that forcing incompatible people to remain married would achieve the social goals traditionally associated with family life. Desertion remained the single most important reason for granting divorce, but what constituted desertion changed. At a time when women presumably had more and better job opportunities, judges were more likely to enforce the common-law support obligations in the form of alimony. In fact, job opportunities and wages for women could not provide a satisfactory alternative to marriage. The statistics show that both men and women married younger and were likely to remarry after divorce.[4]

PUBLIC POLICY AND FAMILY WELFARE

Mothers' Aid

The Progressive era saw an important change in the nature of public policy toward the family. The nineteenth-century solution to marital breakdown and to the failure of families to carry out their social obligations was to give wives control over their separate property and wages and to expand the grounds for divorce. This freed the wife and mother to enter the marketplace and support herself and her children. Progressive era social reformers, however, preferred to strengthen the home life of the poor to enable mothers to fulfill their motherly role. This perspective led to a range of urban reforms, including the creation of the juvenile court, which later became the domestic relations or family court. Illinois, which originated the juvenile court system in 1899, found that in a disproportionately large number of cases there was no father in the house and that mothers had to work. Therefore, in 1911 the state passed the first mothers' aid law. Better known today as Aid to Families with Dependent Children (AFDC), mothers' aid represented an important innovation in welfare policy. Government began to assume some of the responsibilities of the absent father. It grew out of the traditional belief that the home was "the greatest molding force of mind and character," and from the association of home with motherhood.

By 1921 all but five southern states and the District of Columbia had passed Mothers' Aid laws. The selection from the *New York State Report of the Commission on Relief for Widowed Mothers* (1914) states the basic argument used in campaigns for the passage of mothers' pension acts. The report was written by Irene Loeb (1876–1929), a social worker and reporter, who was later appointed president of the New York Child Welfare Board. Although women's groups were vocal in its behalf, its passage rested on other factors. The extraordinary number of deaths each year from industrial accidents and diseases had created pressure for the passage of workmen's compensation and employers' liability laws. Existing conceptions of contract and liability relieved employers from any obligation to invest in safety, because employees were assumed to enter the job at their own risk. The passage of pensions for widows, a substitute for more far reaching legislation, shifted the financial burden of supporting widows from individual employers to taxpayers. The selections from Emma O. Lundberg, *"Aid to Mothers with Dependent Children,"* and the report by the United States Children's Bureau *On Mothers' Aid* (1931), describe the trends in this new policy.

The virtual exclusion of unmarried mothers was done on purpose, to discourage premarital sex. A single girl, like the industrial worker, entered premarital sexual relationships at her own risk. Although primary legal responsibility for support of wife and children rested with the husband, there was no public office or agency to locate husbands who had deserted and compel them to discharge their obligations.[5]

Family Planning

A different approach to preventing women from falling into poverty as the result of a husband's death or desertion was birth control. A new feminism emerged during the Progressive era that saw birth control as a means of freeing women from bondage to the traditional role model of wife/mother. Margaret Sanger recalls, in *My Fight for Birth Control*, the event that transformed her into a missionary, in 1912, and led her to Europe to learn about contraceptive methods. In 1916 she opened a clinic in Brooklyn to help poor women. It was closed by the police and Sanger was convicted of obscenity under a state law. The state court of appeals upheld the conviction but Judge Crane indicated that physicians might be exempt from the restriction on circulating birth control information if they were prescribing it to prevent disease. Later, the American Birth Control League, which Sanger founded in 1921, adopted this strategy; it lobbied to remove state and federal restrictions on the right of doctors to prescribe contraceptive devices and information. Meanwhile, the league's petition for a license to open a "Parents' Clinic" in Chicago was denied by the commissioner of health. The league then went to court and received a favorable ruling in *Helen G. Carpenter* v. *William S. Dever* (1923).

Judge Fisher's opinion in the case is a good example of how the judiciary influenced the direction of the birth-control movement. The courts established the conditions under which contraceptive information and devices could be dispensed, but did so in a way that prevented women from controlling their own bodies. For a long time the reliance on clinics limited the value of birth control as a means of reducing poverty. By 1920 there were only fifty-five clinics in twenty-three cities, in twelve states. The limitations imposed on advertising reduced the size of the clientele. The Voluntary Parenthood League observed that clinics did not reach most women and that a "doctors' bill" merely put the whole subject in the category of crime and indecency. The League sought the repeal of the Comstock Act and a return to the legal situation that prevailed before 1873.[6]

In 1924, the *Cummins-Vaile Bill* was introduced into Congress, to legalize the distribution of contraceptive information. Progressive feminists, who did not oppose making contraception information available on demand, had no enthusiasm for it, and their reasons are stated by Dr. Marguerita A. Stewart, testifying as a representative of the National Christian League for the Promotion of Purity.

As middle-class wives learned how to use contraceptive techniques more effectively during the late nineteenth century, abortion declined as a means of family planning. Nevertheless, for single women who were ignorant of contraceptive techniques, abortion remained the only way of escaping social stigma. *Foster* v. *State of Wisconsin* (1923) shows a judicial unwillingness to treat abortion before the embryo had quickened as manslaughter.

SUFFRAGE AND JURY SERVICE

The Progressive era saw a proliferation of women's organizations dedicated to making the community responsive to the needs of women and the family order. Through clubs, humanitarian societies, and trade unions women became involved in the process of making public policy. As women's organizations increasingly took over the male role of protector and guardian of women and the family, their priorities came into conflict with the economic interests of men. It became apparent that there were serious limitations to an approach that relied on stimulating others to act in their behalf, that is of arousing in men feelings of guilt or gallantry. By 1910, consensus had emerged that suffrage was crucial.

The selections presented here illustrate some of the differing motivations among suffragists. The first document, a *flyer of the New York Suffrage Party,* shows how domestic feminists, concerned with making the physical and social environment of the city conform to the demands of an ideal home, turned traditional conceptions about women's place and role into a rationale for suffrage.[7] In the pamphlet, *"Senators* vs. *Working Women,"* a shirtwaist maker, at a 1912 mass meeting in New York, explains what trade union women hoped to accomplish with suffrage.

The female constituency of the suffrage movement was augmented by a new group of suffrage leaders who introduced strategies for capturing public attention—marches and street rallies. In taking their message outdoors suffragists broke with a cultural model of proper feminine behavior that had supported traditional ideas about women's place and role. On March 3, 1913, for example several thousand women and a few men paraded down Pennsylvania Avenue, appealing to Congress and President-elect Woodrow Wilson, on behalf of the suffrage amendment that had lain dormant in both Houses since 1893. Progressive reform legitimized suffrage, and between 1910 and 1914 six states gave the vote to women: Illinois, Washington, California, Arizona, Kansas, and Oregon. The militant National American Woman Suffrage Association (NAWSA) kept suffrage at the center of political attention in the states, and Alice Paul's newly formed Congressional Union (1913) concentrated on a constitutional amendment; but the issue stalled until World War I, when the massive mobilization of women's groups, in behalf of the war effort, made it difficult for patriotic men to deny women the vote. The Nineteenth Amendment went through Congress and on August 18, 1920, when passed by the Tennessee state legislature, gave all women the right to vote.[8]

Its passage raised the question of whether suffrage carried with it the right or privilege to be jurors. In 1942, for example, only twenty-eight states permitted women to serve on juries and fifteen of these allowed them to claim exemption because of their sex. Twenty other states disqualified female jurors summarily. Jury service differs from suffrage in that it involves participation in the administration of justice. In the selection *Jury Service for Women* (1924) Jennie L. Barron tried to answer all the different reasons put forth for restricting women, and in the process she explained much about how the image of woman as mother operated to limit the concept of women as citizens and peers. Whereas the Supreme Court held that the exclusion of blacks from juries denied them equal protection and due process under the Fourteenth Amendment, it did not come to this conclusion for women until 1975.

DOCUMENTS

WOMAN'S NATURE

Changing Models of Womanhood

[129]

William I. Thomas, "On a Difference in the Metabolism of the Sexes" (1897)

It is increasingly apparent that all sociological manifestations proceed from physiological conditions. . . . Morphologically the development of men is more accentuated in almost every respect than that of women. . . . Anthropologists, indeed, regard woman as intermediate in development between the child and the man. . . . Wagner decided that the brain of woman taken as a whole is uniformly in a more or less embryonic condition. . . . The superior physiological irritability of woman, whether we call it sensibility, feeling, emotionality, or affectability, is due to the fact of the larger development of her abdominal zone, and the activity of the physiological changes located there in connection with the process of reproduction. . . . Both social feeling and social organization are thus primarily feminine in origin. . . .

From William I. Thomas, "On a Difference in the Metabolism of the Sexes," *American Journal of Sociology* 3 (July 1897), 31, 40, 61.

The Feminine Mystique in
Advertising (1920s–1940s)

"The Importance of Our Faces"
Myth America:
Picturing Women, (1865–1945).

Magazine cover,
The Ladies Home Journal.

Responding to scientific ideas that education was bad for girls' health, women's colleges
introduced much physical exercise and many sports. This cartoon seems to be based on this
preoccupation with fitness. Courtesy Graphics Division, Princeton University Library.

[130]
G. Stanley Hall on Physiology and Adolescent Education (1904)

First, the ideal institution for the training of girls from twelve or thirteen on into the twenties, when the period most favorable to motherhood begins, should be in the country. . . . All that can be called environment is even more important for girls than boys, significant as it is for the latter.

The first aim, which should dominate every item, pedagogic method and matter, should be health—a momentous word that looms up besides holiness, to which it is etymologically akin. . . .

Another principle should be to broaden by retarding; to keep the purely mental back and by every method to bring the intuitions to the front; appeals to tact and taste should be incessant. . . . Bookishness is probably a bad sign in a girl; it suggests artificiality, pedantry, the lugging of dead knowledge. . . . The rule should be to keep nothing that is not to become practical; to open no brain tracts which are not to be highways for the daily traffic of thought and conduct; not to overburden the soul with the impedimenta of libraries and records of what is afar off in time or zest, and always to follow truly the guidance of normal and spontaneous interests wisely interpreted.

From *Adolescence: Its Psychology and Its Relations to Physiology, and Education* (New York, 1904), vol. 2, pp. 636–640.

[131]
Popular Song: "Mother, Queen of Home" (1899)

The hand that rocks the cradle
is the hand that sways the world,
In ev'ry land, no matter where
we roam;

And though we may be loyal
to our own dear native land,
Our hearts are true to Mother—
Queen of Home!

Cited in Carol Wald and Judith Papachristou, *Myth America: Picturing Women, 1865–1945* (New York: Pantheon, 1975), p. 139. Courtesy Pantheon Books, a Division of Random House, Inc.

[132]
Edward O'Donnell on "Women as Bread Winners —the Error of the Age" (1897)

Is it a pleasing indication of progress to see the father, the brother and the son displaced as the bread winner by the mother, sister and daughter?

Is not the evolutionary backslide, which certainly modernizes the present wage system in vogue, a menace to prosperity—a foe to our civilized pretensions? . . .

The growing demand for female labor . . . is an insidious assault upon the home; it is the knife of the assassin, aimed at the family circle—the divine injunction. It debars the man, through financial embarrassment from family responsibility, and physically, mentally and socially excludes woman equally from nature's dearest impulse. . . .

Capital thrives not upon the peaceful, united contented family circle; rather are its palaces, pleasures and vices fostered and increased upon the disruption, ruin or abolition of the home, because with its decay and ever glaring privation, manhood loses its dignity, its backbone, its aspirations. . . .

The wholesale employment of women in the various handicrafts must gradually unsex them, as it most assuredly is demoralizing them, or stripping them of that modest demeanor that lends a charm to their kind, while it numerically strengthens the multitudinous army of loafers, paupers, tramps and policemen. . . .

But somebody will say, would you have women pursue lives of shame rather than work? Certainly not; it is to the alarming introduction of women into the mechanical industries, hitherto enjoyed by the sterner sex, at a wage uncommandable by them, that leads so many into that deplorable pursuit. . . .

From *American Federationist*, October 1897, cited in Rosalyn Baxandall et al., eds., *America's Working Women: A Documentary, 1600 to the Present* (New York: Vintage, 1976), pp. 168–69. Courtesy of Random House, Inc.

[133]
Margaret Sanger on Happiness in Marriage (1926)

Sex-love and happiness in marriage, I repeat, do not just happen. . . . Eternal vigilance is the price of marital happiness. . . . The nuptial relation must be kept

From Margaret Sanger, *Happiness in Marriage* (1926), cited in Sheila M. Rothman, *Woman's Proper Place: A History of Changing Ideals and Practices, 1870 to the Present* (New York: Basic Books, 1978), p. 211. Reprinted by permission of Grant Sanger, M.D.

romantic. When either feels that fatigue or monotony is beginning to enter the
relation, he or she must take the initiative of intensifying and rejuvenating it. . . .
Do not be afraid to take the brakes off your heart, to surrender yourself to love. . . .
Unclamp this emotion; let it have full, healthy exercise.

[134]
Dr. Douglas A. Thom on Child Management (1930)

[I]nterest and love alone on her [the mother's] part are not enough to assure
success. . . . The very love of the mother for her child may be the stumbling
block. . . . This love is invariably associated with excessive worry, anxiety, and, at
times, problems of childhood.

United States Children's Bureau *Bulletin,* no. 143, cited in Sheila M. Rothman, *Woman's Proper Place: A
History of Changing Ideals and Practices, 1870 to the Present* (New York: Basic Books, 1978), p. 215.

The New Feminist Perspective

[135]
Helen Thompson (Woolley) on the Mental Traits of Men and Women (1903)

The suggestion that the observed psychological differences of sex may be due to
differences in environment has often been met with derision, but it seems at least
worthy of unbiased consideration. The fact that very genuine and important differences of environment do exist can be denied only by the most superficial observer.
Even in our own country, where boys and girls are allowed to go to the same schools
and to play together to some extent, the social atmosphere is different from the
cradle. Different toys are given them, different occupations and games are taught
them, different ideals of conduct are held up to them. The question for the moment
is . . . what effect they have on the individuals who are subjected to them?

   The difference in physical training is very evident. Boys are encouraged in all

Cited in Rosalind Rosenberg, "The Academic Prism: The New View of American Women," in Carol
   Ruth Berkin and Mary Beth Norton, eds., *Women of America: A History* (Boston: Houghton Mifflin,
   1979), pp. 340–41. Copyright © 1979 by Houghton Mifflin Company.

forms of exercise and in out-of-door life, while girls are restricted in physical exercise
at a very early age. . . . Rough games and violent exercise of all sorts are discouraged.
Girls are kept in the house and taught household occupations. The development in
physical strength is not held up to girls as an ideal, while it is made one of the chief
ambitions of boys. . . .

When we consider the other important respect in which men are supposed to be
superior to women—ingenuity and inventiveness—we find equally important differences in social surroundings which would tend to bring about this result. Boys are
encouraged to individuality. They are trained to be independent in thought and
action. This is the ideal of manliness held up before them. . . . Girls are taught
obedience, dependence, and deference. They are made to feel that too much independence of opinion or action is a drawback to them—not becoming or womanly. A boy
is made to feel that his success in life, his place in the world, will depend upon his
ability to go ahead with his chosen occupation on his own responsibility, and to
accomplish something new and valuable. No such social spur is given to girls.

MARRIAGE AND DIVORCE

[136]

George Elliott Howard, "Is the Freer Granting of Divorce an Evil?" (1908)

First of all, it is significant that liberty of divorce has a peculiar interest for woman.
The wife more frequently than the husband is seeking in divorce an escape from
marital ills. During the two decades (1887–1906) in the whole country over 66
percent of all decrees were granted on the wife's petition. . . .

A glance at the tables showing the relative number of decrees on each principal
ground granted to the husband or to the wife, respectively, reveals the deep interest
which the woman has in the divorce remedy. In 83 percent of all decrees granted for
cruelty, in 90.6 percent of those granted for drunkenness, and 100 percent of those
granted for neglect to provide, the husband was the offender and the wife the
plaintiff. That the sources of the divorce movement are bad social conditions which
may be remedied is illustrated by the sinister fact that directly or indirectly 184,568
divorces, or nearly 20 percent of the entire number reported for the two decades,
were granted for intemperance; and in nine-tenths of these cases the culprit was the

From *Papers and Proceedings of the American Sociological Society* 3 (1908), pp. 156–60. By permission of The
American Sociological Association.

man. Surely the situation calls loudly, not for less divorce, but for less liquor and fewer saloons.

The extent to which divorce is due to desertion challenges our most serious attention. The number of decrees on this ground reaches the astounding total of 367,502 or nearly 38.9 per cent, of the entire number on all grounds for the two decades. Moreover, of the whole number of decrees granted to the husband for all causes, 49.4 per cent (156,283) or nearly half were for desertion; while 33.6 per cent (211,219) or one-third of all those granted to the wife were for the same cause. . . . Now for the abandoned family desertion often involves the bread-and-butter problem which the aggrieved spouse must have full liberty to solve. What is the remedy? Assuredly not the restriction of divorce, but the proper punishment of the deserter and the civilization of the sociological frontier.

There remains for consideration one more source of the divorce movement, and that the most prolific source of all. . . . No one who in full detail has carefully studied American matrimonial legislation can doubt for an instant that, faulty as are divorce laws, our marriage laws are far worse. . . . We are far more careful in breeding cattle or fruit trees than in breeding men and women. . . .

To the sixteenth-century reformer divorce is the medicine for the disease of marriage. Emphatically it remains so today. The wise reformer . . . will not waste his energy in unjustly punishing divorced people although some of them may deserve punishment. . . . It is needful to apply the radical or preventive remedy. That remedy is proper social control; but adequate social control can be achieved only through socialization of education. We are in sore need of a rational system of education broad enough to embrace the whole complex problem of sex, marriage, and the family. . . .

PUBLIC POLICY AND FAMILY WELFARE
Mothers' Aid

[137]

Report of the Commission on Relief for Widowed Mothers (New York, 1914)

BASIC PRINCIPLES

The Commission believes it to be fundamentally true that:

1. The mother is the best guardian of her children.

2. Poverty is too big a problem for private philanthropy.

3. No woman, save in exceptional circumstances, can be both the home-maker and the bread-winner of her family.

4. Preventive work to be successful must concern itself with the child and the home.

5. Normal family life is the foundation of the State, and its conservation an inherent duty of government.

THE GENERAL SITUATION

The Commission finds that:

1. Widowhood is the second greatest cause of dependency, the first being the incapacity of the bread-winner.

2. The widowed mother is in peculiar need of adequate assistance, and is uniquely open to constructive educational endeavors.

3. Public aid to dependent fatherless children is quite different in theory and effect from "charity" or "outdoor relief."

4. The experience of twenty-one other states in the Union, and of the larger countries of Europe, proves that it is feasible to administer such aid wisely and efficiently by public officials.

5. The experience elsewhere has shown that such aid is the most economical as well as the most socially advanced method of caring for dependent children.

Cited in Robert Bremner et al., eds., *Children and Youth in America: A Documentary History* (Cambridge, Mass.: Harvard University Press, 1971), vol. 2, pp. 379–80.

[138]

Emma O. Lundberg, "Aid to Mothers with Dependent Children" (1921)

APPLICATION OF THE LAW

The central idea in the propaganda, and the most common inclusion in the earlier laws, was aid to widows. Gradually this conception has widened, until now only six states of the forty limit the grant to children of widows, though all states include widows directly or by implication. . . . In seventeen states children of deserted mothers may be granted aid, and in six states, children of divorced mothers. Families where the father is totally incapacitated may be helped in eighteen states; fifteen states permit aid if the father is in an institution for the insane or is feeble-minded. . . .

INADEQUACY OF GRANTS

Amounts paid for the care of children in boarding homes by private child-caring agencies in 1920 approximately averaged $4.50 a week per child; for three children, this would be approximately $60 a month. For the states in which a legal allowance is specified, the maximum grants for three dependent children in their own home are as follows: $19 to $20, seven states; $22 to $29, nine states; $30 to $39, eight states; $40 to $49, four states; $50 to $55, four states.

In boarding homes the family would necessarily have some other income; the families granted mothers' pensions are much less likely to have other resources. Yet the standard set in mothers' pension laws is approximately from one-third to two-thirds the amount found requisite by agencies for boarding children in family homes. Again it should be emphasized that even the inadequate maximum permitted by the terms of the law is seldom granted. . . .

From *The Annals* of the American Academy of Political and Social Science (November, 1921) in Robert Bremner et al., eds., *Children and Youth in America: A Documentary History* (Cambridge, Mass.: Harvard University Press, 1971), pp. 389–91. Courtesy American Academy of Political and Social Science.

[139]

U.S. Children's Bureau Report on Mothers' Aid (1931)

TYPES OF FAMILIES AIDED

Families for which status of father was reported

Father dead	
Number	49,477
Per cent	82
Father deserting	3,296
Parents divorced	1,369
Father disabled physically	2,325
Father disabled mentally	1,984
Father imprisoned	1,596
Mother unmarried	55
Other status	17
Total	60,119

Even when the statutory provision is liberal, it is the willingness of the community or its administrative agency to provide, through mothers' aid, for families with different types of problems that influences the number of such families aided. The cases reported by administrative agencies in 17 States and the District of Columbia having liberal laws showed that in many localities widows constitute a large majority of the mothers aided. In these States the percentage of the families in which the father was dead varied from 54 in Washington to 93 in New Hampshire. Much difference is found in the willingness of agencies in different States to provide for families in which the father has deserted or has been divorced. In 5 States (Colorado, Florida, Kansas, Nebraska, and Washington) from 21 to 35 percent of the families assisted had needed aid because of desertion or divorce, whereas in 5 other States (Missouri, Nevada, New Hampshire, North Carolina, and Rhode Island) less than 10 percent of the families aided presented these domestic difficulties. In States having legal provisions allowing aid to deserted but not divorced mothers the number of deserted families receiving aid varied from 2 per cent of the families in New York to 13 per cent of the families in Wyoming. The percentage of mothers aided who were deserted by the fathers seems little affected by the specific provisions (which are found in 10 States) as to the length of time the father must have been away from the family before aid is granted.

From United States Children's Bureau publication, *Mothers' Aid* (1931) cited in Robert Bremner et al.,
Children and Youth in America: A Documentary History (Cambridge, Mass.: Harvard University Press,
1971), pp. 394–97.

The proportion of families aided in which the father was unable to support his family by reason of his imprisonment or physical or mental disability was usually small, but in 6 States (Arkansas, Massachusetts, Michigan, Minnesota, Missouri, and North Carolina) and the District of Columbia, from 15 to 22 percent of the families belonged in these groups. In North Carolina the State appropriation has been divided so that a special fund has been made available for assistance to prisoners' families. Proportionately the State fund for prisoners' families was much more liberal than the State grant for other mothers' aid cases. . . .

RACE OF MOTHERS

Information as to the race of the mothers aided was obtained from all reporting agencies in 18 States and the District of Columbia, but from only a part of those in 20 States. No information on race of mother was available for 6 States. Of the total number of families (46,597), 96 per cent were white, 3 per cent were Negro, and 1 per cent belonged to other races. About half of the Negro families aided were reported by counties in Ohio and Pennsylvania.

Comparison of the percentage of Negro families in the total population of the counties reporting race, with the percentage of the families aided that were Negro, shows that provision for Negro families was limited in a number of States. The disproportion between probable need and provision is even greater when the lower income level of Negro families is taken into consideration.

EXPENDITURES FOR MOTHERS' AID
BY STATES

During the year ended June 30, 1931, $33,885,487.36 was expended for grants to mothers in the 44 States and the District of Columbia reporting to the Children's Bureau. This amount is an understatement of what was actually spent in grants in aid, as complete figures were not available for California and New Jersey, and no information was received from a few localities known to be granting aid. . . .

In a large proportion of the administrative units that reported figures, funds were too limited to provide adequately for all the families made eligible for assistance by the statutes. In localities in which standards of administration were high and in which other agencies were available to care for dependent families, there was a definite tendency, under these circumstances, to limit the number of families accepted for care, in order that allowances for families should not fall below an amount necessary to assure normal and satisfactory development for the children for whom the public had accepted responsibility. Average monthly grants for all administrative areas in the different States varied from $4.33 to $69.31. With average monthly grants in 21 States falling below the median grant of $21.78 per family, it is evident that allowances in many localities had been affected by the attempt to divide limited funds among many families. Such allowances bear no relation to the actual needs of the families. Mothers' aid is not an emergency measure. It is a long-time program to prevent the breaking up of families and to assure care for dependent children in their own homes, often during the most formative years of their lives. Every effort should be made to provide allowances that will maintain a satisfactory standard of living in these families.

Family Planning

[140]
My Fight for Birth Control, by Margaret Sanger (1912–1916)

AWAKENING AND REVOLT

Early in the year 1912 I came to a sudden realization that my work as a nurse and my activities in social service were entirely palliative and consequently futile and useless to relieve the misery I saw all about me. . . .

Were it possible for me to depict the revolting conditions existing in the homes of some of the women I attended in that one year, one would find it hard to believe. There was at that time, and doubtless is still today, a sub-stratum of men and women whose lives are absolutely untouched by social agencies.

The way they live is almost beyond belief. They hate and fear any prying into their homes or into their lives. They resent being talked to. The women slink in and out of their homes on their way to market like rats from their holes. The men beat their wives sometimes black and blue, but no one interferes. The children are cuffed, kicked and chased about, but woe to the child who dares to tell tales out of the home! Crime or drink is often the source of this secret aloofness, usually there is something to hide, a skeleton in the closet somewhere. The men are sullen, un-skilled workers, picking up odd jobs now and then, unemployed usually, sauntering in and out of the house at all hours of the day and night.

The women keep apart from other women in the neighborhood. Often they are suspected of picking a pocket or "lifting" an article when occasion arises. Pregnancy is an almost chronic condition amongst them. I knew one woman who had given birth to eight children with no professional care whatever. The last one was born in the kitchen, witnessed by a son of ten years who, under his mother's direction cleaned the bed, wrapped the placenta and soiled articles in paper, and threw them out the window into the court below. . . .

From Margaret Sanger, *My Fight for Birth Control* (New York: Farrar & Rhinehart, 1931), pp. 46–56, 152–60. Reprinted by permission of Grant Sanger, M.D.

Margaret Sanger (left), with
her sister, in court after
their arrest in 1916.

In this atmosphere abortions and birth become the main theme of conversation.
On Saturday nights I have seen groups of fifty to one hundred women going into
questionable offices well known in the community for cheap abortions. I asked
several women what took place there, and they all gave the same reply: a quick
examination, a probe inserted into the uterus and turned a few times to disturb the
fertilized ovum, and then the woman was sent home. Usually the flow began the
next day and often continued four or five weeks. Sometimes an ambulance carried the
victim to the hospital for a curetage, and if she returned home at all she was looked
upon as a lucky woman. . . .

   "It's the rich that know the tricks," they'd say, "while we have all the kids."
Then, if the women were Roman Catholics, they talked about "Yankee tricks," and
asked me if I knew what the Protestants did to keep their families down. When I
said that I didn't believe that the rich knew much more than they did I was laughed
at and suspected of holding back information for money. They would nudge each
other and say something about paying me before I left the case if I would reveal the
"secret". . . .

Finally the thing began to shape itself, to become accumulative during the three weeks I spent in the home of a desperately sick woman living on Grand Street, a lower section of New York's East Side. Mrs. Sacks was only twenty-eight years old; her husband an unskilled worker, thirty-two. Three children, aged five, three and one, were none too strong nor sturdy, and it took all the earnings of the father and the ingenuity of the mother to keep them clean, provide them with air and proper food, and give them a chance to grow into decent manhood and woman-hood.

Both parents were devoted to these children and to each other. The woman had become pregnant and had taken various drugs and purgatives, as advised by her neighbors. Then, in desperation, she had used some instrument lent to her by a friend. She was found prostrate on the floor amidst the crying children when her husband returned from work. Neighbors advised against the ambulance, and a friendly doctor was called. The husband would not hear of her going to a hospital, and as a little money had been saved in the bank a nurse was called and the battle for the precious life began.

It was in the middle of July. The three-room apartment was turned into a hospital for the dying patient. Never had I worked so fast, never so concentratedly as I did to keep alive that little mother. Neighbor women came and went during the day doing the odds and ends necessary for our comfort. The children were sent to friends and relatives and the doctor and I settled ourselves to outdo the force and power of an outraged nature. . . .

At the end of two weeks recovery was in sight, and at the end of three weeks I was preparing to leave the fragile patient to take up the ordinary duties of her life, including those of wifehood and motherhood. Everyone was congratulating her on her recovery. All the kindness of sympathetic and understanding neighbors poured in upon her in the shape of convalescent dishes, soups, custards, and drinks. Still she appeared to be despondent and worried. She seemed to sit apart in her thoughts as if she had no part in these congratulatory messages and endearing welcomes. I thought at first that she still retained some of her unconscious memories and dwelt upon them in her silences.

But as the hour for my departure came nearer, her anxiety increased, and finally with trembling voice she said: "Another baby will finish me, I suppose."

"It's too early to talk about that," I said, and resolved that I would turn the question over to the doctor for his advice. When he came I said: "Mrs. Sacks is worried about having another baby."

"She well might be," replied the doctor, and then he stood before her and said: "Any more such capers, you woman, and there will be no need to call me."

"Yes, yes—I know, Doctor," said the patient with trembling voice, "but," and she hesitated as if it took all of her courage to say it, "*what* can I do to prevent getting that way again?"

"Oh ho!" laughed the doctor good naturedly, "You want your cake while you eat it too, do you? Well, it can't be done." Then, familiarly slapping her on the back and picking up his hat and bag to depart, he said: "I'll tell you the only sure thing to do. Tell Jake to sleep on the roof!"

With those words he closed the door and went down the stairs, leaving us both petrified and stunned.

Tears sprang to my eyes, and a lump came in my throat as I looked at that face before me. It was stamped with sheer horror. I thought for a moment she might have gone insane, but she conquered her feelings, whatever they may have been, and turning to me in desperation said: "He can't understand, can he?—he's a man after all—but you do, don't you? You're a woman and you'll tell me the secret and I'll never tell it to a soul."

She clasped her hands as if in prayer, she leaned over and looked straight into my eyes and beseechingly implored me to tell her something—something *I really did not know*. . . .

. . . I was about to retire one night three months later when the telephone rang and an agitated man's voice begged me to come at once to help his wife who was sick again. It was the husband of Mrs. Sacks, and I intuitively knew before I left the telephone that it was almost useless to go.

. . . I arrived a few minutes after the doctor, the same one who had given her such noble advice. The woman was dying. She was unconscious. She died within ten minutes after my arrival. It was the same result, the same story told a thousand times before—death from abortion. She had become pregnant, had used drugs, and then consulted a five-dollar professional abortionist, and death followed.

The doctor shook his head as he rose from listening for the heart beat. I knew she had already passed on; without a groan, a sigh or recognition of our belated presence she had gone into the Great Beyond as thousands of mothers go every year. I looked at that drawn face now stilled in death. I placed her thin hands across her breast and recalled how hard they had pleaded with me on that last memorable occasion of parting. The gentle woman, the devoted mother, the loving wife had passed on leaving behind her a frantic husband, helpless in his loneliness, bewildered in his helplessness as he paced up and down the room, hands clenching his head moaning "My God! My God! My God!"

The Revolution came—but not as it has been pictured nor as history relates that revolutions have come. It came in my own life. It began in my very being as I walked home that night after I had closed the eyes and covered with a sheet the body of that little helpless mother whose life had been sacrificed to ignorance. . . .

A "PUBLIC NUISANCE"

The selection of a place for the first birth control clinic was of the greatest importance. No one could actually tell how it would be received in any neighborhood. I thought of all the possible difficulties: The indifference of women's organizations, the ignorance of the workers themselves, the resentment of social agencies, the opposition of the medical profession. Then there was the law—the law of New York State.

Section 1142 was definite. It stated that no one could give information to prevent conception to anyone for any reason. There was, however, Section 1145, which distinctly stated that physicians (only) could give advice to prevent conception for the cure or prevention of disease. I inquired about the section, and was told by two attorneys and several physicians that this clause was an exception to 1142 referring only to venereal disease. But anyway, as I was not a physician, it could not protect me. Dared I risk it? . . .

We determined to open a birth control clinic at 46 Amboy Street to disseminate information where it was poignantly required by human beings. Our inspiration was the mothers of the poor; our object to help them.

With a small bundle of handbills and a large amount of zeal, we fared forth each morning in a house-to-house canvass of the district in which the clinic was located. Every family in that great district received a "dodger" printed in English, Yiddish and Italian. . . .

It was on October 16, 1916, that the three of us—Fania Mindell, Ethel Byrne and myself—opened the doors of the first birth control clinic in America. I believed then and do today, that the opening of those doors to the mothers of Brownsville was an event of social significance in the lives of American womanhood.

News of our work spread like wildfire. Within a few days there was not a darkened tenement, hovel or flat but was brightened by the knowledge that mother-hood could be voluntary; that children need not be born into the world unless they are wanted and have a place provided for them. For the first time, women talked openly of this terror of unwanted pregnancy which had haunted their lives since time immemorial. The newspapers, in glaring headlines, used the words "birth control," and carried the message that somewhere in Brooklyn there was a place where contraceptive information could be obtained by all overburdened mothers who wanted it. . . .

It was whispered about that the police were to raid the place for abortions. We had no fear of that accusation. We were trying to spare mothers the necessity of that ordeal by giving them proper contraceptive information. It was well that so many of the women in the neighborhood knew the truth of our doings. Hundreds of them who had witnessed the facts came to the courtroom afterward, eager to testify in our behalf. . . .

The arrest and raid on the Brooklyn clinic was spectacular. There was no need of a large force of plain clothes men to drag off a trio of decent, serious women who were testing out a law on a fundamental principle. My federal arrest, on the contrary, had been assigned to intelligent men. One had to respect the dignity of their mission; but the New York city officials seem to use tactics suitable only for crooks, bandits and burglars. We were not surprised at being arrested, but the shock and horror of it was that a woman, with a squad of five plain clothes men, conducted the raid and made the arrest. A woman—the irony of it!

I refused to close down the clinic, hoping that a court decision would allow us to continue such necessary work. I was to be disappointed. Pressure was brought upon the landlord, and we were dispossessed by the law as a "public nuisance." In Holland the clinics were called "public utilities."

When the policewoman entered the clinic with her squad of plain clothes men and announced the arrest of Miss Mindell and myself (Mrs. Byrne was not present at the time and her arrest followed later), the room was crowded to suffocation with women waiting in the outer room. The police began bullying these mothers, asking them questions, writing down their names in order to subpoena them to testify against us at the trial. These women, always afraid of trouble which the very presence of a policeman signifies, screamed and cried aloud. The children on their laps screamed, too. It was like a panic for a few minutes until I walked into the room where they were stampeding and begged them to be quiet and not to get excited. I assured them that nothing could happen to them, that I was under arrest but they would be allowed to return home in a few minutes. That quieted them. The men were blocking the door to prevent anyone from leaving, but I finally persuaded them to allow these women to return to their homes, unmolested though terribly frightened by it all.

Crowds began to gather outside. A long line of women with baby carriages and children had been waiting to get into the clinic. Now the streets were filled, and police had to see that traffic was not blocked. The patrol wagon came rattling through the streets to our door, and at length Miss Mindell and I took our seats within and were taken to the police station.

As I sat in the rear of the car and looked out on that seething mob of humans, I wondered, and asked myself what had gone out of the race. Something had gone from them which silenced them, made them impotent to defend their rights. I thought of the suffragists in England, and pictured the results of a similar arrest there, but as I sat in this mood the car started to go. I looked out at the mass and heard a scream. It came from a woman wheeling a baby carriage, who had just come around the corner preparing to visit the clinic. She saw the patrol wagon, realized what had happened, left the baby carriage on the walk, rushed through the crowd to the wagon and cried to me: "Come back! Come back and save me!" The woman looked wild. She ran after the car for a dozen yards or so, when some friends caught her weeping form in their arms and led her back to the sidewalk. That was the last thing I saw as the Black Maria dashed off to the station.

[141]

Helen G. Carpenter *v.* William S. Dever
(Cook County, Illinois, 1923)

The petitioner in this case prays for the issuance of a writ of mandamus against the Mayor and the Commissioner of Health of the City of Chicago, to compel them to grant a license, under the provisions of the City Ordinance, for the maintenance of a clinic to be known as "Parents' Clinic."

The petition sets forth . . . the application made by petitioner for a license, correspondence between petitioner and defendants, and their refusal to issue the license. In the application the nature and kind of treatment to be given to patients in the proposed clinic is stated to consist of "approved methods of contraception and advice consistent with family welfare in each case."

The location for such a clinic is alleged to have been selected at 1347 North Lincoln Street, in the city of Chicago; and a named physician, whose qualifications are not questioned by the respondents, is to be in charge. . . .

A number of eminent physicians testified on behalf of petitioner, to the effect that there were generally accepted and approved methods of contraception; that two specific devices, which they named, were reasonably reliable and generally approved by the profession; that their use was not injurious to health; and that contraception was a medical as well as a sociological problem. The physicians to be in charge of the proposed clinic testified that only married women whose physical, mental, or economic conditions required it, would be given advice and treatment there; that no effort, by advertisement or otherwise, would be made to attract patients; and that, in the main, treatment and advice would be given to persons referred by physicians and social agencies. Only one witness took the stand on behalf of respondents. He testified that he is a physician in the employ of the City, that he specializes in neurological diseases, and has in the past engaged in general practice of medicine. On direct examination, he testified that the methods of contraception referred to by petitioner's witnesses were injurious to the health of the users but on cross examination he admitted that they were not injurious per se but only when improperly applied; that improper use of contraceptive devices was generally due to advice promiscuously received from laymen; that proper medical advice would minimize the injurious effects, not only by discouraging the use of admittedly harmful devices, but also by removing the dangers incident to improper use of instruments not otherwise harmful.

This same witness testified that many cases present themselves in which, from a purely medical viewpoint, contraception is decidedly indicated; that, in such cases,

Circuit Court of Cook County, Illinois, B-102638, Nov. 23, 1923, published as *Birth Control and Public Policy* (Chicago: Illinois Birth Control League, 1924).

medical examinations are necessary, and often surgical operations are advisable to effect sterility.

From a consideration of the foregoing testimony, it was difficult for the Court to follow the reasoning of the learned counsel for respondents on an issue raised by his argument, namely; that the service proposed to be rendered by the Parents' Clinic did not constitute *medical treatment or advice* such as is contemplated by the ordinances regulating clinics; therefore, it would not be a clinic within the meaning of the ordinance, and if the things proposed to be done there were otherwise lawful, no license was necessary. He supported this argument by the rather surprising assertion that contraceptive methods were now so universally known to laymen that advice as to their use no longer constitutes medical or expert advice.

No more complete answer to this broad statement can be made than is to be found in the testimony of his own expert, above recited. The further argument, that contraception is a sociological question, if true, does not make it less a medical one.

From all the evidence adduced, the Court is forced to the conclusion that the establishment of a public place where medical treatment and advice is given comes within the definition of a clinic under the ordinances of the City of Chicago, and that it may not be operated without license. The Court is equally satisfied, from the evidence that there are generally approved methods of contraception which are not injurious to health when applied under proper medical instruction and guidance, such as is proposed to be given in the clinic in question, if permitted to be established; and that if legally permissible, the establishment of a clinic for the examination and the giving of advice to mothers, properly in need of it, would be distinctly in the interest of public health.

Having decided all questions of fact raised by the pleadings and argument (on what the Court regards as undisputed testimony) in favor of petitioner, the proper question for the Court now to determine is whether or not there is any reason in law why no license should issue.

The standing and character of the people who propose to establish this clinic, and the qualification of the physician to be in charge of it, are not questioned.

In a letter of the Health Commissioner, addressed to the petitioner, which is set forth verbatim in the petition, the refusal of the license is based upon a number of technical objections to the application . . . and upon the additional ground that "the purpose for which it is desired to establish the clinic is against public policy, tends to corrupt morals, and is unlawful." In support of that the Commissioner makes reference to Section 211 of the Penal Laws of the United States, which declares as non-mailable any article which may be used for the prevention of conception or any written matter in connection therewith; and, also to Sections 2672 and 2673 of the Chicago City Code of 1922, which prohibits the dissemination of information on contraceptive methods, by hand bills, circulars, newspapers or other publications, and points to these enactments as expressions of a public policy. He also cites biblical passages, which he interprets as divine commandments for unlimited procreation.

Under our system of government, courts cannot be called upon to judicially interpet the Bible or to lend or withhold their processes to enforce biblical injunctions. However much the courts may respect religious doctrines, they must look to the law of the land alone for guidance in their judicial action, leaving the enforcement of purely theological principles to the power of moral persuasion of the ministers of the church. The Court, is, therefore, spared the necessity of interpreting the biblical quotations relied upon by the Health Commissioner.

As to the provisions of the federal statutes and the city ordinances, above mentioned, it is clear that the only matters they seek to repress are promiscuous distribution of written information of birth-preventive methods. If the legislative bodies desired to do more, they would, without doubt, have incorporated their prohibitions in direct language in these statutes and ordinances. Surely, it is not possible to read in these enactments an intent to prohibit oral advice or scientific treatment by competent medical authorities. It is as reasonable to believe that these provisions were prompted by a desire to safeguard health by making it necessary to seek information on the subject from competent sources, as by a desire to prevent the spread of contraception. If the latter were the prime motives, literature advocating contraception would be repressed. As it is, only such as describe the methods are prohibited.

It is past dispute that there is no law specifically prohibiting oral instruction on birth-preventive methods or medical aid in applying mechanical devices to accomplish the desired results. But it is argued for respondents that the purpose of petitioner, in establishing the clinic in question, is not so much with a view to giving medical advice or treatment to married people standing in need of it, but generally, to advocate the claimed social value of what is now commonly termed "birth control."

Nothing in the petition filed in this case, in the application for a license addressed to the Health Commissioner, in the correspondence between the petitioner and the defendants and nothing which appeared in all the evidence before me, gives the slightest justification for this contention on the part of the learned corporation counsel. But, even if that was admittedly the motive prompting petitioner's action, still the Court is at a loss to see how that should defeat her right to have the relief prayed for, if, otherwise, she is in law entitled to it. Counsel for respondents does not contend that the advocacy of birth control, whether done orally or in writing, if methods are not published, is prohibited either by law or by any principle of public policy. Like any other social problem, its value to society may be freely advocated by its proponents within or without a clinic. It may be done in the privacy of a home or an office, from the public forum, by discussion in the press, or by any other method of conveying thought. Those who believe birth control a public benefit may as freely advocate it as those who, on moral or religious grounds, may point to it as a public menace. Both sides to the controversy have perfect liberty to place their views openly before the public. Whatever question of right there may be involved does not go to the advocacy of the theory of birth control as a social benefit, but to the giving of information as to the methods to be employed to effect control. The only real question to be decided is *whether or not the applying of contraceptive devices or giving instructions on methods to be used by married people whose circumstances in life make limited families advisable, is contrary to public policy.*

Public policy is, in its nature, so uncertain and fluctuating, varying with the habits, fashions, and mode of thought of the day, that it is difficult to determine its limits with any degree of exactness.

In Story *On Contracts* 546, it is said:

> It [the expression *public policy*] has never been defined by the courts, but has been left loose and free of definition in the same manner as fraud. This rule may, however, be safely laid down, that wherever any contract conflicts with the morals of the time and contravenes any established interest of society, it is against public policy.

Bouvier's Law Dictionary gives this definition:

> Public policy: That principle of law which holds that no subject can lawfully do that which has a tendency to be injurious to the public or against the public good. . . . "it is a variable quantity; it must and does vary with the habits, capacities and opportunities of the public" . . . . It is manifested by public acts, legislative and judicial, and not by private opinion, however eminent.

In *Wakefield* vs. *Van Tassell,* 202 Ill. 41, our Supreme Court says:

> . . . It is not the interest of the parties alone which is to be considered the true test, but in each particular case, under the facts, the judicial inquiry is, will the enforcement of the condition be inimical to the public interests.

And in the same opinion, the Court quotes the following from *People* vs. *Chicago Gas Trust,* 130 Ill. 268:

> Public policy is that principle of law which holds that no subject or citizen can lawfully do that which has a tendency to be injurious to the public or against the public good.

But what the public policy to be applied to a given case is, is not to be arbitrarily determined by the personal views of the judge. What might appear to one as being against public policy, would to another be excellent public policy. Before an act is condemned as against public policy, the principle justifying such condemnation must be found in the Constitution, statutory law, or judicial pronouncement in conformity with the common law.

It is, therefore, a safe rule for the guidance of courts to refrain from applying the power to declare an act contrary to public policy, in the absence of legislative enactment, unless precedent is found in former judicial decisions of respectable authority. . . .

I do not mean to be understood that acts heretofore unknown, which the legislature has not foreseen and prohibited, or upon which the courts have not had occasion to pronounce judgment, may not be so clearly a violation of public morality or injurious to public interest that the courts would pronounce them as being contrary to public policy; but the courts should certainly refrain from declaring a thing immoral and in violation of a policy of the State where reasonable minds differ as to its morality or immorality, or as to its public benefit or detriment. Particularly is this true of acts which a large and respectable portion of the community regard not only as moral and proper but as a decided benefit to society. Such acts, if they are to be prohibited at all, should be prohibited by legislative action and not by judicial interpretation.

The question of birth control, though, as a matter of public and open discussion, it is of very recent origin, has occupied the minds of eminent scientists and profound students in every land of the universe. Its most enthusiastic advocates see in it the salvation of the race. Many, whose public interest is keen and genuine, view with alarm the constant decrease of births to parents whose moral, physical and material conditions of life are such as make them best fitted to raise families; and a corresponding multiplication of issue to parents who, through physical, moral, or economic handicaps, are the least fit to raise large families. The suffering endured by mothers, unable to prevent the coming of unwelcome children, is graphically described. The effect upon society of the continued increase of this type of children is said to be most threatening. Unfortunately, but for the feeble efforts made by the public schools, society does little to change the condition of its children from that which is predetermined for them by the condition of their parents. Those who are born with sound and healthy bodies and minds are often condemned to lives of stunted development by the moral or economic position of their parents. The child of the drunkard, the immoral woman, the gambler, the user of narcotics, or general antisocial individual is, with rare exceptions, compelled by law to grow up under the influence of such a parent. Still we demand of such a child the same degree of obedience to law, loyalty and devotion to the ideals of our Nation, as we expect of the child born to parents to whom nature has been much more kind.

It is universally admitted that ignorance of contraceptive methods prevails mostly there where smaller rather than large families should be most desired. The sad fact is pointed to also, that for want of knowledge of preventive means, criminal abortions are resorted to in astonishingly large numbers of instances, with resulting deterioration of the health of the mothers and even death.

On the other hand, it is earnestly contended on behalf of respondents, that knowledge of methods of contraception would remove, to a great extent, the only restraining influence against sex immorality on the part of unmarried women. The fear of resulting pregnancy is said to be a great deterrent to immorality. I fear that argument proceeds from an assumption that there are circumstances where ignorance more than knowledge can be relied on to bring greater good. That cannot be true. In fact, so far as this case is concerned, the logic of this position is destroyed by the very argument of counsel for respondent. He boldly declares that methods of contraception are so generally known that medical advice is no longer necessary on the subject. In this statement he is supported by his witness. If this be true no added harm can come to the cause of sex morality by scientific supervision and control. In fact, if petitioner's position is accepted, it would serve the cause of morality. She would have the world know that contraceptive methods are unreliable and injurious to health, except when used under proper medical advice, and that such advice should be given only to married people standing in need of it.

I am loath to subscribe, however, to the proposition that knowledge of birth-preventive methods would materially lessen morality among our young women. If true, it would be sad to contemplate the weakness of our moral sense, of the influence of home environment, and of our moral and spiritual teachers, the clergy included.

The young woman who refrains from sex impropriety, simply because she fears pregnancy, will seek and obtain information on the subject sufficient to allay her fears. On the other hand, the girl in whose consciousness is deeply imbedded a respect for morality, will neither seek the information nor yield her principles upon obtaining it. Morality, in a healthy state of society, must depend upon the acceptance of it as a principle of life, and not upon fear and ignorance.

The desire to establish the clinic in question is an earnest one. The men and women supporting it sincerely believe that they are rendering a great public service. They believe that the application of modern science to the saving of lives in being, and those who are to come as a result of the natural instinct for motherhood, will keep mankind as numerous as it would be had the normal processes of nature with its child mortality and devastating epidemics not been interfered with by science. They urge that, at least until some means can be found of compensating parents by removing the economic difficulties that each new child adds to the poor, none have the right to compel new births where they are not welcome and the added burden is feared.

By offering the opportunity of obtaining knowledge on contraceptive methods the use of them is left entirely to the wishes of the patients. The mother who, by natural instinct or though religious devotion, desires a large family, cannot be affected by this information, but the mother whose physical or economic condition makes childbearing dangerous or difficult, is only doomed to suffering by lack of it.

At least in the light of the honest difference of opinion on this subject, courts should not by judicial pronouncement, without legislation, condemn such an earnest movement as immoral and against public policy.

[142]
Congressional Hearings on the Cummins-Vaile Bill
(1924)

Statement of Hon. William N. VAILE, a Representative From Colorado

Mr. VAILE. Mr. Chairman and gentlemen, I want to remove a little misapprehension concerning this bill, or these bills, which seems to have been spread about pretty largely. These bills do not propose any new or strange legislation, and these bills themselves do not propose to teach birth control, although, of course, it is hoped and expected by the advocates of this legislation that it will be possible, by legalizing this information, to give it where it may be needed, and it really may be needed, to protect the health of women. . . . The legislation on this matter consists of our statute classifying contraceptives as obscene of themselves. We are the only country in the world having this legislation. We did not have it prior to 1873. The bill, therefore, proposes no new or affirmative doctrine. It simply proposes to make lawful what was lawful in the United States prior to 1873, and what is lawful in every other country of the world, so far as I am able to determine; namely, the giving of information under medical supervision concerning methods of preventing conception, and giving the means to do so. It does not propose to do this by any new or affirmative legislation, but by simply striking those provisions from five sections of our Penal Code.

Let me, at the outset, refer to a question which immediately bobs up in the minds of everybody with whom you discuss this subject. They say, "It will promote immorality." Let me ask the committee, in all fairness, if the morality of this country is strikingly superior now to what it was before 1873. You can not pick up a daily paper, you can not go into a church, you can not hear a subject of public morals discussed to any great length by any speaker but what you will be advised that we are at a lower stage of morals than we were 50 years ago. Fifty years ago we did not have such a statute on our books. Certainly the insertion of this proviso in our statutes has not noticeably increased the morality of the United States. It is common knowledge that methods of contraception are used by the educated, the well-to-do classes of the community. Would anybody say that those classes are conspicuously less moral than those who can not obtain this information and have no knowledge of it? I think that would be a great reflection on many people with certainly a highly developed civic consciousness, people prominent in every good work of the community, all of whom as a matter of common knowledge, of which this committee can take judicial notice, do have and use this information.

From testimony before the U.S. Congress, Sub-committee of the Committees on the Judiciary, Joint Hearings on H.R. 6542 and S.2290, Cummins-Vaile Bill (86th Congress, First Session, 1924) in Robert Bremner et al., eds., *Children and Youth in America: A Documentary History* (Cambridge, Mass.: Harvard University Press, 1981), vol. 2 pp. 161, 164, 65.

Let me ask also if this country is conspicuously more moral or less immoral than other countries of the world? . . .

I submit in all fairness that those who charge that this bill will promote immorality should judge by what has happened.

To summarize, the United States is certainly not conspicuously more moral now than it was 50 years ago. Is church attendance, are divorces, is prevalence of crime any test of public morality? Our church attendance certainly does not exceed that of, we will say, Italy. I will admit birth-control methods are not generally practiced in Italy, but neither are they unlawful in Italy. Our church attendance is not less than it is in Holland or New Zealand. Is prevalence of divorce any index of immorality in America? We have the highest divorce rate in the world. Is crime any index of public morality? We have the highest record of homicides in the civilized world. And so, I submit, in all fairness, by merely removing the provisions which were put into the code 50 years ago, and which did not exist theretofore, we won't be rushing on a downward path, so far as we can judge by our own experience or that of any other country.

Statement of Marguerita A. STEWART, Representing the National Christian League for the Promotion of Purity, New York City

Doctor STEWART. Mr. Chairman and gentlemen of the committee, I hope this bill will not be reported for legislative action. Its intent is to give legal sanction to a practice which has been outlawed in this Nation for 50 years. The prevention of conception is a practice which is hoary with age. We can trace it at least as far back as the days of Onan, where we find record of its practice by the man in Genesis, thirty-eighth chapter and ninth verse. It is a practice which is wrong in principle and violates the moral law of the universe. If legalized, it maintains for a man a standard of sex ethics below that of all the nobler species of the animal kingdom. In the animal kingdom below man no noble male approaches the female except at her invitation.

That woman should be driven to protect herself from undesired conceptions by contraceptive methods is degrading to both the man and the woman. (Parenthetically, I may say here that I have been told that modern teachers of this practice put the onus entirely upon the woman by advising her to great secrecy lest the man's moral sense be disturbed.)

Woman is the race carrier, and should be free to conserve to the uttermost her life-giving value to the race. In the periodic functioning of her reproductive organs is written the law of control over that function. Within that law once every month, at her discretion, she may receive the embraces of her man. The woman's control over reproductive functioning would conserve for man the precious vitality of his loins and give to woman her self-respect as a free moral agent in the reproduction of the race. Under these conditions shame would be removed, parentage would become voluntary, and motherhood become the supreme service and joy of woman's life.

To hold up before the young people of our land through legal sanction a standard of sex ethics below that of the nobler beasts of the field would be to debase the character of our Nation and finally disintegrate all morality. And so, gentlemen of the committee, I pray you that this bill may not be reported for legislative action. It would give legal sanction to an unmoral practice which has grown out of woman's age-long sex slavery to man, known in common law as "marital rights."

[143]
Foster *v.* State *(Wisconsin, 1923)*

Plaintiff in error, hereinafter called the defendant, was prosecuted . . . and convicted of having feloniously produced the death of the child of one Anna Jung. The evidence showed among other things that Miss Jung was advanced in pregnancy from six to eight weeks; that she consulted the defendant; that he made an examination and pronounced her pregnant, and performed a criminal operation upon her resulting in a premature expulsion of the foetus. He claimed the evidence fails to show that Miss Jung was pregnant; that there is not sufficient proof of his having performed an operation; and that if guilty at all he should have been prosecuted under the provisions of sec. 4583, Stats., relating to producing a miscarriage. . . .

VINJE, C. J. We shall not devote any time to the discussion or recital of the evidence further than to say that it sustains a finding that Miss Jung was pregnant; that the defendant performed a criminal operation upon her by means of which the embryo or foetus was prematurely expelled; and that there were no prejudicial errors in the trial of the case.

The really serious question in the case is whether the defendant was prosecuted under the proper section of the statute. Sec. 4352, under which he was prosecuted, reads as follows:

> Any person who shall administer to any woman pregnant with a child any medicine, drug or substance whatever, or shall use or employ any instrument or other means with intent thereby to destroy such child, unless the same shall have been necessary to preserve the life of such mother or shall have been advised by two physicians to be necessary for such purpose, shall, in case the death of such child or of such mother be thereby produced, be deemed guilty of manslaughter in the second degree.

It is found in the chapter relating to "Offenses against Lives and Persons." The penalty for its violation is imprisonment in the state prison from four to seven years.
Sec. 4583 reads as follows:

182 (Wisc.) 298 (1923) in Robert Bremner et al., eds., *Children and Youth in America: A Documentary History* (Cambridge, Mass.: Harvard University Press, 1981), vol. 2, pp. 168–170.

> Any person who shall administer to any pregnant woman, or prescribe for such woman, or advise or procure any such woman to take any medicine, drug or substance or thing whatever, or shall use or employ any instrument or other means whatever, or advise or procure the same to be used, with intent thereby to procure the miscarriage of any such woman shall be punished by imprisonment in the county jail not more than one year nor less than six months or by fine not exceeding five hundred dollars nor less than two hundred and fifty dollars, or by both such fine and imprisonment in the discretion of the court.

It is found in the chapter entitled "Offenses against Chastity, Morality, and Decency." It is evident that the legislature did not intend to define the same offense in the two sections. In the latter it defines the offense of an act intended to produce miscarriage or one that does produce miscarriage. . . .

In order to commit such an offense there must be a pregnant woman. A normal pregnancy can exist only where there is embryonic life in the womb of the pregnant woman; therefore, in order to commit the offense of producing a miscarriage, there must be a destruction and expulsion of embryonic life. So we have a statute covering the offense of destroying and expelling from the womb embryonic life. This offense is one not against a person because the law does not recognize a mere embryo as a person or human being, but is an offense against morality because it is against good morals to destroy that which otherwise presumably would develop into a human being. It interferes with the normal functions of nature in the perpetuation of the race.

The offense described in sec. 4352 constitutes manslaughter in the second degree and is by statute included under the denomination of "homicide," which means the killing of a human being. . . . Neither in popular nor in scientific language is the embryo in its early stages called a human being. Popularly it is regarded as such, for some purposes, only after it has become "quick," which does not occur till four or five months of pregnancy have elapsed. In contemplation of law, says Blackstone, life begins as soon as an infant is able to stir in its mother's womb. . . . It is obvious that no death of a child can be produced where there is no living child. Sec. 4352 requires the existence of a living child and the causing of its death, or that of the mother, before the offense there defined is committed. If pregnancy has not advanced sufficiently so that there is a living child, that is, a quick child, then felonious destruction of the foetus constitutes a criminal miscarriage only. This construction gives full force and effect to each section as defining a distinct separate offense, is in accordance with the common conception of the beginning of life, and is sustained by authority. . . .

In a strictly scientific and psychological sense there is life in an embryo from the time of conception, and in such sense there is also life in the male and female elements that unite to form the embryo. But law, for obvious reasons, cannot in its classifications follow the latest or ultimate declarations of science. It must for purposes of practical efficiency proceed upon more every-day and popular conceptions, especially as to definitions of crimes that are *malum in se*. These must be of such a nature that the ordinary normal adult knows it is morally wrong to commit them. That it should be less of an offense to destroy an embryo in a stage where human life in its common acceptance has not yet begun than to destroy a *quick* child, is a conclusion that commends itself to most men. The legislature saw fit to enact sec. 4583, a law making it an offense to produce a criminal miscarriage. It also made it a graver offense by sec. 4352 to produce a criminal abortion resulting in the death of a quick child or of its mother. Both the quick child and the mother are human beings—hence to unlawfully kill either constitutes manslaughter. A two months' embryo is not a human being in the eye of the law and therefore its destruction constitutes an offense against morality and not against lives and persons. Defendant should have been prosecuted under the provisions of sec. 4583. The evidence does not sustain a conviction under sec. 4352.

SUFFRAGE AND JURY SERVICE

[144]
Flyer, New York Suffrage Party (1917)

A FOOLISH MOTHER loves her children only in the house. A WISE MOTHER loves her children wherever they go. AN EFFICIENT MOTHER follows her children out of the house, into the street, to the school, to the movie, the factory, and stands between the child and evil influences, low standards, bad sanitation, disease, and vice.

THESE CONDITIONS ARE CONTROLLED BY VOTES. HOW MUCH DO YOU LOVE YOUR CHILDREN? Answer by joining the women who LOVE CHILDREN EVERYWHERE. JOIN THE NEW YORK WOMAN SUFFRAGE PARTY.

Cited in Marlene Stein Wortman, "Domesticating the Nineteenth-Century American City," *Prospects: An Annual of American Cultural Studies* 3 (1977), 564–65.

Demonstrating for Change: Suffrage Parade, Chicago, June 7, 1916. Courtesy Chicago Historical Society.

Picketing the White House, 1917: An innovative strategy developed by the Woman's Party.

[145]

"Senators vs. Working Women," by Mollie Schepps (1912)

Mollie Schepps, Shirt Waist Maker, answers the New York Senator who says: "Now there is nobody to whom I yield in respect and admiration and devotion to the sex."

We want man's admiration, but we do not think that is all there is to live for. Since economic conditions force us to fight our battle side by side with man in the industrial field, we do not see why we should not have the same privileges in the political field, in order to better the conditions under which we must work. . . . We demand a voice as to how politics shall be conducted. Yes, we want man's admiration, but not the kind that looks well on paper or sounds good when you say it. (Applause.) What we want men to do is to practice, to stop talking, of the great comforts that they have provided for us; we know in most of the cases we are the providers; we also want them to know that in these days they will have to try to win our admiration. . . .

Don't you gentlemen worry, our minds are already made up as to what we are going to do with our vote when we get it. Another reason is given against woman suffrage; it is said that equal say will enable the women to get equal pay, and equal pay is dangerous. Why? Because it would keep the women from getting married. Well, then, if long, miserable hours and starvation wages are the only means man can find to encourage marriage it is a very poor compliment to themselves. In the name of a purer marriage we must have equal voice in making the laws, for we have found out from experience that it is not only men who have to get married.

There are a few facts from the shirt-waist strike I would like to call to your attention. . . . When we sent a committee to Mayor McClellan to speak for protection for 30,000 women on strike in the shirt-waist industry, and to protest against the brutality of the police, what answer did the Mayor give the committee? This: He could not be bothered with any striking shirt-waist makers. Had that same committee represented 30,000 men, men who would have a vote at the next election, you can bet that the committee would have received a different answer, for that would mean 30,000 votes at the next election. This is the kind of respect, admiration and devotion we receive from our admirers the politicians when we fight for a better condition and a decent wage.

One year later, when we had the terrible disaster of the Triangle Shirt-waist factory, where our bodies were burned by the wholesale and many jumped from the tenth floor and smashed their poor bodies rather than be roasted, then again those

From a 1912 pamphlet of the Wage Earners League of New York, in Rosalyn Baxandall et al., *America's Working Women: A Documentary, 1600 to the Present* (New York: Vintage, 1976), pp. 216–218. Courtesy Random House, Inc.

very same gentlemen, that a year ago tried to break our ranks when we fought for a safer place to work in, shed tears over the bodies on the sidewalk crushed to pieces. . . . We cannot, and must not, wait until our sisters that live in comfort get the votes for us. We know they have everything that their heart desires in order to make life worthwhile. That is no reason why they should not have the ballot, but working women must use the ballot in order to bring about conditions where all may be able to live and grow because they work. The ballot used as we mean to use it will abolish the burning and crushing of our bodies for the profit of a very few.

[146]
The Nineteenth Amendment of the U.S. Constitution (1920)

1. The right of citizens of the United States to vote shall not be denied or abridged by the United States or by any State on account of sex.
2. Congress shall have power to enforce this article by appropriate legislation.

[147]
"Jury Service for Women," by Jennie Loitman Barron

The purpose of this article is . . . to show the advisability of admitting women to jury service, and to answer some of the objections which are commonly given. . . .

The right of a trial by jury is one of the most firmly rooted of the fundamental principles of our nation and of all our states. It is considered more important than any other one guarantee of liberty because it protects the common people from the power of their officials. Juries have always been an essential part of our administration of justice. The Constitution of the United States and of every state in the Union guarantees the right to public trial by an impartial jury.

Appropriate exemptions from jury service should be provided for women, as appropriate exemptions for men are now provided. Among the men who are exempted are doctors, lawyers, dentists, pharmacists, veterinarians, preachers, school teachers, city officials, ship captains, and engineers. In addition to these classes, the following women should be exempt: women trained nurses, women nursing sick

From a pamphlet published by the Committee on the Legal Status of Women of the National League of Women Voters, 1924.

members of their own family, and mothers having a child or children under twelve years of age, or women having the legal custody of such children. Of course all persons, whether men or women, if ill or otherwise physically incapacitated, are exempt.

Our juries consist of citizens who listen to the evidence and merely pass upon the facts presented. They do not have to have any knowledge of the law, nor do they need any specific training. Broadly, they must be citizens of the United States, of good moral character and sound judgment. Nobody has ever contended that the men have a monopoly of these qualities.

Is a hod-carrier better equipped than a housekeeper to decide a case involving the guilt or innocence of one accused of offering for sale decayed foods to the public? Is a ribbon salesman better equipped than a mother to estimate the damages suffered by a young girl who has been seriously injured in an automobile accident? Is a bank clerk better equipped than a woman buyer to decide a dispute involving the quality of clothing material? Is a man better equipped than a woman to judge the sanity or insanity of a person whose will is being questioned on that ground?

Of course it is true, as is contended by some, that there are women who have not the sense even to judge these things. It is equally true that there are also men who haven't the sense to judge these things. As Mrs. Poyser has so aptly said, "I do not deny that women are foolish. God Almighty made them to match the men."

Justice to women, and even to the community, demands that women should be eligible to sit as jurors, for if women are like men, they surely should serve; and if women are not like men, their point of view, different from that of the men, should be represented on our juries. . . . Women certainly do not want to be denied it if a privilege, nor evade it if a duty. Every advance in civilization means responsibility as well as privilege. Citizenship implies responsibility. Women are ready to assume the burdens as well as the benefits of citizenship.

How would a man feel if he had to be tried by a jury of all women? As voters, taxpayers, and litigants, it is unjust to deny women the right to sit on juries which decide questions affecting their property and their liberty. Is it fair to the woman victim who has suffered at the hands of some man to have her case tried by a jury composed only of men?

Shall we say that a woman shall have a right to make wills, a right to collect her own wages, a right to do business, a right to speak in public, a right to go to college, a right to enter the professions, a right to hold office, a right to vote, a right to practice law in the courts, a right to testify in court, a right to sue and be sued, and yet not have a right to sit in the jury box?

The right of trial by jury was intended to give every citizen a trial by an impartial jury and judgment by one's peers. Can we say that a woman or girl on trial is receiving a trial by an impartial jury, when women are not eligible as jurors? To say that a woman before the Bar is entitled to judgment by her peers, and then to exclude women from the jury room, is to misinterpret the spirit which underlies our

What women would do in the community with suffrage: A cartoonist's vision from *Civics Magazine*. Courtesy Manuscript Collection, University of Illinois, Chicago Circle Campus.

Jeanette Rankin of Montana, elected the first United States Congresswoman, 1917. Montana had passed suffrage in 1914.

institutions. Jury service for women is another step toward the attainment of that universal justice for which the American nation stands. . . .

A jury should represent a cross-section of the community. No cross-section of the community is complete without women.

Women jurors are specially needed in cases involving women and girls, and in cases affecting public morals; first, because women can appreciate women's conditions best; and second, because women are generally more interested than men in the morals of their community. A shabby, poverty-stricken, adolescent girl victim is not as interesting to some male jurors as is a clever, well-dressed, handsome adventuress. . . .

Women on the witness stand speak more frankly and freely to a jury where there are women. . . .

Mothers in rearing their children, are constantly acting as jurors. They are continually called upon to make decisions requiring sound judgment. We want the mother instinct which is used in the closeted nursery to be used also in the big troubled nursery of the world.

Women as a class are respectors of law and champions of equality and justice. These qualities in the jury room will naturally lead to verdicts greatly helping the enforcement of the law. . . .

"But," say others, "women have no time to serve on juries." How much time does it take? There are different rules in each of the states, but generally one cannot be drafted for jury service more than once in two or three years. This means that one probably will not be drafted more than once in several years, and it is very frequently the case that one is never drafted in a lifetime, because the number of jurors necessary, in proportion to the entire population is extremely small. Opening jury service to women would give us an increased number of jurors to draw upon. It would halve the responsibilities of men and women for jury service.

Women may be divided into two classes; those in the home, and those in industry. As mentioned before, about one-fifth of all our women are engaged in gainful occupations. They can leave their occupations as easily as the men, from point of view of time, and probably better from the point of view of remuneration. As a whole, their wages are not as high as those of the men, and, therefore, are nearer the compensation they receive as jurors.

As regards the women in the home, "Who is going to look after the baby?" The "babies" of many women are school teachers, clerks, doctors, and in our stores and factories. These babies probably would not miss mother's care more than usual, and, of course, the mothers of young babies should be exempted.

The other women in the home may be divided into two classes, those who do not have household duties weighing very heavily upon them, because they can afford to keep help; and those of the poorer class, who must perform all their housework themselves. Women of the poorer classes would probably welcome jury service as much and even more than those of the richer class, because it would give them an opportunity for relaxation and recreation away from the home. With the compensation received from jury duty they could easily hire others to do their housework. To these women jury service, with its short hours and reasonable compensation, would be an educational and an interesting diversion from the monotonous routine of household drudgery. It is better that the sweeping and dishwashing should suffer temporarily at the hands of the high school girl next door, than that the state should be deprived of splendid jury material.

Those with household help can easily find time for jury service. Many cases in court do not last longer than the average bridge party or church festival. There is no danger to the home from women serving on juries. The home has not suffered because of thousands of women's clubs of every possible political and humanitarian complexion, nor because women have sat on city councils, or on boards of directors. Grace and charm have not departed from the American home; family life has not been destroyed; domestic arts have not been neglected; children have not gone, in greater numbers than before, breakfastless to school. There is no recorded increase in the burning of soups. Indeed, women's outside interests have helped to develop the home. Homemaking is something more than housekeeping. Many homes are hurt by the trivialities and lack of interest of mothers in the affairs of life.

The most common objection to women jurors is that they will be subjected to pass on cases of a disagreeable nature. The percentage of cases involving presentation of unsavory testimony is extremely small. The number of women who will hear such testimony is infinitesimal, because very few civil cases raise such questions, and even the percentage of criminal cases of such a nature is very small. . . .

The opportunity for women to read unsavory stories in yellow journals is greater in one day than jury service would afford them in a lifetime.

The contact of woman with life does not diminish her elevating and refining influence, but brings it to the jury. This will certainly be the effect, since only women of good moral character and sound judgment are allowed to serve on juries.

We have women litigants, women court stenographers, women witnesses, and in some states, even women judges, and these have not suffered from contact with the court room. Women doctors, nurses, and social workers are probably best acquainted with evil social conditions, yet this has in no way undermined their morals. Yet some would call it indecent to have men and women who are selected for good mentality and morals, discuss the weight of facts in the halls of justice. Many of the disagreeable cases involve women; therefore, women should help decide them, in order to reach just verdicts. . . .

In an exaggerated attempt to find objections, some have even placed jury service on a par with military and volunteer fire service. It is ridiculous to claim that because women do not run with the fire horses, they cannot sit in the jury box.

In the rare cases where a mixed jury would be kept over night, they would be given separate quarters in a hotel. Since our country has survived the test of men and women traveling together in sleeping cars, in the care of a male porter, we ought to have nothing to fear from the very rare necessity of men and women jurors spending a night in hotels, in separate quarters, in the care of sheriffs and matrons. The additional expense of women jurors would be neglible, for women jurors would not increase the number, but only change the personnel of jurors.

The fundamental question is not one of expense but whether it preserves our system of justice. If it does, all admit that no expense is too great. Has the objection of expense prevented the passage of the Women's Compensation Act, the Minimum Wage Law, Woman Suffrage, or any other progressive movement?

UNIT 2

[*Occupational Choice*]

FROM PROTECTION TO RESTRICTION

This section explores the process by which the concept of protective legislation became transformed into the concept that gender was a valid basis for employment discrimination. Organized women's groups such as The Federation of Women's Clubs, the Women's Trade Union League, and the National Consumers' League, among others, provided effective and persistent pressure on state legislatures and on the courts in behalf of maximum-hour and minimum-wage laws for women. In examining these documents we must distinguish the motives of proponents both from the effects of regulation, and from the motives of supporters. We must also distinguish between the temporary historical circumstances that gave rise to the need for protective legislation and permanent factors that became the basis for continuing policies in a very different set of circumstances. Finally we must look at the impact of the judicial process itself.

Maximum-Hour Legislation

Toward the end of the nineteenth century the Supreme Court turned away from the deferential attitude toward state legislative authority that had produced the Slaughter-house and Bradwell decisions, and started declaring various pieces of state economic legislation unconstitutional, on the grounds that they clashed with the due process clause of the Fourteenth Amendment. One such case was *Lochner* v. *New York* (1905) which endangered the maximum-hour legislation that had been passed by twenty-one states. That issue came before the Supreme Court in *Muller* v. *Oregon,* 1908. Louis Brandeis, the counsel for Oregon, had to persuade the court that the circumstances of the present case were distinguishable from Lochner and therefore not controlled by it. He had to show a compelling state interest in limiting freedom of contract for women, since this was the most obvious difference between the New York and Oregon laws. His brief, which was written with Josephine Goldmark, became the model for introducing sociological data and statistics to establish a factual connection between the law and the conditions of life that gave rise to it. It presented 113 pages of evidence on the physical differences between men and women, on the bad effects of long hours on the health and morals of women workers, and on the way this undermined the health and welfare of future generations. The brief did not establish causal connections between long hours and ill health and failed to distinguish physical causes from economic ones. In large measure this arises from the reports of doctors, workers, government investigators on which they had to rely. It allows two quite different conclusions: that working women suffered because of their biological structure; or that they suffered because the only jobs open to them were particularly dangerous and unpleasant.

The Muller decision is a landmark case not only for its relevance to women's rights, but for its implications for economic regulation in general. Justice Brewer, judicial conservative, presented the opinion of the court. His argument rested on the same view that sustained common law restrictions on married women's property rights and on divorce, and that underpinned the growth of morals regulation: women may be denied rights that men enjoy, both for what the state considers their own benefit and in the interests of preserving the race. The principle enunciated by the court in Muller became a binding precedent and was later used to justify other kinds of special women's labor legislation, as well as the exclusion of women from juries, state-supported universities, and certain types of jobs.

Night-Work Legislation

The case of *Radice* v. *New York,* 1924, illustrates the way protective legislation could be turned into an instrument to restrict occupational opportunity and choice. It involved the type of legislation that led Alice Paul and the National Woman's Party to introduce the Equal Rights Amendment in Congress that same year. New York, like many other states, passed maximum-hour legislation that was filled with exceptions; in this case waitresses in small restaurants could not work between 10 p.m. and 6 a.m., but could in small hotels, where, presumably, their health and morals were not compromised. The night work rule was applied in some places to professionals such as pharmacists and nurses, but not to student nurses.

Radice, the owner of a small restaurant in Buffalo, New York, was convicted of the crime of employing a woman in his restaurant after 10 p.m. In his defense he argued that the law violated the due process and the equal protection clauses of the Fourteenth Amendment. Liberty, the Supreme Court had often said, could be limited only to the degree it was necessary to promote public welfare. Statutory classifications that distinguished among groups of people had to be based on a reasonable connection to the public good. The question raised by this case was whether a statute limiting night work for some waitresses, but not others, bore a rational relationship to public welfare. The evidence in the court records showed only a tenuous relationship between night work and health and safety hazards, but a significant relationship to restriction on occupational choice. Some women found night work more compatible with their family responsibilities than day work, and more lucrative as well. Women printers fought for eight years to become an exception, since the law took away their livelihood.

The U.S. Supreme Court, citing the Muller precedent, upheld the Radice conviction. The decision represented the beginning of an important shift in the Court's policy toward reviewing state legislation that restricted women's occupational choice. In *Muller,* the Court required compelling evidence to justify a law limiting women's occupational freedom. In Radice, the Court seems to be saying that, if the legislature deemed the physical differences between the sexes to warrant special legislative limitations on women, the Court would defer to that judgment unless it saw no apparent justification for the law.

Minimum-Wage Legislation

The Supreme Court took a very different stance, however, in regard to minimum-wage statutes for women. Between 1912 and 1915 a number of states passed such laws, largely as a result of crusades against the white slave trade. *The Report of the Illinois State Senate Committee on Vice* (1916) is representative of investigations conducted in many states that demonstrated a link between substandard wages and the growth of prostitution. The wage structure, the committee found, was based on the legal assumption that women were not the primary breadwinners, and not on the value of the work they performed. The recommendations of the committee followed those of the Women's Legislative Congress, in 1914, which consisted of various women's organizations and had been established to advise the committee.

In the years after World War I, employers organized to oppose the minimum wage. Adopting the methods of their opponents, they marshalled statistics and cited "contented" workers who protested against a statute that would cost them their jobs. All this impressed the legislatures, and the courts as well. Investigations by the women's bureau and various state agencies showed that despite *rises* in pay, women workers in factories, laundries, and other mercantile establishments did not earn a living wage. Real wages had frequently dropped in relation to the cost of living.

In 1918 Congress authorized the establishment of a minimum wage for adult women in the District of Columbia. A year later the women's bureau investigators found that in the District the average rate of pay for women hotel, restaurant, and hospital workers was $15.40 per week, compared to an estimate by the Bureau of Labor Statistics that the minimum cost of living was $18.43 per week. In March, 1920 the wage board established the minimum wage at $16.50. The Children's Hospital of the District of Columbia and a woman elevator operator in a hotel sued to enjoin enforcement.

In *Adkins* v. *Children's Hospital* (1923) the Court faced a 1,000-page brief prepared by Felix Frankfurter and Josephine Goldmark of the National Consumers' League. The Court invalidated the minimum-wage law, relying on the notion of freedom of contract established in the Lochner case. The Adkins decision must be read together with Radice, which followed it by only a few months. Both involved legislation to mitigate a physical and moral health problem. In Adkins, much evidence was introduced to demonstrate the relationship between substandard wages and physical and moral health of women. Since women's wages never equaled men's in the same job, a minimum-wage act clearly provided protection without restricting opportunity. The reverse, however, was true of the night-work statute, which the court upheld. Did the Court mean that women should be protected only so far as it did not encourage their participation in the workforce?

The Court continued to oppose minimum-wage legislation through the Depression and the first Roosevelt administration. As late as 1936 they invalidated a women's minimum-wage law of the state of New York, on the grounds that the due process clause forbade laws that unfairly regulated property. They also invalidated most of Roosevelt's New Deal program in the area of social welfare. It had become more and more difficult to believe that in the absence of strong unions, a wage was the result of free bargaining between employees and employers. After Roosevelt's overwhelming victory in 1936 he introduced in Congress his famous (or infamous) Court-packing plan. As the debate progressed in Congress the Supreme Court dramatically reversed itself on a number of legal issues. The reversal on minimum wages for women occurred in the case of *West Coast Hotel* v. *Parrish* (1937). The law at issue, enacted by Washington state in 1913, had been consistently enforced, despite the Adkins case.

The decision relied on Muller for its precedent but went further. It demoted freedom of contract from its position as a fundamental constitutional right, immune from all but the most urgently needed restriction. In the light of post-1937 constitutional developments, the demotion of freedom of contract became extremely significant. The Supreme Court began to develop a two-tier theory of "liberty" within the meaning of the due process clause of the Fourteenth Amendment. The first or lower tier of liberty consisted basically of the individual's right to do whatever he or she wanted. Restraints in this were presumed by the Court to be constitutional if they met certain standards of "reasonableness." The second or higher tier of rights contained "fundamental" rights. Infringements of these liberties were presumed to be unconstitutional, unless there was proof of compelling state interest in abridging the right. One significant result of the Parrish case was that freedom of contract did not receive the benefit of the tougher standards. Economic rights gained virtually no judicial protection after 1937. Freedom of contract could now be curtailed as long as the restriction had some reasonable relation to a legitimate governmental purpose. In the employment cases involving women after 1937, the courts did not even apply this lesser scrutiny. They interpreted the unbroken line of decisions from *Muller* to *Parrish* as having established the principle that permanent, rather than situation-bound, distinctions between the sexes justified any gender-based employment discrimination.[9]

DOCUMENTS

FROM PROTECTION TO RESTRICTION
Maximum-Hour Legislation

[148]
Lochner v. New York, *U.S. Supreme Court (1905)*

Mr. Justice PECKHAM delivered the opinion of the Court:
[The labor law of the State of New York] is not an act merely fixing the number of hours which shall constitute a legal day's work, but an absolute prohibition upon the employer permitting, under any circumstances, more than ten hours work to be done in his establishment. The employee may desire to earn the extra money, which would arise from his working more than the prescribed time, but this statute forbids the employer from permitting the employee to earn it.

The statute necessarily interferes with the right of contract between the employer and employees, concerning the number of hours in which the latter may labor in the bakery of the employer. The general right to make a contract in relation to his business is part of the liberty of the individual protected by the Fourteenth Amendment of the Federal Constitution. Under that provision no State can deprive any person of life, liberty or property without due process of law. . . . There are, however, certain powers, existing in the sovereignty of each State in the Union, somewhat vaguely termed police powers [which] relate to the safety, health, morals and general welfare of the public. . . .

It must of course be conceded that there is a limit to the valid exercise of the police power by the State. . . . In every case that comes before this court . . . where

198 U.S. 45 (1905).

During World War I, women eagerly accepted well-paid jobs in machine shops and heavy industry plants. After the war, with the return to "normalcy," their occupational choices were once against restricted to female-dominated industries, where the pay was lower.

Woman machinist. Courtesy National Archives, Washington, DC

Women weighing coils. Courtesy National Archives, Washington, DC

legislation of this character is concerned . . . the question necessarily arises: Is this a fair, reasonable and appropriate exercise of the police power of the State, or is it an unreasonable, unnecessary and arbitrary interference with the right of the individual to his personal liberty or to enter into these contracts in relation to labor which may seem to him appropriate or necessary for the support of himself and his family? . . .

The question whether this act is valid as a labor law . . . may be dismissed in a few words. There is no reasonable ground for interfering with the liberty of person or the right of free contact, by determining the hours of labor, in the occupation of a baker. There is no contention that bakers as a class are not equal in intelligence and capacity to men in other trades or manual occupations, or that they are not able to assert their rights and care for themselves without the protecting arm of the State. . . . They are in no sense wards of the State. . . . We think that a law like the one before us involves neither the safety, the morals nor the welfare of the public. . . . The law must be upheld, if at all, as a law pertaining to the health of the individual engaged in the occupation of a baker. It does not affect any other portion of the public. . . . Clean and wholesome bread does not depend upon whether the baker works but ten hours per day or only sixty hours a week. . . .

. . . The mere assertion that the subject relates though but in a remote degree to the public health does not necessarily render the enactment valid. The act must have a more direct relation, as a means to an end, and the end itself must be appropriate and legitimate. . . .

. . . This case has caused much diversity of opinion in the state courts. . . . The Court of Appeals has upheld the act as . . . a health law. One of the judges of the Court of Appeals, in upholding the law, stated that . . . the regulation in question could not be sustained unless they were able to say, from common knowledge, that working in a bakery or candy factory was an unhealthy employment. The judge held that, while the evidence was not uniform, it still led him to the conclusion that the occupation of a baker or confectioner was unhealthy and tended to result in diseases of the respiratory organs. Three of the judges dissented from that view, and they thought the occupation of a baker was not to such an extent unhealthy as to warrant the interference of the legislature with the liberty of the individual.

We think the limit of the police power has been reached and passed in this case. . . .

. . . To the common understanding the trade of a baker has never been regarded as an unhealthy one. Very likely physicians would not recommend the exercise of that or of any other trade as a remedy for ill health. . . . There must be more than the mere fact of the possible existence of some small amount of unhealthiness to warrant legislative interference with liberty. It is unfortunately true that labor, even in any department, may possibly carry with it the seeds of unhealthiness. But are we all, on that account, at the mercy of legislative majorities? . . . No trade, no occupation, no mode of earning one's living could escape this all-pervading power, and the acts of the legislature in limiting the hours of labor in all employments would be valid, although such limitation might seriously cripple the ability of the laborer to support himself and his family. . . .

It is also urged, pursuing the same line of argument, that it is to the interest of the State that its population should be strong and robust, and therefore any legislation which may be said to tend to make people healthy must be valid as health laws, enacted under the police power. If this be a valid argument and a justification for this kind of legislation, it follows that the protection of the Federal Constitution from undue interference with liberty of person and freedom of contract is visionary. . . . [There is] scarcely any law but might find shelter under such assumptions. . . . Not only the hours of employees, but the hours of employers, could be regulated, and doctors, lawyers, scientists, all professional men, as well as athletes and artisans, could be forbidden to fatigue their brains and bodies by prolonged hours of exercise, lest the fighting strength of the State be impaired. We mention these extreme cases because the contention is extreme. . . . We think that such a law as this, although passed in the assumed exercise of the police power, and as relating to the public health, or the health of the employees named, is not within that power, and is invalid. . . . Statutes of the nature of that under review, limiting the hours in which grown and intelligent men may labor to earn their living, are mere meddlesome interferences with the rights of the individual. . . . All that it could properly do has been done . . . with regard to the conduct of bakeries, as provided for in the other sections of the act. . . . These several sections provide for the inspection of the premises where the bakery is carried on, with regard to furnishing proper washrooms and water-closets, apart from the bake-room, also with regard to providing proper drainage, plumbing and painting. . . .

[149]
Muller *v.* Oregon, *U.S. Supreme Court (1908)*

Mr. Justice BREWER delivered the opinion of the court:

On February 19, 1903, the legislature of the State of Oregon passed an act (Session Laws, 1903), the first section of which is in these words:

"Sec. 1. That no female (shall) be employed in any mechanical establishment, or factory, or laundry in this State more than ten hours during any one day."

Section 3 made a violation of the provisions of the prior sections a misdemeanor, subject to a fine of not less than $10 nor more than $25. On September 18, 1905, an information was filed in the Circuit Court of the State for the county of Multanomah, charging that the defendant ". . . require[d] a female, to wit, one Mrs. E. Gotcher, to work more than ten hours. . . ."

208 U.S. 412 (1908).

A trial resulted in a verdict against the defendant, who was sentenced to pay a fine of $10. The Supreme Court of the State affirmed the conviction, *State* v. *Muller*, 43 Oregon 252, whereupon the case was brought here on writ of error.

The single question is the constitutionality of the statute under which the defendant was convicted so far as it affects the work of a female in a laundry. That it does not conflict with any provisions of the state constitution is settled by the decision of the Supreme Court of the State. The contentions of the defendant, now plaintiff in error, are thus stated in his brief:

(1) Because the statute attempts to prevent persons, *sui juris,* from making their own contracts, and thus violates the provisions of the Fourteenth Amendment.
(2) Because the statute does not apply equally to all persons similarly situated, and is class legislation.
(3) The statute is not a valid exercise of the police power.

It is the law of Oregon that women, whether married or single, have equal contractual and personal rights with men. . . .

It thus appears that, putting to one side the elective franchise, in the matter of personal and contractual rights they stand on the same plane as the other sex. Their rights in these respects can no more be infringed than the equal rights of their brothers. We held in *Lochner* v. *New York,* 198 U.S. 45, that a law providing that no laborer shall be required or permitted to work in a bakery more than sixty hours in a week or ten hours in a day was not as to men a legitimate exercise of the police power of the State, but an unreasonable, unnecessary and arbitrary interference with the right and liberty of the individual to contract in relation to his labor, and as such was in conflict with, and void under, the Federal Constitution. That decision is invoked by plaintiff in error as decisive of the question before us. But this assumes that the difference between the sexes does not justify a different rule respecting a restriction of the hours of labor.

In patent cases counsel are apt to open the argument with a discussion of the state of the art. It may not be amiss, in the present case, before examining the constitutional question, to notice the course of legislation as well as expressions of opinion from other than judicial sources. In the brief filed by Mr. Louis D. Brandeis, for the defendant in error, is a very copious collection of all these matters, an epitome of which is found in the margin.

The legislation and opinions referred to in the margin may not be, technically speaking, authorities, and in them is little or no discussion of the constitutional question presented to us for determination, yet they are significant of a widespread belief that woman's physical structure, and the functions she performs in consequence thereof, justify special legislation restricting or qualifying the conditions under which she should be permitted to toil. Constitutional questions, it is true, are not settled by even a consensus of present public opinion, for it is the peculiar value of a written constitution that it places in unchanging form limitations upon legislative action, and thus gives a permanence and stability to popular government which otherwise would be lacking. At the same time, when a question of fact is debated and debatable, and the extent to which a special constitutional limitation is affected by the truth in respect to that fact, a widespread and long continued belief concerning it is worthy of consideration. We take judicial cognizance of all matters of general knowledge. . . .

That woman's physical structure and the performance of maternal functions place her at a disadvantage in the struggle for subsistence is obvious. This is especially true when the burdens of motherhood are upon her. Even when they are not, by abundant testimony of the medical fraternity continuance for a long time on her feet at work, repeating this from day to day, tends to injurious effects upon the body, and as healthy mothers are essential to vigorous offspring, the physical well-being of woman becomes an object of public interest and care in order to preserve the strength and vigor of the race.

Still again, history discloses the fact that woman has always been dependent upon man. He established his control at the outset by superior physical strength, and this control in various forms, with diminishing intensity, has continued to the present. As minors, though not to the same extent, she has been looked upon in the courts as needing especial care that her rights may be preserved. Education was long denied her, and while now the doors of the school room are opened and her opportunities for acquiring knowledge are great, yet even with that and the consequent increase of capacity for business affairs it is still true that in the struggle for subsistence she is not an equal competitor with her brother. Though limitations upon personal and contractual rights may be removed by legislation, there is that in her disposition and habits of life which will operate against a full assertion of those rights. She will still be where some legislation to protect her seems necessary to secure a real equality of right. Doubtless there are individual exceptions, and there are many respects in which she has an advantage over him; but looking at it from the viewpoint of the effort to maintain an independent position in life, she is not upon an equality. Differentiated by these matters from the other sex, she is properly placed in a class by herself, and legislation designed for her protection may be sustained, even when like legislation is not necessary for men and could not be sustained. It is impossible to close one's eyes to the fact that she still looks to her brother and depends upon him. Even though all restrictions on political, personal and contractual rights were taken away, and she stood, so far as statutes are concerned, upon an absolutely equal plane with him, it would still be true that she is so constituted that she will rest upon and look to him for protection; that her physical structure and a proper discharge of her material functions—having in view not merely her own health, but the well-being of the race—justify legislation to protect her from the greed as well as the passion of man. The limitations which this statute places upon her contractual powers, upon her right to agree with her employer as to the time she shall labor, are not imposed solely for her benefit, but also largely for the benefit of all. Many words cannot make this plainer. The two sexes differ in structure of body, in the functions to be performed by each, in the amount of physical strength, in the capacity for long-continued labor particularly when done standing, the influence of vigorous health upon the future well-being of the race, the self-reliance which enables one to assert full rights, and in the capacity to maintain the struggle for subsistence. This difference justifies a difference in legislation and upholds that which is designed to compensate for some of the burdens which rest upon her.

We have not referred in this discussion to the denial of the elective franchise in the State of Oregon, for while it may disclose a lack of political equality in all things with her brother, that is not of itself decisive. The reason runs deeper, and rests in the inherent difference between the two sexes, and in the different functions in life which they perform.

For these reasons, and without questioning in any respect the decision in *Lochner* v. *New York,* we are of the opinion that it cannot be adjudged that the act in question is in conflict with the Federal Constitution, so far as it respects the work of a female in a laundry, and the judgment of the Supreme Court of Oregon is affirmed.

Night-Work Legislation

[150]
Radice *v.* People of the State of New York, U.S. *Supreme Court (1924)*

Mr. Justice SUTHERLAND delivered the opinion of the Court:

The validity of the statute is challenged upon the ground that it contravenes the provisions of the Fourteenth Amendment, in that it violates (1) the due process clause, by depriving the employer and employee of their liberty of contract, and (2) the equal protection clause, by an unreasonable and arbitrary classification.

1. The basis of the first contention is that the statute unduly and arbitrarily interferes with the liberty of two adult persons to make a contract of employment for themselves. The answer of the State is that night work of the kind prohibited, so injuriously affects the physical condition of women, and so threatens to impair their peculiar and natural functions, and so exposes them to the dangers and menaces incident to night life in large cities, that a statute prohibiting such work falls within the police power of the State to preserve and promote the public health and welfare.

The legislature had before it a mass of information from which it concluded that night work is substantially and especially detrimental to the health of women. We

264 U.S. 292 (1924).

cannot say that the conclusion is without warrant. The loss of restful night's sleep cannot be fully made up by sleep in the day time, especially in busy cities, subject to the disturbances incident to modern life. The injurious consequences were thought by the legislature to bear more heavily against women than men, and, considering their more delicate organism, there would seem to be good reason for so thinking. The fact, assuming it to be such, properly may be made the basis of legislation applicable only to women. Testimony was given upon the trial to the effect that the night work in question was not harmful; but we do not find it convincing. Where the constitutional validity of a statute depends upon the existence of facts, courts must be cautious about reaching a conclusion respecting them contrary to that reached by the legislature; and if the question of what the facts establish be a fairly debatable one, it is not permissible for the judge to set up his opinion in respect of it against the opinion of the lawmaker. The state legislature here determined that night employment of the character specified, was sufficiently detrimental to the health and welfare of women engaging in it to justify its suppression; and, since we are unable to say that the finding is clearly unfounded, we are precluded from reviewing the legislative determination. The language used by this Court in *Muller* v. *Oregon*, in respect of the physical limitations of women, is applicable and controlling:

> The limitations which this statute places upon her contractual powers, upon her right to agree with her employer as to the time she shall labor, are not imposed solely for her benefit, but also largely for the benefit of all. Many words cannot make this plainer. The two sexes differ in structure of body, in the functions to be performed by each, in the amount of physical strength, in the capacity for long-continued labor, particularly when done standing, the influence of vigorous health upon the future well-being of the race, the self-reliance which enables one to assert full rights, and in the capacity to maintain the struggle for subsistence. This difference justifies a difference in legislation and upholds that which is designed to compensate for some of the burdens which rest upon her.

Adkins v. *Children's Hospital*, is cited and relied upon; but that case presented a question entirely different from that now being considered. The statute in the Adkins Case was a wage-fixing law, pure and simple. It had nothing to do with the hours or conditions of labor. We held that it exacted from the employer "an arbitrary payment for a purpose and upon a basis having no causal connection with his business, or the contract or the work" of the employee; but, referring to the Muller Case, we said that "the physical differences (between men and women) must be recognized in appropriate cases, and legislation fixing hours or conditions of work may properly take them into account."

2. Nor is the statute vulnerable to the objection that it constitutes a denial of the equal protection of the laws. The points urged under this head are (a) that the act discriminates between cities of the first and second class and other cities and communities; and (b) excludes from its operation women employed in restaurants as singers and performers, attendants in ladies' cloak rooms and parlors, as well as those

employed in dining rooms and kitchens of hotels and in lunch rooms or restaurants conducted by employers solely for the benefit of their employees.

The limitation of the legislative prohibition to cities of the first and second class does not bring about an unreasonable and arbitrary classification. Nor is there substance in the contention that the exclusion of restaurant employees of a special kind, and of hotels and employees' lunch rooms, renders the statute obnoxious to the Constitution. The statute does not present a case where some persons of a class are selected for special restraint from which others of the same class are left free; but a case where all in the same class of work, are included in the restraint. Of course, the mere fact of classification is not enough to put a statute beyond the reach of the equality provision of the Fourteenth Amendment. Such classification must not be "purely arbitrary, oppressive or capricious." But the mere production of inequality is not enough. Every selection of persons for regulation so results, in some degree. The inequality produced, in order to encounter the challenge of the Constitution, must be "actually and palpably unreasonable and arbitrary." Directly applicable are recent decisions of this Court sustaining hours of labor for women in hotels but omitting women employees of boarding houses, lodging houses, etc., *Miller* v. *Wilson;* and limiting the hours of labor of women pharmacists and student nurses in hospitals but excepting graduate nurses. *Bosley* v. *McLaughlin.* The opinion in the first of these cases was delivered by Mr. Justice Hughes, who, after pointing out that in hotels women employees are for the most part chambermaids and waitresses; that it cannot be said that the conditions of work are the same as those which obtain in the other establishments; and that it is not beyond the power of the legislature to recognize the differences, said:

> The contention as to the various omissions which are noted in the objections here urged ignores the well-established principle that the legislature is not bound, in order to support the constitutional validity of its regulation, to extend it to all cases which it might possibly reach. Dealing with practical exigencies, the legislature may be guided by experience. It is free to recognize degrees of harm, and it may confine its restrictions to those classes of cases where the need is deemed to be clearest. As has been said, it may 'proceed cautiously, step by step,' and 'if an evil is specially experienced in a particular branch of business' it is not necessary that the prohibition 'should be couched in all-embracing terms.' If the law presumably hits the evil where it is most felt, it is not to be overthrown because there are other instances to which it might have been applied. Upon this principle which has had abundant illustration in the decisions cited below, it cannot be concluded that the failure to extend the act to other and distant lines of business, having their own circumstances and conditions, or to domestic service, created an arbitrary discrimination as against the proprietors of hotels.

The judgment below is Affirmed.

Minimum-Wage Legislation

[151]
Report of the Senate Vice Committee, Illinois General Assembly (1916)

Your Committee finds:

1. *That poverty is the principal cause, direct and indirect, of prostitution.*

Throughout this inquiry, as with every other inquiry of public or private undertaking that has come to our attention, one fact has stood forth distinctly, although in some reports no prominence is accorded it, nor has it the dignity of commentary. It is the all-significant fact that the toll of many thousands of girls annually fed to commercialized vice is entirely exacted from the very poorest groups. Seventy percent of the mothers of girls at the Geneva home, who were in employment, were either washwomen or scrubwomen, "which means hard work with low earnings" *(Sophonisba P. Breckinridge in "The Delinquent Child and the Home")*. Slightly under 70 percent of the delinquent girls brought into the Juvenile Court of Cook county were from families not supported by the fathers, where the mother had become the wage-earner, and the conditions of poverty were extreme. Twenty-one percent were from very poor families, where "the father was able to bear the burden of support but there was a hard struggle while the children were small, to make both ends meet" *(Same Authority)*. This committee was unable to learn of a single prostitute, in any city in Illinois visited or in which its investigators operated, who had come from a home of even modest prosperity. Women do not seek lives of prostitution, except under economic pressure, or economic expediency, or under the handicap of moral and mental defects resulting from previous family economic conditions.

This, your committee respectfully submits, is the fundamental, the first truth to be accepted in the diagnosis and intelligent treatment of the social disease of prostitution. . . .

There is much other testimony of the actual practice of prostitution being preceded by an experience in ignorance or deception or force, in which virtue was sacrificed without either the receipt or the expectation of money. But even in this respect the line of demarkation between the actual sale of virtue and the loss of virtue through deception and force is many times difficult to trace. The familiar experience of the girl decoyed to her infamy through promise of marriage may be on her part either an error of affection or a transgression born solely of desire to escape an intolerable economic condition. The presumption is incontrovertible that the girl,

Pp. 23–24, 28, 30, 33, 38–40, 52–55, 815–21.

whose means are inadequate properly to meet the items of a bare existence, is least fortified to resist prenuptial demands, the denial of which she may fear will cost a husband while the granting might open the matrimonial door of escape from all the miseries of starvation. In the absence of love, therefore, such experiences may partake of many of the elements of prostitution, virtue being given, not indeed for a price in money, but for a promise of future support. The girl gambles rather than makes open sale.

Your Committee respectfully recommends:

1. *The immediate enactment of a minimum-wage law, prohibiting the payment of less than a living wage to any woman, or minor, except during a period of apprenticeship not exceeding six months.*

After nearly three years of inquiry, seeking statistics and viewpoints, reducing arguments to mathematics, applying accepted rules of economics and logic, your Committee is arrived at the firm conclusion that the enactment of the proposed minimum wage law is the essential initial step in the intelligent treatment of the problems under survey.

2. *The repeal of all laws that have fallen into disuse, and the strict enforcement of all others. A permanent committee on law enforcement recommended.*

In laws prohibitory of immoral and indecent conduct, Illinois is entitled to foremost rank among her sister states. This Committee, indeed, has discovered no offense against good morals that could not adequately be reached by existing statutes.

3. *The encouragement of joint action by the states, looking toward uniform state legislation.*

A congress of legislative committees, acting in an advisory capacity on matters of distinctly State legislation, would unquestionably exert a beneficial influence in making uniform the enactments of the sister states. This movement, long recognized as essential in the handling of moral problems as divorce and industrial problems as minimum wage, was responsible for the creation of a joint committee for this purpose by the Forty-ninth General Assembly.

4. *Improvement of the conditions of girls in domestic service, and of girls from homes offering inadequate social opportunities, by the opening of school houses and all other available public buildings as social centers; hours of labor of girls in domestic employment to be regulated to permit of participation.*

5. *Establishment of homes for the adequate moral and industrial schooling of women during the period of reformation.*

6. *Extension of vocational education in the public schools.*

7. *Abolition of the obnoxious fining system in the treatment of immoral women convicted in the courts.*

8. *Registration of all girls under 18 and of boys under 21, in employment; notice of engagement and of discharge, and reason therefore, mandatory on both employer and employee. A woman, under the state factory inspector, to investigate, without publication, all complaints against moral conditions.*

9. *Newspapers and all other publications of general circulation prohibited from printing and circulating the details of any breach of promise, divorce or other proceeding in which moral lapse or immoral conduct is charged, until final adjudication has been had in the trial court; and then, such publication to be restricted to an unvarnished statement of the charge and the finding of the court.*

No one will question the harmful impression on the immature mind of the narrated details of moral erring, as recorded in connection with divorce, and similar proceedings. Without the slightest infringement on the liberty of the press, a much needed reformation in this regard may easily be accomplished.

10. *Creation of a state athletic commission for the encouragement of healthy and non-professional sports and pastimes.*

As a counter influence to dance halls, poolrooms and other places indoors where either girls or boys, or both, are attracted, your Committee recommends the encouragement by the state of all manner of sports, pastimes and athletics. A state commission, actively engaged in instructing boys and girls in the various games, organizing them into teams, arranging inter-urban, inter-county and finally inter-sectional contests, would, in the judgment of your Committee, prove an invaluable factor.

The reasons given for each recommendation have been shortened or deleted.—Ed.

"EVIDENCE"

The Vice Committee sent investigators into the field, around the state, who interviewed prostitutes. Below is a sample of their reports, which were supplemented by those of social workers and prostitutes who appeared openly before the committee and were cross-examined.

No. 2—Domestic. Age 25. Swedish. Left home at 16, upon the death of her mother, to earn her own living. In her first position as a servant, she fell a victim of a son of the family, with whom she cohabited whenever they were left alone in the house for an evening. Caught in a compromising situation by her mistress, she was discharged. Soon after she entered the home of a woman who was an invalid. Here she was paid $4 a week by her mistress and says she received more than that from the woman's husband. She remained with this family for about a year. Then upon the departure of her own father from the city, she gave herself up to a life of prostitution "for the money there was in it," she said. "Nobody really cares what becomes of me, so why should I starve to be decent? Only one week this year have I made less than $30.00 and so far I haven't spent a cent on doctors either." Is a very attractive blonde with clear skin; takes a great pride in dressing fashionably. Moral sense never developed.

No. 12—Age 23. Sales clerk in a department store. Father dead and her wages support an invalid mother and two smaller children. Keeps company with a young man, who hands her a little money each week and makes more money on the side. Says she must do wrong or see her mother die. Her story corroborated by investigator. Low wages in this case appear to be the sole cause of the girl's downfall, as she seems to find no enjoyment or pleasure in her habits. Cried bitterly while confiding her story and seemed devoted to her family. Declares she will some day end her life.

No. 23—Waitress in the dining room of a prosperous hotel. About 27 years old. Has not seen her husband for four years. Attends faithfully to her duties in the dining room and is probably not suspected by the management of the immoral diversions in which she engages with transient guests after working hours. Was "dated up" for the investigator by the news stand clerk and promptly agreed to meet him on a distant corner to spend a couple of hours with him anywhere.

In conversation she admitted immoral habits and declared she had to make extra money to pay for the care of her child in another city. Depends for money upon four or five traveling men who "make" it regularly, and avers she does not and will not entertain men who live in the city.

No. 27—Polish. Age 22. Works in a laundry. Wages $7 a week. Married at 19 and deserted five months later by her husband. Has not seen him since. Child died soon after birth. Unable to read or write and with no training for any kind of work she found employment in a laundry and had worked in several of them. "Men don't hunt in laundries for wives," was the explanation with which she justified her loose morals.

This girl refuses to go to a hotel lest she might be seen by some friend, but offered to show the investigator a lonely spot in the north end of the city.

No. 28—Age 16, and looks younger. Saleslady in a retail store. Very shrewd and wise for her years; profane but will not drink. Earns $4 a week and tells her family that she earns $9 to account for the good clothes which are furnished to her by her "friend," who is married. Is not faithful to him, however, and declares she will "jump the town" with the first man that will take her where she does not have to fear discovery by her parents and doesn't have to go home every night. This girl graduated from grammar school, but was unable to obtain any better position than the job she holds as saleslady at $4 a week. Home conditions bad.

No. 29—Age 22. Is kept as a "widow with means" in a respectable home by a prosperous married business man who calls for her one or two evenings each week and takes her for automobile rides into the country where she has immoral relations with him. Between his visits she entertains three other young men, but will not let them come to her room. When the investigator was introduced by one of her friends she consented to go for a ride in the country for a "good time" if she could get another girl to go along. Formerly worked as a domestic in the home of the man who now keeps her.

No. 31—A frequenter of cafes in the red light district. Recently came from Chicago, where she worked in a tailoring shop and earned $6 a week at piecework. Russian. Twenty-two years old. Seduced and deserted in Chicago by her fiance; her sister had supplied her with money to leave home and escape the slander of neighbors. She had been advised by women of the tenderloin to go where things were "wide open," and the girls were making "good money." She is bright and is ambitious to save enough money to open a flat.

[152]
Adkins *v.* Children's Hospital of the District of Columbia, *U.S. Supreme Court (1923)*

Mr. Justice SUTHERLAND delivered the opinion of the Court:

The question presented for determination by these appeals is the constitutionality of the Act of September 19, 1918, providing for the fixing of minimum wages for women and children in the District of Columbia. . . .

The appellee in the first case is a corporation maintaining a hospital for children in the District. It employs a large number of women in various capacities, with whom it had agreed upon rates of wages and compensation satisfactory to such employees, but which in some instances were less than the minimum wage fixed by an order of the board made in pursuance of the act. The women with whom appellee had so contracted were all of full age and under no legal disability. . . .

In the second case the appellee, a woman 21 years of age, was employed by the Congress Hall Hotel Company as an elevator operator, at a salary of $35 per month and two meals a day. She alleges that the work was light and healthful, the hours short, with surroundings clean and moral, and that she was anxious to continue it for the compensation she was receiving, and that she did not earn more. Her services were satisfactory to the Hotel Company, and it would have been glad to retain her, but was obliged to dispense with her services by reason of the order of the board and on account of the penalties prescribed by the act. The wages received by this appellee were the best she was able to obtain for any work she was capable of performing, and the enforcement of the order, she alleges, deprived her of such employment and wages. She further averred that she could not secure any other position at which she could make a living with as good physical and moral surroundings, and earn as good wages, and that she was desirous of continuing and would continue the employment, but for the order of the board. . . .

The statute now under consideration is attacked upon the ground that it authorizes an unconstitutional interference with the freedom of contract included within the guarantees of the Due Process clause of the Fifth Amendment. That the right to contract about one's affairs is a part of the liberty of the individual protected by this clause is settled by the decisions of this court and is no longer open to

261 U.S. 525 (1923).

question. . . . Within this liberty are contracts of employment of labor. In making such contracts, generally speaking, the parties have an equal right to obtain from each other the best terms they can as the result of private bargaining. . . . There is, of course, no such thing as absolute freedom of contract. It is subject to a great variety of restraints. But freedom of contract is, nevertheless, the general rule and restraint the exception, and the exercise of legislative authority to abridge it can be justified only by the existence of exceptional circumstances. Whether these circumstances exist in the present case constitutes the question to be answered. It will be helpful to this end to review some of the decisions where the interference has been upheld. . . .

Statutes fixing hours of labor. . . . In some instances the statute limited the hours of labor for men in certain occupations, and in others it was confined in its application to women. No statute has thus far been brought to the attention of this court which by its terms applied to all occupations. In *Holden* v. *Hardy,* the court considered an act of the Utah Legislature, restricting the hours of labor in mines and smelters. This statute was sustained as a legitimate exercise of the police power, on the ground that the Legislature had determined that these particular employments, when too long pursued, were injurious to the health of the employees, and that, as there were reasonable grounds for supporting this determination on the part of the Legislature, its decision in that respect was beyond the reviewing power of the federal courts.

That this constituted the basis of the decision is emphasized by the subsequent decision in *Lochner* v. *New York* reviewing a state statute which restricted the employment of all persons in bakeries to 10 hours in any one day. The court referred to *Holden* v. *Hardy, supra,* and declared it to be inapplicable. . . .

In *Bunting* v. *Oregon,* . . . since the state Legislature and state Supreme Court had found such a law necessary for the preservation of the health of employees in these industries [mills, factories, and manufacturing establishments], this court . . . accepted their judgment, in the absence of facts to support the contrary conclusion. . . .

In addition to the cases cited above, there are decisions of this court dealing with laws especially relating to hours of labor for women.

In the Muller Case the validity of an Oregon statute, forbidding the employment of any female in certain industries more than 10 hours during any one day, was upheld. The decision proceeded upon the theory that the difference between the sexes may justify a different rule respecting hours of labor in the case of women than in the case of men. It is pointed out that these consist in differences of physical structure, especially in respect of the maternal functions, and also in the fact that historically woman has always been dependent upon man, who has established his control by superior physical strength. . . . But the ancient inequality of the sexes, otherwise than physical, as suggested in the Muller Case has continued "with diminishing intensity." In view of the great—not to say revolutionary—changes which have taken place since that utterance, in the contractual, political, and civil status of

women, culminating in the Nineteenth Amendment, it is not unreasonable to say
that these differences have now come almost, if not quite, to the vanishing point. In
this aspect of the matter, while the physical differences must be recognized in
appropriate cases, and legislation fixing hours or conditions of work may properly
take them into account, we cannot accept the doctrine that women of mature age
. . . require or may be subjected to restrictions upon their liberty of contract which
could not lawfully be imposed in the case of men under similar circumstances. To do
so would be to ignore all the implications to be drawn from the present-day trend of
legislation as well as that of common thought and usage, by which woman is
accorded emancipation from the old doctrine that she must be given special protection or be subjected to special restraint in her contractual and civil relationships. In
passing, it may be noted that the instant statute applies in the case of a woman
employer contracting with a woman employee as it does when the former is a man.

    . . . A law forbidding work to continue beyond a given number of hours leaves
the parties free to contract about wages and thereby equalize whatever additional
burdens may be imposed upon the employer as a result of the restrictions as to hours,
by an adjustment in respect of the amount of wages. Enough has been said to show
that the authority to fix hours of labor cannot be exercised except in respect of those
occupations where work of long continued duration is detrimental to health. This
court has been careful in every case where the question has been raised, to place its
decision upon this limited authority of the Legislature to regulate hours of labor and
to disclaim any purpose to uphold the legislation as fixing wages, thus recognizing
an essential difference between the two. It seems plain that these decisions afford no
real support for any form of law establishing minimum wages.

    If now, in the light furnished by the foregoing exceptions to the general rule
forbidding legislative interference with freedom of contract, we examine and analyze
the statute in question, we shall see that it differs from them in every material
respect. It is not a law dealing with any business charged with a public interest or
with public work, or to meet and tide over a temporary emergency. It has to do with
the character, methods or periods of wage payments. It does not prescribe hours of
labor or conditions under which labor is to be done. It is not for the protection of
persons under legal disability or for the prevention of fraud. It is simply and
exclusively a price-fixing law, confined to adult women (for we are not now considering the provisions relating to minors), who are legally as capable of contracting
for themselves as men. It forbids two parties having lawful capacity—under penalties as to the employer—to freely contract with one another in respect of price for
which one shall render service to the other in a purely private employment where
both are willing, perhaps anxious, to agree, even though the consequence may be to
oblige one to surrender a desirable engagement and the other to dispense with the
services of a desirable employee. The price fixed by the board need have no relation to
the capacity or earning power of the employee, the number of hours which may
happen to constitute the day's work, the character of the place where the work is to

be done, or the circumstances or surroundings of the employment, and, while it has no other basis to support its validity than the assumed necessities of the employee, it takes no account of any independent resources she may have. It is based wholly on the opinions of the members of the board and their advisors—perhaps an average of their opinions, if they do not precisely agree—as to what will be necessary to provide a living for a woman, keep her in health and preserve her morals. It applies to any and every occupation in the District, without regard to its nature or the character of the work.

The standard furnished by the statute for the guidance of the board is so vague as to be impossible of practical application with any reasonable degree of accuracy. What is sufficient to supply the necessary cost of living for a woman worker and maintain her in good health and protect her morals is obviously not a precise or unvarying sum—not even approximately so. The amount will depend upon a variety of circumstances. . . . The relation between earnings and morals is not capable of standardization. It cannot be shown that well-paid women safeguard their morals more carefully than those who are poorly paid. Morality rests upon other considerations than wages, and there is certainly no such prevalent connection between the two as to justify a broad attempt to adjust the latter with reference to the former. As a means of safeguarding morals the attempted classification, in our opinion, is without reasonable basis. . . . Nor is there ground for distinction between women and men, for certainly if women require a minimum wage to preserve their morals men require it to preserve their honesty. . . .

The law takes account of the necessities of only one party to the contract. It ignores the necessities of the employer by compelling him to pay not less than a certain sum, not only whether the employee is capable of earning it, but irrespective of the ability of his business to sustain the burden, generously leaving him, of course, the privilege of abandoning his business as an alternative for going on at a loss. Within the limits of the minimum sum, he is precluded, under penalty of fine and imprisonment, from adjusting compensation to the differing merits of his employees. It compels him to pay at least the sum fixed in any event, because the employee needs it, but requires no service of equivalent value from the employee. . . . The law is not confined to the great and powerful employers but embraces those whose bargaining power may be as weak as that of the employee. It takes no account of periods of stress and business depression, of crippling losses, which may leave the employer himself without adequate means of livelihood. To the extent that the sum fixed exceeds the fair value of the services rendered, it amounts to a compulsory exaction from the employer for the support of a partially indigent person, for whose condition there rests upon him no peculiar responsibility, and therefore, in effect, arbitrarily shifts to his shoulders a burden which, if it belongs to anybody, belongs to society as a whole.

. . . The ethical right of every worker, man or woman, to a living wage may be conceded. One of the declared and important purposes of trade organizations is to secure it. And with that principle and with every legitimate effort to realize it in fact, no one can quarrel; but the fallacy of the proposed method of attaining it is that it assumes that every employer is bound at all events to furnish it. . . .

It is said that great benefits have resulted from the operation of such statutes, not alone in the District of Columbia but in the several states, where they have been in force. A mass of reports, opinions of special observers and students of the subject . . . has been brought before us in support of this statement, all of which we have found interesting, but only mildly persuasive. That the earnings of women are now greater than they were formerly, and that conditions affecting women have become better in other respects, may be conceded; but convincing indications of the logical relation of these desirable changes to the law in question are significantly lacking. . . . No real test of the economic value of the law can be had during periods of maximum employment, when general causes keep wages up to or above the minimum; that will come in periods of depression and struggle for employment, when the efficient will be employed at the minimum rate, while the less capable may not be employed at all. . . .

It follows, from what has been said, that the act in question passes the limit prescribed by the Constitution, and accordingly the decrees of the court below are affirmed.

Mr. Justice HOLMES, dissenting:

The question in this case is the broad one. Whether Congress can establish minimum rates of wages for women in the District of Columbia, with due provision for special circumstances, or whether we must say that Congress had no power to meddle with the matter at all. To me, notwithstanding the deference due to the prevailing judgment of the Court, the power of Congress seems absolutely free from doubt. . . .

. . . [P]retty much all law consists in forbidding men to do some things that they want to do, and contract is no more exempt from law than other acts. Without enumerating all the restrictive laws that have been upheld I will mention a few that seem to me to have interfered with liberty of contract quite as seriously and directly as the one before us. Usury laws prohibit contracts by which a man receives more than so much interest for the money he lends. . . . Some Sunday laws prohibit practically all contracts during one-seventh of our whole life. Insurance rates may be regulated. . . .

I confess that I do not understand the principle on which the power to fix a minimum for the wages of women can be denied by those who admit the power to fix a maximum for their hours of work. . . . I perceive no difference in the kind or degree of interference with liberty. . . . The bargain is equally affected whichever half you regulate. *Muller* v. *Oregon,* I take it is as good law today as it was in 1908. It will need more than the Nineteenth Amendment to convince me that there are no differences between men and women, or that legislation cannot take those differences into account. I should not hesitate to take them into account if I thought it necessary to sustain this Act.

I am of the opinion that the statute is valid and that the decree should be reversed.

[153]

West Coast Hotel Co. *v.* Parrish, *U.S. Supreme Court (1937)*

Mr. Chief Justice HUGHES delivered the opinion of the Court.

This case presents the question of the constitutional validity of the minimum-wage law of the state of Washington. . . .

"Sec. 3. There is hereby created a commission to be known as the 'Industrial Welfare Commission' for the State of Washington, to establish such standards of wages and conditions of labor for women and minors employed within the State of Washington, as shall be held hereunder to be reasonable and not detrimental to health and morals, and which shall be sufficient for the decent maintenance of women."

Further provisions required the commission to ascertain the wages and conditions of labor of women and minors within the state. Public hearings were to be held. If after investigation the commission found that in any occupation, trade or industry the wages paid to women were "inadequate to supply them necessary cost of living and to maintain the workers in health," the commission was empowered to call a conference of representatives of employers and employees together with disinterested persons representing the public. The conference was to recommend to the commission, to issue an obligatory order fixing minimum wages. Any such order might be reopened and the question reconsidered with the aid of the former conference or a new one. . . .

The appellant conducts a hotel. The appellee Elsie Parrish was employed as chambermaid and (with her husband) brought suit to recover the difference between the wages paid her and the minimum wages fixed pursuant to the state law. The minimum wage was $14.50 per week of 48 hours. The appellant challenged the act as repugnant to the due process clause of the Fourteenth Amendment of the Constitution of the United States. . . .

The appellant relies upon the decision of this Court in *Adkins* v. *Children's Hospital.*

300 U.S. 379 (1937).

Mrs Catherine Waugh McCulloch, Chair of the Committee on Uniform Laws concerning Women, was admitted to the Illinois bar in 1886 and was active in both the temperance and suffrage movements.

The Supreme Court of Washington has . . . refused to regard the decision in the Adkins case as determinative and has pointed to our decisions both before and since that case as justifying its position. We are of the opinion that this ruling of the state court demands on our part a re-examination of the Adkins case. . . .

The point that has been strongly stressed, that adult employees should be deemed competent to make their own contracts, was decisively met nearly forty years ago in *Holden* v. *Hardy* where we pointed out the inequality in the footing of the parties. We said:

> The legislature has also recognized the fact, which the experience of legislators in many states has corroborated, that the proprietors of these establishments and their operatives do not stand upon an equality, and that their interests are, to a certain extent, conflicting. The former naturally desire to obtain as much labor as possible from their employes, while the latter are often induced by the fear of discharge to conform to regulation which their judgment, fairly exercised, would pronounce to be detrimental to their health or strength. In other words, the proprietors lay down the rules, and the laborers are practically constrained to obey them. In such cases

self interest is often an unsafe guide; and the legislature may properly interpose its authority.

And we added the fact "that both parties are of full age, and competent to contract, does not necessarily deprive the state of the power to interfere, where the parties do not stand upon an equality, or where the public health demands that one party to the contract shall be protected against himself." "The state still retains an interest in his welfare, however reckless he may be. The whole is no greater than the sum of all the parts, and when the individual health, safety, and welfare are sacrificed or neglected, the state must suffer."

It is manifest that this established principle is peculiarly applicable in relation to the employment of women in whose protection the state has a special interest. That phase of the subject received elaborate consideration in *Muller* v. *Oregon* (1908) where the constitutional authority of the state to limit the working hours of women was sustained. . . . [I]n *Quong Wing* v. *Kirkendall,* in referring to a differentiation with respect to the employment of women, we said that the Fourteenth Amendment did not interfere with state power by creating a "fictitious equality." . . .

. . . The validity of the distinction made by the Court between a minimum wage and a maximum of hours in limiting liberty of contract was especially challenged [by the dissenting justices in the Adkins case]. That challenge persists and is without any satisfactory answer. . . .

We think that the . . . *Adkins* case was a departure from the true application of the principles governing the regulation by the state of the relation of employer and employed. Those principles have been re-enforced by our subsequent decisions. Thus in *Radice* v. *New York,* we sustained the New York statute which restricted the employment of women in restaurants at night. . . .

. . . What can be closer to the public interest than the health of women and their protection from unscrupulous and overreaching employers? And if the protection of women is a legitimate end of the exercise of state power, how can it be said that the requirement of the payment of a minimum wage fairly fixed in order to meet the very necessities of existence is not an admissible means to that end? The Legislature of the state was clearly entitled to consider the situation of women in employment, the fact that they are in the class receiving the least pay, that their bargaining power is relatively weak, and that they are the ready victims of those who would take advantage of their necessitous circumstances. The Legislature was entitled to adopt measures to reduce the evils of the "sweating system," the exploiting of workers at wages so low as to be insufficient to meet the bare cost of living, thus making their very helplessness the occasion of a most injurious competition. The Legislature had the right to consider that its minimum-wage requirements would be an important aid in carrying out its policy of protection. The adoption of similar requirements by many states evidences a deepseated conviction both as to the presence of the evil and as to the means adapted to check it. Legislative response to that conviction cannot be regarded as arbitrary or capricious and that is all we have to decide. Even if the wisdom of the policy be regarded as debatable and its effects uncertain, still the Legislature is entitled to its judgment.

There is an additional and compelling consideration which recent economic experience has brought into a strong light. The exploitation of a class of workers who are in an unequal position with respect to bargaining power and are thus relatively defenseless against the denial of a living wage is not only detrimental to their health and well being, but casts a direct burden for their support on the community. What these workers lose in wages the taxpayers are called upon to pay. The bare cost of living must be met. We may take judicial notice of the unparalleled demands for relief which arose during the recent period of depression and still continue to an alarming extent despite the degree of economic recovery which has been achieved. It is unnecessary to cite official statistics to establish what is of common knowledge through the length and breadth of the land. While in the instant case no factual brief has been presented, there is no reason to doubt that the state of Washington has encountered the same social problem that is present elsewhere. The community is not bound to provide what is in effect a subsidy for unconscionable employers. The community may direct its lawmaking power to correct the abuse which springs from their selfish disregard of the public interest. The argument that the legislation in question constitutes an arbitrary discrimination, because it does not extend to men, is unavailing. This Court has frequently held that the legislative authority, acting within its proper field, is not bound to extend its regulation to all cases which it might possibly reach. The Legislature "is free to recognize degrees of harm and it may confine its restrictions to those classes of cases where the need is deemed to be clearest." If "the law presumably hits the evil where it is most felt, it is not to be overthrown because there are other instances to which it might have been applied." . . . This familiar principle has repeatedly been applied to legislation which singles out women, and particularly classes of women, in the exercise of the state's protective power. . . . Their relative need in the presence of the evil, no less than the existence of the evil itself, is a matter for the legislative judgment.

Our conclusion is that the case of *Adkins* v. *Children's Hospital, supra,* should be, and it is, overruled. The judgment of the Supreme Court of the state of Washington is affirmed.

Mr. Justice SUTHERLAND, dissenting.

Mr. Justice Van Devanter, Mr. Justice McReynolds, Mr. Justice Butler, and I think the judgment of the court below should be reversed. . . .

The Washington statute, like the one for the District of Columbia, fixes minimum wages for adult women. Adult men and their employers are left free to bargain as they please; and it is a significant and an important fact that all state statutes to which our attention has been called are of like character. The common-law rules restricting the power of women to make contracts have, under our system, long since practically disappeared. Women today stand upon a legal and political equality with men. There is no longer any reason why they should be put in different classes in respect of their legal right to make contracts; nor should they be denied, in effect, the right to compete with men for work paying lower wages which men may be willing to accept. And it is an arbitrary exercise of the legislative power to do so. In the Tipaldo case [*Morehead* v. *New York ex rel.* Tipaldo], it appeared that the New York Legislature had passed two minimum-wage measures—one dealing with women alone, the other with both men and women. The act which included men was vetoed by the Governor. The other, applying to women alone, was approved. The "factual background" in respect of both measures was substantially the same. In pointing out the arbitrary discrimination which resulted, we said:

> These legislative declarations, in form of findings or recitals of fact, serve well to illustrate why any measure that deprives employers and adult women of freedom to agree upon wages, leaving employers and men employees free to do so, is necessarily arbitrary. Much, if not all that in them is said in justification of the regulations that the act imposes in respect of women's wages apply with equal force in support of the same regulation of men's wages. While men are left free to fix their wages by agreement with employers, it would be fanciful to suppose that the regulation of women's wages would be useful to prevent or lessen the evils listed in the first section of the act. Men in need of work are as likely as women to accept the low wages offered by unscrupulous employers. Men in greater number than women support themselves and dependents and because of need will work for whatever wages they can get and that without regard to the value of the service and even though the pay is less than minima prescribed in accordance with this act. It is plain that, under circumstances such as those portrayed in the "factual background," prescribing of minimum wages for women alone would unreasonably restrain them in competition with men and tend arbitrarily to deprive them of employment and a fair chance to find work.

. . . Since the contractual rights of men and women are the same, does the legislation here invoked, by restricting only the rights of women to make contracts as to wages, create an arbitrary discrimination? We think it does. Differences of sex afford no reasonable ground for making a restriction applicable to the wage contracts of all working women from which like contracts of all working men are left free. Certainly a suggestion that the bargaining ability of the average woman is not equal to that of the average man would lack substance. The ability to make a fair bargain, as every one knows, does not depend upon sex.

If, in the light of the facts, the state legislation, without reason or for reasons of mere expediency, excluded men from the provisions of the legislation, the power was exercised arbitrarily. . . .

Finally, it may be said that a statute absolutely fixing wages in the various industries at definite sums and forbidding employers and employees from contracting for any other than those designated would probably not be thought to be constitutional. It is hard to see why the power to fix minimum wages does not connote a like power in respect of maximum wages. . . .

UNIT 3

$$\left[\textit{Crime and Deviance} \right]$$

JUVENILE JUSTICE

During the Progressive era most states introduced a separate juvenile justice system and adopted modern correctional machinery. They sharply increased investment in institutions for female delinquents. Whereas between 1850 and 1910 only about five reformatories for girls were built by states per decade, between 1910 and 1920 twenty-three were built.

The aim of the juvenile court was to prevent the formation of a criminal class by rescuing children from immoral environments. The court had the power to remove children from family situations which might lead to criminality. This power of the state was not new, although it was invoked far more extensively than in the past. The concept was based on the medieval English doctrine of *parens patriae*, which sanctioned the right of the crown to intervene in natural family relations wherever a child's welfare was threatened. The juvenile courts were empowered to take truants, child beggars, children working under age, children in bars, dance halls, or in the company of criminals from their homes and commit them to a public or private reformatory for an indefinite number of years, through the offender's twenty-first year of age.

Juvenile courts differed from adult courts by collapsing the distinction between delinquent and predelinquent behavior and not providing the child with the traditional procedural safeguards against deprivation of liberty. They had no arraignment and plea, no trial by jury and no rule prohibiting a defendant from being a witness against him or herself. They also had no strict rules of evidence. Parents, neighbors, schools, and police sent reports to the court about "incorrigible children." The child was brought before the court with a parent, after investigation of the family by a probation officer. The judge, after discussion with the family, could send the erring youth home under the supervision of a probation officer, or to a reformatory. A reformatory was defined as a residential school to train children in industry, morality, and the means to earn a living. In theory, therefore, the child was not being imprisoned without due process of law.

The juvenile court system viewed probation as the main rehabilitation tool. In theory, probation officers functioned less as agents of law enforcement than as visiting teachers who would instruct parents and children on how to eliminate family stress and use community resources to increase economic security and recreation. The juvenile court was integral to the design of domestic feminists who sought to preserve the lower-class family and make the city conform to the needs of the home. To aid the family, reformers promoted mothers' aid, neighborhood parks and community centers, school and sanitation reform, and crusaded against vice and saloons. When judges believed that the home could not properly carry out its function, they sent children to reformatories, which took on that role. Many of the new institutions were built on a cottage model, with a matron in charge of each cottage, so as to create a home environment.[10]

In this system of justice the judge had a great deal of personal discretion. The type of justice varied, depending on the judge's moral attitudes. The documents in this section explore the impact of concepts about woman's nature and gender role on the administration of justice. The selection by Sophonisba P. Breckinridge and Edith Abbott on *Adolescent Male and Female Delinquent Behavior* describes the way social workers and judges evaluated the antisocial behavior of boys and girls. The attitude towards boys was largely shaped by the new psychology of G. Stanley Hall and his work on adolescence. His description of girls gave the imprimatur of science to the Victorian perspective that sexually precocious girls were morally and biologically perverse. "The Table of Offenses Committed by Adolescent Boys and Girls" with the "Table on the Disposition of their Cases in the Illinois Juvenile Court, 1899–1909" shows that girls were less likely than boys to commit offenses defined as crimes under adult criminal codes, but more likely to be sent away to reformatories than be placed on probation. Girls tended to commit victimless crimes involving transgressions in personal behavior. This is consistent with the discussion of Breckinridge and Abbott on the social meaning of delinquent offenses of boys and girls. The documents raise an important question: was the female crime wave, that was used to justify increased public investment in female reformatories, real or merely the result of a change in terminology?

The new penology of rehabilitation relied on the indeterminate sentence, which transferred the power to decide the actual period of incarceration to an administrative board; their decision relied on the recommendations of the superintendent and staff who provided the reports.

The new penology also developed, but did not create, the system of work parole as a test of whether an individual was ready to return permanently to society. A juvenile could not be held, however, past the age of twenty-one, when he or she legally became an adult. "The Case Histories of Frank and Nellie" from the *Annual Report of the Massachussetts Training Schools* (1923) illustrate the law in practice after sentencing. They show the way the same cultural stereotypes which shaped sentencing practices influenced rehabilitation programs and parole practices.

SEX AND MENTAL RETARDATION

The same nineteenth-century concepts about sexual norms and gender roles that produced the new penology led physicians to treat deviant female sexual behavior as evidence of mental retardation.[11] The Progressive era's preoccupation with race progress found expression not only in policies of immigration restriction and racial segregation, but in the creation of custodial facilities for mentally retarded women. Until the development of intelligence tests, there was no agreed upon method of determining the degree of mental abilities, except in the case of those with physical lesions such as cretins and mongoloids. Physicians relied on their personal judgment of an individual's mental and social capabilities.

The *Abstracts of Case Records from the Wisconsin Home for the Feeble-Minded* (1906–1920) provide a rare glimpse into the way sexual and behavioral norms were used in admissions and to justify long periods of retention. Peter Tyor's quantitative analysis of the records of twelve institutions shows both a disproportionate number of women in the inmate population and a trend, in the late nineteenth century, toward admitting girls at a later age and keeping them longer through the child bearing years. *The Fifty-Sixth Annual Report of the Trustees of the Massachusetts School for the Feeble-Minded* (1904) raises questions about the indiscriminate use of sexual passion for classifying girls as feeble-minded.

The rationale for segregating feeble-minded girls shifted in emphasis as scientific studies linked heredity and deviant behavior. In the eyes of administrators, institutions were intended to protect retarded women from male sexual advances and to protect society from the women. Eugenics-minded physicians and administrators, armed after 1910 with the IQ test, increasingly urged that the segregation of feeble-minded women be supplemented with sterilization to prevent the procreation and spread of a criminal class and to relieve overcrowding. *The Second Annual Report of the Trustees of New York State Custodial Asylum for the Feeble-Minded* (1887) and the *Letter from Frank P. Norbury to the Illinois General Assembly, Senate Committee on Vice* (1916) illustrate this theme.

DOCUMENTS

JUVENILE JUSTICE

[154]

*Sophonisba P. Breckinridge and Edith Abbott on
Adolescent Male and Female Delinquent Behavior*

BOYS

It is clear that the larger offenses of burglary and larceny and the other more seriou
depredations are committed by boys in groups, but often the purely mischievous act
are likewise manifestations of the spirit of the gang. In fact, there is scarcely a type o
delinquent boy who is not associated with others in his wrongdoing. . . . The bo
who is brought in because he will not give in all his wages undoubtedly wants t
spend them in social ways. The impression made by a study of the actual reasons fo
bringing boys into court is that the delinquency is in many instances distinctly on
of a social character and is due to the organization of a little group whose purpos
may be harmless enough but whose social effort is misdirected.

. . . [Offenses which are called] . . . "incorrigible" in the case of boys . . . cove
such misdemeanors as loitering about the streets and using vulgar language, receiv
ing money embezzled by another boy, and running away with it, refusing either t
work or to go to school, roaming the street late at night, going up on the roof of
building and throwing stones at passers-by, riding on railroad trains, keeping ba
company, refusing to obey parents, and staying away from home. . . . The offens

From Sophonisba P. Breckinridge and Edith Abbott, *The Delinquent Child and the Home* (New Yor
1912), pp. 30–31, 35, 36–38. Copyright © 1912 (renewed 1940) by the Russell Sage Foundatio
Reprinted by permission of the publisher.

described as "disorderly conduct" . . . covers such acts as climbing the structures of the elevated railroad, starting a fight with another boy on a streetcar, loitering on the street corner, shooting bullets from a revolver on the street the day before the Fourth, "attempting to strike his mother, . . ." assaulting a boy and creating a disturbance, earning money and then running away and spending it, . . . wandering about downtown streets without lawful occupation, being afraid to go home, . . . throwing stones at actors in a West Side music hall, calling a neighbor names, and a larger number of other offenses varying greatly in seriousness of character.

GIRLS

Turning from the offenses of the delinquent boy to the question of the delinquent girl, some quite different problems present themselves. . . . The terms which are used in classifying the girls' offenses are the same as those which were used in the corresponding table of boys' offenses, but the offenses covered by these terms are very different. Stealing, of course, continues to indicate the taking of property; but the forms of stealing change. The girl is most frequently charged with shoplifting or stealing from the person by whom she is employed. She seldom makes stealing a form of recreation, as the boy does who breaks into empty houses or attempts a raid on a store or a freight car.

These words, [disorderly and incorrigible,] however, have an entirely different meaning when applied to girls. Perhaps the most frequent charge against the incorrigible girl is that she has been "staying away from home or going out at night in company with vicious people." Sometimes she refuses to stay at home and keeps a room in the disreputable quarter of the city; she attends tough dances and does not come home until two or three o'clock in the morning; she associates with vicious persons, refuses to work and brings money home without working; goes away and stays for days, is strongly suspected of being immoral, uses vulgar and obscene language; she is on the streets day and night, stays out with a rough crowd of boys until three o'clock in the morning; or she stays out all night and "admits that one night she stayed at a hotel with a young man." In general, the incorrigible or disorderly girl is one who "has a bad reputation."

No explanation of the term "immorality" is necessary. . . . The word "immorality" is never used in the petition or the statement of the case if it can be avoided, and when it is used it is probable that the experience of the girl has not been either an isolated or an accidental one. . . . It has already been explained that the offenses disguised in the court records under the terms "incorrigibility" or "disorderly conduct" are in substance much the same as those plainly described as immoral. . . .

More than 80 percent of the delinquent girls are brought to court because their virtue is in peril, if it has not been already lost. . . . Even such incomplete reports of home conditions as are contained in the court records show that in a large number of these cases when a girl is charged with some offense like stealing or running away, which is apparently free from moral peril, there is in reality grave moral danger in the conditions under which she lives. . . . It is obvious that even if, because of the conditions surrounding her home life or the failure of the school or of the city to guard her, the girl herself should be held blameless, yet if she has had intimate knowledge of vice or of vicious persons and of vicious conditions, she is not a safe companion for the child who is still ignorant and innocent.

[155]

The Juvenile Court in Action (Chicago, 1899–1909)

TABLE 1
Delinquent Boys and Girls Brought Before the Illinois Juvenile Court
from July 1899–June 30, 1909.
Totals and Percentages—By Offense

OFFENSES	Number		Percent	
	BOYS	GIRLS	BOYS	GIRLS
Stealing	5,795	417	50.8	15.0
Incorrigibility	2,478	1,186	21.7	42.8
Disorderly conduct	1,851	184	16.2	6.7
Malicious mischief	740	4	6.5	0.2
Vagrancy	265	3	2.3	0.1
Immorality	178	871	1.6	31.4
Dependent charges	90	90	0.8	3.3
Truancy	85	1	0.7	0.0
Miscellaneous offenses	159	3	1.4	0.1
Offense not given	..	11	0.0	0.4
Total	11,641	2,770	102.0	100.0
Two offenses	228	..	2.0	..
Total	11,413	2,770	100.0	100.0

TABLE 2
Disposition of Cases of All Children Brought to Court Between
July 1, 1899, and June 30, 1909

DISPOSITION OF CASE	Number		Percent	
	BOYS	GIRLS	BOYS	GIRLS
Continued indefinitely or dismissed	1,928	278	16.9	10.0
Put on probation	6,770	1,039	59.3	37.5
Committed to institutions	2,430	1,416	21.3	51.1
Held to the Grand Jury or Municipal Court	95	2	0.8	0.1
Other disposition	34	..	0.3	0.0
Disposition of cases not recorded	156	35	1.4	1.3
Total	11,413	2,770	100.0	100.0

From Sophonisba P. Breckinridge and Edith Abbott, *The Delinquent Child and the Home* (New York, 1912), pp. 39–40. Copyright © 1912 (renewed 1940 by The Russell Sage Foundation. Reprinted by permission of the publisher.

[156]
Reform School Parole:
The Case Histories of Frank and Nellie
(Massachusetts, 1923)

The following are two typical cases of wards who have received honorable discharges in accordance with this statute:

FRANK

"Frank was born in 1904 in one our mill cities, the son of poor but respectable foreign-born people. His mother was unable to speak English. The home surroundings were fair, but as both parents worked all the time, Frank did not receive much attention, and twice in his 9th year was before the court and placed on probation for delinquency.

"As his delinquency and truancy continued, he was then committed, at nine years of age, to a county training school, where he remained for over five years. During this time he ran away frequently and at last was committed to the Lyman School when he was about 15 for not obeying the rules of the county training school.

"After a stay of about 7 months in the Lyman School, he ran away from that institution and joined the United States Navy, where he served 9 months. His father secured his release from the Navy by proving that he was under age at the time of enlistment.

"The following year (the boy being then 16 years old) he was before the court on three counts of robbery and was committed to the Industrial School for Boys at Shirley. The police reported that he had been hanging around with the toughest gang in the city and was considered a very bad boy.

"After a stay of about 11 months at the Industrial School for Boys, he was paroled to his home. The old gang that he had associated with in the past was waiting for him when he was paroled, but he would not have anything to do with them. He immediately got work in one of the local mills and continued steadily at work whenever the mill was in operation. He finally changed his work to that of teamster for an ice company.

"In a little over two years from the date of his parole he was given an honorable discharge. He was then 19 years of age and excellent reports had been received regarding his conduct covering the preceding two years.

"Notwithstanding the weakness of home conditions and his long period of delinquency, the boy made good from the time he was paroled from the Industrial School for Boys."

From *Annual Report of the Trustees of The Massachusetts Training Schools*, 1923, pp. 7–9.

NELLIE

"Nellie was the daughter of a man of heavy drinking habits and a mother who was feeble-minded. The mother died when Nellie was about 16 years of age. For several years previous to the mother's death, the family had been under observation on account of the neglected condition of the children due to the father's drinking and the mother's carelessness and inability to care for them. Previous to her mother's death Nellie had been working about in several different families at housework.

"After her mother's death, complaint was made that Nellie and her sister (two years younger) were living at home in a condition of extreme neglect. Both girls were in a deplorable condition of filthiness and raggedness, with heads infested with vermin. It was found that Nellie had had immoral experiences while at housework in families and that she was diseased. At the age of 16½ she was committed to the Industrial School for Girls on a charge of lewdness. It was felt, however, that she was not essentially a bad girl, but rather the victim of extremely unfavorable circumstances.

"After remaining in the Industrial School for Girls about a year and a half, Nellie was placed at housework on a farm in a family where there were several children. This home was exactly suited to Nellie, who loved the freedom and outdoor life of the country. She was fond of children and on the whole did very well indeed. She was rather slow about her work, but showed a wonderful spirit of willingness and her behavior was entirely satisfactory. She remained in this home over a year and was then placed in another home where she could receive more pay. She remained here about a year. She did exceedingly well in this home also—was abolutely trustworthy and honest and much loved by her employer and her children.

"Nellie had a brother older than herself who was a hopeless invalid and a charity patient in a hospital in her home county. Nellie was exceedingly fond of this brother and constantly, during the period she had been placed out, had kept in touch with him and visited him from time to time. An opportunity was obtained for Nellie to become a ward maid in this hospital where she could have the privilege of being with her brother and caring for him. He had by this time become totally blind and Nellie showed a most unselfish devotion in looking out for him and making life as happy as possible for him. Her younger sister, who had meanwhile been placed in various families in the community, also obtained work at the same hospital, so that the two sisters were together with their invalid brother.

"Just before Nellie was 21, she was given an honorable discharge. Her conduct and work had been exceedingly good and her attitude toward her brother and sister most remarkable. Shortly after her honorable discharge she was married and is now keeping house on a farm. She seems happy and very well married."

SEX AND MENTAL RETARDATION

[157]
Abstracts of Case Records from the Wisconsin Home for the Feeble-Minded (1906–1920)

a. *Elsie Weiner.* Age 14. Admitted 1907. Epileptic. A rather good natured epileptic of about the middle grade of imbecile. Had already been taken from a house of ill fame. Short but stout in figure. Physically well formed. Quarrelsome, tattling, mischief making, untruthful. Makes fair progress in manual work.

1911: Still fretful and quarrelsome.

1915: Quarrels more and irritable. Otherwise nothing new to note.

1916: Wasserman test—negative.

1918: Has frequent epileptic attacks. Otherwise in good health.

1920: Transferred to X County Asylum. *School Report:* Moral sense: Has seemed reliable in what I have seen of her. Reading—Good. Spelling—Pretty good in writing words but poor in spelling orally. Writing, fairly good.

b. *Mary Shenks.* Age 16. Admitted 1906. Very large in frame. Slow in thought and action. Physically well developed. Said to have been the subject of improper sexual attentions from stepfather. Takes up simple house duties fairly well.

1909: Self-willed to obstinacy. Impossible if not closely watched. Has attained some proficiency in kitchen work.

1911: Will lie when to her advantage.

1913: Good strong worker in kitchen. Her temperamental condition remains the same.

1914: Has been on rebellious strikes against those in authority so she has to be restrained. Previously, however, she was given a change in work so as to bring her back to a better condition. This seemed to have no effect.

1916: Wasserman test—negative. Physically well. Mentally unchanged.

1917: Had a number of severe colds during the winter and was taken from the laundry and given work in the sewing room at No. 1. Her health is good now and her work is satisfactory.

1918: Had a severe attack of variola of the confluent type, last winter. Made a

Abstracts of Case Records from the Wisconsin Home for the Feeble-Minded, 1906–1920, Chippewa Falls. This material has been edited to protect the privacy of the individuals mentioned and their families. The names, although fictitious, reflect the ethnic backgrounds of the inmates. With permission of Northern Wisconsin Center for the Developmentally Disabled, Chippewa Falls, Wisconsin.

perfect recovery except that she was badly pitted. A few months ago she developed a deep-seated abscess of the left breast and later one developed over the right ankle. She has been in the hospital for some time and is still there receiving treatment. Her general physical condition is good.

c. *Mollie McCarthy*. Age 20. Admitted 1898. Middle Grade Imbecile. Short almost to dwarfishness. Stout in frame. Industrious and quiet. Was put in jail for lewd behavior and transferred here. Simple minded and probably without much moral sense. (See judge's letter regarding mother.) Does very well here under guardianship. Entertaining in manner as she is "cute" in some ways. Willing and industrious, but childish.

1909: Takes to music pretty well. Is a member of the band but does not rank among the best players.

1911: About one year ago she had a series of 4 or 5 spasms. Has had more since, but her digestion and bowel condition must be constantly looked after.

1913: Assisting in kindergarten. We believe this work suitable to her physical needs.

1916: Wassserman test—negative.

d. *Paula Worthman*. Age 21. Admitted 1907. Strong and good natured. Committed here after having been arrested for infanticide. Left a dead baby in the entrance of the Omaha station in this city. Either born dead or died of neglect. Evidently morally irresponsible. A graduate of the Industrial school for girls.

1909: Amiable and industrious. No great reasoning power. Robust in health.

1910: Still continues in good health. Does quite a little manual work. Takes a good deal of interest in earning money to pay for her dental work. Apt to allow her mind to dwell on sentimental subjects if those in charge will permit it. Is not a healthy attitude for her.

1912: A good helper on ward in care of other children. Was found to be communicating with one of the boys a short time ago.

1914: Dismissed by court. December 1913.

1915: Report came to us that about a year after release she had a child. When asked who the father was she could not tell as she had been with some thirty men. She has since married one of those men.

1920: Never returned.

[158]
Second Annual Report of the Trustees of the New York State Custodial Asylum for Feeble-Minded Women (1887)

[The purpose of the asylum is to take women] "who grade in mind from being erratic to idiotic, one fifth of whom being mothers from no wedlock," [who are] "ungoverned and easily yielding to lust," and "see them sheltered and shielded from the vices of vicious men."

Cited in Peter Tyor, "'Denied the Power to Choose the Good': Sexuality and Mental Defect in American Medical Practice, 1850–1920," *Journal of Social History* 10 (1977), p. 480.

[159]
Fifty-sixth Annual Report of the Trustees of the Massachusetts School for the Feeble-Minded (1904)

It is difficult to draw the line between the girl who has gone astray, or may be led astray, by reason of mental defect, and one who is merely a person of uncontrollable sexual desire. But be the line a broad or a narrow one, is this school to become a convenient "home" for girls of confessedly the latter description? In other words, is inordinate sexual passion on the part of a young woman to be regarded by the trustees as sufficient evidence of feeble-mindedness to have her as an inmate of this institution?

Cited in Peter Tyor, "'Denied the Power to Choose the Good,': Sexuality and Mental Defect in American Medical Practice, 1850–1920," *Journal of Social History* 10 (June 1977), p. 481.

[160]

Letter from Frank P. Norbury, Psychiatrist, to the Illinois General Assembly (1916)

I beg leave to enclose an extract from my report as alienist [psychiatrist] of the Board of Administration, discussing certain features of the special problems of the feeble-minded, and I would respectfully call your attention to the suggested need of appropriate legislation to solve some of the questions of parole of the feeble-minded. In the investigations of your Committee, no doubt, you have been impressed by this time with the fact that most of the young women with whom you have to deal in your problems belong to the group known as moron, or high grade feeble-minded. It is from this group that most of the moral delinquencies occur, and we have found that girls of this type are paroled from the feeble-minded institutions and are lost sight of. . . . Another fact which you must bear in mind is that from this same group are recruited the mothers of the feeble-minded, and it is quite important that there should be segregation and legal control to properly regulate this class. . . .

SPECIAL PROBLEMS OF THE FEEBLE-MINDED

The Board of Administration deals with concrete problems in its daily administration of the needs of the wards of the State entrusted to its care. . . . The needs of the feeble-minded and epileptics are of especially grave concern to this board. We believe legislation is needed, relating to the legal status of the feeble-minded (authority to control) both as to commitment and parole, and also the segregation of feeble-minded during the child-bearing period. The first provision should be made with much forethought, in order that the rights of the individual may be conserved, including a legal definition of feeble-mindedness, and then throwing such safeguards about this procedure as will protect the individual during parole from residence in the institution. . . . We need definite regulations of procreation of the feeble-minded, and especially so with reference to the segregation of the feeble-minded female during the child-bearing period. It is a biological fact that seldom does a feeble-minded woman give birth to a normal-minded child. This implies the biological fact that feeble-minded is a transmissable hereditary unit and that to prevent the reproduction of feeble-minded children the State must, as far as possible, prevent their procreation. This burden of the feeble-minded is social, biological and economic, and the State should concern itself in all three aspects of the burden. . . . This Board feels that legislation along these lines is one of the most important considerations which can claim the attention of the legislative assembly.

From Illinois General Assembly, *Report of the Senate Vice Committee*, 1916, pp. 829–30.

UNIT 4

$$\left[\begin{array}{c} Protection\ v. \\ Equal\ Rights \end{array}\right]$$

SEVENTY-FIVE YEARS AFTER SENECA FALLS

Women's personal autonomy and sense of self-worth were advanced by the nineteenth-century conception of womanhood, which established a cultural model that contrasted with the image embodied in common law. Women participated more fully in community decision making and professional opportunities, largely by increasing the social importance of their sphere and expanding its boundaries. In the name of home and motherhood they promoted environmental reforms such as housing, sanitation, and parks, along with the expansion of community social services to women, children, and family, which also opened up professional opportunities in teaching, library work, social work, nursing. They gained training in self-assertion and political skills through women's clubs, temperance societies, trade unions, and colleges.[12]

Feminists adapted to social realities and pursued what can only be described in retrospect as an apartheid strategy. This was not fully their own choice, for the economic and educational system provided only token integration, and the political system, which made and administered the laws, resisted completely. Women could come as petitioners, but to succeed they had to persuade some group of men to take up their cause. Women seeking to help disadvantaged women made full use of the image of weakness and purity. Here too they were adapting to reality to accomplish improvements in the workplace. Most working women, concentrated in the lowest paying jobs and industries, worked long hours and lacked proper health care. The women's trade union movement was itself a product of the resistance of male unions to women's participation. Its working-class leaders, who had come from the ranks, believed in class action and strikes, but eventually turned to protective legislation to compensate for their economic powerlessness.[13]

Women activists, assuming the role of men as protectors of women and the home, had, by the end of the first decade of the twentieth century, gained political recognition as the representatives of this interest group. Their goal in the 1920s was to eliminate the remaining legal disabilities through state legislative action and to mobilize the power of the state to accomplish reforms in health and the workplace that had initially been undertaken through private agencies.

In 1922 the National League of Women Voters established a Committee on Uniform Laws Concerning Women, to collect information on the legal status of women in all the states and pinpoint where discrimination remained and action needed to be taken. The first document—an excerpt from *A League of Women Voters Survey of the Legal Status of Women* published by the National League of Women Voters, 1924—is a "summary of the legal status of women" on the issues of contractual and property rights, guardianship, marriage and divorce, and jury duty. The excerpts from the laws of Alabama, Arizona, Idaho, Iowa, and Washington show the lack of uniformity among states in different regions, with regard to contractual property rights.

Most suffrage activists were committed to promoting family welfare policies that would help mothers perform their role more effectively. This reflected both a reality and an ideology that identified women and their rights with their role as mothers. In 1919 a number of women's organizations joined together in the Women's Joint Congressional Committee, to work as a common lobby. The national committee, along with similar state legislative councils that emerged, worked for improved education, maternal and infant care, the Child Labor Amendment, and increased funding for the Children's Bureau and the Women's Bureau.

The first major triumph of the Women's Joint Congressional Committee was the Sheppard-Towner Act (1921). Intended to reduce the infant and maternal mortality rate, the act provided states with matching federal funds to establish prenatal and child health clinics that would train expectant mothers in personal hygiene and the scientific care of children. It expanded the responsibility of the state to guard the health of its citizens and give women the primary, if not exclusive role in the field of community health and welfare. The services offered by the clinics did not conflict with private medicine; at the time, the medical profession viewed its mission as curing, not preventing illness. But after the passage of the act leaders of the profession moved to expand the domain of the private family physician and specialist to include the provision of preventive health services.

The doctors denigrated the skills of women—mothers, nurses, and social workers—and then moved in 1930 to cut off public funds to community health clinics. The 1930 White House Conference on the Health and Protection of Children highlighted the changes taking place in women's status during the 1920s. Whereas the 1909 and 1919 White House conferences had been dominated by child welfare reformers and educated women, the 1930 Conference on the Health and Protection of Children was controlled by medical specialists. The demise of the Sheppard-Towner Act represented only one example of the general appropriation by professionals, overwhelmingly men, of the field of child welfare. As a segment of the medical profession women declined from 6 percent in 1910 to 4.4 percent in 1930.

The Sheppard-Towner episode, because it involved activities so closely associated with womanhood, suggests the limits of a strategy that sought to expand women's status and options by using, rather than questioning, social definitions of women's biology and sex-roles. Social feminists, hoping that this act, along with protective labor legislation and mothers' aid, would improve the conditions of women in the working class and in rural areas, opposed the Equal Rights Amendment put forth by Alice Paul's National Woman's Party (NWP). To the NWP the elimination of legal inequality was the logical outgrowth of the suffrage victory, a carrying forward of the original Seneca Falls Convention platform that demanded full social and economic equality for women. The editor of the NWP's official publication, *Equal Rights,* was Harriet Stanton Blatch, daughter of Elizabeth Cady Stanton; and the man who introduced the ERA into the House of Representatives in 1923 was Republican representative of Kansas, Daniel R. Anthony, nephew of Susan B. Anthony. Senator Charles Curtis, Republican from Kansas, introduced the bill in the Senate.

Proponents of the ERA started from the proposition that women were persons and that to define them exclusively through their roles as mothers denied them freedom of choice. Supporters of the ERA therefore opposed the range of special protective laws based on gender, but not special legislation based on different categories. The small, but highly vocal group that supported this amendment did so on principle, but were particularly sensitive to this image because they were professionals. To be a professional woman in 1920 meant putting career before marriage; only 12.2 percent of all professional women were married. For middle-class women a career outside the home remained socially taboo. When married women from the working class labored, they did so because they needed to support families, and they were locked into jobs identified as woman's work.[14]

The document presented here, on the debate among feminists on the

Equal Rights Amendment in *Good Housekeeping Magazine* (1924), captures the essence of the split. Inez Hayes Irwin, a novelist, explained "Why the Woman's Party is For It." She used court cases to evoke the personal dimension of partial rights, in the traditional areas of property, guardianship, and contract. She explained why the amendment would not affect maternity legislation. Her argument against protective legislation for women alone is theoretical, since the evidence of its impact was not in until a few years later. Florence Kelley explained "Why Other Women's Groups Oppose the Amendment." Although many suffragists and social feminists would not be called feminists by modern definitions, this was not true of Florence Kelley. She highlights the investment her generation had in implementing the programs they worked for thirty years to put in place.[15]

DOCUMENTS

SEVENTY-FIVE YEARS AFTER SENECA FALLS

[161]
A League of Women Voters Survey of the Legal Status of Women (1924)

Sections of the codes have been deleted, and the sentences run together.—Ed.

CONTRACTUAL RIGHTS

There are sixteen states in which married women have an absolute right of contract, without any restrictions. There are four more states where the only restriction is as to her right to convey real estate without her husband joining, and in three of these there is a similar restriction against the husband. There are eight community property states, in which the married woman may make contracts freely as to community property, which is under the control of the husband. In four of the community property states, the wife must join in the conveyance of any real estate which constitutes a part of the community property. In four states, in which her general right to contract has been asserted, her right to convey her real estate without her husband joining in the deed is denied without any reciprocal requirement concerning the husband's real estate. In eight states, a married woman is specifically denied the right to become a surety. This is also true of those states in which there has been no statute giving the general right of contract, and there are nine such states. There are several states in which a decree in court is required before she can become a free trader. There are two states in which women are now living practically under the common law.

Prepared by the Committee on Uniform Laws Concerning Women, of the National League of Women Voters, 1924.

PROPERTY RIGHTS

There are eight community property states in which the husband has control of the community property during his lifetime, but in four of these states the wife must join in a conveyance of real estate. In these states, husband and wife have no interest whatever in each other's separate estates. Of the remaining forty states, the laws of twenty-five provide for an equal interest by married persons in each other's real estate. In four states, a married woman has a right to a certain interest in her husband's real estate, where no reciprocal right is granted to the husband.

In seven states, the common law rights of dower and curtesy still subsist.

In fifteen states, there are differences which cannot well be summarized, but which are set out in the body of this pamphlet.

No state by law accords to wives any portion of the family income, except such as they may have earned outside the home, and in six states the husband also takes her wages. In no state may a wife collect for services performed in the home.

In nineteen states, the wife is given the family clothing after the husband's death, and in seven others it may be awarded to her as a part of the special allowance made to the husband's estate.

In forty-three states, parents inherit equally from a deceased child. In only seventeen states, does a wife share equally with the husband in the children's earnings, and there is no state in which the wife is entitled to a voice in the choice of a family home or in which there is a joint headship in husband and wife.

EQUAL GUARDIANSHIP OF CHILDREN

In thirty-seven states, an equal guardianship law has been passed. Some of these laws are not so broad as that which has been suggested by the League Committee, and in other states, interpretations have not been wholly satisfactory, but in most of the states, where laws have been passed, interpretations are satisfactory. In one state there is added a proviso that in case of dispute the father's authority shall prevail.

In one, and possibly two states, a father may will a child, born or unborn, away from the custody of the mother, and in one more state, may do so in case of the insanity of the mother. Another state permits the father to appoint a guardian, by his will for a child over fourteen. In nine states, such a will is recognized where the consent of the mother has been obtained.

MARRIAGE AND DIVORCE

In fourteen states, common law marriages have been abolished by statute. In five states, some form of provision for a health certificate is made. In six states, a law has been passed prohibiting the evasion of marriage laws.

In thirty-eight states, men must be 21 years of age before they may marry without the consent of parents or guardian, while only nine states have the same requirement for women. In seven states men are required to be 18 years of age before they can marry without the consent of parents or guardian, in one state 20 years, one at 17, and one at 16. In thirty-one states, women must be 18 years of age before they may marry without consent of the parents or guardian, three at 16, one at 15, and one at 14.

With consent, there are five states where boys marry as young as 16 and six states in which they may marry at 14. As to girls, with consent of parents and guardians, in six states they may marry at 12, in seven at 14, in five at 15, and in ten at 16. The other states maintain a higher standard.

In twenty-one states women are received as jurors.

COMMITTEE'S PRESENTATION

1. *Contractual Rights of Married Women*

a. *Alabama.* The 1907 Code of Alabama provides that a wife has full legal capacity to contract as if she were unmarried, except as otherwise provided by law. She cannot sell or mortgage her real estate unless her husband joins with her in the deed. She cannot, directly or indirectly, become a surety for her husband. If, however, the husband is a deserter for two years, is insane, a criminal, or a non-resident, she may convey as if unmarried.

b. *Arizona.* The 1913 Revised Statutes of Arizona provide that married women shall have the same legal rights as men of the age of twenty-one years and upwards, except the right to make contracts binding the common property of the husband and wife, and shall be subject to the same legal liabilities as men of the age of twenty-one years and upwards.

[Arizona] is a community property state. Of this community property the husband has complete control during his lifetime. No real estate held as community property can be conveyed without both spouses joining, with the exception of unpatented mining claims, which are not included in community property although acquired subsequently to marriage.

c. *Idaho.* The 1919 Statutes of Idaho grant the right of absolute management, control and power of disposition of a married woman's separate estate, but it has been specifically held by the courts that the common law disability of married women to enter into contracts still remains, except in contracts for their own use or in management of their separate estates. A married woman may not make contracts to become surety or guarantor for debts of others.

d. *Indiana.* The Revision of 1914 removes all legal disabilities of married women to contract, except as elsewhere in the statutes provided, and until the session of the legislature of 1923 the only provisions were restrictions alike upon husband and wife, and were therefore not discriminations. The session of 1923 passed a law providing that a married woman cannot enter into any executory contract to sell or convey or mortgage her real estate, nor shall she convey or mortgage the same, unless her husband joins in such contract, conveyance or mortgage.

e. *Iowa*. The 1919 compiled Code of Iowa provides for the right of married women to contract as if unmarried, without restriction.

f. *Washington*. The Statutes of 1922, provide for the freedom of contract on the part of married women and state: "All laws which impose or recognize civil disabilities upon a wife which are not imposed or recognized as existing as to the husband are hereby abolished." This is a community property state, and the wife has no control of such community property and cannot contract concerning it, except that she must join with her husband if community real estate is to be conveyed.

2. Property Rights of Married Women

a. By the 1907 Code of Alabama, if a wife dies leaving a separate estate, the husband takes one-half of the personal property absolutely, and has the use of all the real estate for life.

If a husband dies and his estate is solvent, the wife takes one-half if there are no lineal descendants; if insolvent, one-third; and if there are lineal descendants, whether his estate is solvent or insolvent, she takes one-third; provided, however, that if her separate estate amounts to more than her dower right, she takes nothing, and if less, she takes the difference between the amount of her separate estate, and the dower allowed to her.

During her lifetime she cannot convey her separate real estate, unless he joins in the deed, but, the husband may handle his real estate without regard to his wife's consent.

b. *Arizona*. Under the 1913 Revised Statutes of Arizona, the surviving spouse (the other spouse having died intestate), whether husband or wife, takes the same measure of interest in the deceased spouse's estate, real, personal, or mixed.

This is a community property state and the statutes provide that upon the death of either husband or wife, one-half of the community property shall be taken by the surviving spouse, and the other half is subject to testamentary disposition, in the absence of which it goes to the legal descendants of the deceased.

The only distinction in property rights seems to be that the husband has the absolute control of the personal property belonging to the community, and absolute right of disposition thereof during his lifetime.

c. *Idaho*. Statutes of Idaho, abolishes curtesy and dower, and husband and wife may handle their separate estates without regard to each other.

The rights of husband and wife are reciprocal as to intestate estate. If spouse dies, leaving surviving spouse and one child, estate is equally divided; if spouse and more than one child survive, surviving spouse takes one-third; if no child, surviving spouse takes one-half.

This is a community property state, under the law of which the husband has control and management of the community property, but "he cannot sell, convey or encumber the community real estate unless the wife joins with him in executing and acknowledging the deed or other instrument of conveyance."

Upon the death of either husband or wife, one-half of all the community property shall go to the survivor, subject to the community debts, and the other half shall be subject to the testamentary disposition of the deceased husband or wife, in favor only of his, her, or their children, or a parent of either spouse, subject also to the community debts; community property may be left by will to a parent or parents. In case no such testamentary disposition shall have been made by the deceased husband or wife, it shall go to the survivor, subject to the community debts, the family allowance, and the charges and expenses of administration.

d. *Indiana.* Neither husband nor wife has a present interest in the other's real estate. The Revision of 1914 abolishes curtesy and dower.

There shall descend to a widow one-third of the real estate in fee simple, free from all demands of creditors, provided that where the real estate exceeds in value ten thousand dollars, she shall take one-fourth, and where it exceeds twenty thousand, one-fifth only as against creditors.

There shall descend to a widower one-third of his wife's real estate, subject to its proportion of debts of the wife contracted before marriage.

If a widow shall marry a second or any subsequent time, holding real estate in virtue of any previous marriage, and there be a child or children or their descendants alive by such marriage, such widow may not during such second or subsequent marriage, with or without the assent of her husband, alienate such real estate; and if, during such marriage, such widow shall die, such real estate shall go to her children by the marriage in virtue of which such real estate came to her. No such restriction attaches to property inherited by a husband.

Where a husband dies intestate, leaving a widow and one child, each shall take one-half of his real estate, but no such provision is made concerning the husband, in case of the death of his wife.

The only way that husband or wife can bar the interest of the other in real estate after death of the other is by joint conveyance. The interest of the wife extends to lands in which her husband has an equitable title, but no such provision is made in favor of the husband.

If a man dies intestate, leaving surviving a second or other subsequent wife, without children by him, but leaving a child or children, or their descendants alive by a previous wife, such surviving childless second or other subsequent wife shall take only a life estate in one-third of the lands of her deceased husband, and the fee thereof shall at the death of such husband vest at once in such child or children, or their descendants, subject to the life estate of such widow.

If a husband or wife dies intestate, leaving no child, and no father or mother, the whole of his or her property, real or personal, shall go to the survivor.

e. *Iowa.* The 1919 compiled Code of Iowa gives the surviving spouse one-third in the value of all legal and equitable estates in real property possessed by descendant at any time during marriage, providing no relinquishment of the same has been made, and which has not been sold on execution or at judicial sale.

If there are no children, the whole estate, up to the sum of $75,000, goes to the surviving spouse, after the payment of debts and costs of administration, and also one-half of all of the estate in excess of said sum.

f. *Washington.* Curtesy and dower abolished, and neither husband nor wife has any interest in the other's real estate acquired before marriage, nor in such real estate as may be acquired by gift, devise, and bequest subsequent to marriage. All property acquired after marriage (except by gift, devise, or bequest) is community property, of which the husband has the management and control with such power of disposition as he has over his separate estate, except that he cannot devise more than one-half, and the signature of the wife is required upon any conveyance of the community real estate. At the death of either spouse, one-half of the community property goes to the survivor and the remainder is subject to testamentary disposition.

In cases of intestacy, if the deceased leave a spouse and one child or the descendants of one child living, the surviving spouse takes one-half of the estate; if more than one child or the descendants of such children, then one-third of the estate; where there is no issue, one-half of the estate.

[162]
Debate on the ERA: Inez Hayes Irwin, "Why the Woman's Party Is for It" (1924)

Before this article sees the light of print, Senator Curtis of Kansas will have introduced into the Senate, and Representative Anthony, also of Kansas, into the House, an amendment to the Constitution of the United States, called the Lucretia Mott amendment. That amendment is the present platform of the Woman's Party. It reads, "Men and women shall have equal rights throughout the United States and every place subject to its jurisdiction."

In the last two years the Woman's Party has been engaged in an exhaustive research of both the federal and state laws as they discriminate against women. The work is being done in the Law Library of the Supreme Court of the United States by a corps of women trained in the law. From these digests the summaries of twelve states have already been put in pamphlet form. I cite laws as typical of four states—a southern, an eastern, a middle-western and a far-western state.

In Florida, one discovers that women cannot serve on juries and are not admitted to the State University, except the Normal Department, on equal terms with men. A married woman's services belong to her husband. She cannot choose her legal residence; does not control her own property; has practically no right to contract or

Good Housekeeping (March 24, 1924), pp. 18–19.

do business on her own responsibility. The father controls the services and earnings of children. The inheritance laws discriminate against women. In Massachusetts women are disqualified for jury service. The right of married women to carry on business is restricted, and mothers have not equal rights with fathers to the services and the earnings of their children. In Michigan married women have no general capacity to contract; they have not equal right with husbands over joint property. The husband owns his wife's services in the home and controls her right to work outside the home. Mothers have not equal rights with fathers over their children. In Nevada, marriage revokes a woman's will. Married women have no general capacity to contract or to sue, and are restricted in the right to carry on a business. The husband has the exclusive control of community property and a widow's share in community property is less than a widower's share. . . . In less than fifteen states is prostitution a crime for the male as well as the female. More than half the states do not permit women to serve on juries. . . .

I commend these twelve pamphlets to the women of the United States for reading matter. I commend them not only as a woman and a feminist but as a novelist. They illustrate the laws which they cite by court cases. And these cases form as poignant a collection of stories as any fictionist has ever turned out; compressed to a brevity which makes a Balzac or a Turgenev seem verbose.

This happened in Virginia:

"Another case is that of Mrs. Y., who was living separate from her husband. She contended that the separation was due to his mistreatment of her, while he contended that the separation was her fault. They had two children, one only three months old and the other two years old. The fitness of the wife to have the care of their two children was never questioned, but the court decided that these babies should go to the father because of his paramount right to his children and because he had a little property, while the young mother had none."

This happened in Louisiana:

"A woman was married in Alexandria . . . to X, and two and one-half years later they came to New Orleans, where they established a domicile. X's trade . . . was that of fireman upon ocean going steamships, and his absences from home were of four or five months duration, while the intervals between them did not usually extend beyond that many days. His wife engaged in the business of renting rooms and for the purpose of that business retained her maiden name. She also bought real estate in that name, imposed mortgages upon it to secure money borrowed in that name, and made other transactions in the course of her business. By her labor this energetic woman acquired property and money amounting to fifteen thousand dollars ($15,000). The 'ignorant sea-faring man' (husband) learned of his wife's business. He also learned that although she had acquired $15,000, it belonged to the community; that she had no legal right to mortgage it and that since he was 'head and master' of the community, it was under his sole control. He objected to her contracts, mortgages and transactions, as being without 'the knowledge or consent of her husband,' and the courts decided in his favor by sustaining his objection, so that her business transactions concerning the money she had earned were held to be void."

This happened in Mississippi:

"Colonel X refused to allow his stepson, the only child of Mrs. X., to visit her. The court upheld him, stating that he had a perfect right, as master of the house, to 'exclude any person from his doors, and to determine as to whom should be received, as a visitor' by his wife, 'whether or not the grounds upon which he acted were sufficient to justify him in a moral point of view.'"

This happened in New York:

"Mrs. Reynolds, a married woman in Washington County, for eight years cared for an old man who boarded with her in her home. This boarder, who was suffering from cancer, promised to pay her for her services. The work was difficult and disagreeable, including nursing, bathing, extra washing and, for six years, dressing the cancer twice daily. Upon the boarder's death the court decided that Mr. Reynolds was the proper person to collect the compensation for his wife's labor as in the absence of some arrangement . . . the inference of law and of fact would be that she was working for her husband in the discharge of her marital duties."

"A Japanese dancing studio on Riverside Drive was raided by the police and nineteen white girls who were employed there, receiving a commission for each dance, were arrested. Although the girls were found not guilty of any offense, they were subjected to many indignities before the trial. The older girls were put in cells at the police station and the younger girls were sent to the Crittenden Home, where they were garbed in work clothes and made to scrub the floors. At the court they were kept in a room with disreputable persons, both colored and white, while their names and addresses were published in the newspapers. The men were not detained, there being no law under which they could be held."

THE WOMAN'S PARTY TAKES A STAND

The Woman's Party finally decided that just as in their fight for votes for women they had demanded an amendment to the Constitution, they would in their fight for Equal Rights also demand an amendment to the Constitution. They adopted this method for several reasons, one being that a federal amendment is permanent and that it prevents the thing which has twice happened in the case of state laws, that a right has been given and then taken away. Again, a federal amendment means the saving of time, money, and strength of women which forty-eight separate campaigns would enormously dissipate. Then too, the work in the states—where the fight centers around each point of inequality with its personal angle instead of around a fundamental principle—is very difficult. Finally, the Constitution is the supreme law of the land. At one stroke it wipes out past discriminations and prevents new ones. However, the Woman's Party has already been working, though with great difficulty, with state legislatures. It will take every method to get Equal Rights incorporated into the law of the land.

The Woman's Party calls the attention of American women to the fact that all interpretations of the law involving women in our country today are based upon the subject position of women under the English common law instead of on the equal position of women with men. New situations and conditions are always arising which demand a legal interpretation based on equality between men and women rather than on that subject position.

There are few women, I take it, in the United States today . . . who will deny to women the equal right with their husbands to the guardianship of their children. There are few who will deny women the right to their own earnings; the right to make contracts, to inherit property, to control their own property; the right to equal opportunities in schools, universities, government service, the industries, the professions, the arts; the right to their own identity after marriage. We do not anticipate . . . much argument on any one of these scores. If there is a fight . . . it may come on the subject of welfare legislation. . . .

The Lucretia Mott amendment will make impossible any legislation with a sex bias; so that the law demanding an eight-hour day for women only, and the law prohibiting night work for women only, will apply to women and men equally. . . . The Woman's Party believes that there is a fallacy in special legislation, by which it may not work definitely for the betterment of women. In brief, it may result in preventing them from engaging in certain gainful occupations. For instance, where women are enjoined from night work, they may be forced to give up superior night jobs—which are of course eagerly snapped up by men—to take inferior day jobs.

THE AMENDMENT DOES NOT AFFECT MATERNITY LEGISLATION

The Lucretia Mott amendment will not affect maternity legislation, as it is designed to remove inequalities based on sex, not those based on motherhood. It will not interfere with so-called motherhood pensions, because these pensions are not given to mothers alone. There is an increasing modern tendency toward granting this aid to whichever parent is legally responsible for the child.

[163]
Debate on the ERA: Florence Kelley, "Why Other Women's Groups Oppose the Amendment" (1924)

As a fortunate and aspiring grandmother, I am hopeful that the doors of the law schools of Harvard and Columbia may be open to all grandchildren, girls and boys alike, perhaps even the portals of the Supreme Court of the United States. . . . But

Good Housekeeping (March 24, 1924), pp. 158–65.

wisdom born of experience teaches all alike the lesson of caution. Slow and wearisome though the process may be, it is better to keep what has been won and go steadily on getting good laws by votes backed by organization, than to gamble upon the chance of hoped for quick winnings and then lose.

Let us consider some gains which are too precious to be hazarded, among them, equal guardianship, widow's pensions, and the maternity and infancy law.

All good citizens who regard the home as the foundation of this Republic are logically committed to widows' pensions. Before they were established, the alternative to overwork and, too often, broken health for the mother accompanied by insufficient care for the children, was the surrender of the children to strangers even though their mother was loving and skillful and their home a model.

A quarter-century of vigorous organized effort underlies the almost nation-wide spread of this eminently modern, humane and enlightened provision for the care of those who throughout all history have been the most appealing figures, the mother and her little ones deprived by death of their breadwinner.

Under the proposed amendment would the community pay widowers' pensions? Or would widowed mothers be deprived of theirs? . . .

THE SHEPPARD-TOWNER LAW

Until Jeanette Rankin, in August, 1918, introduced in Congress her bill for the Hygiene and Welfare of Maternity and Infancy, the great mass of grieving mothers accepted with what resignation they could command the deaths of their little ones, which they commonly attributed to the will of God. So widespread, intensive, and enlightening was the campaign for this bill that, in the brief space of five years since Miss Rankin forced the subject upon a most reluctant War Congress, her measure has, under the above title, been accepted by forty states, and death rates of infants have fallen beyond the hopes of her followers and of the Children's Bureau which has been administering the law since it took effect in March 1922.

The Sheppard-Towner law applies explicitly to mothers and babies. In some places the maternal death rate, which had been slowly rising throughout several years, is stationary. In others it has begun to fall slightly.

There is, however, no possible assurance that this beneficent measure could survive the passage of the proposed equal rights amendment. Talk of its being safe from annulment because it applies solely to children is folly while mothers are expressly included in it. Moreover the two federal child labor laws have found no charmed life by reason of applying to children. Let us expose this safeguard of the home to no risks. It discriminates indisputably in favor of women. . . .

THE GUARDIANSHIP PROBLEM

The guardianship problem is not yet satisfactorily solved in all the states. In a few the statutes are not even yet modernized. So vast, however, is the progress in the direction of justice and mercy, in this extremely important field, since Miss Anthony first aroused public sentiment, that there is every encouragement for continuing to apply her method.

Before we had votes, progress halted or was slow wherever there was no unique spectacular evil result crying aloud for the equal guardianship of the mother. Since the enfranchisement of women no sin of omission can burden the consciences of the new voters so heavily as delay in finishing this crusade in every state where it is still needed. The speediest method possible is recourse to the legislatures. To await a federal amendment would be cruel folly.

A good illustration of this cheerful fact is Virginia, whose legislature passed, in 1922, seventeen of twenty-eight bills introduced chiefly for improving the lot of children. It is confidently expected by the cooperating organizations of men and women who achieved this beneficent success, that the remaining eleven measures will be adopted during the present year.

This procedure commends itself to men and women of experience in the field of legislation for several reasons, of which two are especially obvious. The first is that modifications in state laws can be made with relative ease when needed as social conditions change. But an amendment can hardly be repealed. It can be changed only by the long, slow process of judicial interpretation. The other is that statutes can be obtained without the delays which attend every federal amendment, even one on a subject so popular for instance, as child labor. It is nearly two years since the second adverse decision of the United States Supreme Court in the child labor cases, and no joint resolution for a federal amendment has yet been referred to the states for ratification.

Living with Miss Jane Addams at Hull House, seven of its early years, inspecting during four of them, with my assistant and deputies, the labor of women, girls and children in the Chicago stockyards and sweatshops of thirty years ago, seeing the interminable hours worked in the rural fruit and vegetable canneries, and the night work in glassworks in the smaller manufacturing cities, I must have been dull, indeed, of mind and heart if I had failed to appreciate the cruel suffering among those quickly increasing tens of thousands of workers.

Nowhere in 1893 was there an effective industrial code such as every modern civilized land is compelled to establish. . . . Night work during part of the year, for all engaged in manufacture, was the rule in seasonal occupations.

Heart-breaking stories were brought to Hull House by terrified mothers, of the experiences of young women in their families on the way home in the cold dark of the winter mornings after working to the point of exhaustion in hot rooms at speeded machines all night. . . .

Clearly no sentimental folly animated the settlements throughout the industrial states, when one after another enlisted in behalf of the eight-hour day and night-work laws for women and girls.

HARD WORK AND DELAYED RESULTS

The struggle for every gain in statutes and judicial decisions for women and girls in industry has been hard fought and costly in money, time and effort. It was in the light of twentieth-century decisions of the United States Supreme Court that New York's court of last resort reversed in 1914 its own adverse decision of 1907, thus permanently establishing a night-work law for women in the greatest of all the industrial states. In New Jersey, after many years of persistent effort, women obtained in 1923 a night-work law so amended at the last moment as to take effect at New Year's 1925. The delay was explained by legislators as intended to enable mill owners to expand their plants to accommodate the women who would be transferred to enlarged day shifts. Rhode Island is due for successful action in 1924.

In New York, organized workingmen help pass whatever bills women in industry endorse. There, since 1886, men and women wage-earners have pursued increasingly the policy of cooperation in promoting labor laws. They have, for instance, procured statutes concerning fire, cleanliness, lighting, ventilation and one day's rest in seven, which apply alike to men, women and children. They have obtained measures exclusively for men, safeguarding those (commonly known as sand hogs) who work in tunnels under rivers and harbors and bills applying to men in the train service of railroads, and on scaffolds in the building trades.

. . . Women obviously do not work in mines and tunnels or on scaffolds. They form no part of train crews under the full-crew laws. Their oldest, most wide-spread, and most insistent demands have been for seats, for more adequate wages, and short, firmly regulated working hours. . . . Whenever union men feel no need of laws, well and good. No one wishes to interfere with them any more than professional women are interfered with today by labor legislation.

On this subject we are immovable. If there are no other reasons for opposing the proposed amendment, we should concentrate all our efforts upon this. . . .

Under the proposed amendment, women could change their hours and other working conditions by law only when men were ready and willing to make the changes for themselves. This would be a new subjection of wage-earning women to wage-earning men, and to that subjection we are opposed on principle and in practice.

NEGLECTED ROOTS OF TROUBLE

In the long history of human experience there is no record of a quick, sure remedy for an injustice involving fundamental social relations. It becomes daily clearer that much injustice to women is attributable to the general absence from the courts of competent, thoroughly trained women judges. This situation is obviously not remediable by amending the federal Constitution. It requires systematic effort in a different field of activity. The trouble lies oftener in judicial misinterpretation of laws, federal and state, than in the measures themselves. And this is curable by the voters whenever the judiciary is elective.

We cannot eat our cake and have it, too. We cannot subject ourselves by a constitutional amendment to compulsory equality with men forevermore, yet keep our most needed special laws, for lack of which, throughout the long terrible past, women and children have suffered and died.

In this kaleidoscopic world, we are confronted by the perpetual necessity of making choices. The ballot is our most recently acquired instrument of choice and change. With it statutes can be fitted precisely, skilfully, to the needs of every group in the community, as each need is clearly recognized.

LET US MAKE HASTE SLOWLY

If, moreover, the proposed amendment were desirable, its enactment in the near future would be premature. The Nineteenth Amendment is not yet four years old. The uses of the ballot, which it conferred upon women, have not begun to be tested. . . . We demand ample opportunity for trying out the possibilities of the ballot in the hands of all the citizens of the whole voting constituency of men and women, before limits are placed upon the freest conceivable use of it. We stand firmly upon the inalienable right of men and women to differ.

NOTES

1. Sheila M. Rothman, *Woman's Proper Place: A History of Changing Ideals and Practices, 1870 to the Present* (New York: Basic Books, 1978), pp. 177–88.

2. Rosalind Rosenberg, "The Academic Prism: The New View of American Women," in *Women of America: A History*, ed. Carol Ruth Berkin and Mary Beth Norton (Boston: Houghton Mifflin, 1979), pp. 319–41.

3. Nelson M. Blake, *The Road to Reno: A History of Divorce in the United States* (New York: Macmillan, 1962), pp. 130–51, 226–29.

4. Elaine Tyler May, *Great Expectations: Marriage and Divorce in Post-Victorian America* (Chicago: University of Chicago Press, 1980), pp. 1–181.

5. Sophonisba P. Breckinridge and Edith Abbott, *The Delinquent Child and the Home* (New York, 1912), pp. 170–74; Robert H. Bremner, et al., eds., *Children and Youth in America: A Documentary History, 1866–1932*, vol. 2 (Cambridge, Mass.: Harvard University Press, 1971) pp. 348–97.

6. Linda Gordon, *Woman's Body, Woman's Right: A Social History of Birth Control in America* (New York: Penguin, 1977), pp. 186–300.

7. Marlene Stein Wortman, "Domesticating the Nineteenth-Century American City," *Prospects: An Annual of American Cultural Studies* 3 (1977), 531–72.

8. Eleanor Flexner, *Century of Struggle: The Woman's Rights Movement in the United States* (1st. ed. 1959; New York: Atheneum, 1970), pp. 248–93, 306–24.

9. Judith A. Baer, *The Chains of Protection: The Judicial Response to Women's Labor Legislation* (Westport, Conn.: Greenwood Press, 1978), pp. 75–135; Karen O'Connor, *Women's Organizations' Use of the Courts* (New York: Lexington Books, 1980), pp. 65–91.

10. Steven L. Schlossman, *Love and the American Delinquent: The Theory and*

Practice of "Progressive" Juvenile Justice, 1825–1920 (Chicago: University of Chicago Press, 1977), pp. 7–193.

11. Peter Tyor, " 'Denied the Power to Choose the Good': Sexuality and Mental Defect in American Medical Practice, 1850–1920," *Journal of Social History* 10 (June 1977), 472–489; Steven Schlossman and Stephanie Wallach, "The Crime of Precocious Sexuality: Female Juvenile Delinquency in the Progressive Era," *Harvard Educational Review* 48 (February 1978), 65–94.

12. Wortman, "Domesticating the Nineteenth-Century City," pp. 547–65.

13. Nancy Schrom Dye, "Creating a Feminist Alliance: Sisterhood and Class Conflict in the New York Women's Trade Union League, 1903–1914," *Feminist Studies* 2 (1975), 24–38.

14. Rothman, *Woman's Proper Place*, pp. 135–164.

15. Dorothy Rose Blumberg, *Florence Kelley: The Making of a Social Pioneer* (New York: Augustus M. Kelley, 1966), pp. 1–180.

Glossary of Legal Terms

ADJUDICATION. The determination of a controversy and a pronouncement of a judgment based on evidence presented.

A MENSA ET THORO. Relating to a judicial separation in which the parties remain husband and wife without cohabitation.

AMICUS CURIAE. Friend of the court; one who gives information to the court on some matter of law which is in doubt.

APPELLANT. The party in a legal action who takes the case to the next highest court.

BONA FIDE. In good faith.

CHANCERY. See EQUITY

CHATTEL. An article of movable personal property, as opposed to real property, which is not usually movable. It may refer to animate as well as inanimate property. A slave, for example, was chattel property.

CHATTEL MORTGAGE. A mortgage on personal property, such as furniture.

CHOSE. A French term referring to a CHATTEL or article of personal property.

CHOSE IN ACTION. Right of proceeding in a court of law to procure payment of a sum of money, or right to recover a personal chattel. The phrase includes all personal chattels which are not in possession of the owner; and all property in action which depends entirely on contracts, express or implied.

CIVIL. That branch of law that pertains to suits outside of criminal practice, pertaining to the rights and duties of persons in contract, tort, etc.; also refers to civil law as opposed to common law.

CIVIL ACTION. Action maintained to protect a private, civil right, or to compel a civil remedy, as distinguished from a criminal prosecution.

CIVIL RIGHTS. Rights given, defined, and circumscribed by positive laws enacted by civilized communities. Civil rights differ from CIVIL LIBERTIES in that civil rights are positive in nature, and civil liberties are negative in nature; that is, civil liberties are immunities from governmental interference or limitations on governmental action (such as those embodied in the First Amendment) which have the effect of reserving rights to individuals.

CIVIL LAW. Roman law embodied in the Justinian Code (Codex Justinianeus) and presently prevailing in most Western European States. It is also the foundation of the law of Louisiana. The term may also be used to distinguish that part of the law concerned with noncriminal matters, or may refer to the body of laws prescribed by the supreme power of the state, as opposed to natural law.

CLASS ACTION. A lawsuit brought by representative member(s) of a large group of persons on behalf of all the members of the group. The class must be ascertainable, the members must share a common interest in the issues of law and fact raised by the plaintiff(s), and the action must satisfy a variety of other special requirements applicable to class actions before the trial court will specifically certify the action to be one maintainable as a class action. If so certified, all members of the class must receive notice of the pendency of the action and an opportunity to exclude themselves from the class if they so desire. Members not so excluding themselves are bound by the judgment. Subclasses may be formed to reach an identifiable and manageable class size for purposes of litigation.

CLEAN HANDS. The concept in equity that claimants who seek equitable relief must not themselves have indulged in any impropriety in relation to the transaction upon which relief is sought; freedom from participation in unfair conduct. A party with "unclean hands" cannot ask a court of conscience (the equity court) to come to his aid.

COHABITATION. Literally, the act of living together. Often statutorily expanded to include living together publicly, as husband and wife; indulgence in sexual intercourse. Cohabitation among unmarried persons of the opposite sex is often proscribed by local laws. Such cohabitation will produce an inference of criminal fornication.

COMMON LAW. The system of jurisprudence, which originated in England and was later applied in the United States, which is based on judicial precedent rather than legislative enactments; it is to be contrasted with civil law (the descendant of Roman Law prevalent in other Western countries). Originally based on the unwritten laws of England, the common law is generally derived from principles rather than rules; it does not consist of absolute, fixed, and inflexible rules, but rather of broad and comprehensive principles based on justice, reason, and common sense. It is of judicial origin and promulgation. Its principles have been determined by the social needs of the community and have changed with changes in such needs. These principles are susceptible of adaptation to new conditions, interests, relations, and usages as the progress of society may require.

COMMUNITY PROPERTY. Community property, or "common" property, as it was called in early American statutes, included everything acquired by either spouse after marriage, except for gifts and inheritances—a startling contrast to the common law in which all was vested in the husband.

COMPLAINANT. The party who initiates the complaint in an action or proceeding.

CONVEYANCE. The transfer of the title of land from one person to another.

COVENANT. An agreement or promise to do or not to do a particular thing; to enter into a formal agreement; to bind oneself in contract.

COVERTURE. The condition or state of a married woman.

CURTESY. An estate for life which a husband takes at the death of his wife in all the lands which she owned during the marriage, if a child who could inherit such lands was born to her during the marriage.

DECEDENT. Term used in wills and estates to denote the deceased person whose estate is involved.

DEFENDANT. In civil proceedings, the party responding to the complaint; one who is sued and called upon to make satisfaction for a wrong complained of by another.

DEFENDANT IN ERROR. The prevailing party in the lower court who is the adverse party in the appellate proceeding wherein review has been sought on a writ of error.

DE MINIMUS. Insignificant; minute, frivolous. Something or some act which is "de minimus" in interest is one which does not rise to a level of sufficient importance to be dealt with judicially.

DEMURRER. The answer to a charge in which a defendant denies legal responsibility although he or she may concede the plaintiff's contention.

DOMICILE. The place of permanent resident of an individual.

DEVISE. A testamentary disposition of land or realty; a gift of real property by last will and testament of the donor. When used as a verb, devise means to dispose of real or personal property by will.

DOWER RIGHTS. The interest of a wife in her husband's real estate. At common law it amounted to a life interest in one third.

DUE PROCESS OF LAW. A judicial proceeding conducted according to the established rules. The phrase means that no person shall be deprived of life, liberty, property, or of any right granted by statute, without such a proceeding. The constitutional guarantee demands only that the law shall not be unreasonable, arbitrary, or capricious and that the means selected to achieve the goal of the law shall have a real and substantial relation to the object being sought. There are two due process clauses in the U.S. Constitution. One in the Fifth Amendment pertains to federal action; the other is in the Fourteenth Amendment and protects persons from state action. Similar clauses are in state constitutions. Due process, unlike some legal rules, is not a technical concept with a fixed content. What constitutes due process has changed in relationship to time, place, and circumstances.

EQUAL PROTECTION OF THE LAWS. This constitutional guarantee means that no person or class of persons shall be denied the same protection of the laws which is enjoyed by other persons or other classes in like circumstances in their lives. The equal protection of the laws of a state is extended to persons within its jurisdiction within the meaning of the Fourteenth Amendment requirement, when its courts are open to them on the same conditions as to others, with like rules of evidence and modes of procedures, for the security of their persons and property, the prevention and redress of wrongs, and the enforcement of contracts; when they are subjected to no restrictions in the acquisition of property, the enjoyment of personal liberty, and the pursuit of happiness, which do not generally affect others; when they are liable to no other or greater burdens and charges than are laid upon others; and when no different or greater punishment is enforced against them for a violation of the laws. The equal protection clause does not take from the State the power to classify in the adoption of police laws. It does, however, require that there be a reasonable basis for the classification. For a description of what constitutes a SUSPECT CLASSIFICATION and situations that lead the Court to subject a law to STRICT SCRUTINY currently see the Introduction.

EQUITY. Most generally, "justice." Historically, "equity" developed as a separate body of law in England in reaction to the inability of the common law courts, in their strict adherence to rigid writs and forms of action, to entertain or provide a remedy for every injury. The king therefore established the high court of CHANCERY, the purpose of which was to do justice between parties in those cases where the common law would give no or inadequate redress. EQUITY also refers to the value of property minus encumbrances. For example, one's EQUITY in a home is the value of the property beyond the amount of the mortgage to be paid.

EXCULPATORY. Refers to evidence and/or statements which tend to clear, justify, or excuse a defendant from alleged fault or guilt.

EX PARTE. The application of one party. An EX PARTE judicial proceeding is one brought for the benefit of one party only without notice to or challenge by an adverse party.

EX REL. Refers to legal proceedings which are instituted by the attorney general or other proper person in the name and in behalf of the state, but on the information and at the instigation of an individual who has a private interest in the matter. That person is called the "relator." Such a cause is entitled sometimes, as in this book: *People ex rel. Barry* v. *Mercein,* or more usually *"State ex rel Doe* v. *Roe."*

FEE OR FEE SIMPLE. An estate of inheritance, generally of land, clear of any condition, limitation, or restriction to particular heirs.

FELONY. Generic term employed to distinguish certain high crimes from minor offenses known as MISDEMEANORS; crimes declared to be such by statute or regarded as "true crimes" by the common law. Statutes often define felony in terms of an offense punishable by death or imprisonment generally or by death or imprisonment for more than one year.

FEME SOLE. An unmarried woman.

FEME SOLE TRADER. A married woman who qualifies by a special statutory provision to do business on her own account, independently of her husband.

HABEAS CORPUS. Known as the "great writ" and means literally, "you have the body." The WRIT OF HABEAS CORPUS has a varied use in criminal and civil contexts. It is basically a procedure for obtaining a judicial determination of the legality of an individual's custody. In the criminal context, it is used to bring the petitioner before the court to inquire into the legality of his or her confinement. The writ is used in civil context to challenge the validity of child custody.

INDICTMENT. Formal, written statement charging a person with an offense, based on findings by the grand jury.

INTESTATE. Without making a will.

JOINT TENANTS. Persons who each own an equal interest in the same property, real or personal.

LITIGATION. A lawsuit.

MESNE CONVEYANCE. A CONVEYANCE is a transfer of title to land from one person, or class of persons, to another by deed, assignment, lease, mortgage, etc. MESNE CONVEYANCE is one occupying an intermediate position in a chain of title between the first grantee and the present holder.

MESSUAGE. Dwelling house with adjacent buildings and surrounding grounds that belong to it.

MISDEMEANOR. A crime which is less than a FELONY.

MOOT CASE. A case which seeks to determine an abstract question that does not rest upon existing facts or rights, or which seeks a judgment in a pretended controversy when in reality there is none.

MORTGAGE. The conveyance of property to be held as security for the payment of an indebtedness. The debtor remains in possession of the property unless scheduled payments are not made.

NE EXEAT. A writ to restrain a person from leaving the jurisdiction of the court in which an action is pending.

NON SUI JURIS. A Latin phrase indicating that a person who is not of legal age does not have legal capacity.

NONSUIT. A judgment taken against a plaintiff who has failed to appear or failed to prove his or her case. Under current rules of practice, the applicable term is "dismissal."

NULLITY. Legally null or void.

OBITER DICTA. Statements made or decisions reached in a court opinion which were not necessary to the disposition of the case.

PENDENTE LITE. Suspended by the lawsuit; pending the lawsuit. Matters which are PENDENTE LITE are contingent upon the determination of a pending lawsuit.

PENOLOGY. The study of punishment for crime.

PER CURIAM OPINION. An opinion by the court which expresses its decision in the case but whose author is not identified.

PERSONALY. Personal property; movable property; chattels.

PLAINTIFF. The one who initially brings the suit; the one who, in a personal action, seeks a remedy in a court for an injury.

PLAINTIFF IN ERROR. One who appeals from a judgment in a lower court. The PLAINTIFF IN ERROR may have been either the defendant or plaintiff in the lower court.

PRIMA FACIE EVIDENCE. Evidence sufficient to establish the fact in question unless rebutted.

PROPRIETARY INTEREST. Any right in relation to a thing which enables a person to retain its possession indefinitely or for a period of time.

RE. A Latin term used to designate judicial proceedings in which there is only one party. Thus, *In re Lockwood* simply means Lockwood's Case.

RECIDIVIST. An "habitual criminal" who is often subject to extended terms of imprisonment.

RELATOR. See EX REL.

REMIT. To release one from guilt or penalty.

RESPONDENT. In equity, the party who answers a bill or other pleading. The term also refers to the party against whom an appeal is brought.

SAEVITIA. In the law of divorce, cruelty—anything which tends to bodily harm and in that manner renders cohabitation unsafe.

SEIZE. To be seized of or in, is to be legal possessor of, or to be holder in FEE SIMPLE.

STRICT SCRUTINY. See EQUAL PROTECTION

SUPRA. Above; in a written work, it refers the reader to something previously written.

SURETY. A person who agrees to pay the debt of another, in case the person primarily liable shall fail to pay.

TENANTS BY THE ENTIRETY. A husband and wife who have an equal interest and ownership in property. On the death of one spouse the other takes the whole to the exclusion of the deceased's other heirs.

TENANTS IN COMMON. Persons who share ownership in the same property. Unlike a tenancy by entirety or a joint tenancy the interest of a tenant in common does not terminate upon his or her death, but passes to the estate or heirs.

VEST. To give an immediate, fixed right of present or future enjoyment.

WASTE. A destruction or material alteration of property by tenant. The early English doctrine held that any change in the character or nature of the land, even improvements, constituted "waste."

WRIT OF ERROR. An early common law writ issued out of the appellate court and served on trial judges ordering them to send up the record in the case. Those who sought the review, whether plaintiffs or defendants in the trial court are designated as PLAINTIFFS IN ERROR. Their opponents are DEFENDANTS IN ERROR.

Selected Bibliography

WORKS ON SOCIAL HISTORY
Anthologies

Bardwick, Judith M., ed. *Readings on the Psychology of Women*. New York: Harper & Row, 1972.

Berkin, Carol Ruth, and Norton, Mary Beth, eds. *Women of America: A History*. Boston: Houghton Mifflin, 1979.

———, and Lovett, Clara M., eds. *Women, War and Revolution*. New York: Holmes & Meier, 1980.

Cantor, Milton, and Laurie, Bruce, eds. *Class, Sex and the Woman Worker*. Westport, Conn.: Greenwood Press, 1977.

Carroll, Bernice A., ed. *Liberating Women's History: Theoretical and Critical Essays*. Urbana: University of Illinois Press, 1976.

Cott, Nancy F., and Pleck, Elizabeth H., eds. *A Heritage of Her Own: Toward a New Social History of American Women*. New York: Simon and Schuster, 1979.

Friedman, Jean E., and Shade, William G., eds. *Our American Sisters: Women in American Life and Thought*. 2d. ed. Boston: Allyn & Bacon, 1977.

Gordon, Michael, ed. *The American Family in Social and Historical Perspective*. New York: St. Martin's, 1978.

Hartman, Mary, and Banner, Lois W., eds. *Clio's Consciousness Raised: New Perspectives on the History of Women*. New York: Harper & Row, 1974.

James, Edward T; James, Janet Wilson; and Boyer, Paul S.; eds. *Notable American Women 1607–1950*. 3 vols. Cambridge, Mass.: The Belknap Press, 1971.

Lerner, Gerda. *The Majority Finds Its Past: Placing Women in History*. New York: Oxford University Press, 1979.

Pleck, Elizabeth, and Pleck, Joseph H., eds. *The American Man*. Englewood Cliffs, N.J.: Prentice-Hall, 1980.

Sicherman, Barbara, and Green, Carol Hurd, eds. *Notable American Women: The Modern Period*. Cambridge, Mass.: The Belknap Press, 1980.

Books

Banner, Lois. *Elizabeth Cady Stanton: A Radical for Women's Rights*. Boston: Little Brown & Co., 1980.
———. *Women in Modern America: A Brief History*. New York: Harcourt Brace Jovanovich, 1974.
Barker-Benfield, G. J. *The Horrors of the Half-Known Life: Male Attitudes Toward Women and Sexuality in Nineteenth Century America*. New York: Harper & Row, 1976.
Beard, Mary Ritter. *Women as Force in History: A Study in Traditions and Reality*. New York: The Macmillan Company, 1946.
Bernard, Jessie. *The Future of Motherhood*. New York: Penguin, 1975.
Bird, Caroline. *Enterprising Women*. New York: W. W. Norton, 1976.
Blair, Karen. *The Club Woman as Feminist: True Womanhood Redefined, 1868–1914*. New York: Holmes & Meier, 1980.
Bordin, Ruth. *Woman and Temperance: The Quest for Power and Liberty*. Philadelphia: Temple University Press, 1981.
Breckinridge, Sophonisba P. *Women In The Twentieth Century: A Study of Their Political, Social and Economic Activities*. New York: McGraw-Hill, 1933.
Brownmiller, Susan. *Against Our Will: Men, Women and Rape*. New York: Bantam, 1975.
Calhoun, Arthur W. *A Social History of the American Family From Colonial Times To the Present*. New York: Barnes & Noble, 1945.
Campbell, Barbara Kuhn. *The "Liberated Woman" of 1914: Prominent Women in the Progressive Era*. Ann Arbor, Michigan: UMI Research Press, 1979.
Chafe, William. *The American Woman: Her Changing Social, Economic and Political Roles, 1920–1970*. New York: Oxford University Press, 1972.
———. *Women and Equality: Changing Patterns in American Culture* New York: Oxford University Press, 1977.
Cott, Nancy F. *The Bonds of Womanhood: "Woman's Sphere" in New England, 1780–1835*. New Haven: Yale University Press, 1977.
Daly, Mary. *The Church and the Second Sex*. New York: Harper & Row, 1975.
Degler, Carl. *At Odds: Women and the Family in America from the Revolution to the Present*. New York: Oxford University Press, 1980.
Demos, John. *A Little Commonwealth: Family Life in Plymouth Colony*. New York: Oxford University Press, 1971.
Dexter, Elizabeth Anthony, *Career Women of America, 1776–1840*. Francestown, N.H.: Marshall Jones Co., 1950.
———. *Colonial Women of Affairs*. Cambridge, Mass.: The Riverside Press, 1931.
Donegan, Jane B. *Women and Men Mid-Wives: Medical Morality and Misogyny in Early America*. Westport, Conn.: Greenwood Press, 1978.
Dublin, Thomas. *Women at Work: The Transformation of Work and Community in Lowell Massachusetts, 1826–1869*. New York: Columbia University Press, 1979.
Dubois, Ellen Carol. *Feminism and Suffrage: The Emergence of an Independent Women's Movement in America, 1848–1869*. Ithaca, N.Y.: Cornell University Press, 1978.

Ehrenreich, Barbara, and English, Deirdra. *Complaints and Disorders: The Sexual Politics of Sickness.* Old Westbury, N.Y.: Feminist Press, 1974.

Epstein, Cynthia Fuchs. *Woman's Place: Options and Limits in Professional Careers.* Berkeley: University of California Press, 1970.

Erikson, Kai. *Wayward Puritans: A Study in the Sociology of Deviance.* New York: Wiley & Sons, 1966.

Faragher, John Mack. *Women and Men on the Overland Trail.*New Haven, Conn.: Yale University Press, 1979.

Fass, Paul S. *The Damned and the Beautiful: American Youth in the 1920's.* New York: Oxford University Press, 1977.

Filene, Peter Gabriel. *Him/Her/Self: Sex Roles in Modern America.* New York: New American Library, 1976.

Flexner, Eleanor. *Century of Struggle: The Woman's Rights Movement in the United States.* New York: Atheneum, 1970.

Foner, Philip. *Women and the American Labor Movement.* New York: Macmillan, 1979.

Foster, Lawrence. *Religion and Sexuality: Three American Communal Experiments of the Nineteeth Century.* New York: Oxford University Press, 1981.

Fox, Richard W. *So Far Disordered in Mind: Insanity in California, 1870–1930.* Berkeley: University of California Press, 1978.

Frankfort, Roberta. *Collegiate Women: Domesticity and Career in Turn of the Century America.* New York: New York University Press, 1978.

Freedman, Estelle B. *The Sisters' Keepers: Women's Prison Reform in America, 1830–1930.* Ann Arbor: University of Michigan Press, 1981.

Genovese, Eugene. *Roll, Jordon, Roll: The World the Slaves Made.* New York: Pantheon, 1974.

Gordon, Linda. *Woman's Body, Women's Right: A Social History of Birth Control in America.* Penguin Books, 1977.

Greenwald, Maurine. *Women, War and Work: The Impact of World War I on Women Workers in the United States.* Westport, Conn.: Greenwood Press, 1980.

Griffen, Clyde, and Griffen, Sally. *Natives and Newcomers: The Ordering of Opportunity in Mid-Nineteenth Century Poughkeepsie.* Cambridge, Mass.: Harvard University Press, 1978.

Grimes, Alan P. *The Puritan Ethic and Women Suffrage.* New York: Oxford University Press, 1967.

Gutman, Herbert G. *The Black Family in Slavery and Freedom, 1750–1925.* New York: Vintage, 1976.

Hagood, Margaret J. *Mothers of the South: Portraiture of the White Tenant Farm Woman.* New York: W. W. Norton, 1977.

Haller, John S., and Haller, Robin M. *The Physician and Sexuality in Victorian America.* Urbana: University of Illinois Press, 1976.

Hayden, Dolores. *The Grand Domestic Revolution: A History of Feminist Designs for American Homes, Neighborhoods and Cities.* Cambridge, Mass: M.I.T. Press, 1981.

Hersh, Blanche Glassman. *The Slavery of Sex: Feminist-Abolitionists in America.* Urbana: University of Illinois Press, 1968.

Hill, Mary A. *Charlotte Perkins Gilman: The Making of a Radical Feminist, 1860–1896.* Philadelphia: Temple University Press, 1979.

Hummer, Patricia. *The Decade of Elusive Promise: Professional Women in the United States, 1920–1930*. Ann Arbor, Michigan: UMI Research Press, 1979.

Jacobson, Paul H. *American Marriage and Divorce*. New York: Rinehart & Co., 1959.

Jeffrey, Julie Roy. *Frontier Women: The Trans-Mississippi West, 1840–1880*. New York: Hill & Wang, 1979.

Johnson, Marilyn and Carroll Susan with Stanwick, Kathy and Korenblit, Lynn. *Profile of Women Holding Office, II* Center for the American Woman and Politics Eagleton Institute of Politics-Rutgers, The State University, New Brunswick, N.J. 1978.

Katzman, David M. *Seven Days a Week: Women and Domestic Service in Industrializing America*. New York: Oxford University Press, 1978.

Kerber, Linda. *Women of the Republic: Intellect and Ideology in Revolutionary America*. Chapel Hill: University of North Carolina Press, 1980.

Koehler, Lyle. *A Search for Power: The 'Weaker Sex' in Seventeenth-Century New England*. Urbana: University of Illinois Press, 1980.

Komarovsky, Mirra. *Blue-Collar Marriage*. New York: Random House, 1964.

Kraditor, Aileen S. *The Ideas of the Woman Suffrage Movement, 1890–1920*. New York: Columbia University Press, 1965.

Lemons, J. Stanley. *The Woman Citizen: Social Feminism in the 1920's*. Urbana: University of Illinois Press, 1975.

Lerner, Gerda. *The Grimké Sisters from South Carolina: Rebels Against Slavery*. Boston: Houghton Mifflin, 1967.

Litoff, Judy Barret. *American Midwives, 1860 to the Present*. Westport, Conn.: Greenwood Press, 1978.

Litwak, Leon F. *Been in the Storm So Long: The Aftermath of Slavery*. New York: Knopf, 1979.

Lockridge, Kenneth A. *Literacy in Colonial New England: An Enquiry into the Social Context of Literacy in the Early Modern West*. New York: W. W. Norton, 1974.

Lopata, Helena Z. *Occupation: Housewife*. New York: Oxford University Press, 1971.

Mandel, Ruth B. *In the Running: Women as Political Candidates*. New York: Ticknor & Fields, 1981.

Marsh, Margaret S. *Anarchist Women, 1870–1920*. Philadelphia: Temple University Press, 1981.

Martin, Del. *Battered Wives*. New York: Pocket Books, 1976.

May, Elaine Tyler. *Great Expectations: Marriage and Divorce in Post-Victorian America*. Chicago: University of Chicago Press, 1980.

Melder, Keith E. *Beginnings of Sisterhood: The American Woman's Rights Movement, 1800–1850*. New York: Schocken Books, 1977.

Mohr, James C. *Abortion in America: The Origins and Evolution of National Policy*. New York: Oxford University Press, 1976.

Morgan, Edmund S. *The Puritan Family: Religion and Domestic Relations in Seventeenth Century New England*. New York: Harper & Row, 1966.

Morgan, David. *Suffragists and Democrats: The Politics of Women's Suffrage in America*. East Lansing: Michigan State University Press, 1972.

Norton, Mary Beth. *Liberty's Daughters: The Revolutionary Experience of American Women, 1750–1800*. Boston: Little Brown, 1980.

O'Neill, William L. *Divorce in the Progressive Era*. New York: Franklin Watts, 1978.

Pivar, David J. *Purity Crusade: Sexual Morality and Social Control, 1868–1900*. Westport, Conn.: Greenwood Press, 1973.

Reed, James. *From Private Vice to Public Virtue: The Birth Control Movement and American Society since 1830*. New York: Basic Books, 1978.

Rothman, Sheila M. *Woman's Proper Place: A History of Changing Ideals and Practices*. New York: Basic Books, 1978.

Ryan, Mary. *Womanhood in America: From Colonial Times to the Present*. 2d. ed. New York: New Viewpoints, 1979.

Scharf, Lois. *To Work or Wed: Female Employment, Feminism and the Great Depression*. Westport, Conn.: Greenwood Press, 1980.

Scott, Anne Firor. *The Southern Lady: From Pedestal to Politics, 1830–1930*. Chicago: University of Chicago Press, 1970.

Sklar, Kathryn Kish. *Catharine Beecher: A Study in American Domesticity*. New York: W. W. Norton, 1973.

Sochen, June. *The New Woman in Greenwich Village, 1910–1920*. New York: Quadrangle Books, 1972.

Spruill, Julia Cherry. *Women's Life and Work in the Southern Colonies*. New York: W. W. Norton, 1972.

Tentler, Leslie W. *Wage-Earning Women: Industrial Work and Family Life in the United States, 1900–1930*. New York: Oxford University Press, 1979.

Walsh, Mary Roth. *"Doctors Wanted: No Women Need Apply": Sexual Barriers in the Medical Profession, 1835–1975*. New Haven: Yale University Press, 1977.

Wandersee, Winifred D. *Women's Work and Family Values, 1920–1940*. Cambridge, Mass.: Harvard University Press, 1981.

Ware, Susan. *Beyond Suffrage: Women in the New Deal*. Cambridge, Mass.: Harvard University Press, 1981.

Wheeler, Adade Michell, with Wortman, Marlene Stein. *The Roads They Made: Women in Illinois History*. Chicago: Charles H. Kerr, 1972.

Yans-McLaughlin, Virginia. *Family and Community: Italian Immigrants in Buffalo, 1880–1930*. Ithaca, N.Y.: Cornell University Press, 1977.

Yates, Gayle Graham. *What Women Want: The Ideas of the Movement*. Cambridge, Mass.: Harvard University Press, 1975.

Zaretsky, Eli. *Capitalism, The Family and Personal Life*. New York: Harper & Row, 1976.

Documentary Sources

Addams, Jane. *Twenty Years at Hull House with Autobiographical Notes*. New York: New American Library, 1961.

Baxandall, Rosalyn; Gordon, Linda; and Reverby, Susan, eds. *America's Working Women: A Documentary History—1600 to the Present*. New York: Vintage Books, 1976.

Beard, Mary, ed. *America Through Women's Eyes*. Westport, Conn.: Greenwood Press, 1969.

Blackwell, Dr. Elizabeth. *Pioneer Work in Opening the Medical Profession to Women: Autobiographical Sketches*. New York: Schocken Books, 1977.

Brownlee, W. Elliot, and Brownlee, Mary M., eds. *Women in the American Economy: A Documentary History, 1625–1929.* New Haven, Conn.: Yale University Press, 1976.

Buhle, Mari Jo, and Buhle, Paul, eds. *The Concise History of Woman Suffrage: Selections from the Classic Work of Stanton, Anthony, Gage and Harper.* Urbana: University of Illinois, 1978.

Cade, Toni, ed. *The Black Woman: An Anthology.* New York: Signet Books, 1970.

Chapman, Anne, ed. *Approaches to Women's History: A Resource Book and Teaching Guide.* Washington, D.C.: American Historical Association, 1979.

Clark, Elizabeth, and Richardson, Herbert W., eds. *Women and Religion: A Feminist Sourcebook of Christian Thought.* New York: Harper & Row, 1977.

Cott, Nancy F., ed. *Root of Bitterness: Documents of the Social History of American Women.* New York: E. P. Dutton, 1972.

Drinnon, Richard, and Drinnon, Anna, eds. *Emma Goldman: Living My Life.* New York: New American Library, 1977.

Dublin, Thomas. *Farm and Factory: The Mill Experience and Women's Lives, 1830–1860.* New York: Columbia University Press, 1981.

Dubois, Ellen Carol. *Elizabeth Cady Stanton–Susan B. Anthony: Correspondence, Writings, Speeches.* New York: Schocken Books, 1981.

Duster, Alfreda M., ed. *Crusade for Justice: The Autobiography of Ida B. Wells.* Chicago: University of Chicago Press, 1970.

Fischer, Christiane, ed. *Let Them Speak for Themselves: women in the American West, 1849–1900.* E. P. Dutton, 1977.

Flynn, Elizabeth Gurley. *The Rebel Girl, An Autobiography: My First Life, 1906–1926.* New York: International Publishers, 1973.

Hamilton, Alice. *Exploring the Dangerous Trades.* Boston: Little Brown, 1943.

Harley, Sharon, and Terborg-Penn, Rosalyn, eds. *The Afro-American Woman: Struggles and Images.* Port Washington, N.Y.: Kennikat Press, 1978.

Kraditor, Aileen S., ed. *Up From the Pedestal: Selected Writings in the History of American Feminism.* Chicago: Quadrangle Books, 1968.

Lerner, Gerda, ed. *The Female Experience: An American Documentary.* Indianapolis: Bobbs-Merrill, 1977.

———. *Black Women in White America: A Documentary History.* New York: Vintage Books, 1973.

Morgan, Robin, ed. *Sisterhood is Powerful: An Anthology of Writings from the Women's Liberation Movement.* New York: Vintage Books, 1970.

O'Hare, Kate Richards. *In Prison.* Seattle: University of Washington Press, 1976.

O'Neill, William L., ed. *Women at Work including The Long Day: The Story of a New York Working Girl by Dorothy Richardson (1905) and Inside the New York Telephone Company by Elinor Langer (1970).* New York: Quadrangle Books, 1972.

Rose, Willie Lee, ed. *A Documentary History of Slavery in North America.* New York: Oxford University Press, 1976.

Sanger, Margaret. *My Fight for Birth Control.* New York: Farrar, Rhinehart, 1931.

Schneir, Miriam, ed. *Feminism: The Essential Historical Writings.* New York: Vintage Books, 1972.

Wald, Carol, and Papachristou, Judith. *Myth America: Picturing Women, 1865–1945.* New York: Pantheon Books, 1975.

Walters, Ronald G., ed. *Primers for Prudery: Sexual Advice to Victorian America.* Englewood Cliffs, N.J.: Prentice-Hall, 1974.

Articles

Bernard, Richard M., and Vinovskis, Maris A. "The Female School Teacher in Antebellum Massachusetts." *Journal of Social History* 10 (Spring 1977): 332–45.

Biemer, Linda. "Business Letters of Alida Schuyler Livingston, 1680–1726." *New York History* 63 (April 1982): 183–207.

Bloch, Ruth H. "American Feminine Ideals in Transition: The Rise of the Moral Mother, 1785–1815." *Feminist Studies* 4 (June 1978): 101–26.

Bularzik, Mary. "Sexual Harassment at the Work Place: Historical Notes." *Radical America* 12 (July–August 1978): 25–44.

Burnham, Dorothy. "The Life of the Afro-American Woman in Slavery." *International Journal of Woman's Studies* 1 (July–August 1978): 363–77.

Campbell, D'Ann. "Was the West Different? Values and Attitudes of Young Women in 1943." *Pacific History Review* (August 1978): 453–63.

Carroll, Bernice A. "Political Science, Part I: American Politics and Political Behavior." *Signs* 5 (Winter 1979): 289–306.

Conway, Jill. "Perspectives on the History of Women's Education in the United States," *History of Education Quarterly* 14 (Spring 1974): 1–12.

———. "Women Reformers and American Culture, 1870–1930." *Journal of Social History* 5 (1971–1972): 164–77.

Doherty, Robert E. "Tempest on the Hudson: The Struggle for 'Equal Pay for Equal Work' in the New York City Public Schools, 1907–1911." *History of Education Quarterly* 19 (Winter 1979): 413–34.

Foster, Lawrence, "From Frontier Activism to Neo-Victorian Domesticity: Mormon Women in the Nineteenth and Twentieth Centuries." *Journal of Mormon History* 6 (1979): 3–21.

Fraundord, Martha Norby. "The Labor Force Participation of Turn-of-the Century Married Women." *Journal of Economic History* 39 (June 1979): 401–18.

Freedman, Estelle. "Separatism as Strategy: Female Institution Building and American Feminism, 1870–1930." *Feminist Studies* 5 (Fall 1979): 512–29.

Furman, Necah S. "Women's Campaign for Equality: A National and State Perspective." *New Mexico History Review* 53 (October 1978): 317–36.

Garcia, Mario T. "The Chicana in American History: The Mexican Women of El Paso, 1880–1920—A Case Study." *Pacific Historical Review* 49 (May 1980): 315–37.

Geidel, Peter. "The National Woman's Party and the Origins of the Equal Rights Amendment, 1920–1923." *Historian* 42 (August 1980): 557–82.

Gelb, Joyce, and Palley, Marian L. "Women and Interest-Group Politics: A Comparative Analysis of Federal Decision-Making." *Journal of Politics* 41 (May 1979): 369–92.

Glenn, Ellen Nakano. "The Dialectics of Wage Work: Japanese-American Women and Domestic Service, 1905–1940." *Feminist Studies* 6 (Fall 1980): 432–71.

Goldin, Claudia. "Female Labor Force Participation: The Origin of Black and White Differences, 1876 and 1880." *Journal of Economic History* 37 (March 1977): 87–108.

Graham, Patricia Albjerg. "Expansion and Exclusion: A History of Women in American Higher Education." *Signs* 3 (Summer 1978), 759–73.

Griswold, Robert L. "Apart but Not Adrift: Wives, Divorce, and Independence in California, 1850–1890." *Pacific Historical Review* 49 (May 1980): 265–84.

Harris, Katherine, "A Study of Feminine and Class Identity in the Women's Christian Temperance Union, 1920–1979: A Case Study." *Historicus* 2 (Fall–Winter 1981): 55–87.

Harrison, Cynthia E. "A 'New Frontier' for Women: The Public Policy of the Kennedy Administration." *Journal of American History* 67 (December 1980): 630–46.

Hirata, Sucie Cheng. "Free, Indentured, Enclaved: Chinese Prostitutes in Nineteenth-Century America." *Signs* 5 (Autumn, 1979): 3–29.

Ichiaka, Yuji. "*Amerika Nadeshiko:* Japanese Immigrant Women in the United States, 1900–1924." *Pacific Historical Review* 49 (May 1980): 339–57.

Jensan, Joan M., and Darlis, A. Miller. "The Gentle Tamers Revisited: New Approaches to the History of Women in the American West." *Pacific Historical Review* 49 (May 1980): 173–214.

Johnson, R. C. "Feminism, Philanthropy and Science in the Development of the Oral Contraceptive Pill." *Pharmacy History* 19 (1977): 63–68.

Keller, Rosemary Skinner. "Creating A Sphere for Women in the Church: How Consequential an Accommodation?" *Methodist History* 18 (January 1980): 83–91.

Kelly-Gadol, Joan. "The Social Relation of the Sexes: Methodological Implications of Women's History." *Signs* 1 (Summer, 1976): 809–24.

———. "The Doubled Vision of Feminist Theory." *Feminist Studies* 5 (1979): 216–27.

Kessler-Harris, Alice. "Women's Wage Work as Myth and History." *Labor History* 19 (Spring 1978): 285–307.

Keyssar, Alexander. "Widowhood in Eighteenth Century Massachusetts: A Problem in the History of the Family." *Perspectives in American History* 8 (1974): 83–119.

Klaczynska, Barbara. "Why Women Work: A Comparison of Various Groups—Philadelphia, 1910–1930." *Labor History* 17 (Winter 1976): 73–87.

Kleinberg, Susan J. "Technology and Women's Work: The Lives of Working Class Women in Pittsburgh, 1870–1900." *Labor History* 17 (Winter 1976): 58–72.

Larson, T. A. "Emancipating the West's Dolls, Vassals and Hopeless Drudges: The Origins of Woman Suffrage in the West." In *Essays in Honor of Professor T. A. Larson,* edited by Roger Daniels. Laramie: University of Wyoming Publications 37 (October 1971): 1–16.

Lunardini, Christine, and Knock, Thomas J. "Woodrow Wilson and Woman Suffrage: A New Look." *Political Science Quarterly* 95 (Winter 1980–81): 655–71.

Morantz, Regina Markell, and Zschoche, Sue. "Professionalism, Feminism and Gender Roles: A Comparative Study of Nineteenth-Century Medical Therapeutics." *Journal of American History* 67 (December 1980): 568–88.

Miller, Marc. "Working Women and World War II." *The New England Quarterly* 53 (March 1980): 42–61.

Neu, Irene D. "The Jewish Business Woman in America." *American Jewish Historical Quarterly* 66 (September 1976): 137–54.

Penfield, Janet Harbison, "Women in the Presbyterian Church—An Historical Overview." *Journal of Presbyterian History* 52 (Summer 1977): 107–24.

Riley, Glenda. "Images of the Frontierswoman: Iowa as A Case Study." *Western History Quarterly* 8 (April 1977): 189–202.

Rosaldo, M. Z. "The Use and Abuse of Anthropology: Reflections on Feminism and Cross Cultural Understanding." *Signs* 5 (Spring 1980): 389–417.

Schaffer, Ronald. "The Problem of Consciousness in the Woman Suffrage Movement: A California Perspective." *Pacific History Review* 45 (November, 1976): 469–93.

Scott, Anne Firor. "The Ever-Widening Circle: The Diffusion of Feminist Values from the Troy Female Seminary, 1822–1872." *History of Education Quarterly* 19 (Spring 1979): 3–25.

Smith-Rosenberg, Carroll, and Rosenberg, Charles. "The Female Animal: Medical and Biological Views of Women and Her Role in Nineteenth-Century America." *The Journal of American History* 60 (September 1973): 332–56

Turner, Edward R. "Women's Suffrage in New Jersey: 1790–1807." *Smith College Studies in History* 1 (June 1916) 165–87.

Tyor, Peter. " 'Denied the Power to Choose the Good': Sexuality and Mental Defect in American Medical Practice, 1850–1920." *Journal of Social History* 10 (June 1977): 472–89.

Vanek, Joann. "Household Technology and Social Status: Rising Living Standards and Status and Residence Differences in Housework." *Technology and Culture* 19 (June 1978): 361–75.

———. "Work, Leisure and Family Roles: Farm Households in the United States, 1920–1955." *Journal of Family History* 5 (Winter 1980), 422–31.

Webster, Janice Reiff. "Domestication and Americanization: Scandinavian Women in Seattle, 1888–1900." *Journal of Urban History* 4 (May 1978), 275–96.

Wilson, Joan Hoff. "The Illusion of Change: Women and the American Revolution." In *The American Revolution: Explorations in the History of American Radicalism,* edited by Alfred F. Young. DeKalb: Northern Illinois Press, 1976.

Women and the American City: A Special Issue of Signs. Journal of Women in Culture and Society 5 (Spring, 1980).

Wortman, Marlene Stein. "Domesticating the Nineteenth Century American City." *Prospects: An Annual of American Cultural Studies* 3. New York: Burt Franklin & Company, 1977.

Young, Louise M. "Women's Place in American Politics: The Historical Perspective." *Journal of Politics* 38 (August 1976): 295–335.

WORKS ON LAW

Cases and Materials

Babcock, Barbara Allen; Freedman, Anne E.; Norton, Eleanor Holmes; and Ross, Susan C. *Sex Discrimination and the Law: Causes and Remedies.* Boston: Little Brown, 1975. 1978 supplement edited by Wendy Williams.

Bell, Derrick A. Jr. *Race Racism and American Law.* Boston: Little Brown, 1973.

California State Library, comp. *California Laws of Interest to Women and Children, 1917.* Sacramento: California State Printing Office, 1918.

Catterall, Helen T. *Judicial Cases Concerning American Slavery and the Negro.* 5 vols. Washington, D.C.: Carnegie Institution of Washington, 1926–1937.

Davidson, Kenneth M.; Ginsburg, Ruth B.; and Kay, Herma H. *Sex-Based Discrimination.* St. Paul, Minn.: West Publishing Co., 1974. 1978 supplement by Ruth Bader Ginsberg and Herma Hill Kay.

Goldstein, Leslie Friedman. *The Constitutional Rights of Women: Cases in Law and Social Change.* New York: Longman, 1979.

Kanowitz, Leo. *Sex Roles in Law and Society.* Albuquerque: University of New Mexico Press, 1973.

Books and Pamphlets

Auerbach, Jerold S. *Unequal Justice: Lawyers and Social Change in Modern America.* New York: Oxford University Press, 1976.

Baer, Judith A. *The Chains of Protection: The Judicial Response to Women's Labor Legislation.* Westport, Conn.: Greenwood Press, 1978.

Baker, Elizabeth. *Protective Labor Legislation.* New York: Columbia University Press, 1925.

Basch, Norma. *In the Eyes of the Law: Women, Marriage and Property in Nineteenth-Century New York.* Ithaca, N.Y.: Cornell University Press, 1982.

Bishop, Joel Prentice. *Commentaries on the Law of Married Women under the Statutes of the Several States and at Common Law and in Equity.* 2 vols. Boston, 1873–75.

Blackstone, Sir William. *Commentaries on the Laws of England, in Four Books.* Edited by Thomas M. Cooley. 4th ed. 2 vols. Chicago, 1899.

Blake, Nelson Manfred. *The Road to Reno: A History of Divorce in the United States.* New York: Macmillan & Co., 1962.

Bloomfield, Maxwell. *American Lawyers in a Changing Society, 1776–1875.* Cambridge, Mass.: Harvard University Press, 1976.

Boorstin, Daniel. *The Mysterious Science of the Law: An Essay on Blackstone's Commentaries.* Cambridge, Mass.: Harvard University Press, 1941.

Bowditch, William I. *Taxation of Women in Massachusetts.* Boston, 1884.

Brown, Barbara A.; Freedman, Ann E.; Katz, Harriet N.; and Price, Alice M. *Women's Rights and the Law: The Impact of the ERA on State Laws.* New York: Praeger Publishers, 1977.

Bullock, William E. *A Treatise on the Law of Husband and Wife in the State of New York Including Chapters on Divorce and Dower.* Albany, 1897.

Dall, Caroline. *Woman's Rights under the Law.* Boston, 1861.

Endlich, G. A. and Richards, Louis. *The Rights and Liabilities of Married Women Concerning Property, Contracts and Torts under the Common and Statute Law of Pennsylvania.* Philadelphia, 1889.

Feinman, Clarice. *Women in the Criminal Justice System.* New York: Praeger Publishers, 1980.

Flaherty, David, ed. *Essays in the History of Early American Law.* Chapel Hill: University of North Carolina Press, 1969.

Friedman, Lawrence N. *A History of American Law.* New York: Simon and Schuster, 1973.

Fuller, Lon L. *Legal Fictions.* Palo Alto, Calif.: Stanford University Press, 1967.

Gallaher, Ruth A. *Legal and Political Status of Women in Iowa: An Historical*

Account of the Rights of Women in Iowa from 1838–1918. Iowa City: State Historical Society of Iowa, 1918.

Gilmore, Grant. *The Ages of American Law.* New Haven: Yale University Press, 1977.

Greenberg, Douglas. *Crime and Law Enforcement in the Colony of New York, 1691–1776.* Ithaca, N.Y.: Cornell University Press, 1976.

Grossberg, Michael. "Law and the Family in Nineteenth Century America." Ph.D. diss., Brandeis University, 1979.

Haar, Charles M., ed. *The Golden Age of American Law.* New York: George Braziller, 1965.

Herttell, Thomas. *The Right of Married Women to Hold and Contract Property Sustained by the Constitution of the State of New York.* New York, 1839.

Hindus, Michael. *Prison and Plantation: Crime, Justice and Authority in Massachusetts and South Carolina, 1767–1878.* Chapel Hill: University of North Carolina Press, 1930.

Holt, Wythe, ed. *Essays in Nineteenth-Century Legal History.* Westport, Conn.: Greenwood Press, 1976.

Horwitz, Morton J. *The Transformation of American Law, 1790–1860.* Cambridge, Mass.: Harvard University Press, 1978.

Howard, George Eliot. *A History of Matrimonial Institutions.* 3 vols., Chicago: University of Chicago Press, 1904.

Hurst, J. Willard. *Law and the Conditions of Freedom in the Nineteenth Century United States.* Madison: University of Wisconsin Press, 1956.

Kairys, David, ed. *The Politics of Law: A Progressive Critique.* New York: Pantheon, 1982.

Kanowitz, Leo. *Women and the Law: The Unfinished Revolution.* Albuquerque: University of New Mexico Press, 1969.

Kent, James. *Commentaries on American Law.* 4 vols. 11th ed., Boston, 1867.

MacKinnon, Catharine. *Sexual Harassment of Working Women: A Case of Sex Discrimination.* New Haven, Conn.: Yale University Press, 1979.

Miller, Casey, and Swift, Kate. *Words and Women: New Language and New Times.* Garden City, N.Y.: Anchor Press, 1977.

Morris, Richard B. *Government and Labor in Early America.* New York: Harper Torchbook, 1965.

———. *Studies in the History of American Law: With Special Reference to the Seventeenth and Eighteenth Centuries.* 2nd ed. Philadelphia: Mitchell, 1959.

Nelson, William E. *Americanization of the Common Law: The Impact of Legal Change on Massachusetts Society, 1760–1830.* Cambridge, Mass.: Harvard University Press, 1975.

Nicholas, Susan Cary; Price, Alice M.; and Rubin, Rachel. *Rights and Wrongs: Women's Struggle for Legal Equality.* Old Westbury, N.Y.: Feminist Press, 1979.

O'Conner, Karen. *Women's Organizations' Use of the Courts.* New York: Lexington Books, 1980.

Petrick, Barbara. *Mary Philbrook: The Radical Feminist in New Jersey.* Trenton: New Jersey Historical Commission, 1981.

Pound, Roscoe. *The Formative Era of American Law.* New York: Peter Smith, 1950.

Rabkin, Peggy A. *Fathers to Daughters: The Legal Foundations of Female Emancipation.* Westport, Conn.: Greenwood Press, 1980.

Reeve, Tapping. *The Law of Baron and Feme, of Parent and Child, of Guardian and Ward, of Master and Servant, and of the Powers of Courts of Chancery.* New Haven, 1816.

Rosenhein, Margaret K., ed. *Pursuing Justice for the Child.* Chicago: University of Chicago Press, 1976.

Sachs, Albie, and Wilson, Joan Hoff. *Sexism and the Law: Male Beliefs and Legal Bias in Britain and the United States.* New York: The Free Press, 1978.

Salmon, Marylynn. "The Property Rights of Married Women in Early America: A Comparative Study," Ph.D. diss., Bryn Mawr College, 1980.

Schlossman, Steven L. *Love and the American Delinquent: The Theory and Practice of Progressive Juvenile Justice, 1825–1920.* Chicago: University of Chicago Press, 1977.

Schouler, James. *A Treatise on the Law of Domestic Relations.* Boston, 1873.

Schur, Edwin M. *Law and Society: A Sociological View.* New York: Random House, 1968.

Smart, Carol. *Women, Crime and Criminology: A Feminist Critique.* Boston, Routledge & Kegan Paul, 1978.

Story, Joseph. *Commentaries on Equity Jurisprudence.* 2 vols. Boston, 1839.

Stow, Mrs. J. W. *Probate Confiscation: Unjust Laws Which Govern Women.* 1878.

Thurman, Kay Ellen. "The Married Women's Property Acts." L.L.M. diss., University of Wisconsin Law School, 1966.

Vernier, Chester G. *American Family Law.* Vol. 3. Stanford, California: Stanford University Press, 1935.

Warbasse, Elizabeth Bowles. "The Changing Legal Rights of Married Women, 1800–1861." Ph.D. diss., Radcliffe College, 1960.

Wells, J. C. *A Treatise on the Separate Property of Married Women, Under the Recent Enabling Statutes.* Cincinnati, 1878.

White, Edward G. *The American Judicial Tradition: Profiles of Leading American Judges.* New York: Oxford University Press, 1976.

Articles

Basch, Norma. "Invisible Women: The Legal Fiction of Marital Unity in Nineteenth-Century America." *Feminist Studies* 5 (Summer, 1979): 346–66.

Bienen, Leigh. "Rape III—National Developments in Rape Reform Legislation." *Women's Rights Law Reporter* 6 (Spring 1980): 171–213.

―――. "A Question of Credibility: John Henry Wigmore's Use of Scientific Authority in Section 924a of the Treatise on Evidence." *California Western Law Review* 19 (1983): 235–68.

Bittenbender, Ada M. "Women in Law." *Chicago Law Times* II (1888), 301–2.

Blatch, Harriot Stanton. "Do Women Want Protection? Wrapping Women in Cotton-Wool." *The Nation* 116 (January 31, 1923), 115–16.

Blumrosen, Ruth G. "Wage Discrimination, Job Segregation and Women Workers." *Women's Rights Law Reporter* 6 (Fall/Winter 1979–80): 21–57.

Boatright, Eleanor. "Political and Civil Status of Women in Georgia, 1783–1860." *Georgia Historical Quarterly* 25 (December 1941): 301–24.

Breckinridge, Sophonisba P. "Legislative Control of Women's Work." *Journal of Political Economy* (January–February 1906): 107–9.

Brown, Barbara A.; Emerson, Thomas I.; Falk, Gail; and Freeman, Ann E. "The Equal Rights Amendment: A Constitutional Basis for Equal Rights for Women." *Yale Law Journal* (1971).

Brown, Robert C. "The Duty of the Husband to Support the Wife." *Virginia Law Review* 18 (1932): 823–49.

Childs, Marjorie M. "The Women Lawyers Centennial." *ABA Journal* 56 (January 1970): 68–70.

Cohn, Henry. "Connecticut's Divorce Mechanism: 1636–1969." *American Journal of Legal History* 14 (1970): 35–54.

Deen, James W., Jr. "Patterns of Testation: Four Tidewater Counties in Colonial Virginia." *American Journal of Legal History* 16 (1972): 154–76.

Dellopenna, Joseph W. "The History of Abortions: Technology, Morality and Law." *University of Pittsburgh Law Review* 40 (September 1979): 359–428.

Drinker, Sophie. "Votes for Women in Eighteenth-Century New Jersey." *New Jersey Historical Society Proceedings* 80 (1962): 31–45.

Erickson, Nancy S. "Kahn, Ballard and Wiesenfeld: A New Equal Protection Test in 'Reverse' Sex Discrimination." *Brooklyn Law Review* 42 (Summer 1975): 1–54.

Erickson, Nancy S. "Women and the Supreme Court: Anatomy Is Destiny." *Brooklyn Law Review* 41 (Fall 1974): 209–82.

Faber, Eli. "Puritan Criminals: The Economic, Social and Intellectual Background to Crime in Seventeenth-Century Massachusetts." *Perspectives in American History* 11 (1977–1978): 81–144.

Friedman, Lawrence M. "Patterns of Testation in the 19th Century: A Study of Essex County (New Jersey) Wills." *American Journal of Legal History* 8 (1964): 34–53.

Gampel, Gwen Victor, with Joan Gunderson. "Married Women's Legal Status in 18th-Century New York and Virginia." *William and Mary Quarterly* 39 (January 1982): 114–34.

Grossberg, Michael. "Guarding the Altar: Physiological Restrictions and the Rise of State Intervention in Matrimony." *American Journal of Legal History* 26 (1982): 197–226.

Hemphill, C. Dallet. "Women in Court: Sex-Role Differentiation in Salem, Massachusetts, 1636 to 1683." *William and Mary Quarterly* 39 (January 1982): 231–43.

Jensen, Carol Elizabeth. "The Equity Jurisdiction and Married Women's Property in Ante-Bellum America: A Revisionist View." *International Journal of Women's Studies* 2 (March–April 1979): 144–54.

Johnston, John D., Jr. "Sex and Property: The Common Law Tradition, the Law School Curriculum, and Developments Towards Equality." *New York University Law Review* 47 (1972), 1033–93.

Johnston, John D., Jr., and Knapp, Charles L. "Sex-Discrimination by Law: A Study in Judicial Perspective." *New York University Law Review* 46 (1971).

Klein, Doris. "The Etiology of Female Crime: A Review of the Literature." *Issues in Criminology* 8 (Fall 1973): 3–30.

Kurtz, Paul M. "The State Equal Rights Amendments and Their Impact on Domestic Relations Law." *Family Law Quarterly* 11 (Summer 1977): 101–50.

Lazarou, Kathleen E. "Fettered Portias: Obstacles Facing Nineteenth-Century Women Lawyers." *Women Lawyer's Journal* 64 (Winter 1978): 21–30.

Lebsock, Suzanne D. "Radical Reconstruction and Property Rights of Southern Women." *Journal of Southern History* 43 (May 1977): 195–216.

Martin, Ellen A. "Admission of Women to the Bar" *Chicago Law Times* 1 (November 1886): 76–92.

Meehan, Thomas R. "Not 'Not Made Out of Levity': Evolution of Divorce in Early Pennsylvania." *Pennsylvania Magazine of History and Biography* 92 (1968): 441–64.

Mies, Frank P. "Statutory Regulation of Women's Employment—Codification of Statutes." *Journal of Political Economy* (Jan.–Feb. 1906): 109–18.

Nemeth, Charles P. "Character Evidence in Rape Trials in Nineteenth Century New York: Chastity and the Admissibility of Specific Facts." *Women's Rights Law Reporter* 6 (Spring 1980): 214–25.

Philbrook, Mary. "Woman's Suffrage in New Jersey Prior to 1807." *New Jersey Historical Society Proceedings* 57 (1939): 87–98.

Pierce, Christine. "Natural Law Language and Women." in *Women in Sexist Society: Studies in Power and Powerlessness,* edited by Vivian Gornick and Barbara K. Moran, pp. 242–58. New York: New American Library, 1972.

Polikoff, Nancy D. "Why Are Mothers Losing: A Brief Analysis of Criteria Used in Child Custody Determinations." *Women's Rights Law Reporter* 7 (Spring 1982): 235–43.

Popiel, Marianne. "Sentencing Women: Equal Protection in the Context of Discretionary Decisionmaking." *Women's Rights Law Reporter* 6 (Fall/Winter, 1979–80): 85–106.

Rivers, Theodore. "Widows' Rights in Anglo-Saxon Law." *American Journal of Legal History* 19 (July 1975).

Rogers, Kristine. " 'For Her Own Protection . . .': Conditions of Incarceration for Female Juvenile Offenders in the State of Connecticut." *Law and Society Review* 7 (1972): 223–46.

Roth, Allan, "The Tender Years Presumption in Child Custody Disputes." *Journal of Family Law* 15 (1977): 423–62.

Salmon, Marylynn. "Equality or Submersion? Feme Covert Status in Early Pennsylvania." In *Women of America: A History,* edited by Carol R. Berkin and Mary Beth Norton, pp. 93–113. Boston, Mass: Houghton Mifflin, 1979.

———. " 'Life, Liberty, and Dower': The Legal Status of Women after the American Revolution." In *Women, War and Revolution,* edited by Carol R. Berkin and Clara M. Lovett, pp. 85–106. New York: Holmes & Meier, 1980.

Sayre, Paul. "A Reconsideration of Husband's Duty to Support and Wife's Duty to Render Services." *Virginia Law Review* 29 (1943): 857–78.

Schlossman, Steven, and Wallach, Stephanie. "The Crime of Precocious Sexuality: Female Juvenile Delinquency in the Progressive Era." *Harvard Educational Review* 48 (February 1978): 65–94.

Semonche, John E. "Common Law Marriage in North Carolina: A Study in Legal History." *American Journal of Legal History* 9 (1965): 320–49.

Shepard, Annamay T. "Unspoken Premises in Custody Litigation." *Women's Rights Law Reporter* 7 (Spring 1982): 229–34.

Spaeletta, Matteo. "Divorce in Colonial New York." *The New York Historical Society Quarterly* 39 (October 1955): 422–40.

Strickland, Martha. "The Common Law and the Statutory Right of Women to Office." *American Law Review* 17 (Jan.–Feb. 1883): 670–83.

Taub, Nadine, and Schneider, Elizabeth M. "Perspectives on Women's Subordination and the Role of Law." *The Politics of Law: A Progressive Critique.* Edited by David Kairys. New York: Pantheon Books, 1982, 117–39.

Warren, Joseph. "Husband's Right to Wife's Services." *Harvard Law Review* 38 (1925): 421–39.

Weisberg, D. Kelly. "'Under Greet Temptations Heer': Women and Divorce in Puritan Massachusetts." *Feminist Studies* 2 (1975): 183–93.

Weisberg, D. Kelly. "Barred from the Bar: Woman and Legal Education in the United States, 1870–1890." *Journal of Legal Education* 28 (1977): 485–507.

Williams, Wendy. "The Equality Crisis: Some Reflections on Culture, Courts and Feminism." *Women's Rights Law Reporter* 7 (Spring 1982): 175–200.

"Women as Advocates." *American Law Review* 18 (Jan.–Feb. 1884): 478–79.

Zainaldin, Jamil. "The Emergence of a Modern American Family Law." *Northwestern University Law Review* 73 (1979): 1038–89.

Index

References to illustrations are printed in boldface type.